War Crimes
and Realpolitik

WAR CRIMES AND REALPOLITIK

International Justice from World War I to the 21st Century

Jackson Nyamuya Maogoto

LYNNE
RIENNER
PUBLISHERS

BOULDER
LONDON

Published in the United States of America in 2004 by
Lynne Rienner Publishers, Inc.
1800 30th Street, Boulder, Colorado 80301
www.rienner.com

and in the United Kingdom by
Lynne Rienner Publishers, Inc.
3 Henrietta Street, Covent Garden, London WC2E 8LU

Library of Congress Cataloging-in-Publication Data
Maogoto, Jackson Nyamuya, 1975–
    War crimes and realpolitik : international justice from World War I to
the 21st century / Jackson Nyamuya Maogoto.
      p.   cm.
    Includes bibliographical references and index.
    ISBN 1-58826-276-6 (hardcover : alk. paper) — ISBN 1-58826-252-9
(pbk. : alk. paper)
    1. War crimes—History. 2. War crime trials—History. 3. War (International
law). 4. International criminal courts—History. I. Title.
K5301.M36 2004
341.6'9'09—dc22   2003023330

British Cataloguing in Publication Data
A Cataloguing in Publication record for this book
is available from the British Library.

Printed and bound in the United States of America

⊗   The paper used in this publication meets the requirements
     of the American National Standard for Permanence of
     Paper for Printed Library Materials Z39.48-1992.

     5 4 3 2 1

Contents

Acknowledgments   vii

Introduction   1

1 Toward the Modern International Penal Process   15

   The Development of the Modern Laws of War *16*
   The Birth of the International Penal Process *20*
   Conclusion *27*

Part 1: The World Wars

2 A False Dawn: The Failure to Enforce International
   Justice After World War I   37

   The Coming of the War *38*
   Germany and Turkey:
       Championing Nationalism Through Destruction *40*
   The Paris Peace Conference *44*
   Frustrated Justice:
       The Peace Treaties of Versailles and Sevres *51*
   Conclusion *62*

3 A New Dawn: The Birth of the Modern International
   Penal Process   77

   The Breakdown of Collective Security Efforts *79*
   Germany and Japan:
       Emptying the Content of the Laws of War *83*
   The United Nations War Crimes Commission *88*
   The London International Conference *92*
   The Roar of the Victors: The International Military Tribunals *98*
   Tokyo in the Shadow of Nuremberg *100*
   Conclusion *106*

Part 2: The Cold War and the 1990s

4 Cold War: International Justice in the Shadow of Realpolitik   125

People First, Nations Second:
    Developments in the International Law Regime *127*
A New Plank in International Enforcement:
    The Rise of NGOs *133*
Conclusion *136*

5 Crisis in the Balkans: Raising the Nuremberg Precedent   143

Death of a State:
    The Dissolution of the Yugoslav Federation *145*
Enemies of Promise: NATO and the Security Council *155*
Fulfilling a Mandate: Developments in the ICTY *159*
Conclusion *163*

6 Rwanda: Portrait of a Reluctant International Community   179

A People Betrayed:
    The International Community's Indifference *180*
Redeeming the World's Conscience:
    Responding Through the International Penal Process *185*
Fulfilling a Mandate: Developments in the ICTR *188*
Conclusion *192*

Part 3: Into the New Millennium

7 The International Criminal Court:
    Challenges and Concessions to the State   203

The Road to Rome *204*
Structure and Competence of the ICC *206*
The Lonely Superpower: U.S. Opposition to the ICC *216*
Reflections on the ICC *221*
Conclusion *223*

8 International Justice: Retrospect and Prospect   235

List of Acronyms   245
Glossary   247
Selected Bibliography   253
Index   263
About the Book   267

Acknowledgments

This book is dedicated to the two central women in my life, my sister, Lillian Kerubo Maogoto, a keen admirer and ardent supporter; and my mother, Mary S. G. Maogoto, a constant pillar of support and motivation.

I wish to acknowledge the moral and material support of the University of Newcastle Law School and especially the enthusiasm of the dean, Ted Wright, professor and Belle Weise Chair of Legal Ethics. The assistance of Catherine Blake Neville made a daunting task much less intimidating.

I also appreciate the support of Lynne Rienner Publishers and particularly Lynne Rienner, whose suggestions proved enlightening and informative.

War Crimes
and Realpolitik

Introduction

In the past five millennia, thousands of wars have been fought and billions of lives extinguished. Ironically, it was in the modern era, characterized by a codification of laws and customs of war and a growing body of international norms, that war achieved unprecedented destructive capacity. The twentieth century has the infamy of being the bloodiest century in the history of mankind. This legacy does not show any loss of momentum today. Total war made its way into the international vocabulary, with the two world wars alone claiming some 50 million lives, including many civilians who had little or no role in their governments' bloody adventures.[1] Given the grim statistics and the history of armed conflict, the importance of regulation of the conduct of war cannot be doubted. The law of war—with its unique role in preserving rights, creating a body of rules that are realistic for the exigencies of combat situations, and providing further regulations that are meaningful to those facing armed conflicts—is irreplaceable.

The law of war (in general parlance today, "international humanitarian law") is as old as war itself and remains the umbrella term covering all laws that govern the conduct of states, individuals, and other entities during armed conflict. The law of war historically developed in two separate categories, and this separation remains largely intact. The first category, *jus ad bellum* (the right to initiate war),[2] refers to the legality of purpose of the war. The second category, *jus in bello* (the law during war), regulates the conduct of war, independent of the war's legality.[3] *Jus in bello* laws matured primarily through custom and military manuals, until the atrocities of late-nineteenth-century warfare, spurred by the technological advances of industrialism, led to public outcry and a desire to centralize the laws of war. This second aspect is the focus of this book.

The modern trail of warfare dates to the middle of the seventeenth century, when the independent nation-state was founded upon a reverence for sovereignty, emanating from the Peace of Westphalia of 1648 that ended the wars of religion between the Protestant and Catholic states. The Westphalia Treaty completed a process that had begun toward the end of the Middle Ages, which focused upon the establishment of single overriding authorities in the growing national areas of Europe.[4] We now know of course, that despite the promise of the Westphalian peace, the advent of the sovereign independent nation-state did not usher in a new era of peace and stability but rather inaugurated the modern nation-state—the most monopolistic and exacting of all associations, one that made devotion to national interest the most revered of all virtues. The post-Westphalian era reinforced the government's duty to maximize the assets of their states (through militarism and conquest) without regard to the consequences (real or hypothetical) to society. Although international law was seen as an essential institution to reinforce reason against passion, the impatience of the nation-state invoked national interest to justify violation of legal or ethical rules and win support for a calculated gain in material or geopolitical advantage.

And even though force, diplomacy, and law[5] predate the modern nation-state, its birth at Westphalia[6] and the growing maturity of international society elevated these institutions in light of insecurity and fear of other states, necessitating individual states to look after their own security and possibly dominate others by extending their own power. As international society developed, war was seen as a normal feature of international relations and an important attribute of the state. International law aimed to regulate war as an institution rather than to sanction the act of war. The institutions of force, diplomacy, and law were gradually established as central techniques of influence in international relations through which states attempted to change their environment in accordance with determined aims and objectives or attempted to adapt to the environment. There was not a great deal of theorizing on the causes of war in general because most people thought that the causes of war were obvious. "States went to war for gain, or in self-defense because they were attacked by some other state acting for gain."[7] Put simply, war was inherent in the nature of sovereignty; it was what states did. Yet attempts to regulate war are as old as war itself. From ancient societies until today, some have purported to limit the conduct of war with legal codes. Proponents of such efforts assume that bringing war within the bounds of rational rules may somehow "humanize" war and contain its brutalities.[8] As Michael Walzer comments, "War is so awful that it makes us cynical about the possibility of restraint, and then it is so much worse that it makes us indignant at the absence of restraint."[9]

Post-Westphalia international law, such as it was, imposed no effective restraints on nation-states and their leaders in starting and carrying out aggression. Foreign policy was premised on a need to protect and advance something that was called "national interest," and the tendency then and now was to define that notion primarily in terms of the state's power[10] and well-being, and secondarily in terms of the citizenry's welfare. Thus national interests rather than moral "abstractions" of principles and norms guided state action—a mode that favored political expedience over appreciable gain in norms and principles. With imperialistic ambitions taking root, national interest came to encapsulate the extension of a state's territory and the consolidation of hegemonic power. What varied was the degree of shrewdness in the calculating self-interest of diplomats and politicians. The post-Westphalia era was a world with minimal constraints on national leaders and almost no constraints on the state's treatment of its own nationals. Leaders of nation-states were not accountable for alleged violations of international law and the strongest states—militarily, economically, and politically—prevailed.

In the formative period of the modern international community, war, especially between states, was seen and held to be the ultimate mechanism for the resolution of conflict. The paradox is that law and war seem to occupy mutually exclusive terrain. As Cicero wrote, *inter arma silent leges*—"in time of war the law is silent."[11] Law implies order and restraint; war epitomizes the absence of both. It is precisely when the legal system fails that conflict turns to violence. Law may act to deter war, but it has no practical role once the fighting has begun.[12] The paradox in regulating the conduct of armed conflict is best expressed in the contrasting views of Montesquieu (a jurist) and Clausewitz (a military general). Montesquieu gives the humanistic perspective—the parties to an armed conflict (war) should inflict on each other the least possible harm. In contrast, Carl von Clausewitz, in his celebrated book *On War*, affirms that "in war the party seeking to win should inflict upon his enemy as much harm as is necessary to ensure a decisive victory."[13] Though one can assume that Clausewitz's approach may theoretically lead to reduced victimization, it is not the primary goal in the conduct of war. The reduction of victimization was, however, Montesquieu's primary goal. In time, Montesquieu's humanistic view was to prevail and be expressed in the international community's commonly shared values, as reflected in conventional and customary international humanitarian law, as well as in the domestic laws of a number of states. "Regrettably, however, the practices of states remained consistent with the teachings of von Clausewitz as opposed to those of Montesquieu."[14]

The establishment of formal enforcement mechanisms to govern the international system has long been sought by those who believe that the nature of the modern international legal order demands clear rules governing international behavior[15] and especially the unilateral use of force, as this threatens the legitimacy of international law by diminishing the rule of law. The hope of "civilized society" has long been that nations would cease to pursue interests through violence and coercion and attempt instead to negotiate in quest of agreement and enshrine this in settled norms that would condition the behavior of states in the international system. Yet from the early development of the laws of war and enforcement mechanisms, the nature of the state-centric international system dictated that law played second fiddle to the hard reality of power politics. Strong domestic-based political, moral, or ideological motivations (the hallmark of realpolitik)[16] crippled the early development of international humanitarian law and subsequently hobbled its enforcement in the twentieth century, when the legitimacy of war was first put in question and its use subjected to legal constraints.

Prior to the twentieth century, war was a formal business with uniformed armies occupying delineated territory, a code of conduct that was usually (though not always) observed, a formal declaration, and a formal end in the peace treaty.[17] The "decisive battle" was a feature of Clausewitzian war—formal fighting and formal peace—but technological and strategic developments increasingly displaced this formal warfare dominated by set-piece battles, paving the way for an epoch of unbridled ferocity. Victory at whatever cost replaced politically inspired calculus, and end objectives and virulent nationalism replaced "rational" state egoism as the basis of war.

In the twentieth century technological advancements and the birth of total war combined with a strong body of multilateral rules and norms governing war—and the challenge of Clausewitzian conceptions of war. The landscape of war had undergone dramatic transformation. The combatant/noncombatant distinction had been blurred, and the immense power of new weapons and the indiscriminate tactics of warfare inspired a need to discipline excesses occurring beyond delineated battlefields. Previous conceptions of war (i.e., legitimate and/or rational as long as the warmaking state had the authority to act) were put in doubt as the common-sense view gained ascendance that war represents a breakdown, a malfunctioning, of the international system. It took the senseless mayhem of World War I—the destruction of economic structures, dissipation of financial resources, and undermining of political stability—to erase the traditional notion that war was a rational political act. World War I was disastrous for its initiators and the victims. Millions died pointlessly, and regimes fell. The carnage forced modern industrial societies to question war as an instrument of national policy in which the benefits of conquest seemed trivial compared to the costs of war: large-scale death and destruction, political instability, and economic turmoil. It seemed obvious that war was no longer a profitable enterprise. Resultant economic and political chaos, reinforced by increasing moral disquiet over the idea that states had free rein, focused minds on the moral and legal responsibilities for the outbreak of this war.

World War I was a watershed. Apart from marking the maturation of total war, the postwar peace saw an unsuccessful process of penalization by individualizing criminal responsibility for violations of laws of war and for crimes against humanity. The punishment provisions of the peace treaties signed at Versailles and Sevres sought to limit sovereign immunity by punishing military and civilian officials while extending universal jurisdiction to cover war crimes and crimes against humanity. In the end, this international penal process yielded to national sovereignty, leading to sham national trials in Germany and in Turkey against a relative handful of defendants. The political concessions that translated into immunity for wartime atrocities reignited the debate on whether international law was simply a convenience leading to free rein in diplomacy.[18] The hypocrisy of the victor as well as the vanquished raised crucial questions. Was international humanitarian law a useful mechanism in the international system, or just another weapon in the game of diplomacy? Was international humanitarian law a vital component of international relations, or an acceptable minor obstacle in the pursuit of policy offering no significant restraint on a nation's freedom to pursue national interests? The international system began to establish mechanisms to ensure the practical application and enforcement of international humanitarian law. But it took another round of state-orchestrated carnage two decades hence to spur states into giving international humanitarian law life and vitality.

At Nuremberg (and later at Tokyo) the modern international penal process was practically inaugurated. Nuremberg was designed to change the anarchic context in which nations and peoples of the world related to one another. Nuremberg and Tokyo demonstrated that national leaders as well as state officials and personnel could be held responsible for their actions under international law, revealing the enforceability of international norms governing the conduct of armed conflict. Despite the successful establishment of the tribunals pursuant to international law invocations, the process demonstrated that international law, though affording a crucial framework for international society, was not a self-contained abstraction. It is a force in international affairs, but its influence can be understood only in light of other forces governing the behavior of nations and governments.

Despite the dominance of geopolitical interests at the end of World War I, which shadowed the post–World War II international trials, Nuremburg and Tokyo marked a turning point in the understanding of sovereignty and the protection that it afforded. The traditional state-centered view of personality—predicated on the view of the state as the relevant subject of the international regime—experienced a radial shift after World War II when the concept of individual criminal responsibility was laid down as the cardinal principle governing international law violations. With international humanitarian law interlocking with the emerging law of human rights, the shift away from states to the individual became a dominant development. The nation-state was no longer the sole subject of international law because international law was expanding its frontiers and extending to domestic areas jealously guarded by Westphalian sovereignty. International law was moving toward direct applicability to individuals—endowing them with rights and protections and in return demanding adherence to international norms.

These developments in the transforming juridical discourse reflected a paradigm shift in the conceptualization of the international rule of law. This new subjectivity was evident in the later enforcement of expanded norms, which are directed beyond states to persons and peoples with new enforcement structures based on institutionalization. However, this movement was to be first checked and then routinely interrupted by the volatile politics of the Cold War, preventing an immediate fulfillment of its lofty ideals.

The precedent set at Nuremberg and amplified at Tokyo—pointing to a restrained state disciplined by international law norms—was curtailed with the onset of the Cold War. The Cold War largely put an end to the spurt of international judicial activity inaugurated at Nuremberg and Tokyo and contributed to the preservation of a statist international order. But even amid the dominant ideological rivalry of the Cold War, the United Nations (UN) was beginning to move, tentatively but assuredly, from mere standard-setting to implementing those standards. The Cold War era involved mixed blessings for the international penal process. Tremendous advances were made in the codification and broadening of international humanitarian law, but East-West rivalries prevented meaningful enforcement at the international level. The resultant bipolar politics rendered the United Nations powerless to deal with many of the humanitarian crises accompanied by gross human rights violations.

The moral abdication of states during the Cold War era set the stage for the series of internecine conflicts in Rwanda, Somalia, Liberia, Bosnia, and elsewhere that occurred in the immediate aftermath of the Cold War. States and individuals had come to regard international humanitarian law as more of a moral code of conduct than as binding obligations on states and individuals. The lack of an enforcement regime contributed to cynicism and a lack of respect for the legitimacy of international justice. The ad hoc international criminal tribunals in the 1990s represented an international effort to put in place such a regime. In that same decade, states voted to adopt the Rome Statute establishing the International Criminal Court (ICC), seemingly closing the circle on the efforts first inaugurated after World War I.

The wave of accountability has in recent times gathered strength. At no point in history has so much attention been focused on human wrongs: by global media, by nongovernmental organizations (NGOs), and by the organs of national and international law. Holding individuals accountable for those wrongs—criminal prosecution—has become popular. Though prosecution for human rights offenses had been a historical rarity, in 2000 former officials from at least fourteen countries were under indictment for violations of international humanitarian law. The institutions currently commanding the most attention for ongoing international prosecutions are the International Criminal Tribunal for the Former Yugoslavia (ICTY) and the International Criminal Tribunal for Rwanda (ICTR). With the entry into force of the Rome Statute, the ICC promises to be a powerful new institution for ensuring accountability. Much is expected of the nascent ICC, but promise may yet outstrip reality in light of international realpolitik.

From the optimists' standpoint, the new international spirit for corralling international outlaws is gathering pace. The recent design innovations of the Special Court for Sierra Leone (SCSL)[19] provide an encouraging model for generating a tighter weave of international norms and the reality of enforcing them. Established in 2000,[20] the SCSL is part of a growing attempt to more effectively meet the goals of international justice through incremental changes in the familiar institutions of prosecution. Prosecution seems the sole presumptive response to violations of international humanitarian law. Yet it is just one tool in the toolbox of accountability. While one tool—international prosecution—has gained ascendance, it has the potential to distract attention and take away resources from more suitable mechanisms. Those seeking accountability should know what they seek to accomplish, employ well-designed prosecutions to satisfy the highest priorities, and supplement tribunals with other mechanisms to address the things that prosecution does not.

The complexities of ensuring clear-cut international justice in the international system will be evident throughout this book. Politicians and diplomats responsible for setting up bodies mandated to investigate and prosecute violations of international humanitarian law often favor political expedience. And trials occur only when and in the manner dictated by prevailing political currents. Justice is compromised through a series of mechanisms, both legal and political. Often, timely investigations can lead to politically undesired results. Indeed, the investigation of the alleged criminal conduct by military and political leaders who are essential to achieving a peaceful settlement can impede the process, creating major dilemmas in which political settlements are favored over justice. That is why so many international and noninternational conflicts have resulted in de jure or de facto immunity for the leaders, as well as most of the perpetrators of international humanitarian law and international human rights violations.[21]

Important changes have occurred in the international legal regime, driven by international humanitarian law in its quest to discipline sovereign excesses. Legal rhetoric reflects changing conceptions of legitimacy in contemporary international politics and represents a paradigm shift toward a definite conception of rule of law in the international domain with greater significance for the juridicization of international affairs discourse. A distinct dimension of the juridical transformation is its enforcement and entrenchment through international institutionalization. The 1990s witnessed a remarkable expansion in the institutionalization of international law. New institutions ranging from international courts to nongovernmental organizations mediated both public and private realms. And though the dual purpose of criminalization of atrocious wartime conduct is to deliver justice and deter future atrocities, in practice principles of justice are often subjugated to the vagaries of realpolitik, and sovereignty overrides the laws of war.

The humanitarian regime has been entrenched through codifications chartering new international judicial institutions that make criminal justice the primary means of enforcing international rights law. Although international criminal tribunals began on an ad hoc basis, they have become the international community's primary response to humanitarian crises. A consensus on establishing a new institution dedicated to ongoing international adjudication of violations of humanitarian law is seen in the ICTY and ICTR, leading to the establishment of the permanent ICC. The expanded discourse of international criminal justice has revised traditional understandings of the law of war, the parameters of war and peace, and the state's duties to its citizens by extending international jurisdiction beyond national borders and situations of conflict to penetrate states during times of peace.

Establishing an international regime that contemplates the coercive enforcement of humanitarian law reflects a reconceptualization of the rule of law in the international order. The aim of the newly established enforcement machinery in the form of independent international institutions dedicated to enforcing humanitarian law supports the perception of a heightened international rule of law. These new international institutions incorporate criminal sanctions into the international legal system. Criminal sanctions are a distinctive dimension of legal norms and can plausibly be used to signal and reinforce the difference between general and positive law norms.[22]

Contemporary developments point to a reliance on law, legal processes, and judicial structures in international politics, which raises a question about how to interpret these judicial developments. The international humanitarian legal regime supports a transformation of global politics through its articulation of an international discourse of rule of law. Global rules of law enable and restrain power in today's political circumstances in order to manage new conditions of political disorder through the rubric of law. In the absence of a common world government it is the humanitarian legal regime that is used to lend authority and legitimacy to the international realm through its tribunals, proceedings, juridical language, and public justificatory processes. Humanitarian law and courts are the preeminent institutions and processes aimed at managing current global politics and at representing the legalist view on how to advance the core goal of ending political violence.

The international penal process is intended to advance the goal of rationalizing foreign policy decisionmaking and to assist in the legitimization of globalizing an international rule of law order. However, the enterprise has troubling ramifications. To a large extent, international penal process aims to ensure minimal preservative rights that rationalize the erosion of the territorial status quo in favor of the protection of human rights. Beyond the role of the law as constraint, the concept of international justice would allow for military interventions beyond their historical goal (protecting national sovereignty) to the broader goal of protecting peoples who are facing atrocities.

Often prosecution at the international level may become a tool for political gain. This motivation may arise most prominently in the decision to establish tribunals or target regional conflicts for prosecution. Once a prosecutorial structure is in place, the possibility for political gain depends more directly on the prosecutor's susceptibility to political influences. Tribunals may provide an avenue to reduce the political influence of indictees or to enhance public opinion of regimes helping to deliver "justice." In addition, tribunals may provide a symbol for international power brokers to show that they are remedying humanitarian deprivations but without having to muster resources more suitable to the task at hand.[23] The international penal process is often caught in the unhealthy grip of bureaucratic self-preservation. The institutions of international prosecution may have a vested self-interest in the prominence and perceived efficacy of international prosecution as a mechanism of accountability. Although it is true that preserving a prosecutorial institution as an institution may be necessary to achieve long-term ends, self-preservation also has the potential to crowd out an institution's original aims and to emerge as an end unto itself. In tribunals, this self-preservation may manifest itself as a concern for institutional growth and credibility for their own sake.

The history and record of international criminal investigation and adjudication bodies, from the Treaty of Versailles to the Rome Statute, demonstrate the dominance of competing interests of politics or the influence of a changed geopolitical situation. The ad hoc tribunals and investigations have suffered from the competing interests of politics or the influence of a changed geopolitical situation. In the observation of renowned international criminal law scholar M. C. Bassiouni:

> Between 1919 and 1994 there were five *ad hoc* international investigation commissions, four *ad hoc* international criminal tribunals, and three internationally mandated or authorized national prosecutions arising out of World War I and World War II. These processes were established by different legal means with varying mandates, many of them producing results contrary to those originally contemplated. The investigations and prosecutions were established to appease public demand for a response to the tragic events and shocking conduct during armed conflicts. Despite public

pressure demanding justice, investigative and adjudicating bodies were established for only a few international conflicts. Domestic conflicts, no matter how brutal, drew even less attention from the world's major powers, whose political will has been imperative to the establishment of such bodies.[24]

The interplay between law and politics characteristic of the twentieth century's ad hoc international tribunals is manifest in the allocation of responsibility during the different trial stages. Frequently, there is total separation between the establishment of the bodies and their administration. Similarly, the investigation stage is separated from the adjudication stage, and in each case, without exception, the judicial bodies that pronounce sentences are terminated immediately afterward. The fact that diplomats and politicians are largely entrusted with authority to establish international tribunals and delineate their mandates and authority means that important decisions are not necessarily motivated by justice concerns.[25] "Often, institutional records documenting the various stages seldom reflect the activity occurring behind the political curtain."[26]

Pursuing political settlements while concurrently seeking to obtain justice is an incongruent goal. Pursuing each contemporaneously compromises justice in favor of political settlements because nations are the actors, the legislators, the executives, as well as the judges of international law. Despite norms, standards, and obligations, the implementation or enforceability of this is inevitably policy-oriented, informed by a process of authoritative state decisionmaking based on calculations of self- as well as collective interest or disinterest. The law then is in many ways part of the political process; law is made and agreements are given meaning by the total political process—when governments act and other governments react, when courts (national or international) decide cases, when political bodies debate and pass resolutions and nations act in their light. International law, then, is in many aspects an "architecture of political compromise."[27]

In the twentieth century, international trials occurred at different times and places. The singling out of certain conflicts in a world full of aggression and inhumanity highlights the hypocritical selectivity of major powers. The complacency of government leaders results in inaction, compelling the occasional ad hoc tribunals that have ethical weaknesses and present legal and practical difficulties. "The phenomenon of political complacency in the face of repeated atrocities in various parts of the world is regrettably a feature of international realpolitik."[28] After every conflict or event during which the perceived need arises to prosecute and punish those who commit international crimes, "the world community ultimately settles for the legal status quo ante."[29] Of course, to dismiss international norms and standards as entirely hostage to politics would be a misleading simplicity. The whole body of the law, including the legal framework of international society, shapes and limits the behavior of nations and determines the alternatives available to them. Even as to the norms of the law, their influence on diplomacy is subtler and more complex than merely to deter violation or induce compliance. However, the domineering influence of realpolitik in the international order is frequent, as law intersects with state interests, necessitating the need for political accommodation. In the words of L. Henkin:

> Relations between nations are primarily the responsibility neither of generals nor of judges; they remain the domain of diplomacy between representatives of nations promoting national policies . . . diplomacy, and law do not represent discrete stages in international history. They have long coexisted, waxing and waning, in different "proportions" at different times, among different nations in different contexts.[30]

This overview and general introduction of war and the vagaries of realpolitik introduces the two dominant themes of this book. In subsequent chapters, a detailed analysis looks at the interplay of justice requirements in the face of political expedience. The central point is that nations, though relying on the rubric of international humanitarian law in establishing international penal mechanisms, nonetheless seek to concurrently promote individual interests through various techniques of influence that lead to compromises and political accommodation.

This book is divided into three parts. Chapter 1 introduces war generally as a sovereign right and the development of the laws of war regime to address sovereign excesses. It sets the stage for the subsequent analysis, which focuses on the manner in which the international penal process has developed over time. Chapter 2 considers World War I and the efforts to secure international criminal accountability as envisaged under the peace treaties of Versailles and Sevres. While the envisaged international efforts failed to materialize, important principles were established. Chapter 3 deals with World War II and the groundbreaking international penal processes at Nuremberg and Tokyo. The chapter notes that the Nuremberg judgments, by establishing individual accountability for violations of international law, explicitly rejected the argument that state sovereignty was an acceptable defense for unconscionable violations of human rights.

In Part 2, we'll discuss the Cold War and the ad hoc international criminal tribunals of the 1990s that symbolized a move from the old diplomacy grounded in power and politics to a new diplomacy based on law and authority. Chapter 4 is a general commentary on the Cold War era, discussing the manner in which the Nuremberg principles crossed over into the national sphere, as well as the disappointment created when international humanitarian law was consigned to the backseat. Chapters 5 and 6 focus on the two ad hoc international criminal tribunals created under UN auspices in the 1990s to prosecute those responsible for grave violations in the former Yugoslavia and Rwanda.

Part 3 includes an extended discussion on the International Criminal Court, the last great institution to be established in the twentieth century and a crowning achievement. It establishes a permanent international penal mechanism and thus seals a major lacuna in the international system. Chapter 7 discusses efforts to establish a permanent tribunal for crimes violating international law and examines the organization and operating principles of the ICC. The chapter explores the politics of establishing the court and the reflection of this in the Rome Statute. Chapter 8 concludes with a discussion of international justice in retrospect and prospect.

Notes

1. See Jean Pictet, *Developments and Principles of International Humanitarian Law* (Dordrecht, Netherlands, and Boston: M. Nijhoff, 1985), 79.

2. Remigiusz Bierzanek traces the origin of this distinction to the Romans in "The Prosecution of War Crimes," in *A Treatise on International Criminal Law,* edited by M. Cherif Bassiouni and Ved P. Nanda (Springfield, IL: Thomas, 1973), 559. A modern example of a law of *jus ad bellum* is the United Nations Charter, prohibiting "threat or the use of force" by states against other states (UN Charter, art. 2, para. 4).

3. *Jus in bello* laws are attributed to the Greeks. See Bierzanek, "The Prosecution of War Crimes," 559.

4. The intention of the treaty was the termination of conflicts between private and public jurisdictions as well as the more general conflict all over Europe between ecclesiastical and secular claims for the citizenry's obedience and allegiance.

5. Louis Henkin, *How Nations Behave: Law and Foreign Policy* (London: Pall Mall, 1968), 4. Broadly speaking one can conceive of force as an institution of violence and coercion, diplomacy as an institution of problem-solving and negotiation, and law as an institution of rules and norms that aims to manage interaction, be it in the sociopolitical or economic sphere.

6. See Adam Watson, *The Evolution of International Society: A Comparative Historical Analysis* (London and New York: Routledge, 1992), which is one of the best guides to the origins of the Westphalia system.

7. Chris Brown, *Understanding International Relations* (New York: Palgrave, 2001), 9.

8. Ibid., 55.

9. Michael Walzer, *Just and Unjust Wars: A Moral Argument with Historical Illustrations,* 2nd ed. (New York: Basic Books, 1992), 46.

10. "State power" is a multifaceted and complex notion. State power in international relations may be defined as the ability of an actor on the international stage to use tangible and intangible resources and assets in such a way as to influence the outcomes of international events to its own satisfaction. For a discussion of the dimensions of state power, see Brown, *Understanding International Relations,* 89–99; Walter S. Jones, *The Logic of International Relations,* 5th ed. (Boston: Little, Brown, 1985), 245–248.

11. Quoted in Quincy Wright, *A Study of War* (Chicago: University of Chicago Press, 1965), 863.

12. Chris A. F. Jochnick and Roger Normand, "The Legitimation of Violence: A Critical History of the Laws of War," *Harvard International Law Journal* (1994): 49.

13. M. Cherif Bassiouni, *Crimes Against Humanity in International Criminal Law*, 2nd rev. ed. (The Hague and Boston: Kluwer Law International, 1999), 44.

14. Ibid., 42.

15. See for example T. L. H. McCormack and G. Simpson, "The International Law Commission's Draft Code of Crimes Against the Peace and Security of Mankind," *Criminal Law Forum* 5 (1994): 10; M. Cherif Bassiouni and C. L. Blakesley, "The Need for an International Criminal Court in the New International World Order," *Vanderbilt Journal of Transnational Law* 25 (1992): 54.

16. "Realpolitik" is a word of German origin and literally means "practical politics." It is broadly used here to denote power politics designed to produce or achieve certain desired outcomes whether based on legal, moral, or ideological considerations.

17. Brown, *Understanding International Relations*.

18. Henkin, *How Nations Behave*, 5.

19. United Nations Security Council Resolutions (UN SCOR), *Report of the Secretary-General on the Establishment of a Special Court for Sierra Leone*, 55th sess., UN Doc. S/2000/915, 2000.

20. Ibid.

21. M. Cherif Bassiouni, "Former Yugoslavia: Investigating Violations of International Humanitarian Law and Establishing an International Criminal Court," *Fordham International Law Journal* 18 (1995): 1191, 1209.

22. See generally H. L. A. Hart, *The Concept of Law* (Oxford: Oxford University Press, 1961), 213–214 (discussing the uses of sanctions for norm-strengthening functions in domestic law); Judith N. Shklar, *Legalism: Law, Morals, and Political Trials* (Cambridge, MA: Harvard University Press, 1986) (discussing legalism as an ideology internal to the legal profession and, more important, as political ideology). Growing emphasis on positivism in international law has tended to derive largely from U.S. jurisprudence.

23. See, for example, United Nations General Assembly Resolutions (UN GAOR), *Annual Report of the International Tribunal for the Prosecution of Persons Responsible for Serious Violations of International Humanitarian Law Committed in the Territory of the Former Yugoslavia Since 1991*, 49th sess., Agenda Item 152, UN Docs. A/49/342, S/1994/1007, 1994, 44, para. 7 (admitting that the tribunal was created to fill the "need to demonstrate to the international community that the United Nations was not sitting back idly while thousands were being brutally abused or massacred"); see also Jackson Nyamuya Maogoto, "International Justice in the Shadow of Realpolitik: Re-Visiting the Establishment of the Ad Hoc International Criminal Tribunals," *Flinders Journal of Legal Reform* 161 (2001) (arguing that the establishment of the two ad hoc international criminal tribunals was an act of tokenism by the world community, which was largely unwilling to intervene in either the former Yugoslavia or Rwanda but did not mind creating institutions that would give the appearance of moral concern).

24. M. Cherif Bassiouni, "From Versailles to Rwanda in Seventy-Five Years: The Need to Establish a Permanent International Criminal Court," *Harvard Human Rights Journal* 10 (1997): 11–12.

25. Ibid.

26. Ibid.

27. Gerry Simpson, "'Throwing a Little Remembering on the Past': The International Criminal Court and the Politics of Sovereignty," *University of California Davis Journal of International Law and Policy* 5 (1999): 133, 142.

28. M. Cherif Bassiouni, "'Crimes Against Humanity': The Need for a Specialized Convention," *Columbia Journal of Transnational Law* 31 (1994): 458.

29. Ibid.

30. Henkin, *How Nations Behave*, 4.

1

Toward the Modern
International Penal Process

Many acts committed during the course of hostilities—acts that we now consider to be conventional war crimes—were a normal incident of warfare during the earliest days of recorded history. The prospects of a free run of a soldier's "lusts for blood, spoil and women was a major incentive to a soldier to persevere in the rigors which were likely to attend a protracted siege."[1] It was at approximately this period that the doctrine of "just war" evolved. According to this, the side fighting the just war was engaged in a lawful war and was not bound by the law of war, whereas (theoretically) the adversary, fighting an unjust war, was so bound. The unsparing cruelty of war during the greater part of the Middle Ages was gradually modified through the influence of Christianity and chivalry.[2] The development of the just war doctrine by the church in the Middle Ages marked a serious attempt to regulate conduct during war. The roots of contemporary laws of war[3] arose and grew gradually during the latter part of the Middle Ages with the rationale of seeking to humanize war by balancing military necessity with concerns for humanity. The enforcement of laws of war dates to this same era, when the first known war crimes trials were held.[4] However, the just war doctrine was easily subject to manipulation owing to its highly subjective nature; both sides almost invariably contended that they were fighting the just war, often backed by a high church official. The application of such a doctrine meant that the laws of war would cease to be meaningful. In order to enhance the application of the laws of war, a custom arose whereby even the just-fighting state was bound by humanitarian law. In other words, both sides were equally bound to obey the laws of war without regard to claims of justness.

Over a period of many centuries, humanitarian principles regulating armed conflicts evolved. In the course of this, certain principles emerged that restricted what a combatant could do during war. It was the beginning of what became known as *jus ad bellum*. In time, humanitarian principles formed an interwoven fabric of norms and rules preventing certain forms of physical harm and hardships from befalling noncombatants, as well as certain categories of combatants such as the sick, wounded, shipwrecked, and prisoners of war. As the protective scheme of prescriptions and proscriptions increased qualitatively and quantitatively, the most serious breaches were criminalized. As imperialistic ambitions took root in Europe, multistate conflict displaced interstate conflict, providing the impetus toward multilateral regulation of war within the framework of developing international legal norms.

The process of normative development in international humanitarian law was dominated by politicians and diplomats who held sway over the substantive content of international law generally (and regulation of war specifically), as well as the obligations the state undertook. Thus the development of international humanitarian law frequently occurred amid the politically oriented authoritative processes of international lawmaking, in which political expedience and geopolitical reality were the determinant factors.[5] Amid the endeavors of publicists, politicians, and diplomats to craft the structure and content of international law, this historical phase was also founded upon the emerging shared values of the world community to limit resort to war and regulate its conduct to minimize its harmful human consequences. Thereafter, bilateral and multilateral treaties, particularly after the Peace of Westphalia in 1648, sought to regulate relations among states for the prevention of war and to give tangible expression to these shared values and concerns. It was during this era (after Westphalia and before the two world wars)—wherein sovereign absolutist states operated without any superior authority or body—that the development and codification of modern international humanitarian law began.

This chapter is a *tour de horizon* of the development of laws of war and the concept of supranational adjudication of war crimes.

The Development of the Modern Laws of War

International law as one between sovereign and equal states based on the common consent of these states is a product of modern Christian civilization; it may be said to be about 500 years old. When the Roman Empire collapsed, the Christian church moved in to fill the vacuum as an umbrella authority over Europe. This form of international order—the Respublica Christiana—was founded upon natural law, with a distinctly theological twist as a system of norms emanating, ultimately, from God. As the church grew to exercise temporal power in Europe, it abandoned its early commitment to pacifism but sought to humanize war.[6]

The Respublica Christiana endured for 1,000 years, but it could not withstand the changes brought on by the Renaissance and the Reformation. It ended violently with the Thirty Years' War (1618–1648), which itself ended with the Peace of Westphalia.[7] The origin of the international community in its current structure and configuration is usually traced back to the Peace of Westphalia.[8] Thus 1648 marked the end of the Thirty Years' War, the fracture of the Holy Roman Empire, the emergence of sovereign states in Europe, and the rise of international law.[9] More significant, the affirmation of national states in modern societies generated a monopoly of domestic criminal justice systems keen to assert absolute sovereignty to ward off interference by the papacy.

During the Thirty Years' War, in 1625, Hugo Grotius published his seminal work, *De Jure Belli ac Pacis Libris Tres* (On the Law of War and Peace).[10] In it, Grotius maintained that the laws governing relations among nations must first safeguard the sovereignty of states; he was of the view that rules preventing interference in another state's jurisdiction would help safeguard sovereignty. Grotius concluded that the practice of states reflected natural law through the reasoned judgment of men.[11] Most important from the modern perspective, he insisted that war should be governed by a strict set of laws.[12] Grotius maintained that violence beyond that necessary to secure the military goal was not justified and that suffering should be minimized within the parameters of military requirements.[13]

The Peace of Westphalia attempted to codify an international system based on the coexistence of a plurality of states exercising unimpeded sovereignty within their territories, thereby making untrammeled state sovereignty and freedom from outside interference the foundation of modern international law. In the absence of any higher authority deriving from the community of states, restraints in the international arena were mostly self-imposed, voluntarily observed, and enforced principally by the threat of retaliation. In the absence of an international mechanism for enforcing international law, war was a means of self-help for giving effect to claims based on international law. War was viewed as a natural function of the state and a prerogative of its unrestricted sovereignty. Such was the legal and moral authority that war, when resorted to, was described as being undertaken to defend a legal right.[14] War was in effect a sanction looked upon as a legal remedy of self-help.[15] This conception was intimately connected with the distinction between just and unjust wars. As long as war was a recognized instrument of national policy (both giving effect to existing rights and changing the law), the justness or otherwise of the war was legally irrelevant.[16]

Customary international law has always and still permits belligerent states to prosecute enemy soldiers in their custody for breach of the laws and customs of war.[17] And in the peace treaties ending the wars of the seventeenth century and thereafter, the custom of the amnesty (or oblivion) provision developed. This forgave, among other things, war crimes committed during the hostilities that the treaty terminated.[18] This practice continued until the twentieth century when the Treaty of Versailles and the other peace treaties that ended World War I swept aside the practice in favor of international accountability through the penal process.

In the period 1648–1815, with the state in ascendance, there were few significant developments in international humanitarian law. Although there existed a functioning system of international law, this system served the interests of states to coexist peacefully, rather than to pursue the interests of international cooperation.[19] International humanitarian law would have only a very limited role in the post–Westphalian era system where state sovereignty took preeminence, interstate conflict was regular, and international cooperation was minimal. Aside from a few narrow rules prohibiting certain means and methods of war, norms of international humanitarian law could not arise before there existed a certain level of solidarity, community, and development on the international scene. International humanitarian law would not possibly be effective if state action remained largely unfettered and unregulated. Thus not only was the state largely free to do as it wished; the individual acting as agent of the state was shielded from sanction by the privileges and immunities based in sovereignty.

The regulation of war continued to remain on the international agenda, but the emphasis was pragmatism in regulating the conduct of war rather than seeking means to formally enforce the norms and rules, a process that was seen as anachronistic to the state's sovereign right to engage in war. More than a century after the watershed Peace of Westphalia, publicists continued to recognize war as a right of the state, though arguing for the humanization of conflict. Thus, Jean-Jacques Rousseau argued in his seminal work *Le Contrat Social* (The Social Contract) that:

> Since the aim of war is to subdue a hostile state, a combatant has the right to kill the defenders of that state while they are armed; but as soon as they lay down their arms and surrender, they cease to be either enemies or instruments of the enemy; they become simply men once more, and no one has any longer the right to take their lives. It is sometimes possible to destroy a state without killing their lives. It is sometimes possible to destroy a state without killing a single one of its members, and war gives no right to inflict any more destruction than is necessary for victory. These principles were not invented by Grotius, nor are they founded on the authority of the poets; they are derived from the nature of things; they are based on reason.[20]

It was not until 1815 that the first steps toward dynamic and practical international cooperation were taken within the framework of the Congress of Vienna.[21] The Congress of Vienna, beyond formalizing the new balance of power following the defeat of Napoleon's armies by Austria, Britain,

Prussia, and Russia, represents the first international collective security arrangement. More significant for the development of international law, it was also the first joint state action to prohibit the slave trade and piracy by imposing individual criminal responsibility. The pertinent provisions of the Final Act obliged every state signatory to prosecute the alleged offender under its own criminal laws.[22]

Laws of war continued to be embodied in accepted norms and rules, with few formal multilateral agreements. Considering this lack of precision, progress was made during the nineteenth century after the close of the Napoleonic Wars, especially from 1850 to 1899, to codify the rules and norms and thus accelerate their development. The codification reached new heights in this era (the heyday of legal positivism), setting the stage for the development of a formal international regime. The laws of war evolved through an isolation of military practices that became usages; these usages, through custom and treaties, turned into legal rules. The growth of the laws and usages of war was determined by the basic principle of military necessity, which stated that all violence not necessary to overpower the opponent should not be permitted to belligerents. The influence of this principle of military necessity had enormous influence upon the practice and methods of warfare in seeking to regulate the cruel and unsparing nature of war under the then ascendant doctrine of raison d'etat.[23]

In many respects, the evolution of humanitarianism in armed conflicts came to fruition in the middle of the nineteenth century, more specifically after the Battle of Solferino in June 1859, where France defeated Austro-Hungary.[24] Henri Dunant, a Swiss businessman who happened to be in the vicinity of the battlefield, was deeply moved by the sight of the many wounded men left to suffer and die for lack of medical attention. In 1862 Dunant published *Un Souvenir de Solferino*,[25] which inspired the conclusion two years later of the first Geneva Convention on the treatment of the sick and wounded during battle.[26] Four years later came the first multilateral agreement to ban the use of a particular weapon in war.[27] And in 1863, before either of these agreements had been concluded, the earliest official government codification of the laws of war was promulgated by the United States during the Civil War. This was the first modern codification of the laws of war to be officially adopted by a warring belligerent.[28] This codification was issued as General Orders no. 100 (Instructions for the Government of Armies of the United States in the Field, more commonly known as the Lieber Code).[29] It was drafted by an academic intent on drawing general principles of human morality from empirical evidence, and it was issued by a president determined to found his policies on human reason. The Lieber Code can thus be considered the final product of the eighteenth-century movement to humanize war through the application of reason.[30] It gave the concept of laws of humanity explicit recognition, provided a blueprint for similar international efforts in the second half of the century, and has been widely praised as a humanitarian milestone for implementing the rule of law in an actual war.[31] The Lieber Code's greatest contribution was its identification of military necessity as a general legal principle to limit violence, in the absence of any other rule, a principle that was soon to achieve international recognition.[32]

Even if destined only for American soldiers and binding only on them, the Lieber Code had an important influence on military regulations in other armies. As "the first attempt to check the whole conduct of armies by precise written rules"[33] and "a persuasively written essay on the ethics of conducting war,"[34] the Lieber Code projected influence far beyond the ranks of the United States Army. In 1868 an international commission meeting in St. Petersburg, Russia, applied the code's principle of military necessity to ban the use of small-caliber explosive bullets because they would cause "unnecessary suffering."[35] In 1870 the Prussian government adapted the code as guidance for its army during the Franco-Prussian War.[36] Concerning the evolution of the humanitarian law of war during this period, one moralist has written:

> It was not until the middle of the nineteenth century that the idea began to take hold in military law—though theologians and moralists had often made the point before—that certain practices should be forbidden, regardless of their military utility, because they were inhumane. As the laws of war continued to evolve during this period and were gradually codified in national military law and in international treaties, humanitarian considerations increasingly took their place beside those of expedience.[37]

The humanitarian considerations that increasingly began to eclipse military expedience found practical manifestation after the Franco-Prussian War. The atrocities of that war and the seeming determination of the parties to ensure impunity by ignoring the need for diligent prosecution of war criminals led Gustave Moynier (one of the founders of the International Committee of the Red Cross [ICRC]) to present a proposal for a permanent international criminal court. The atrocities committed during the Franco-Prussian War convinced Moynier, a humanist, that public opinion alone was inadequate absent a formal supranational mechanism to enforce international humanitarian law. Next we consider this proposal.

The Birth of the International Penal Process

Before discussing Gustave Moynier's proposal for an international criminal court, we should review the enforcement of humanitarian rules and norms through supranational mechanisms.

Prior to the twentieth century, trials through joint military jurisdiction were rare, based on the ancient *jus militaire* and knightly code of honor, an era when the laws of war were tied to religious particularism. As the laws of chivalry developed during the Middle Ages in Western Europe, so did rules limiting the means and manner of conducting war. Heraldic courts developed a code of chivalry that regulated a knight's conduct in battle; Christian princes enforced these in their own courts. The goal of these principles, norms, and rules was to protect noncombatants, innocent civilians, and those who were hors de combat from unnecessary harm.

The enforcement of modern international humanitarian law[38] dates back to the Middle Ages, when the first known war crimes trials were held.[39] The first international criminal tribunal to bring to justice someone responsible for crimes against humanity was convened in 1474. An ad hoc criminal tribunal of twenty-eight judges from different states allied to the Roman Empire tried and convicted Peter Von Hagenbach for murder, rape, perjury, and other crimes in violation of "the laws of God and man" during the occupation of the town of Breisach on behalf of Charles, Duke of Burgundy, at a time when there were no hostilities.[40] M. C. Bassiouni cites this as the "first documented prosecution for initiating an unjust war,"[41] essentially as the first ad hoc international criminal tribunal.[42] After the Middle Ages, additional norms and rules were developed to strengthen basic principles of humanity. And until the nineteenth century these residual remains of chivalry, the nonbinding theoretical treatises of the publicists, and the slow accretions of customary restraints derived from state practice represented the extent of the legal framework governing conduct during war. However, the changing nature of warfare spurred by technological advancement and heightened rivalries among nation-states revealed their impotence and compelled revision. The French Revolution and the Napoleonic Wars heralded an unbridled ferocity and the birth of the nation at arms, in which entire populations and industrial bases were mobilized in support of the war effort, blurring the combatant/noncombatant distinction and jeopardizing any civilian claims to immunity.[43]

As the modern international system developed in the nineteenth century and multilateralism found its voice, there were efforts to increase voluntary compliance and to hold states responsible for violations of certain international obligations. Unilateral political or military retaliation and economic sanctions continued to be the main vehicles whereby states were censured for offensive conduct. It was the failure of this informal international enforcement mechanism that led Moynier, on 3 January 1872, to present a proposal to the International Committee of the Red Cross calling for the establishment by treaty of an international tribunal to enforce laws of war and other humanitarian norms.[44] Until Moynier suggested a permanent court, almost all trials for such violations were conducted by ad hoc tribunals constituted by one of the belligerents—usually the victor—rather than by ordinary courts or by an international criminal court.

Moynier was not originally in favor of establishing an international criminal court. Like many humanists of the era, he shared the belief that reason, an emotional appeal, and the gritty descriptions of individual suffering would shock the public into humanitarian outrage and by extension pressure warring states to adhere to humanitarian norms and rules.[45] Indeed, in his 1870 commentary on the 1864 Geneva Convention concerning the treatment of wounded soldiers,[46] he considered whether an international criminal court should be created to enforce it. However, he rejected this approach in favor of relying on the pressure of public opinion, which he thought would be sufficient. He noted that

> a treaty was not a law imposed by a superior authority on its subordinates (but) only a contract whose signatories cannot decree penalties against themselves since there would be no one to implement them. The only reasonable guarantee would lie in the creation of international jurisdiction with the necessary power to compel obedience, but in this respect, the 1864 Geneva Convention shares an imperfection that is inherent in all treaties.[47]

Nevertheless, he believed that public criticism of violations of the 1864 Geneva Convention would be sufficient, observing that

> public opinion is ultimately the best guardian of the limits it has itself imposed. The 1864 Geneva Convention in particular, is due to the influence of public opinion on which we can rely to carry out the orders it has laid down. . . . The prospect of those concerned of being arraigned before the tribunal of public conscience if they do not keep to their commitments, and of being ostracized by civilized nations, constitutes a powerful enough deterrent for us to believe ourselves correct in thinking it better than any other.[48]

He also hoped that each of the state parties to the 1864 Geneva Convention would enact legislation imposing serious penalties for violations. He was to be disappointed on both accounts.[49] Several months after Moynier's commentary, the Franco-Prussian War broke out. Fundamentally, the origin of the war lay in a collision of national interests. For the sake of Prussian (German) unification and expansion, Chancellor Otto von Bismarck had taken up the cause of German national self-determination, its fulfillment possible only at the cost of France. Since 1866 the French had dreaded the consolidation of a powerful state on their northern frontier, at least without compensation sufficient to preserve their own relative weight in the European balance. These were the ingredients of an explosive compound. The trigger was the abrupt announcement by Germany in the summer of 1870 that a Hohenzollern prince was to become king of Spain.[50] Subsequent events created an atmosphere in which reason and compromise were impossible, igniting nationalistic passion in France and sweeping away the particularism and distrust of the two Germanys in a flood of patriotic exaltation.[51]

On 15 July 1870, France, keen to scuttle Bismarck's unification ambitions and maintain its preponderant political weight, declared war on Germany. By early August, the numerically and militarily superior Prussian forces had penetrated deep into French territory, and in early September France's principal army surrendered and Emperor Napoleon III was captured. Paris fell in January 1871 (by which time the armies of the French National Defense were largely destroyed), an armistice was declared in late January, a preliminary peace was signed in February, and the final peace treaty was signed in Frankfurt on 10 May 1871.[52] The press and public opinion on both sides of the conflict fanned atrocities. Moynier was forced to recognize that "a purely moral sanction" was inadequate "to check unbridled passions."[53] Moreover, although both sides accused each other of violations, they failed to punish those responsible or even to enact the necessary legislation. It was at this point that Moynier developed his proposal for an international criminal court.

It was not surprising that the model for the new court was the arbitral tribunal that had been established the year before in Geneva pursuant to the Treaty of Washington of 8 May 1871 in order to decide claims by the United States against Britain for damage caused to U.S. shipping by the Confederate raider *Alabama*.[54] A major transformation of international relations in this period—that is, the rising tendency to settle international conflicts more frequently than in former times by arbitration—seemed to have influenced Moynier in his conviction of the efficacy of an international criminal court. Ostensibly, the numerous arbitrations were a hint that the international community was inching toward formal adjudication mechanisms in the implementation of international law and rejecting war as the judicial procedure of last resort.[55]

In developing his proposal, Moynier examined legislative, judicial, and executive powers related to criminal law before concluding that an international institution was necessary to replace national courts. Because states had been reluctant to take action on criminal legislation under Geneva, he argued that the creation of an international criminal court was necessary. He did not think that it was appropriate to leave judicial remedies to the belligerents, because no matter how well respected the judges were, they would be subjected to pressure.[56]

Moynier's proposal focused on creating a formal enforcement mechanism for coercive compliance. The criminal trial was to achieve the enforcement of limitations and obligations of international humanitarian law. But for

the international justice system to work, the proposal needed the unequiv-
ocal cooperation of states. States had to feel duty-bound to discharge their
international obligations. Because law by its nature requires compliance,
the successful establishment of an international penal process required that
the dictates of the laws of war be respected and obeyed; in other words, it
would not work if states did not feel obligated to comply. With states rooted
in the traditional notion of state sovereignty, the proposal was doomed.
Moynier's proposal led to a flurry of letters from some of the leading
experts in international law, including Francis Lieber, Achille Morin, de
Holtzendorff, John Westlake, and Antonio Balbin de Unquera and Gregorio
Robledo on behalf of the Central Committee of the Red Cross of Spain.[57]
Although some experts welcomed Moynier's initiative to strengthen implementation of the 1864 Geneva Convention, most argued that the proposal
would not be as effective as other methods, and all were critical of various
aspects of the proposal. This cool reception reflected the fact that enforcement of international law was based on an informal system, relying on voluntary compliance by states rather than formal enforcement. Given the cool
reception by legal experts, no government publicly took up the proposal.[58]

The next significant event came almost three decades after Moynier's
proposal. Technological and industrial advances caused major changes in
warfare and led to the landmark Hague Peace Conferences.

The Hague Peace Conferences

In 1899, European powers reassembled for the first International Peace
Conference of The Hague to discuss comprehensively the codification of
the laws of war resulting in the groundbreaking Hague Conventions on
warfare with the key aim of arms limitation. A second conference was convened eight years later to revise the conventions emanating from the 1899
effort and to further broaden the scope of international humanitarian law.
The Hague Conferences were hailed by many as forming the bedrock of
modern international humanitarian law.

The first Hague Peace Conference followed a half-century of intensifying conflict among the emerging European nation-states. At the close of the
century, warfare had altered dramatically, largely as a result of technological
changes. Industrialization meant that armaments could be mass-produced
and that armies could be sustained in the field.[59] The century witnessed
incremental changes in the technology of weaponry, from inaccurate
smoothbore muskets to more advanced guns like breechloaders, repeating
rifles, and the machine gun, which reshaped the battlefield. Cannons evolved
from muzzleloaders to breechloaders with a far longer range and heavier,
more deadly projectiles.[60] Developments in transportation, particularly the

extension of national railroad systems, also changed the patterns of warfare. States were now able to move large numbers of troops rapidly, meaning that mass armies could be conscripted, mobilized, and deployed. Total war was now a reality. Baron de Staal, the Russian representative, in his opening address to the Hague Conference, acknowledged the gulf between public and diplomatic expectations but urged the delegates to fulfill their historic opportunity.[61] The conference focused on disarmament and the need for arbitration and mediation forums as an alternative to war.[62] The first treaty of the modern era that addressed "the illegality of aggressive force [and its effects on civilians] was embodied in the 1899 Hague Convention for the Pacific Settlement of International Disputes"[63] and was to be amplified at the second Hague Conference. Apart from codifying international customary norms relating to the laws of war, the first conference gave the concept of laws of humanity further explicit recognition.[64]

In 1907 the second Hague Peace Conference was convened to revise the conventions of 1899. The general thrust of this conference, like the first, was to "serve the interests of humanity and the ever progressive needs of civilization by diminish[ing] the evils of war."[65] This was accomplished by revising the general laws and customs of war with greater precision and confining them to mitigate the severities of war. The 1907 Hague Convention (IV) Regarding the Laws and Customs of War on Land[66] had an annex containing a list of restrictions that underscored the principle "that the right of belligerents to fight war is not unlimited."[67] Despite the recognized right of a state to wage war, the signatory powers agreed on the prohibition of certain methods of warfare with the implicit assumption that persons who committed the proscribed acts could be prosecuted for violating these new laws of war. Apart from recognizing international customary norms relating to the laws of war as war crimes, the conference gave the concept of laws of humanity explicit recognition. The history of crimes against humanity begins with the Martens Clause,[68] incorporated in the 1907 Hague Convention Regarding the Laws and Customs of War on Land[69] drafted by Fedor Fedorovitch Martens, a principal expert on international law and the Russian representative to the Hague Conference. The Martens Clause states in part that in cases not covered by the Hague Convention, the "belligerents remain under the protection of the rule of the principles of the laws of nations, as they result from the usages established among civilized peoples, from the laws of humanity, and the dictates of public conscience."[70] The conference unanimously adopted this clause as part of the preamble to the 1907 Hague Convention Regarding the Laws and Customs of War on Land.[71] Although there was agreement on the cataloging of specific war crimes, as well as a general standard (via the Martens Clause) to cover unforeseen circumstances that might arise in the course of war, there was little willingness by the twenty-six sovereign states to "submit to the juris-diction of an international court" to try alleged war criminals.[72] The sugges-tion at the conference of a permanent international criminal court "with compulsory jurisdiction that would transcend national boundaries" met strong opposition, led by the United States.[73]

The lack of collective sanctions and the growing capacity of states to inflict destruction magnified the need for peaceful dispute resolution so that opportunities to avoid war could at least be available. The Hague Peace Conferences of 1899 and 1907 established regular means for the pacific set-tlement of disputes to allow parties to step back from the brink if and when war was about to break out.[74] The Hague Conferences marked the begin-ning of attempts to limit the right of war as an instrument of law and as a recognized means for changing legal rights.[75] Thus the elevation of inter-state and regional relations in the context of the international legal system was marked by the adoption of the Hague Conventions of 1899 and 1907, which sought to codify universal rules and norms regarding warfare and opened the door to arms control.[76] The products of the Hague Conferences formed the bedrock of the modern law of war, a crowning achievement in the effort to humanize war through law.

The first Hague Conference marked the end of the nineteenth century, and the second ushered in the twentieth century. The turn of the century was marked by the existence of a body of formal international humanitar-ian rules and norms. But equally important, it was an age of empires in which the idea of waging rather than regulating war was dominant. Preva-lent among European powers was a common rhetoric and attitude based on a mixture of social Darwinism, militarism, and imperialism. In the first decade, the British reduced threats to their empire by accepting U.S. supremacy in the West, allying with Japan in the East, and coming to agree-ments with the two European powers that posed the most direct threat to their empire—France and Russia. With the conclusion of international agreements, battle lines were drawn between two competing alliances. The fundamental problem facing the core powers in Europe, divided as they were in the rival military alliances, was how to incorporate an increasingly powerful and restless united Germany into an imperial European system that reflected the interests and power of the other European states.[77] By 1912 there were indications that the major powers were prepared to con-sider war as a possible solution. In the 1910s growing Social Democratic strength in Germany convinced many in the elite that war might be the only way to maintain Germany's social and political order, creating an atmos-phere in which the ruling class would rally to support the nation and its bid to expand.[78] Eventually the strategic choices of the two rival European alliances, as well as nationalistic passions, culminated in the cataclysm that became World War I.[79]

Conclusion

Two observations deserve mention. First, while it is not possible to incubate international law from politics, selfish politics of sovereignty all too often scuttled attempts to create a formal international enforcement mechanism. States were keen to see the international legal regime reflect and reify their status, rights, and obligations, a trend that is still strong today.[80] Seemingly, international law operates to shape discourse and lend credence and inevitability to existing arrangements.[81] In the context of war, the basic fact that nations purport to respect the rule of law helps to protect the entire structure of warmaking from more fundamental challenges. Although the laws themselves speak to sovereign nations, their psychosocial effects are visited upon the public at large. If states cannot put in place formal enforcement mechanisms, no rules of law will have any force, since powerful states act according to discretion and disobey the law, as there is no central political authority above sovereign states to enforce the rules and norms of international law.

Second, while the progressive development, codification, and enforcement of international law depend on the political goodwill of the community of states, none can expect international law to function with success without some defined process of international adjudication. The rude reality of international life is that strong international relations are but one of the aspects of maintaining peace in the fraternity of states. International law can be much more effective if formal enforcement mechanisms exist.

We next discuss the two world wars, important not only because they marked the maturity of total war and redrew the world's geopolitical map but also because they swept away the ancient practice of giving amnesty at the end of hostilities. They were the first modern efforts to focus on the issue of moral and legal responsibility for the outbreak of war and the trial of state leaders, personnel, and officials, providing accountability through an international penal process. The seeds were sown at the end of World War I, but the envisaged international process by the victors was swept away by a resurgent tide of nationalism and geopolitical concerns. It was left to the victors in World War II to reap the fruits of the international penal process at the end of World War II.

Notes

1. Howard Levie, *Terrorism in War: The Law of War Crimes* (Dobbs Ferry, NY: Oceana, 1993), 11.

2. Two major factors of importance in the fifteenth century prepared the ground for the growth of principles of a future international law. Considering the centrality of war as a preeminent sovereign right of states, these factors fell within the ambit

of conflict. The first factor was the custom of the great states of keeping standing armies. The uniform and stern discipline in these armies favored the rise of more universal rules and practices of warfare. The second factor was the Reformation. Through its influence the spirit of Christianity took precedence and awoke the conviction everywhere that the principles of Christianity ought to unite the Christian world more than they had done hitherto, and that these principles ought to be observed in matters international as much as in matters national.

3. The forerunner of modern-day international humanitarian law.

4. Professor M. C. Bassiouni mentions, among others, the trial of Comadin Von Hohestafen, tried in Naples in 1268, and Peter Von Hagenbach, tried before an international tribunal in 1474. See M. Cherif Bassiouni, *International Criminal Law* (Dobbs Ferry, NY: Transnational, 1986–1987), 3–4. For a short account of the Von Hagenbach trial, and references to other accounts, see Georg Schwarzenberger, *International Law as Applied by Courts and Tribunals* (London: Stevens, 1968), 462–466. See also Timothy L. H. McCormack, "From Sun Tzu to the Sixth Committee: The Evolution of an International Law Regime," in *The Law of War Crimes: National and International approaches,* edited by Timothy L. H. McCormack and Gerry Simpson (The Hague and Boston: Kluwer Law International, 1997), 32–37.

5. M. Cherif Bassiouni, *Crimes Against Humanity in International Criminal Law,* 2nd rev. ed. (The Hague and Boston: Kluwer Law International, 1999), 45.

6. See for example William Belchor Ballis, *The Legal Position of War: Changes in Its Practice and Theory from Plato to Vattel* (New York: Garland, 1973), 58–59.

7. This was in the form of two treaties signed in the Westphalian towns of Munster and Osnabruck. However, from a legal point of view the two treaties were considered as a single instrument.

8. Antonio Cassese, *International Law in a Divided World* (Oxford: Clarendon, 1994), 34.

9. Although at the Congress at Munster and Osnabruck all the existing European powers, with the exception of Great Britain, Russia, and Poland, were represented, the Westphalian peace of 1648, to which France, Sweden, and the states of the German Empire were parties, and which recognized the independence of Switzerland and the Netherlands as well as the practical sovereignty of the 355 states of the German Empire, was not of worldwide importance, despite the fact that it contained various lawmaking stipulations. And the same may be said of all other treaties of peace between 1648 and 1815.

10. Hugo Grotius, *On the Law of War and Peace: Including the Law of Nature and of Nations,* translated by A. C. Campbell (Washington, DC: M. W. Dunne, 1901).

11. See for example Ian Brownlie, *International Law and the Use of Force by States* (Oxford: Clarendon, 1963), 3–18; Julius Stone, *Legal Control of International Conflict* (Sydney: Maitland, 1954), 3–18; David Kennedy, "Primitive Legal Scholarship," *Harvard International Law Journal* 27 (1986): 1. The early publicists, like the Spanish Dominican Francisco de Vitoria, continued to use the "just war" framework but universalized its principles: Francisco de Vitoria, *Francisci de Victoria de Indis et de Jure Belli Reflectiones,* edited by James Scott Ernest and translated by Ernest Nys (Washington, DC: Carnegie Institute of Washington, 1917).

12. See Grotius, *The Rights of War and Peace,* vol. 3, 323–333, 359–364; Quincy Wright, *A Study in War* (Chicago: University of Chicago Press, 1965), 872–875.

13. Grotius conceded that any act required by military necessity was legal per se. For example, Grotius wrote that military necessity would permit a belligerent to

injure property and persons of an enemy population and even to kill those who had surrendered unconditionally. See Grotius, *The Rights of War and Peace,* vol. 3, 328–330.

14. See for example Herscht Lauterpacht, *The Function of Law in the International Community* (Hamden, CT: Archon Books, 1966), 364–365; Leo Strisower, *Der Kriegund die Volkenechtsordmung* (Wein, Germany: Manz, 1919), 22–25.

15. Herscht Lauterpacht, ed., *Oppenheim's International Law, Volume 2: Disputes, War, and Neutrality* (London: Longmans, 1952), 202.

16. Ibid., 223.

17. Such trials may be held before a military court, either domestic or constituted jointly by more than one state (in which case it would have an international aspect). In one of the leading texts on international law the customary right of belligerent states to try war criminals is explained thus:

> The right of the belligerent to punish, during the war, such war criminals as fall into his hands is a well-recognized principle of international law. It is a right of which he may effectively avail himself after he has occupied all or part of enemy territory, and is thus in the position to seize war criminals who happen to be there [and] may, as a condition of the armistice, impose upon the authorities of the defeated State the duty to hand over persons charged with having committed war crimes, regardless of whether such persons are present in the territory actually occupied by him or in the territory which, at the successful end of hostilities, he is in a position to occupy. For in both cases the accused are, in effect in his power. And although normally the Treaty of Peace brings to an end the right to prosecute war criminals, no rule of international law prevents the victorious belligerent imposing upon the defeated State the duty, as one of the provisions of the armistice or Peace Treaty, to surrender for trial persons accused of war crimes. (Lauterpacht, ed., *Oppenheim's International Law,* 257c.)

18. See, for example, art. 2 of the 1648 Treaty of Westphalia between the Holy Roman Empire and France and Their Allies; art. 3 of the Treaty of Utrecht between Spain and Great Britain; art. 1 of the 1763 Treaty of Paris between Great Britain, France, and Spain. It may logically be inferred that, lacking such a provision, the offenders would have been subject to trial had they subsequently fallen into the hands of the former enemy.

19. Lyal S. Sunga, *The Emerging System of International Criminal Law: Developments in Codification and Implementation* (The Hague and Boston: Kluwer Law Insternational, 1997), 337.

20. Jean-Jacques Rousseau, *The Social Contract and Discourses,* translated by G. D. H. Cole (London: Dent, 1913), 171. Rousseau also argued that "war is not then a relation between men . . . but between states, in war individuals are enemies wholly by chance, not as men, not even as citizens, but only as soldiers, not as members of their country, but also as its defenders."

21. See generally C. K. Webster, *The Congress of Vienna* (London: H.M. Stationery Office, 1920); Harold Wilson, *The Congress of Vienna: A Study in Allied Unity: 1812–1822* (London: Constable, 1946), for details on this landmark Congress.

22. The Final Act of the Vienna Congress, signed on 9 June 1815 by Great Britain, Austria, France, Portugal, Prussia, Russia, Spain, and Sweden-Norway, ranks as the first lawmaking treaty of worldwide importance. It comprised lawmaking stipulations concerning four points: the perpetual neutralization of Switzerland

(art. 108, no. 11); free navigation on the so-called international rivers (arts. 108–117); the abolition of the slave trade (art. 118, no. 15); and the different classes of diplomatic envoys (art. 118, no. 16). See Lassa Oppenheim, *International Law: A Treatise*, Volume 1: *Peace*, 1st ed. (London: Longmans, Green, 1905–1906), 563–564.

23. By the nineteenth century, raison d'etat reigned supreme, as symbolized in the doctrines of Carl von Clausewitz. A Prussian general, von Clausewitz (1780–1831) wrote *Vom Kriege* (On War) between 1816 and 1830, advocating "absolute war." To Clausewitz, war was a natural expression of the competition between states, and its value lay in sorting out the weak from the strong. See Carl von Clausewitz, *On War*, edited and translated by Michael Howard and Peter Paret (Princeton, NJ: Princeton University Press, 1976), 87.

24. See Hilaire McCoubrey, *International Humanitarian Law: The Regulation of Armed Conflicts* (Aldershot, UK: Dartmouth, 1990), 6, 10–11.

25. Henry Dunant, *A Memory of Solferino*, English ed. (Washington, DC: American Red Cross, 1959).

26. Convention for the Amelioration of the Condition of the Wounded in Armies in the Field, 22 August 1864 (Geneva Convention, 1864), reprinted in *The Laws of Armed Conflicts: A Collection of Conventions, Resolutions, and Other Documents*, eds. Dietrich Schindler and Jiri Toman, 3rd rev. ed. (Dordrecht: Nijhoff, 1988), 279. See Arthur Nussbaum, *A Concise History of the Law of Nations*, rev. ed. (New York: Macmillan, 1954), 224–227. In *Un Souvenir de Solferino* (126), Dunant called for "a special congress to formulate" an "international principle, with the sanction of an inviolable Convention, which . . . might constitute a basis for Societies for the relief of the wounded in the various countries of Europe."

27. *Declaration Renouncing the Use, in Time of War, of Explosive Projectiles Under 400 Grams Weight*, 29 November/11 December 1868, reprinted in Schindler and Toman, *The Laws of Armed Conflicts*, 101.

28. President Abraham Lincoln officially signed the Lieber Code for the use of the Union Army in April 1863. The Lieber Code was also known as General Orders no. 100. See Richard S. Hartigan, *Lieber's Code and the Law of War* (Chicago: Precedent, 1983), 1.

29. Ibid.

30. See for example Nussbaum, *A Concise History of the Law of Nations*, 226; Frank Freidel, *Francis Lieber, Nineteenth-Century Liberal* (Baton Rouge: Louisiana State University Press, 1947), 147–151, 332–335; Phillip S. Paludan, "Lincoln and the Rhetoric of Politics," in *A Crisis of Republicanism*, edited by Lloyd E. Ambrosius (Lincoln: University of Nebraska Press, 1990), 73.

31. Telford Taylor, a prosecutor at the Nuremberg Trials, calls the Lieber Code "the germinal document for codification of the laws of land warfare." Telford Taylor, foreword to *The Law of War: A Documentary History*, edited by Leon Friedman, vol. 1 (New York: Random House, 1972), xviii.

32. Military necessity is widely recognized as one of the underlying principles of the modern law of war. See for example Michael Bothe, Karl Partsch, and Waldemar Solf, *New Rules for Victims of Armed Conflicts* (The Hague and Boston: Martinus Nijhoff, 1982), 194–195; U.S. Department of the Air Force, *International Law: The Law of Armed Conflict and Air Operations*, AFP no. 110–31, 1976, para. 1–3a(1); Georg Schwarzenberger, *International Law*, vol. 2 (London: Stevens and Sons, 1957–1986), 9–13; Myres S. Mcdougal and Florentino P. Feliciano, *Law and Minimum World Public Order* (New Haven, CT: Yale University Press, 1961), 521–522; cf. U.S. Department of the Army, *The Law of Land Warfare*, Field Manual no. 27–10, 1956, para. 3.a.

33. Nussbaum, *A Concise History of the Law of Nations*, 227.

34. Freidel, *Francis Lieber*, 335.

35. 1868 St. Petersburg Declaration Renouncing the Use, in Time of War, of Explosive Projectiles Under 400 Grammes Weight, 18 Martens (NRG–1873), 474–475 (Fr.).

36. The code also formed the basis of the Brussels Declaration of 1874, which in turn influenced the Hague Regulations on the Laws and Customs of War on Land of 1899 and 1907, the foundation of the law of land warfare for the entire twentieth century. See *Regulations Annexed to Convention (IV) Respecting the Laws and Customs of War on Land*, 36 Stat. 2227, 18 October 1907, reprinted in Schindler and Toman, *The Laws of Armed Conflicts*, 63; Hartigan, *Lieber's Code*, 22; cf. Nussbaum, *A Concise History of the Law of Nations*, 227.

37. Ellery C. Stowell and Henry C. Munro, eds., *International Cases: Arbitrations and Incidents Illustrative of International Law as Practiced by Independent States* (Boston and New York: Houghton Mifflin, 1916), 222–223, citing *Halleck's International Law or Rules Regulating the Intercourse of States in Peace and War*, edited by G. Sherston Baker and Maurice N. Drucquer, 4th ed. (London: K. Paul, Trench, Trubner, 1908), 350.

38. Schwarzenberger distinguished six meanings of international criminal law: (1) the territorial scope of municipal criminal law; (2) internationally prescribed municipal law (a state's international obligation to criminals); (3) authorized municipal criminal law (internationally authorized exercise of criminal jurisdiction, for example, with regard to piracy in the high seas); (4) municipal criminal law common to civilized nations; (5) international cooperation in the administration of municipal criminal justice; and (6) international criminal law in the material sense of the word. Schwarzenberger, *International Law*, 5–13. Bassiouni defines this "material international criminal law" as "the criminal aspects of international law [which] consist of a body of international prescriptions containing penal characteristics, including criminalization of certain types of conduct irrespective of particular enforcement modalities and mechanisms." Bassiouni, *International Criminal Law*, 1.

39. Bassiouni mentions, among others, the trial of Comadin Von Hohestafen, tried in Naples in 1268, and Peter Von Hagenbach, tried before an international tribunal in 1474. Bassiouni, *International Criminal Law*, 3–4.

40. For a short account of this trial and references to other accounts, see Schwarzenberger, *International Law as Applied by Courts and Tribunals*, 3rd ed. (London: Stevens and Sons, 1957–1986), 462–466.

41. M. Cherif Bassiouni, *Crimes Against Humanity in International Criminal Law* (Boston: M. Nijhoff, 1992), 197. See also M. Cherif Bassiouni, "The Time Has Come for an International Criminal Court," *Indiana International and Comparative Law Review* 1 (1991): 1.

42. Several centuries were to elapse before the foundations were laid for incriminating individuals for war crimes considered to be grave violations of the law applicable in armed conflicts.

43. Wright, *A Study in War*, 291–328.

44. The proposal was published in the *Bulletin International des Societes de Secours aux Militaries Blesses* (the predecessor of the *International Review of the Red Cross*), under the title: "Note sur la creation d'une instituition judiciaire internationale propre a prevenir et a reprimer les infractions a la Convention de Geneve." For a text of the draft convention, see Christopher Keith Hall, "The First Proposal for a Permanent International Criminal Court," *International Review of the Red Cross* 322 (March 1998): 72–74.

45. See Dunant's *A Memory of Solferino*, with its overt appeal to "noble and compassionate hearts and . . . chivalrous spirits" (at 118); it represents a nineteenth-century Romantic approach to limiting war. Many of the Romantics (including Dunant) did not reject the Enlightenment appeal to reason as such but rather attempted to go beyond it to engage the emotions. Cf. Hugh Honor, *Romanticism* (London: Allen Lane, 1979), 280–282.

46. Geneva Convention, 1864.

47. *Etude sur la Convention de Geneve pour l' Amelioration du Sort des Militaires Blesses dans Armees en Campagne* (Paris, 1870), 300. English translation of the quotations in Pierre Boissier, *From Solferino to Tsushima: History of the International Committee of the Red Cross* (Geneva: Henry Dunant Institute, 1963), 282.

48. Hall, "The First Proposal," 59.

49. Ibid.

50. Otto Pflanze, *Bismarck and the Development of Germany: The Period of Unification, 1815–1871* (Princeton, NJ: Princeton University Press, 1963), 433.

51. Gordon A. Craig, *Germany 1866–1945* (Oxford: Clarendon, 1978).

52. See Michael Howard, *Franco-Prussian War: The German Invasion of France 1870–71* (London and New York: Methuen, 1981); A. J. P. Taylor, *The Struggle for Mastery in Europe, 1848–1918* (Oxford: Clarendon, 1954), 206–217; Norman Rich, *Great Power Diplomacy, 1814–1914* (Hanover, NH: University Press of New England, 1992), 213–223.

53. Gustave Moynier, "Note sur la creation d'une insitution judiciaire internationale propre a prevenir et a reprimer les belowctions a la Convention de Geneve," in *Bulletin International des Societes de Secours aux Militaires Blesses,* Comite International, no. 11 (Avril 1872), 122 (translation of the quotations in Hall, "The First Proposal," 59).

54. See Hall, "The First Proposal," 59.

55. Brownlie, *International Law and the Use of Force,* 21.

56. Hall, "The First Proposal," 60.

57. For a commentary on these views, see Hall, "The First Proposal," 63–64.

58. No further significant development in the enforcement of international humanitarian law occurred until the end of World War I, with the peace settlement placing an unprecedented focus on the issue of moral and legal responsibility for the outbreak of the war. The Western Allies went beyond indemnities, territorial concessions, and other measures, customarily demanded at peace conferences, to the issue of individual guilt for crimes committed in breach of international law. See Chapter 2 in this book for a detailed analysis.

59. Clive Ponting, *Progress and Barbarism: The World in the Twentieth Century* (London: Chatto and Windus, 1998), 272.

60. Detlev F. Vagts, "The Hague Conventions and Arms Control," *American Journal of International Law* 94 (2000): 31.

61. James Brown Scott, ed., *The Hague Peace Conference of 1899 and 1907: A Series of Lectures Delivered Before the Johns Hopkins University in the Year 1908* (Baltimore: Johns Hopkins University Press, 1909), 34.

62. For the text and commentary of the conventions adopted at the 1899 conference, see A. Pearce Higgins, *The Hague Peace Conferences and Other International Conferences Concerning the Laws and Usages of War: Texts of Conventions with Commentaries* (Cambridge: Cambridge University Press, 1909).

63. Comment, "The Iraqi Conflict: An Assessment of Possible War Crimes and the Call for Adoption of an International Criminal Code and Permanent International Criminal Tribunal," *New York Law School Journal of International and Comparative Law* (1993): 81.

64. The modern history of crimes against humanity begins with the Martens Clause, incorporated in the 1899 Convention Regarding the Laws and Customs of War on Land. Fedor Fedorovitch Martens was the principal expert on international law and representative to the Hague Conferences on the law of war. He drafted the so-called Martens Clause, which was incorporated into the eighth paragraph of the Hague Convention of 1899. This clause provides:

> Until a more complete code of the laws of war is issued, the High Contracting Parties think it right to declare that, in cases not included in the Regulations adopted by them, populations and belligerents *remain under the protection and empire of the principles of international law, as they result from the usages established between civilized nations, from the laws of humanity and the requirements of public conscience.* (emphasis added)

The 1899 Hague Conference unanimously adopted the Martens Clause as part of the Preamble to the 1907 Hague Convention (IV) Regarding the Laws and Customs of War on Land (1862–1910).

65. Howard Ball, *Prosecuting War Crimes and Genocide: The Twentieth Century Experience* (Lawrence: University Press of Kansas, 1999), 15.

66. Hague Convention (IV), reprinted in Schindler and Toman, *The Laws of Armed Conflicts,* 63.

67. Regulations Respecting the Laws and Customs of War on Land, annex to the Hague Convention (IV), art. 22.

68. See Martens Clause.

69. Hague Convention (IV).

70. See Martens Clause.

71. Hague Convention (IV).

72. Comment, "Security Council Resolution 808: A Step Toward a Permanent International Criminal Court for the Prosecution of International Crimes and Human Rights Violations," *Golden Gate University Law Review* 25 (1996): 443.

73. Ibid.

74. See the Hague Conventions of 1899 and 1907 on the Pacific Settlement of Disputes. The texts are reproduced in International Peace Conference (1st: 1899), *Texts of the Peace Conferences at The Hague, 1899 and 1907* (London: Published for the International School of Peace by Grim, 1908). For reports on the proceedings, see James Brown Scott, ed., *The Reports to the Hague Conferences of 1899 and 1907* (Oxford: Clarendon, 1917).

75. Lauterpacht, *Oppenheim's International Law,*X 179.

76. For a listing and brief commentary on the major conventions in the Hague Law regime, see M. Cherif Bassiouni, *International Crimes: Digest/Index of International Instruments, 1815–1985* (New York: Oceana, 1986). See also European Law Students Association (ELSA), *Handbook on the International Criminal Court* (Brussels: ELSA, 1997), 41–44.

77. Ponting, *Progress and Barbarism,* 252.

78. Ibid.

79. This is discussed in detail in Chapter 2.

80. See Phillip R. Trimble, "International Law, World Order, and Critical Legal Studies," *Stanford Law Review* 42 (1990): 811, 833.

81. Georg Schwarzenberger, *Power Politics: A Study of International Society* (London: Stevens and Sons, 1951), 203.

PART 1

The World Wars

2

A False Dawn:
The Failure to Enforce International
Justice After World War I

The first major effort to curb international crimes through an international penal process arose after World War I. In 1914, Europe, divided by competing military alliances, was a powder keg. The fuse was lit when a Serbian nationalist assassinated Austrian archduke Franz Ferdinand on a bridge in Sarajevo. Lacking any institution with authority to maintain peace, the disputing parties had no choice but to call upon their allies and resort to force. Without effective international law, the only alternative was war. By the time World War I ended, tens of millions of soldiers and civilians lay dead or wounded. Reconciliation could not begin without first bringing to justice those individuals whose unconscionable atrocities had violated "the laws of humanity" and who had been responsible as the authors of the war and "for supreme offences against international morality and sanctity of treaties."[1]

The devastation provided a catalyst for the first serious attempt in modern times at international justice. This new attitude included extending criminal jurisdiction over sovereign states (Germany and Turkey) for the apprehension, trial, and punishment of individuals guilty of committing atrocities under the rubrics of "war crimes" and "crimes against humanity." The peace treaties of Versailles and Sevres envisaged liability for individuals even if crimes were committed in the name of states. However, the emerging commitment to human dignity was derailed and then swept aside by resurgent nationalistic ambitions.

Amid calls for establishing international tribunals, Germany and Turkey advocated against such a move, arguing that sovereignty over territory and authority over nationals would be threatened. Ultimately the significance of these threats prevailed over the imposition of international trials against German and Turkish defendants. The subsequent national trials at Leipzig under the framework of the Peace Treaty of Versailles[2] were largely a public relations exercise by the German Supreme Court (Reichsgericht) rather than an instrument of justice.[3] The victors also gave up on enforcing the principle of individual criminal responsibility for the genocide of Armenians (more than 600,000 victims) with the Peace Treaty of Lausanne, which replaced the Peace Treaty of Sevres and "ratified" the general amnesty adopted by the Turkish government.

The Coming of the War

Military and economic factors prior to 1914 played a central role in fueling European militarism and imperialism.[4] World War I is unlikely to have unfolded without the Anglo-German commercial rivalry, the Franco-Russian alliance, the blank check given to Austro-Hungary to crush Serbia by Germany, and the prior formation of two entangling military alliances. The bifurcation of the multipolar balance-of-power system and the absence of a hegemony to maintain order may have made war inevitable. Thus a world war began, even though

> political leaders in each of the great powers . . . preferred a peaceful settlement of their differences. The primary explanation for the outbreak of the world war, which none of the leading decision-makers of the European great powers wanted, expected, or deliberately sought, lies in the irreconcilable interests defined by State officials, the structure of international power and alliances that created intractable strategic dilemmas, the particular plans for mobilization and war that were generated by these strategic constraints, [and] decision-makers' critical assumptions regarding the likely behavior of their adversaries and the consequences of their own actions.[5]

From a military standpoint, European great powers were aligned against one another on the eve of World War I in a way that made a military struggle irresistible. Europe was dominated by two hostile alliances. They pitted Germany, Austro-Hungary, and the Ottoman Empire, on the one hand, against France, Britain, and Russia on the other.[6] The mutually reinforcing alliances dictated the great powers' reactions to the 1914 Austrian succession crisis occasioned by the assassination of Archduke Franz Ferdinand, creating a momentum that along with "the pull of military schedules" dragged European statesmen toward war.[7] The strategic choices of the two alliances would culminate in the longest European war in a century, leading to millions of deaths, crumbling empires, and the birth of new states that would redraw the geopolitical map.

When the foreign horizon was darkening, Germany was at the apex of military and economic strength, leading some German economists to demand an expansion of the European basis of German power.[8] As the predominant military and industrial power on the continent, Germany sought to compete for international position and status. Russia was also expanding and threatened Germany. Germany's challenge to British dominance was driven by its desire to become a leading state and to keep down lesser challengers, themselves growing in strength.[9]

In spring 1914, French elections brought to power radical socialists. France's militarist, ultranationalist party brooked no rapprochement with Germany (its main continental rival) but instead excited aggression. Coupled with the fact that preventive war was gaining ground in Germany (fueled by the government's deep pessimism about the international situation), the unease and tension that had been simmering soon rose to the boil.

On 28 June 1914, Gavrilo Princip, a Serbian nationalist, shot the Austrian archduke and his consort in Sarajevo. The news of the murder shattered the German kaiser, a close friend of the archduke. On 14 July 1914, Germany convinced Austria to send a severe ultimatum to Serbia, deliberately framed in terms that no self-respecting state could accept.[10] Germany's unconditional support of Austro-Hungary was accompanied by encouragement for Austro-Hungary to crush Serbia. This proved to be a serious miscalculation, provoking an unexpected reaction.

Serbia, backed by the assurance of military support from Russia, rejected the Austrian ultimatum. Austro-Hungary immediately declared war on Serbia, propelling the crisis to its final phase. Russia, infuriated by the Austrian declaration of war on its protégé, implemented significant military measures, no doubt encouraged in this dangerous course by its ally, France.[11] Russia's military measures only served to strengthen Austrian belligerence and led to a general mobilization of Austrian troops. Russian and Austrian mobilization made a great war inevitable. As Basil Liddell Hart noted, "Henceforth the 'statesmen' may continue to send telegrams, but they are merely wastepaper. The military machine has completely taken charge."[12]

As soon as Germany learned of Russian general mobilization, it ordered general mobilization (*Kriegsgefahr*) in Berlin and dispatched an ultimatum to St. Petersburg demanding that Russia cease all military measures against Germany and Austro-Hungary within twelve hours. In the absence of a reply, Germany declared war on Russia.[13] This declaration of war caused France to proclaim general mobilization to support Russia.

Shortly thereafter, Germany put in place the Schlieffen Plan,[14] which advocated a swift thrust into Belgium to strike at France and then a transfer of troops to the Eastern front to crush Russia. On the evening of 2 August an ultimatum requesting passage for the German armies was delivered in Brussels. King Albert and his government categorically rejected the demand the following morning. That evening, Germany declared war on France, and German troops crossed the Belgian frontier on 4 August. A British ultimatum requesting their withdrawal was disregarded, leading Britain to declare war on Germany. With the major European powers at war, it was inevitable that Europe would degenerate into war as minor powers moved in to fulfill treaty commitments of military support and pursued their own national agendas. Europe was now polarized between the Western Powers (or Entente Powers) led by France, Britain, and Russia and the Central Powers, dominated by Germany and the Austro-Hungarian Empire.

World War I witnessed one of the largest military mobilizations in history, with the Western Powers mobilizing more than 40 million soldiers and the Central Powers mobilizing close to 20 million. Four years later, with an armistice in force, the war came to an abrupt halt. The total cost was estimated at 21 million casualties and 8.5 million combatants dead. In monetary terms, the war cost $202 billion, with property destroyed in the war topping $56 billion.[15] Of the civilian death toll, Turkey was the leading perpetrator, massacring 1–2 million Armenians, Greeks, and Syrians, accounting for about 50 percent of civilian wartime casualties.[16]

During the course of World War I there were numerous statements by allied officials that at war's end individuals who had committed war crimes would receive justice.[17] However, the proposed armistice approved by the Supreme War Council had no provision for war crimes prosecutions.[18] Article VI(2) of the 1918 Armistice Agreement that was eventually signed at Compiegne included a paragraph to the effect that "no person shall be prosecuted for having taken part in any military measures previous to the signing of the armistice." This provision, far from clear in meaning, was construed as precluding war crimes arrests or trials until after a peace treaty had entered into force.[19] As a result, no joint action was taken by the victors with respect to war matters pending the conclusion of a peace treaty.

Germany and Turkey: Championing Nationalism Through Destruction

Germany's Unbridled Conduct

The first major offense that Germany committed was the violation of Belgian neutrality (of which Germany was one of the guarantors). In this case it was felt that such a flagrant violation of an international obligation constituted a crime against public law.[20] Germany also committed numerous violations of the rights of combatants and civilians. Not even prisoners, the wounded, women, or children were respected. Murders, massacres, tortures, human shields, collective penalties, arrests, and execution of hostages were part of the toll.

World War I also brought new modes of warfare, notably submarine warfare and aerial bombing. In the run-up to World War I, the submarine was legally considered to be a surface warship and therefore was subject to the rules governing their conduct.[21] The assumption was that submarines would comply with the Declaration of London, drafted at the London Naval Conference in 1908.[22] Germany initially required submarine commanders to attempt to identify neutral shipping in the war zone. This policy became ineffective when the British Admiralty directed British merchant ships to resemble neutrals as closely as possible, to copy neutral lighting systems, and to ram any submarines sighted.[23] Considering that submarines were so vulnerable to deception, surface gunfire, and ramming, Germany by January 1917 had declared unrestricted submarine warfare within the war zone.[24] Within the zone, all sea traffic would be opposed by mines and submarines. All merchants entering without permission could be torpedoed on sight without warning and without providing safety for crew or passengers.[25] With the Western navies in control of the surface during World War I, German submarines dared not escort their prizes to port for adjudication. Their choice was to let ships go unmolested or to destroy them at sea.[26]

Inevitably the latter course was favored by a German command convinced of the humanity of brutal and swift warfare. In following the dictates of military necessity, which entailed maintaining stealth, the submarine was unable to comply with the humanitarian requirements of international law set forth in the London Treaty and Protocol, resulting in well-publicized incidents in which German U-boats sunk innocent ships, including hospital and mail ships.[27] The United States was a strong proponent of neutral shipping rights, and the sinking by German submarines of four U.S. merchant vessels bound for Great Britain and France precipitated U.S. entry into the war.[28] Even as war was coming to an end, on 16 October 1918 (eleven days after a request by Germany to President Woodrow Wilson for mediation to end the war), the Germans torpedoed, off Kingston, the Irish mail steamer *Lenister* with 450 men, women, and children drowned. This eleventh-hour atrocity was to be freshly remembered.

The aerial bombing campaigns of World War I, especially the Zeppelin and Gotha offensives by Germany and the Western Allied counteroffensives (executed or planned), and other bombing operations, were largely indiscriminate.[29] Laws of war received little (if any) consideration, except as propaganda to allege indiscriminate attacks by the enemy. Inaccurate though it was, bombing was not the least discriminate weapon of World War I. Germany's Paris Gun fired from distances up to seventy-five miles could be aimed only at the center of Paris. Used in conjunction with the German offensive of March 1918, it had but one purpose: to attack the morale of Parisians.[30] The use of the highly inaccurate Paris Gun caused many civilian fatalities without much military advantage, drew the ire of the Western Allied powers, and incensed the public in many European states.

Besides the unrestricted submarine warfare and indiscriminate bombing,

> One rarely mentioned action taken by the Germans during World War I, an action that has been said to have caused more worldwide indignation than any other event of that war with the possible exception of unrestricted submarine warfare, was the deportation of Belgian and French men, women and children to be used as forced labor. While it never reached the proportions of the Nazi action along similar lines taken during World War II it probably caused more international concern than did the millions deported as slave labor during the latter war.[31]

The outcry and condemnation of this action was sufficiently serious for the German parliament to form a committee six years after the war to investigate and control the damage from the persisting moral and ethical fallout.[32]

Turkey and the Armenian Genocide

During World War I the Ottoman Empire carried out one of the largest genocides in world history, slaughtering huge portions of its minority Armenian population.[33] The Armenian genocide followed decades of persecution by the Ottomans and came after two similar but smaller rounds of massacres (1894–1996 and 1909) that caused 200,000 Armenian deaths. In all, more than 1 million Armenians were killed. The European powers, who defeated the Turks time and again on the battlefield, were unable or unwilling to prevent the slaughter. Although the European powers did pursue a strategy of "humanitarian intervention" in Ottoman Turkey during the years leading up to World War I, they never had a cohesive unity of interests. Most harmful to the Armenians was the lack of a powerful state to champion their cause. The events have subsequently slipped into the shadows of world history,[34] thus gaining the title "the forgotten genocide."[35] To this day, Turkey denies the genocidal intent of these mass murders.[36]

Evidence suggests that Turkey's entry into World War I was influenced by a desire to resolve lingering domestic conflicts. Vice Field Marshal Joseph Pomiankowski, the Austrian military plenipotentiary attached to the Ottoman general headquarters during the war, alluded in his memoirs to the unabating antagonism between Muslims and non-Muslims. Referring to "the spontaneous utterances of many intelligent Turks," Pomiankowski conveyed their view that these conquered people ought to have been forcibly converted into Muslims or "ought to have been exterminated (*ausrotten*) long ago."[37]

On 16 December 1914, five months after the start of World War I, an imperial rescript canceled the Armenian Reform Agreement of 8 February 1914 (containing international stipulations for the respect of the rights of the Armenian minority that the Turkish government had undertaken to protect).[38] This reflected a general determination during the war to abrogate the international treaties that had resulted from the application of the principle of "humanitarian intervention." This is further reinforced by Ottoman foreign minister Pasa Halil's statement to the German ambassador Count von Wolff-Metternich as the war intensified that "the Ottoman Cabinet had decided to declare null and void the Paris Treaty of 1856, the London Declaration of 1871, and the Berlin Treaty of 1878."[39] As Halil explained, "All three of these international treaties had imposed 'political shackles' on the Ottoman State which the Porte intended to be rid of."[40]

The decisive event reducing the Armenian population to helplessness came five months after the 1914 imperial rescript. In a memorandum dated 26 May 1915, the interior minister requested from the grand vizier the enactment through the cabinet of a special law authorizing deportations. The memorandum was endorsed on 29 May 1915 by the grand vizier; the cabinet on 30 May promulgated a new emergency law, the Temporary Law of Deportation.[41] Pursuant to this law and alleging treason, separatism, and other assorted acts by the Armenians as a national minority, the Ottoman authorities ordered, for national security reasons, the wholesale deportation of Armenians, a measure that was later extended to virtually the entire Armenian population. (This law, it should be noted, was eventually repealed "on account of its unconstitutionality" in a stormy 4 November 1918 session of the postwar Ottoman parliament.)[42] The execution of this order, ostensibly a wartime emergency measure of relocation, actually masked the execution of the Armenian population. The vast majority of the deportees perished through a variety of direct and indirect atrocities perpetrated during the deportations. During this time, Ittihadist leaders secretly formed a unit called the Special Organization (Teskilati Mahsusa) to resolve the Armenian question. Its mission was to deploy in remote areas of Turkey's interior and to ambush and destroy convoys of Armenian deportees. Contrary to the avowals of Ottoman authorities who promulgated the emergency laws, the Armenians did not return from deportation. The deportations proved to be a cover for the ensuing destruction. In Winston Churchill's words,

> In 1915 the Turkish government began and ruthlessly carried out the infamous general massacre and deportation of Armenians in Asia Minor . . . the clearance of the race from Asia Minor was about as complete as such an act, on a scale so great, could well be. . . . There is no reasonable doubt that this crime was planned and executed for political reasons. The opportunity presented itself for clearing Turkish soil of a Christian race opposed to all Turkish ambitions, cherishing national ambitions that could be satisfied only at the expense of Turkey, and planted geographically between Turkish and Caucasian Moslems.[43]

The massive, deliberate, and systematic massacres by Turkey of its Christian subjects under the cover of war did not go unnoticed. As early as 24 May 1915, the Western Powers solemnly condemned these atrocities.[44] The victors were later to exert pressure upon defeated Turkey to prosecute the authors of the Armenian genocide pursuant to the 1915 declaration, threatening that unless the perpetrators were punished the terms of the impending peace settlement could be severe.[45]

The Paris Peace Conference

At the end of World War I empires had fallen, traditions of government had been shaken to the breaking point, and human misery stretched from the Rhine to Vladivostok. In Russia a militant party had displaced the czar as absolute ruler, and among insurgent groups in the West there was agitation that might destroy the very freedoms that made it possible for them to agitate. Woodrow Wilson, architect of the armistice, arrived at Paris in December 1918 with preponderant economic and military power and a dynamic political platform for the world. It was now to be seen whether the war that Wilson tried to justify as making the world "safe for democracy" had indeed achieved that goal. For the first time in the history of Europe, democratic governments were to bear the responsibility of reestablishing the continent's international structure and of ordering its affairs. Democracy, now at an apex in history, would help to construct a durable peace that would prevent a repetition of death, devastation, famine, and debt. But the signing of the armistice in November 1918 undermined the cohesive force that met the common danger. The governments of the Western alliance and their responsible officials, released from the extreme tension that war brought, became less responsive to the cause of peace and instead sought to cultivate a spirit of nationalism fortified by the sacrifices of war. This was to limit the peacemakers in pursuing Wilson's idealism.

Expectations ran high in 1919. World War I had evoked revulsion of war and the logic of realpolitik that rationalized great power rivalry, arms races, secret alliances, and balance-of-power politics. The experience led policymakers at the Versailles Palace to reevaluate assumptions about statecraft and to search for substitute principles with which to build a new world order. They hoped that their deliberations crystallized in policies rooted in the idealism of liberal international relations theory. The problem was not only to build a peace but also to construct a peaceful international order that would manage international conflicts in the future.[46] Idealists also advocated bringing state sovereign excesses under the jurisdiction of international law through an international penal process and the promotion of international justice. Despite lofty expectations, peacemakers were forced to follow the forms and procedures of international intercourse confirmed through history. These forms and procedures had all the force of custom, from which all conventional human relations derive their legitimacy. Peace treaties must be signed, affecting an unprecedented number of nations. Before the terms could be determined in detail, the victors would have to reach a general understanding among themselves; before they could do so, secret negotiations among the great powers would have to run its course. In the meantime Europe would have to wait.

Beginning with the first session of the peace conference on 12 January 1919, and continuing through the year, internal politics of the victorious and defeated nations infringed on the diplomatic labors of the Big Four.[47] The Paris Peace Conference was composed of delegates of all the victorious Western Allies styled as the "Council of Ten," which attempted to agree on the terms of peace with Germany and Austria. Progress was very slow. Consequently, upon a suggestion by Woodrow Wilson, the "Council of Ten" agreed on 24 March 1919 that only the heads of state of the most important allies should meet as the "Council of Four," but commonly called the "Big Four," officially named the "Supreme Council of the Principal Allied and Associated Powers." This council included President Woodrow Wilson of the United States, Prime Ministers David Lloyd George of the British Empire, Georges Clémenceau of France, and Vittorio Orlando of Italy. Throughout Europe and, to a lesser degree, in the United States, similar underlying conditions gave rise to unsettling and urgent political issues and pressures. Soon after the exaltation over the armistice subsided, it became obvious that the war, instead of settling major issues, had actually exacerbated them. Especially now that revolution had swept Russia and threatened other countries, economic and social questions claimed first priority. The socialist revolution hovered over the conference proceedings. The ascent to power of a socialist extremist in Hungary after a revolt stunned and terrified the delegates at Paris.[48] The Hungarian revolt stimulated renewed respect for Wilson's peacemaking project.[49] Until then realists considered Wilson to be unduly alarmist in saying that the imposition of oppressive peace terms could produce catastrophic results. Such warnings could no longer be dismissed quite so lightly, particularly since the event in Hungary was followed elsewhere.[50] Except at great risk, the victors could not afford to drive the enemy to desperation with punitive peace terms and coercive economic measures. However legitimate Europe's security needs, they alone could not dictate policy along the Rhine, in Eastern Europe, and in Russia. The prescription was self-evident: stern but just peace terms, relief in furtherance of governmental stability throughout Central and Eastern Europe, and containment of Bolshevik regimes by all means short of direct military intervention.

The Big Four were concerned that a Germany squeezed by harsh and oppressive peace terms would turn to Bolshevism and clamored for a tough anti-Soviet course to prevent a Russo-German alliance. The caveat against incensing and alienating Germany became the major thrust of the so-called Fontainebleau memorandum drafted by British prime minister Lloyd George.[51] Lloyd George was not primarily concerned about the long-term diplomatic and military consequences of inequities in the treaty between the victors and Germany. What influenced him, by his own admission, was the imminent and impending convergence of the enemy's exasperation with the revolutionary spirit. The memorandum frightened the conference with the twin specter of Bolshevism and a Russo-German alliance. Indeed, this fear drove Lloyd George to press for terms that would induce Germany "both to sign and to resist Bolshevism." Germany received a fair territorial settlement in Europe and a tolerable reparations bill, and it would be assured that disarmament would be the first step toward general disarmament and that it would qualify for admission to the League of Nations.

In settling upon such terms for the Germans, it was not possible to ignore the responsibility of those who first drew the sword and therefore might be held accountable for the horror that ensued. Nor could Germany's violation of Belgian neutrality in 1914 be overlooked. The peacemakers also faced submarine atrocities and other forms of terror, all in disregard of the customs for the conduct of war by civilized nations. Britain was of the opinion that the former emperor of Germany, Wilhelm II, be brought from asylum in Holland and arraigned before an interallied tribunal. France and Italy voiced support for this position, with the United States agreeing to cooperate. But the diplomats of Europe raised fundamental questions. Would the government of the Netherlands give up the accused? If the Western Allied governments set up a tribunal, would the world at large accept the jurisdiction of such a court to try and punish an ex-post-facto felony? Would not lawlessness on the part of the enemy find an excuse in the lawlessness of the victors?[52]

At Paris, Wilson suggested that the question of national and individual crimes against decency be settled in the comparative privacy of the Supreme Council, the Paris Conference's highest organ. But at the insistence of Lloyd George, it was decided to place the subject on the agenda of a plenary session. As a result, the peace conference decided on 25 January 1919 to create a commission, the first international investigative commission to study the question of penal responsibility.[53] The official intergovernmental commission subsequently established was called the Commission on the Responsibilities of the Authors of War and on Enforcement of Penalties.[54] It was composed of delegates of the five great powers and five small states—Belgium, Greece, Poland, Rumania, and Serbia. It was instructed to consider "the responsibility of the authors of the war"; "the fact as to breaches of the laws and customs of war committed by the forces of the German Empire and their allies"; "the degree of responsibility for these offences attaching to particular members of the enemy forces";

and "the constitution and procedure of a tribunal appropriate to the trial of these offences."[55] Based on subsequent developments in the administration of the commission's mandate, however, it is reasonable to question whether the Western Allies' intentions were to pursue justice or whether they only intended to use symbols of justice to achieve political ends.[56] We next consider the groundbreaking work of the commission.

The 1919 Commission

The Commission on the Responsibilities of the Authors of War and on Enforcement of Penalties was charged with an onerous responsibility. It held closed meetings for two months and conducted intensive investigations.[57] This work was supposed to culminate in the charging of named individuals for specific war crimes. Besides German responsibility for the war and its breaches of the laws and customs of war, the commission also sought to charge Turkish officials and other individuals for "crimes against the laws of humanity"[58] based on the Martens Clause contained in the preamble of the 1907 Hague Convention (IV).[59] That clause states:

> Until a more complete code of the laws of war has been issued, the High Contracting Parties deem it expedient to declare that, in cases not included in the Regulations adopted by them, the inhabitants and the belligerents remain under the protection and the rule of the principles of the law of nations, as they result from the usages established among civilized peoples, from the laws of humanity, and the dictates of the public conscience.[60]

It was in this context that Nicolas Politis, a member of the commission and foreign minister of Greece, proposed the adoption of a new category of war crimes meant to cover the massacres against the Armenians, declaring: "Technically these acts [the Armenian massacres] did not come within the provisions of the penal code, but they constituted grave offences against the law of humanity."[61] Despite the objections of U.S. representatives Robert Lansing (the U.S. secretary of state and chairman of the commission) and James Brown Scott (an eminent international jurist), who challenged the ex-post-facto nature of such a law, the majority of the commission concurred with Politis.[62] A 5 March 1919 report by the commission specified the following violations against civilian populations as falling within the purview of grave offenses against the laws of humanity: systematic terror; murders and massacres; dishonoring of women; confiscation of private property; pillage; seizing of goods belonging to communities, educational establishments, and charities; arbitrary destruction of public and private goods; deportation and forced labor; execution of civilians under false allegations of war crimes; and violations against civilians as well as military personnel.

The commission's final report dated 29 March 1919 concluded that the war had been premeditated by Austro-Hungary and Germany, that they had deliberately violated the neutrality of Belgium and Luxembourg, that they had committed massive violations of the laws and customs of war;[63] and determined that "rank, however exalted," including heads of state, should not protect the holder from personal responsibility.[64] The commission also recommended establishing an international court composed of representatives of victors to try certain categories of offenses, but it specifically recommended against charging anyone with the offense of making aggressive war.[65]

In addition, the commission's final report also spoke of "the clear dictates of humanity" that were abused "by the Central Empires together with their allies, Turkey and Bulgaria, by barbarous or illegitimate methods," including "the violation of . . . the laws of humanity." The report concluded that "all persons belonging to enemy countries . . . who have been guilty of offences against the laws and customs of war or the laws of humanity, are liable to criminal prosecution."[66] Prompted by the Belgian jurist Rolin Jaequemeyns, the commission included the crimes that Turkey was accused of having perpetrated against Armenian citizens.[67] The commission concluded that "every belligerent has, according to international law, the power and authority to try the individuals alleged to be guilty of [war crimes] . . . if such persons have been taken prisoners or have otherwise fallen into its power."[68] The commission recommended that any peace treaty provide for an international tribunal to prosecute war criminals.[69] The commission proffered a series of acts deemed war crimes that were subsequently codified into international law.[70] The commission grouped these acts into four categories: (1) offenses committed in prison camps against civilians and soldiers of the Western Allies; (2) offenses committed by officials who issued orders in the German campaign against Western Allied armies; (3) offenses committed by all persons of authority, including the German kaiser, who failed to stop violations of laws and customs of war despite knowledge of those acts; and (4) any other offenses committed by the Central Powers that national courts should not be allowed to adjudicate.[71]

However, the U.S. and Japanese representatives on the commission objected to several key aspects of the commission's report. The commission proposed establishing a high tribunal to try, among others, charges:

> Against all authorities, civil or military, belonging to enemy countries, however high their positions may have been, without distinction of rank, including the heads of state, who ordered, or, with knowledge thereof and with power to intervene, abstained from preventing or taking measures to prevent, putting an end to repressing, violations of the laws or customs of war [it being understood that no such abstention should constitute a defense for the actual perpetrators].[72]

In their reservation to the commission's report, the U.S. representatives, Lansing and Scott, stated, among other things, that

> there were two classes of responsibilities, those of a legal nature and those of a moral nature, that legal offences were justiciable and liable to trial and punishment by appropriate tribunals, but that moral offences, however iniquitous and infamous and however terrible in their results, were beyond the reach of judicial procedure, and subject only to moral sanctions.[73]

Concerning crimes against humanity, they said:

> [The report of the commission] declares that the facts found and acts committed were in violation of the laws [and customs of war] and of the elementary principles of humanity. The laws and customs of war are a standard certain, to be found in books of authority and in the practice of nations. The laws and principles of humanity vary with the individual, which, if for no other reason, should exclude them from consideration in a court of justice, especially one charged with the administration of criminal law. . . . The American representatives are unable to agree with this inclusion, in so far as it subjects to criminal, and, therefore, to legal prosecution, persons accused of offences against "the laws of humanity," and in so far as it subjects chiefs of state to a degree of responsibility hitherto unknown to municipal or international law, which no precedents are to be found in the modern practice of nations.[74]

The U.S. representatives therefore objected to the references to the laws and principles of humanity in what they believed was meant to be a judicial proceeding. In their opinion, the facts found were to be violations or breaches of the laws and customs of war, and the persons singled out for trial and punishment were only to be those persons guilty of acts that should have been committed in violation of the laws and customs of war. The United States (and Japan) opposed "crimes against humanity" on the grounds that the commission's mandate was to investigate violations of the laws and customs of war and not the uncodified laws of humanity.[75] Concerning the criminal liability of heads of state, they argued that

> this does not mean that the head of state, whether he be called emperor, king, or chief executive, is not responsible for breaches of the law, but that he is responsible not to the judicial but to the political authority of his country. His act may and does bind his country and render it responsible for the acts which he has committed in its name and its behalf, or under cover of its authority; but he is, and it is submitted that he should be, only responsible to his country as otherwise to hold would be to subject to foreign countries, a chief executive, thus withdrawing him from the laws of his country, even its organic laws, to which he owes obedience, and subordinating him to foreign jurisdictions to which neither he nor his country owes allegiance or obedience, thus denying the very conception of sovereignty.[76]

Concerning war crimes trials in general, they said: "The American representatives know of no international statute or convention making a violation of the laws and customs of war—not to speak of the laws of humanity—an international crime affixing a punishment to it, and declaring the court which has jurisdiction over it."[77] Finally, concerning the establishment of an international tribunal, Lansing and Scott proposed that it "should be formed by the union of existing military tribunals or commissions of admitted competence in the premises."[78]

There were two difficulties that the U.S. delegates seem not to have considered thoroughly. First, which national procedure would the tribunal apply, and how would attempts to develop a uniform procedure be addressed by national courts? Confusion was bound to emanate from any attempt to amalgamate or adjust the varying procedures of the different tribunals without careful previous preparation. Second, if the laws and customs of war were to be applied, did such implementation exist in domestic legislation of the Western Allies and, if not, was it necessary that it did?[79]

The rest of the commission rejected the U.S. (and Japanese) opposition and insisted on the insertion of penal responsibility provisions in the peace treaty. Having overruled its chairman, Lansing, a large majority of the commission agreed that at the next renewal of the armistice the Germans should be required to deliver certain war criminals as well as relevant documents; furthermore, Western Allied commanders in occupied territory should be ordered to secure wanted persons who lived in regions under their control. However, Lansing refused to transmit these suggestions to the Supreme Council, arguing that as appointees of a plenary session the commission could report only to the full peace conference. He preferred that the conference, instead of trying Germans, issue a severe reprimand. He proposed that a committee of inquiry be appointed to consider the question in light of documents in the archives of the enemy and to report to participating governments.

The work of the commission was to feature prominently in the subsequent peace treaties negotiated by the Western Allies and Germany and Turkey. In a dramatic break with precedent, the treaties were to contain penal provisions as opposed to blanket amnesties. Much of the debate among the Western Allies addressed issues concerning the prosecution of Kaiser Wilhelm II, German war criminals, and Turkish officials for "crimes against the laws of humanity."[80] However, because of serious disagreement among the Western Allies on the desirability of a war crimes tribunal, the recommendations of the commission were incorporated to a limited extent into the peace treaties.[81] Next we look at the peace treaties and the subsequent failure to establish the envisaged international penal mechanisms owing to realpolitik considerations.

Frustrated Justice:
The Peace Treaties of Versailles and Sevres

Secretary of State Robert Lansing and James Brown Scott were the U.S. members of the Commission on the Responsibilities of the Authors of War and on Enforcement of Penalties, with Lansing acting as the commission's chairman. Representing a nation that had suffered less from the misconduct of Germans during the war, they were not eager to cloak the exercise of power in a dubious legal form. They maintained the position that to create an international tribunal to try war crimes committed during World War I "would be extralegal from the viewpoint of international law, . . . contrary to the spirit both of international law and of the municipal law of civilized states and . . . would, in reality, be a political and not a legal creation."[82] The Japanese delegation shared this opposition to penal responsibility advocated by the rest of the commission. This dissent was later to play itself out among the Western Allies, who, keen to cater for political expedience, incorporated only limited penal provisions in the peace treaties of Versailles and Sevres.

The Failure to Establish Prosecutions
Pursuant to the Peace Treaty of Versailles

The commission's final report came to the Supreme Council (which had the final authority on negotiating the peace treaty) on 29 March 1919. The U.S. representatives attached a statement to the effect that the views of the majority contravened U.S. principles. Lansing thought that the British knew the practical impossibility of the action that they were forced by public opinion to advocate and were depending on the United States to block it. Lansing found President Wilson even more strongly opposed to trying the kaiser. Both feared that physical punishment of Wilhelm II would make him a martyr and would lead to the restoration of the dynasty.[83]

On 8 April, the Big Four discussed the question of penal responsibility for wartime atrocities at great length. President Wilson, the chairman of the Supreme Council, opined: "I am afraid, it would be difficult to reach the real culprits. I fear that the evidence would be lacking."[84] Wilson thought that in the violation of Belgium's neutrality a crime had been committed for which eventually the League of Nations would find a remedy. He warned against dignifying the culprit, stooping to his level by flouting the principles of law. When Lloyd George told the Council of Four that he wanted "the man responsible for the greatest crime in history to receive the punishment for it," Wilson replied: "He will be judged by the contempt of the whole world; isn't that the worst punishment for such a man?" He thought the German militarists doomed to "the execration of history."[85] Although Wilson agreed that the Western Allies' populaces might not understand if the kaiser were allowed to go free, he stated: "I can do only what I consider to be just, whether public sentiment be for or against the verdict of my conscience." Seeing political censure rather than criminal prosecution of the kaiser, French prime minister Georges Clemenceau burst into an impassioned appeal that was shrewdly aimed at Wilson:

> For me, one law dominates all others, that of responsibility. Civilization is the organization of human responsibilities. Mr. Orlando [the Italian prime minister] says: "Yes, within the nation." I say: In the international domain. I say this with President Wilson who, when he laid the foundations of the League of Nations, had the honor to carry over into international law the essential principles of national law. . . . We have today a glorious opportunity to bring about the transfer to international law of the principle of responsibility which is at the basis of national law.[86]

Wilson still demurred. He pointed out that there was no legal or other means of forcing Holland to give up the kaiser. At this point Lloyd George declared that the question of the kaiser's prosecution before an international tribunal, like that of reparations, interested British opinion "to the highest degree," and his people could not accept a treaty that left it unsolved. He suggested that they could force Holland to deliver Wilhelm II by threatening its exclusion from the League of Nations. Under this well-directed attack, Wilson, who was about to go into the final meetings of the Commission on the League of Nations to seek approval of an amendment with respect of the Monroe Doctrine, yielded. The next morning he read to the Supreme Council a draft that he had prepared. It satisfied Clemenceau and Lloyd George and provided the substance for articles 227 and 229 of the Peace Treaty of Versailles.[87] In withdrawing from his opposition to the war crimes clauses, Wilson recognized that they were too ineffectual to warrant any determined resistance. When he was asked by the U.S. ambassador to Paris, John Davis, whether he expected to "catch his rabbit," he replied in the negative, quipping that "it was all damned foolishness anyway."[88] Similarly, Lloyd George's enthusiasm was to wane after a strong protest from General Louis Botha, the South African representative, along with a rapidly subsiding vindictive feeling among the British public.[89]

On 25 June, three days before the conclusion of the Peace Treaty of Versailles, Wilson brought up the matter of the kaiser's extradition. Lansing drafted a note that was sent to the Dutch government requesting compliance with article 227 of the peace treaty, under which the five victorious powers were to try Wilhelm II before a "special tribunal" on the charge of "a supreme offence against international morality and the sanctity of treaties." The response from the Netherlands, whose sitting monarch was the kaiser's cousin, was not positive. The Dutch insisted that a grant of political asylum should be respected. The Dutch rejected the concepts of "international policy" and "international morality" upon which the Western Allies proposed to try and punish the kaiser, and they invoked the domestic laws and national traditions of Holland as further justification. The Dutch defined the kaiser's offense as "political" and hence exempt from extradition.[90] As a result, the Western Allies did not formally request his extradition, and there was no formal judicial or administrative process in which the kaiser's extradition was denied.[91] No further action was taken, but British and French leaders could appease their constituencies with evidence that they had tried to satisfy the prevailing demand for retributive "justice."[92] Nevertheless, the assertion by the peace conference of a right to punish war criminals was a novel departure from tradition, one that set a precedent for action at the end of the next world war.

After much compromise, the Western Allied representatives finally agreed on the terms of the Treaty of Peace Between the Allied and Associated Powers and Germany, concluded at Versailles on 28 June 1919.[93] Besides other important matters, including reparations, the treaty in article 227 provided for the creation of an ad hoc international criminal tribunal to prosecute Kaiser Wilhelm II for initiating the war.[94] It further provided in articles 228 and 229 for the prosecution of German military personnel accused of violating the laws and customs of war before interallied military tribunals or before the military courts of any of the Western Allies.[95] The limited incorporation of the recommendations of the commission with regard to penal provisions was to prove fatal because the treaty provisions pertaining to war crimes ultimately proved unworkable in the postwar political context.[96] The attempt to try war criminals failed for a number of reasons, including: the enormity of the undertaking; deficiencies in international law and in the specific provisions of the peace treaty, which proved to be unworkable; the failure of the Western Allies to present a united front to the Germans and to take strong measures to enforce the treaty; and strong German nationalism. The victors' lack of control over affairs within Germany ultimately defeated the attempt to bring accused war criminals to justice.[97]

It is worth noting that the Peace Treaty of Versailles did not link the 1919 commission to eventual prosecutions recognized under articles 228 and 229, resulting in an institutional vacuum between the investigation and prosecution stages. Commenting on the hypocritical reason behind this institutional vacuum, M. C. Bassiouni states:

> The Treaty of Versailles did not link the 1919 Commission to eventual prosecutions recognized under its Articles 228 and 229, resulting in an institutional vacuum between the investigation and prosecution stage.

Therefore, if the outcome of investigating was no longer politically useful, it could be reduced to a report that was easy to ignore and ultimately forget. If, however, the investigation outcome became politically useful, it could be used for eventual prosecutions.[98]

Subsequently, the two major provisions of the Peace Treaty of Versailles, articles 227 and 228, were not implemented as geopolitical considerations dominated the post–World War I era. Regarding prosecution of the kaiser under article 227, the Western Allies blamed the Dutch government for its refusal to extradite, and some saw this as a way to avoid establishing a tribunal pursuant to article 227. The Western Allies were not ready to create the precedent of prosecuting a head of state for a new international crime. Indeed, this was evident in the choice of words used by the Western Allies in drafting article 227, authored primarily by representatives of Great Britain:

> The Allied and Associated Powers publicly arraign William II of Hohenzollern, formerly German Emperor, for a supreme offence against international morality and the sanctity of treaties. A special tribunal will be constituted to try the accused, thereby assuring him the guarantees essential to the right of defense . . . . In its decision the tribunal will be guided by the highest motives of international policy, with a view to vindicating the solemn obligations of international undertakings and the validity of international morality. . . . The Allied and Associated Powers will address a request to the Government of the Netherlands for the surrender to them of the ex-Emperor in order that he may be put on trial.[99]

In an informative critique on the politics behind this provision, Bassiouni opines:

> The provisions of Article 227 . . . were artfully drafted. They define the crime of aggression as the supreme crime against the sanctity of the law of treaties. The question that arises is what is a "crime against the sanctity of the law of treaties"? This inherent vagueness in Article 227 was deliberate and was built into the Article so that, should the Kaiser ever be brought to trial, he would be acquitted based on the fact that his conviction would violate the principles of legality.[100]

Considering that the text of article 227 does not refer to a known international crime, but defines the purported crime of aggression in a manner more analogous to a "political" crime, the Dutch government had a valid legal basis to reject the Western Allies' attempt to secure the surrender of the kaiser for trial. Article 227, quite possibly, was intended to fail. It offered a concession to the European masses, who saw the kaiser as an ogre of war, and to the French and Belgian governments, which wanted to humiliate Germany for initiating the war. Additionally, the very idea of prosecuting the kaiser troubled many. In particular, the British[101] (and obviously some of the Western Allies) feared that their heads of state could be exposed to similar risks, thus subverting one of the cardinal tenets of international law: sovereign immunity.

As for the prosecutions intended by articles 228 and 229, political tussles caused delay. By 1921, when the provisions finally got a realistic chance for implementation, the zest of the Western Allies to set up joint or even separate military tribunals had waned, and new developments in Europe required that Germany not be further humiliated. Though crimes against humanity were not ultimately included in the list of offenses drawn up by the commission,[102] largely due to objections by the United States and Japan,[103] by 1920 the Western Allies had compiled a list of approximately 20,000 Germans who were to be investigated for war crimes.[104] These crimes included torture, use of human shields, rape, and the torpedoing of hospital ships by German submarines.[105] Although there is no question that these terrible crimes were covered by the international law of armed conflict as it then existed, the Western Allies were apprehensive of trying so many German officials and personnel. After all, Germany was trying to reconstruct, and extensive trials might jeopardize the stability of the vulnerable Weimar Republic and expose it to revolutionary Bolshevik influence.[106] "Many politicians argued against prosecution, preferring instead to look to the future."[107] However, because many of these crimes were truly heinous, complete freedom from prosecution was also unacceptable. An alternative solution was therefore proposed. Instead of setting up an international tribunal, Germany would conduct the prosecutions. It was agreed that the German government would prosecute a limited number of war criminals before the German Supreme Court (the Reichsgericht) in Leipzig instead of establishing an interallied tribunal as provided for in article 228.

In response to the request to undertake prosecutions, Germany, which had previously passed a national law to implement provisions of articles 228 and 229 of Versailles, passed new legislation to assume jurisdiction under its national laws to prosecute accused offenders. Under German law, the procurator general of the supreme court had the right to decide which cases would be brought to trial.[108] By refusing to surrender German nationals to the Western Allies for trial, the German government virtually repudiated article 228, which stipulated such a surrender. Field Marshal Rüdiger von der Goltz's scornful declaration that "the world must realize that . . . no catchpoll shall hand Germans over to the Allies"[109] was symptomatic of powerful resistance among Germans. The government was reluctant to accede to foreign pressure and institute criminal proceedings against nationals for crimes against humanity. Although the armistice between Germany and the Western Allies was signed on 11 November 1918, the trials at Leipzig did not begin until 23 May 1921.[110] By then, the Western Allies' political will to pursue justice was dissolving. International public interest was also dissipating, and domestic political concerns in the Western Allied countries overshadowed any remaining concerns that academics, intellectuals, and public-spirited citizens may have had in Belgium, France, and Great Britain.[111]

The Western Allies were required to submit their cases, including evidence, to the German procurator general. The initial list of 20,000 was reduced to 896 by the Western Allies; of these only forty-five were submitted for prosecution.[112] Despite the 1919 commission's extensive report and the Western Allies' supplemental information conveyed to the German procurator general, only twelve military officers were ultimately prosecuted before the supreme court.[113] There were no other national or interallied proceedings against any of those accused of war crimes by the commission or any of the cases rejected for prosecution by the procurator general.

The German public showed indignation that German judges could be found to sentence the war criminals, and the press brought all possible pressure to bear on the court.[114] Many of the defendants were cheered upon entering or leaving the courtroom, whereas representatives of the Western Allies attending the trials were jeered. Those acquitted often departed the courtroom with bouquets of flowers offered by an admiring public. Prison guards who assisted in the escape of some defendants before or after conviction were publicly congratulated.[115] The most famous case involved the *Llandovery Castle* hospital ship, which had been torpedoed and sunk, with two naval lieutenants firing upon survivors in lifeboats. The two lieutenants proudly accepted the *London Times* calling them "barbarians," and the German press hailed them as "U-boat heroes" upon their being sentenced to four years' imprisonment.[116] Thus what was intended to be a deterrent to future violations of international humanitarian law gave rise to nationalistic fervor and a sense of indignation that became a unifying force against the Western Allies.

The outcome of the Leipzig proceedings was dismal by any standard of retributive justice.[117] Only twelve trials were held; half resulted in acquittals and half in convictions with light sentences. Allied disappointment at the popular exaltation of the defendants and subversion of justice led the Western Allies to appoint the Commission of Allied Jurists to examine the effect of the popular response on the proceedings. The commission unanimously recommended to the Supreme Council that the Leipzig trials be suspended and the remaining defendants be tried before interallied courts. The commission's recommendations failed to yield the desired results.[118]

The Leipzig trials exemplified the sacrifice of justice on the altars of international and domestic politics.[119] The treaty commitment to try and punish offenders if Germany failed to do so was never carried out. The political leaders of the major powers were more concerned with ensuring peace in Europe than pursuing justice.[120] Indeed, it was a common belief that World War I was the war to end all wars and that the League of Nations would usher in a new world order that would prevent future wars. The Western Allies, however, missed the opportunity to establish an international system of justice that would have functioned independently of political considerations. These weak attempts to impose international criminal justice failed to deter the military leaders who initiated World War II.

Commenting on the Leipzig trials and its future impact, Bassiouni notes:

> The Leipzig trials, which ended in 1923, were thus a complete farce. The absence of resolute action on the part of the Allies, and the great latitude ceded to Germany regarding these prosecutions may well have set the scene for even greater atrocities in the coming years: the next decade [1923–1932] saw the rise of National Socialism in Germany. By 1936, the Nazi party was in power, and its policies of racial and ethnic discrimination were fully in force.[121]

The events during and after 1939 led to a more pragmatic reaction by the Western Allies, still smarting from the debacle that ended World War I. The failure to implement articles 227, 228, and 229 was a result of political compromise. "This compromise demonstrates that the political will of the world's major powers is paramount over all else."[122] "The post–World War I experience showed the extent to which international justice can be compromised for the sake of political expedience. Conversely, the post–World War II experience was [to reveal] how effective international justice could be when there is political will to support it and the necessary resources to render it effective."[123]

The Failure to Establish Prosecutions
Pursuant to the Peace Treaty of Sevres

When Turkey signed the armistice on 30 October 1918, it was at the mercy of the Western Allies. Winston Churchill described Turkey as being "under the spell of defeat, and of deserved defeat."[124] Similarly, British foreign minister George Curzon denounced Turkey as "a culprit awaiting sentence."[125] Turkey's "culpability," in the eyes of the Western Allies, involved mainly war crimes and crimes against its own citizens. Nine months after the conclusion of Versailles, a treaty of peace was presented to Turkey on 11 May 1920. It was signed on 10 August at Sevres. Besides the matter of mandates for Mesopotamia, Palestine, Syria, and Lebanon, the treaty provided for Turkey's surrender of accused persons to be tried for "crimes against the laws of humanity." Charges were to be brought before an international tribunal against Turkish officials for the large-scale killing of Armenians in Turkey.[126]

Based on the recommendations of the 1919 Allied Commission on the Responsibilities of the Authors of War and on Enforcement of Penalties, several articles stipulating the trial and punishment of those responsible for the Armenian genocide were incorporated into the Peace Treaty of Sevres.[127] Under article 226, the Turkish government recognized the right of trial and punishment by the Western Allies, "notwithstanding any proceedings or prosecution before a tribunal in Turkey."[128] Moreover, Turkey was obligated to surrender "all persons accused of having committed an act in violation of the laws and customs of war, who are specified either by name or by rank, office or employment which they held under Turkish authorities."[129] Under article 230 of the peace treaty, Turkey was further obligated to hand over persons whose surrender might be required by the Western Allies as being responsible for the massacres committed during the continuance of the state of war on territory that formed part of the Turkish Empire on 1 August 1914. The Western Allies reserved the right to designate the tribunal that would try the accused, and the Turkish government was obligated to recognize such a tribunal.[130] The Peace Treaty of Sevres, therefore, provided for international adjudication of the crimes perpetrated by the Ottoman Empire against Armenians during World War I.

The Western Allies, pursuant to their earlier warning in May 1915, were committed to prosecuting Turkish officials and personnel responsible for the Armenian massacres. This initial commitment was reflected in the fact that beginning in January 1919, prior to the conclusion and signing of Sevres, Turkish authorities, directed and often pressured by Western Allied authorities in Istanbul, arrested and detained scores of Turks from four groups: (1) the members of Ittihad's Central Committee; (2) the two wartime cabinet ministers; (3) a host of provincial governors; and (4) high-ranking military officers identified as organizers of wholesale massacres in their zones of authority. The suspects were first taken to the military governor's headquarters and were subsequently transferred to the military prison maintained by the Turkish defense ministry. Custody and the disposal of their cases by the Turkish judiciary, however, posed serious problems.[131]

The Turkish response paralleled the German response. The foreign minister of the Istanbul government objected to surrendering Turkish nationals to the Western Allies, and Mustafa Kemal, the head of the antagonistic Ankara government, rejected the very idea of "recognizing a kind of right of jurisdiction on the part of a foreign government over the acts of a Turkish subject in the interior of Turkey herself."[132] Turkey claimed that such a surrender of Turkish subjects contradicted the sovereign rights of the Ottoman Empire as recognized by Britain in the armistice. As the Turkish foreign minister argued,

> Compliance with the demand for surrender by the Turkish Government would be in direct contradiction with its sovereign rights in view of the fact that by international law each state has [the] right to try its subjects for crimes or misdemeanors committed in its own territory by its own tribunals. Moreover, His Britannic Majesty having by conclusion of an armistice with the Ottoman Empire recognized [the] latter as a *de facto* and *de jure* sovereign State, it is incontestably evident that the Imperial Government possesses all the prerogatives for freely exercising [the] principles inherent in its sovereignty.[133]

Despite this argument, the commission held that trials by national courts should not bar legal proceedings by an international or an interallied national tribunal. On 2 April 1919, the British prime minister stated that should the Turks persist in their recalcitrant attitude, "pressure should at least be brought to bear upon them to refrain from instituting any form of proceedings against [the accused war criminals] until the Peace Conference has decided as to their ultimate disposal."[134] On 28 May 1919, sixty-seven detainees were seized by surprise by the British and removed from the military prison. Twelve of them, mostly former ministers, were taken to the island of Mudros, the rest to Malta. The twelve ministers were eventually transferred to Malta, where the number of prisoners rose to 118 by August 1920.[135]

In the months following the removal of Turkish suspects to Malta, the political climate in Istanbul, particularly in the interior of Turkey, began to change to the Western Allies' detriment. As insurgent Kemalism[136] gained a foothold throughout Turkey, the pro-British sultan's government steadily weakened. Moreover, the Western Allies began to bicker among themselves. Delays in the final peace settlement with Turkey complicated this situation. France and Italy began to court the Kemalists in secret; the Italians lent the new regime substantial military assistance; and both the French and the Italians sabotaged British efforts to restore and strengthen the authority of the sultan and his government.[137] In the face of these developments, Britain's resolve to secure justice in accordance with the 24 May 1915 Western Allied note was attenuated. This was not helped by a defiant Germany. Just as the Netherlands had refused to extradite the German kaiser, a request to Germany to arrest and surrender Talat Pasa, grand vizier and de facto head of the Ottoman State who had fled to Germany at the end of the war, was rebuffed by Germany, which invoked article 5(2) of the 1917 Turko-German Extradition Treaty,[138] with the German foreign minister emphatically proclaiming: "Talat stuck with us faithfully, and our country remains open to him."[139]

Toward the end of September 1919, the demise of prosultan Damad Ferid's cabinet became imminent. On 17 November 1919, the new British high commissioner, Admiral Sir John de Robeck, informed Curzon, the British foreign minister, that "the present Turkish Government . . . [is] so dependent on the toleration of the organizers of the [Kemalist] National Movement that I feel it would be futile to ask for the arrest of any Turk accused of offences against Christians, even though he may be living openly in Constantinople. . . . I do not consider it politically advisable to deport [to Malta] any more prisoners."[140] Notwithstanding, the British admiral stated almost prophetically that unless a legal process was initiated "it may be safely predicted that the question of retribution for the deportations and massacres will be an element of venomous trouble in the life of each of the countries concerned."[141] Political considerations were not the only impediments to the commencement of retributive justice. Turkey's efforts to disguise responsibility and intent under the cover of World War I were insurmountable in the Western Allies' efforts at punishment. In mid-1920, Sir Harry Lamb, the political-legal officer of the British High Commission at Istanbul, enumerated in a detailed memorandum the evidentiary difficulties encumbering the effective prosecution of the authors of the Armenian genocide.[142] Alarmed by the implications of these impediments, Lamb warned his superiors that

> unless there is whole-hearted co-operation and will to act among the Allies, the trials will fall to the ground and the direct and indirect massacres of about one million Christians will get off unscathed. Rather than this should happen, it were better that the Allies had never made their declarations in the matter and had never followed up their declarations by the arrests and deportations that have been made.[143]

In the end, the penal provisions enshrined in the Peace Treaty of Sevres were to prove empty, a hollow threat. Retributive justice gave way to political accommodation. Abandoned by their allies, and pressured domestically to seek the release of some British prisoners held hostage by the Kemalists (who had gained national, political, and military ascendancy), the British sought a deal with Kemalist representatives for the total release of the Malta detainees. However, Mustafa Kemal refused to honor the former government's exchange agreement of 16 March 1921,[144] since it had excluded several Ittihadists implicated in the Armenian massacres, as well as eight others accused of mistreating British prisoners during the war. Instead, new foreign minister Yusuf Kemal (Tengirsek) pressed for an "all-for-all" exchange.[145] The all-for-all exchange agreement ensued on 23 October 1921, and the remaining fifty-three Turks were released on 1 November 1921. British shame and guilt set in immediately. Calling some of the Turks whom they had set free "notorious exterminators" of Armenians,[146] the

British officials involved in the negotiations and decisionmaking appended their reactions to the relevant documents. Foreign Minister Curzon scolded himself for having made a "great mistake" in pushing for the release of the Turks from British custody; he attributed his act "to a pressure which I always felt to be mistaken." Another British official commented as follows:

> The less we say about these people the better. . . . I had to explain why we released the Turkish deportees from Malta, skating over thin ice as quickly as I could. There would have been a row I think. . . . [T]he staunch belief among Members [of the Parliament is] that one British prisoner is worth a shipload of Turks, and so the exchange was excused.[147]

With the British having released the suspected criminals it had in custody, the Ankara government was pressured to deliver on its pledge (made on 11 June 1921 to the British government) that when the Malta internees were released in exchange for British civilian and military persons "those accused of crimes would be put on impartial trial at Ankara in the same way as German prisoners were being tried in Germany."[148] This, as well as subsequent similar assurances, proved to be mere negotiating ploys. Though Turkey established military tribunals to undertake prosecutions, the Turks embarked on an insincere and half-hearted effort at national investigation and prosecution in the expectation of being rewarded by lenient peace terms. By agreeing to try Turkish war criminals, the Ottoman authorities expected to be treated less sternly at the peace conference, a fact confirmed by Turkish historians[149] and the British officials involved.[150] The Ottoman authorities reasoned that the Turkish nation could not be held responsible for the crimes of a political party and its governmental agents. Commenting on the first sentence of capital punishment imposed by the Turkish Military Tribunal, British high commissioner Admiral Sir A. Calthorpe maintained that the Turks, including the grand vizier and his supporters, "consider executions a mere concession to the Entente rather than as punishment justly meted out to criminals." The rise of nationalism, and the Turkish populace's increasingly defiant attitude toward the Western Allies, further weakened the government's resolve in its quest for justice. The efforts to punish those responsible for the genocide were sabotaged.

Despite good intentions, the Turkish tribunals lacked the strength for full prosecution. This weakness reflected the impotence of the postwar government. By assigning blame and fixing punishment, the Turkish courts-martial were expected to alleviate the domestic consequences of military defeat through "catharsis" and also mollify the victors. They were therefore placed in a position that tended to weaken the judicial will to adjudicate the charges. Generally, no nation can adjudge impartially and condemn itself, directly or indirectly, on charges of complicity in atrocities unless it hews to the law and honors that facts of the case.[151]

Although ultimately ineffectual, the attempted prosecution was of extraordinary, though unrecognized, significance. For the first time in history, deliberate mass murder, designated "a crime under international law,"[152] was adjudicated in accordance with domestic penal codes, thus substituting national laws for the rules of international law. Though the Turkish trials were successful in documenting the crimes that had been committed against the Armenian people, they failed dismally in punishing the war criminals.

Domestically, the rise of a strong nationalist movement led by Mustafa Kemal conflicted with legal efforts to prosecute Turkish military and government officials. The nationalist aspirations of unity and national pride were inconsistent with the internal impulse to fix blame and apportion responsibility for the Armenian genocide on Turkish leaders. In the international sphere, political considerations outweighed the Western Allies' desire to force the Turks to acknowledge and prosecute the war criminals. In their zest to win favor with the Kemalist government, France and Italy undermined the efforts of Britain, and to a lesser extent the United States, to bring about retributive justice. Britain, lacking the support of allies and facing Turkish opposition, eventually sacrificed the pursuit of justice to political expediency.

Rising political tensions within the Western Allies and nationalistic passions in Turkey eventually led to the scrapping of the Peace Treaty of Sevres and its subsequent replacement in 1923 by the Peace Treaty of Lausanne,[153] which wiped out the provisions in Sevres relating to the international penal process. Lausanne did not contain any provisions on prosecutions, but rather had an unpublicized annex granting Turkish officials amnesty,[154] thus giving Turkish officials impunity for war crimes and crimes against humanity and burying any hope of prosecution. Many see the lack of action following the Armenian genocide as an important precedent for the subsequent Holocaust of World War II. Indeed, it has been reported that, in trying to reassure doubters of the desirability and viability of his genocidal schemes, Hitler stated, "Who, after all, speaks today of the annihilation of the Armenians?"[155]

Conclusion

At the end of World War I, the Peace Treaty of Versailles provided for the prosecution of Kaiser Wilhelm II and for an international tribunal to try German war criminals. After the war, the kaiser fled to the Netherlands, where he obtained refuge, but the Western Allies, who had no genuine interest in prosecuting him, abandoned the idea of an international court. Instead, they allowed the German Supreme Court sitting at Leipzig to prosecute a few German officers. The Germans criticized the proceedings because they were directed only against them and did not apply to Western Allied personnel who also committed war crimes. More troublesome, however, was the Western Allies' failure to pursue the killing of some 600,000 Armenians in Turkey. A 1919 commission recommended the prosecution of responsible Turkish officials, and "crimes against humanity" became a legal reality. Vocal opposition to the idea from the United States and Japan, using a technical legal argument that no such crime yet existed under positive international law, killed the Peace Treaty of Sevres, which was to serve as a basis for Turkish prosecutions, and was replaced by the Peace Treaty of Lausanne, which gave amnesty. Thus, the first of many mass killings in the twentieth century went unpunished, setting the precedent for later events. In the words of M. C. Bassiouni and C. L. Blakesley, "The short-sightedness and xenophobic tendencies of politicians after World War I had made impossible the advancement of international criminal law and the establishment of an international criminal court, which made the task of establishing Nuremberg and Tokyo more difficult."[156]

There are three main lessons that emerge from the events following World War I. First, nations cannot be expected to effectively police or punish themselves. The post–World War I trials in Turkey, as well those in Germany, reveal the futility of trusting domestic processes to obtain retribution for state-sanctioned crimes. The courts-martial in Turkey documented the crime of organized mass murder against the Armenians, but the trials resulted in only a small number of convictions under Turkish law. The political upheaval attending Turkey's response to military defeat impaired, and ultimately destroyed, the judicial proceedings' effectiveness. The German and Turkish regimes that gained power in the postwar era successfully relied on principles of national sovereignty to reject the authority of the European powers to intervene in the trials. Further, they weakened European resolve by manipulating political tensions. The rise of nationalist feelings conflicted with the purposes behind the prosecution of the accused. The governments and people were unwilling to accept the stigma of collective guilt that was implied by the trials. Rather than accept an international tribunal to try nationals, the vanquished states offered internal proceedings. A parallel can be drawn between the Istanbul and Leipzig trials, where the German war criminals were prosecuted. At Leipzig, domestic and international forces combined to thwart efforts to prosecute alleged war criminals. As with Turkey, nationalist feelings in Germany militated against prosecuting one's own nationals, especially under foreign pressure. The Western Allies, during both the Turkish and Leipzig trials, allowed political considerations to prevail over the efforts to prosecute the enemy's officials.[157]

A second lesson emerging from World War I is that groups of international actors cannot prevent or punish international law violations by another state when they do not remain cohesive and unequivocally committed to such ends. In World War I, the Western Allies decisively defeated the Turkish forces. Further, through their 24 May 1915 declaration expressing the intent to punish the perpetrators of the genocide, Britain, France, and Russia provided a basis for international jurisdiction over the genocidal acts of the Ittihad government of Turkey. Yet the Western Allies were unable to secure retribution for the genocide. Instead, their efforts floundered on political divisions and the inability, or unwillingness, to usurp the Ottomans' sovereign right to punish their own people for acts committed against Ottoman subjects on Ottoman soil. Equally, the Western Allies had decisively defeated Germany. However, in dictating terms through the Peace Treaty of Versailles, they were frightened by the political ramifications of a Bolshevik revolution in Germany and a Russo-German alliance. To this end, they were unprepared to impose the provisions relating to prosecution of war criminals.[158]

The final, and perhaps most daunting, lesson is that enforcement of international law is an "architecture of political compromise."[159] Politics and law are inexorably intertwined. Thus when the international community acts in response to violations of international law, it does so in light of prevailing political currents. All too often different national political agendas cripple the ability for coordination and commitment. The acknowledging of international crimes by states and their subsequent failure to enforce fuels impunity by rogue states. States may take on international obligations merely to appease the international community and enhance their own image and stature. Often states are willing to accept international treaties and conventions at face value and never attempt to ensure compliance; nor do they offer the political support that is required. Political motivations, however benign, tend to create the conditions for a breakdown in international law.

We next turn to the celebrated international military tribunals following World War II. That war was largely the result of the failure by European powers to enforce the provisions of Versailles and the resultant collapse in the collective security regime under the League of Nations. A militarily weak Germany in 1935 militarized and transformed into the military juggernaut of 1939. And with the collapse of the international rule of law, the stage was set once again for international lawlessness by military powers. This time, however, the Western Allies were determined to seek accountability through the international penal process.

Notes

1. Treaty of Peace Between the Allied and Associated Powers and Germany (Peace Treaty of Versailles) concluded at Versailles, 28 June 1919.
2. Ibid.

3. Trials involved only an abridged test list containing no more than forty-five of the 896 names of the suspects accused of war crimes originally supplied by the Western Allies to the German government. Of this only twelve were tried and six convicted in Leipzig, all with small penalties.

4. As L. C. F. Turner notes, "The roots of the war can be traced far back into the nineteenth century, although it is unusual to begin the story of war origins earlier than 1871." L. C. F. Turner, *The First World War* (Melbourne and Canberra: Cheshire, 1967), 1.

5. Jack S. Levy, "Preferences, Constraints, and Choices in July 1914," *International Security* 15 (1990–1991).

6. The Triple Alliance of Germany, Austro-Hungary, and Italy, initiated in 1882 and renewed in 1902, and the Entente Cordiale between Britain and France forged in 1904.

7. Barbara Tuchman, *The Guns of August* (New York: Macmillan, 1962).

8. Associations were formed that pressed for a close economic union with Austro-Hungary, and for the incorporation of other countries in a new customs union. Max Schinkel, director of Germany's second largest bank, the Disconto-Gesellschaft, declared that a broader basis was required "for laying the economic foundations of German world policy." Fritz Fischer, *Germany's Aims in the First World War* (New York: W. W. Norton, 1967), 10. Between 1912 and 1914 the famous Walther Rathenau, the leading figure in Allgemeine-Elektrizitdtsgesellschaft (General Electricity Society), pressed on Bethmann Hollweg the need for a central European customs union and foreshadowed the conception of *Mitteleuropa* (Central Europe) that was to assume such importance during the war.

9. Robert Gilpin, *War and Change in World Politics* (Cambridge: Cambridge University Press, 1981).

10. Serbia was required to suppress all propaganda directed against the monarchy, to dissolve *Narodna Obrana* (the People's Defense), to remove from the army and administration such persons as the Austrian government might stipulate, to arrest certain individuals, to punish severely frontier officials involved in illegal activity, and most important to accept the collaboration in Serbia of representatives of the Austro-Hungarian government for the suppression of subversive activity against the territorial integrity of the monarchy.

11. See A. Von Wegerer, *Der Ausbruch des Weltkrieges, 1914* [The Outbreak of the World War, 1914] (Hamburg: Hanseatische Verlagsanstalt, 1943), 11, 15, quoting Russian documents. Sidney Bradshaw Fay says, "These secret preparatory measures ordered before dawn of the 26th, enabled Russia, when war came, to surprise the world by the rapidity with which she poured her troops into East Prussia and Galicia." Sidney Bradshaw Fay, *The Origins of the World War*, vol. 1 (New York: Macmillan, 1930).

12. B. H. Liddell Hart, *A History of the World War, 1914–1918* (London: Faber and Faber, 1934), 47.

13. Gerhard Ritter explains this "unbelievable haste" by the need to capture Liege at the very outset of the war and comments: "In other words: the gamble of the Schlieffen Plan was so great that it could only succeed as a result of a rapid surprise advance by the German or by a sudden onslaught on Belgium. In the opinion of the General Staff Germany was therefore obliged by purely technical necessities to adopt before the whole world, the role of a brutal aggressor—an evil moral burden which, as is well known, we have not got rid of even today." Gerhard Ritter, *The Schlieffen Plan: Critique of a Myth,* translated by Andrew and Eva Wilson (London: O. Wolff, 1958), 83, 89–90.

14. Drawn by Alfred von Schlieffen, chief of staff (1862–1906), its principal aim was to detach France from the Anglo-French entente of 1904 whose nature Germany had misjudged. The centerpoint of the Schlieffen master plan's thinking was evidently the preference of German elites for a war with France and Russia in order to consolidate Germany's position on the continent and to confirm its status as a world power. The French and Russian staffs were well aware of its general character, and their own plans were aimed at dislocating it by violent offensives of their own. For a detailed discussion, see Ritter, *The Schlieffen Plan.*

15. For war costs at a glance, see Charles F. Horne, ed., *The Great Events of the Great War*, vol. 2 (New York: National Alumni, 1923). A table of costs in human life and money is reproduced in Harold Elk Straubing, ed., *The Last Magnificent War and Eyewitness Accounts of World War I* (New York: Paragon House, 1989), 402–403.

16. Straubing, *The Last Magnificent War.*

17. Probably the last such admonition was that given by the French in October 1918 when the Germans retreating from France were executing a scorched-earth policy, destroying everything that combat had left unscathed. Howard Levie, *Terrorism in War: The Law of War Crimes* (Dobbs Ferry, NY: Oceana, 1993), 22, n. 95.

18. Harry R. Rudin, *Armistice 1918* (New Haven, CT: Yale University Press, 1944), 291–292.

19. James W. Garner, "Punishment of Offenders Against the Laws and Customs of War," *American Journal of International Law* 14 (1920): 81, n. 27.

20. The attributes of neutrality were specifically defined by the Hague Convention (V) of 18 October 1907 in arts. 1, 2, and 10. Belgium's neutrality was not the only neutrality violated. Germany also violated Luxembourg's neutrality, which was guaranteed by art. 2 of the 1867 Treaty of London. For comments by the French and British leaders at the Paris Peace Conference concerning the public outrage at Germany's violation of Belgian neutrality, see Paul Mantoux, *The Deliberations of the Council of Four, March 24–June 28, 1919,* translated and edited by Arthur S. Link and Manfred F. Boemeke, vol. 1 (Princeton, NJ: Princeton University Press, 1992), 189–190.

21. See for example D. P. O'Connell, "International Law and Contemporary Naval Operations," *British Year Book of International Law* 44 (1970), 45; Robert L. Eichelberger, "The Law and the Submarine," *U.S. Naval Inst. Proc.* 77 (1951), 691; Harry E. Barnes, "Submarine Warfare and International Law," *World Polity* 2 (1960): 122.

22. Declaration Concerning the Laws of Naval Warfare (London Declaration), 26 February 1909, 208 Consol. T.S. 338, dictated that a neutral vessel captured by a belligerent vessel could be destroyed only if the safety of the capturing vessel could not be ensured when taking the merchant into port. In order to sink a vessel, a combatant had to provide a place of safety for the crew and passengers. The London Declaration made no reference to armed or unarmed belligerent merchants operating in direct support of the war effort or on a purely commercial mission. Nor did it recognize that a submarine is endangered by taking a prize ship into port.

23. D. P. O'Connell, *The Influence of Law on Sea Power* (Manchester, UK: Manchester University Press, 1975), 45–46.

24. Ibid., 46–47.

25. W. Mallison Jr., *Studies in the Law of Warfare: Submarines in General and Limited Warfare* (Washington, DC: U.S. Government Printing Office, 1966), 62–65. The German strategy of unrestricted submarine warfare nearly defeated the Western Allies in World War I. The German U-boats sank an average of 640,528 gross

registered tons of allied and neutral shipping in the first six months of the campaign. Ibid., 224, n. 2. If sinkings had continued at that rate, Britain probably would have lost the war. Ibid., 224.

26. H. Sprout and M. Sprout, *The Rise of American Naval Power 1776–1918,* 2nd ed. (Princeton, NJ: Princeton University Press, 1967), 330–331.

27. The most famous case involved the *Llandovery Castle* hospital ship, which had been torpedoed and sunk, with two naval lieutenants firing upon the survivors in the lifeboats. Later, after the end of World War I, the two lieutenants proudly accepted the *London Times* calling them "barbarians," while the German press hailed them as "U-boat heroes" upon their being sentenced to four years' imprisonment, *Times* (London), 9 July 1921; "German War Trials: Report of the Proceedings before the Supreme Court in Leipzig," *American Journal of International Law* 16 (1922), 628–640, 674–724; see also C. Mullins, *The Leipzig Trials: An Account of the War Criminals' Trials and a Study of German Mentality* (London: H.F. & G. Witherby, 1921); Reichsgericht, *Annual Digest* 2 (1921): 436.

28. For a more detailed account of the road to war, see E. B. Potter, ed., *Sea Power: A Naval History,* 2nd ed. (Annapolis, MD: Naval Institute Press, 1981), 226.

29. See for example Walter A. Raleigh and H. A. Jones, *The War in the Air: Being the Story of the Part Played in the Great War by the Royal Air Force* (Oxford: Clarendon, 1922–1927); Joseph Morris, *The German Air Raids on Great Britain, 1914–1918* (London: S. Low, Marston, 1920–1969); Kenneth Poolman, *Zeppelins Against London* (New York: John Day Co., 1961); Colin M. White, *The Gotha Summer: The German Daytime Air Raids on England, May to August 1917* (London: R. Hale, 1986).

30. Henry W. Miller, *The Paris Gun: The Bombardment of Paris by the German Long Range Guns and the Great German Offensives of 1918* (New York: J. Cape and H. Smith, 1930), 36.

31. Levie, *Terrorism in War,* 21. One estimate is that 66,000 Belgians were transported to Germany as slave labor and anywhere from 20,000 to 50,000 French. For some reason, perhaps because of the original violation of Belgium's guaranteed neutrality, much more was made of the 66,000 Belgians than of the 100,000 Poles who were similarly treated. James F. Willis, *Prologue to Nuremberg: The Politics and Diplomacy of Punishing War Criminals of the First World War* (Westport, CT: Greenwood, 1982), n. 63, 32–35. For the slave labor problem of World War II, see Levie, *Terrorism in War,* 352–356.

32. As Levie states in *Terrorism in War,* 22:

> The report of a committee of the German Parliament, the *Reichstag,* created in 1919 to investigate the charges of World War I violations of the law of war, justified the action in deporting the Belgians to Germany for labor purposes on the basis of art. 43 of the *1907 Hague Regulations* and with "international law." However, in 1924 the German Government reached agreement with an organization of Belgian deportees under which Germany was to pay a substantial amount of money to the former deportees. Of course, this could have been considered as unpaid wages rather than as damages for the illegal act of deportation.

33. See Vahakn N. Dadrian, "Genocide as a Problem of National and International Law: The World War I Armenian Case and Its Contemporary Legal Ramifications," *Yale Journal of International Law* 14 (1989): 224–226.

34. A prominent expert on genocide describes these shadows as "the United Nations memory hole." L. Kuper, *Genocide: Its Political Use in the Twentieth Century* (New Haven, CT: Yale University Press, 1981), 219.

35. Dickran H. Boyajian, *Armenia: The Case for a Forgotten Genocide* (Westwood, NJ: Educational Book Crafters, 1972); Marjorie Housepian, "The Unremembered Genocide," *Commentary* 42 (September 1966) (published as a pamphlet), reproduced in *Genocide and Human Rights*, J. N. Port, ed., Lanham, MD: University Press of America, 1982), 99–115.

36. See for example Kamuran Gurun, *Ermeni Dosyasi* (Ankara: Turk Tarih Kumuru Basimevi, 1983) (reversing victim-perpetrator roles in Armenian conflict and denying Turkish genocidal intent); Kumuran Gurun, *The Armenian File: The Myth of Innocence Exposed* (London: Published jointly by K. Rustem and Weidenfeld and Nicolson, 1985) (English translation of proceeding); S. Orel and S. Yuca, *Ermenilerce Talat Pasa'ya Atfedilen Telegraflar In Gercek Yuzu* [The Talât Pasha "Telegrams": Historical Fact or Armenian Fiction?] (Nicosia, Cyprus: K. Rustem and Brother, 1983) (denying authenticity of telegrams reflecting central planning of Armenian massacres); N. Ozkaya, *Le Peuple Armenien Et Les Tentatives De Rendre En Servitude Le Peuple Turc* [The Armenian People and the Attempts to Subjugate the Turkish People] (Istanbul: 1971) (blaming Armenian revolutionaries for massacres of Armenians preceding and attending genocide).

37. Joseph Pomiankowski, *Der Zusammenbruch Des Ottamanischen Reiches: Erinnerungen an die Turkei aus der Zeit des Weitkrieges* [The Collapse of the Ottoman Empire: Memories of Turkey During World War II] (Zurich: Amalthea-Verlag, 1928), 162. See also J. Lepsius, *Deutschland und Armenien, 1914–1918: Sammlung Diplomatischer Aktenstücke* [Germany and Armenia, 1914–1918: A Collection of Diplomatic Documents] (Potsdam: Der Tempelverlag, 1919), 84.

38. The Armenian Reform Agreement signed on 8 February 1914 between Turkey and Russia, with the concurrence of the other powers, contained international stipulations with regard to Turkish governmental measures to respect and uphold the rights of the minority Armenians. This agreement was seen by Turkey as shackling the government with regard to the exercise of sovereign prerogatives and policy. See Dadrian, "Genocide as a Problem of National and International Law," 263.

39. Ulrich Trumpener, *Germany and the Ottoman Empire 1914–1918* (Princeton, NJ: Princeton University Press, 1968), 134–135.

40. Ibid. Halil on the same day departed to Berlin to seek German support for the annulments. In informing his government of this move in his 5 September 1916 report, German ambassador Count von Wolff-Metternich directed attention to the Turkish concern for art. 61 of the Berlin Treaty involving Turkey's "engagements for Armenia," and to Halil's justification of the act on grounds of "the effect of war" (*Kriegszustand*). See A. A. Turkei, 183/44, A24061 (Ottoman Archives, Istanbul Research Center). The full text of the repudiation of the treaties in German is in Friedrich Kraelitz-Greifenhorst, "Die Ungultigkeitserklarung des Pariser und Berliner Vertrages durch die osmanische Regierung" [The Declaration of Invalidity of the Paris-Berlin Pact by the Osmanic Government], *Osterreichische Monatsschrift Fur Den Orient* [Austrian Monthly Script for the Orient] 43 (1917), 56–60.

41. For the English text of the law, see R. Hovannisian, *Armenia on the Road to Independence, 1918* (Berkeley: University of California Press, 1967), 51.

42. *Jhamanag* (Istanbul), 5 November 1918.

43. W. Churchill, *The World Crisis: The Aftermath* (London: Thorton Butterworth, 1929), 405. See also Ahmed Refik Altinay, *Iki Komite Iki Kital* [Two Committees and Two Massacres] (Istanbul: Ottoman Script, 1919), 40. Refik focuses on the central theme that under the guise of deportation and wartime relocation Ittihad pursued the goal of "destroying" (*imha*) the Armenians.

44. Declaration of France, Great Britain, and Russia, 24 May 1915, quoted in Egon Schwelb, "Crimes Against Humanity," *British Year Book of International Law* 23 (1946), 181; Dadrian, "Genocide as a Problem of National and International Law," 262.

45. Dadrian, "Genocide as a Problem of National and International Law," 292.

46. Kalevi J. Holsti, *Peace and War: Armed Conflicts and International Order, 1648–1989* (Cambridge: Cambridge University Press, 1991), 175–176, 208–209.

47. Great Britain, the United States, France, and Italy.

48. After a rebellion in Hungary engineered by radical social democrats, the Hungarian leader, Count Michael Karolyi, resigned. Bela Kuhn, a Bolshevik leader took over the reins of power with a band of radical social democrats. For a detailed discussion, see Arno J. Mayer, *Politics and Diplomacy of Peacemaking: Containment and Counterrevolution at Versailles, 1918–1919* (New York: Alfred A. Knopf, 1967).

49. See generally Lord Hankey, *The Supreme Control at the Paris Peace Conference 1919: A Commentary* (London: Allen and Unwin, 1963), George A. R. Riddell, *Lord Riddell's Intimate Diary of the Peace Conference and After, 1918–1923* (London: Gollancz, 1933).

50. There were authentic reports of an imminent collapse in Vienna; a Soviet-type republic was proclaimed in Bavaria; strikes broke out in the Ruhr, in Hamburg, and in Saxony; the sailors of the French squadron at Odessa mutinied, hastening the evacuation of this strategic Black Sea port; and the Red Army stayed Admiral Alexander V. Kolchak's advance and continued to push ahead in the Ukraine. To make matters worse, these worrisome developments in the defeated empires coincided with the upsurge of labor unrest in Britain, France, and Italy.

51. Memorandum, *Some Considerations for the Peace Conference Before They Finally Draft Their Terms,* circulated by the prime minister on 25 March 1919, Cmd. 1614, London, 1922. Close to the full text is cited in Baker, *Woodrow Wilson,* vol. 3, 449–457.

52. David Albert Foltz, *The War Crimes Issue at the Paris Peace Conference, 1919–1920* (New York: Norton, 1925), 49ff; Hankey, *The Supreme Control,* 13.

53. The provisional government of Germany, representing a people told by their rulers that war had been forced on them in 1914 by conspiring enemies, persistently urged the creation of a neutral commission to inquire impartially into the origins of the conflict. The German foreign minister, addressing the foreign offices of the major Western Allies, conjured up the ideals of lasting peace and international confidence. From London and Paris, however, he received blunt rebuffs, asserting that the responsibility of Germany for the war had long ago been incontestably proved. The U.S. State Department, after communicating with the peace mission at Paris, replied in the same tenor. See for example U.S. Department of State, "Papers Relating to the Foreign Relations of the United States" (Paris Peace Conference—F.R., P.P.C., vol. 2), 71–72; Dispatch from Solf to the State Department, forwarded to the House on 11 December 1918, *Yale House Collection and Related Papers,* (Manuscripts and Archives Room, Yale University Library—Y.H.C.).

54. The commission was comprised of two members from each of the five great powers: the United States, Great Britain, France, Italy, and Japan. The additional states composing the allied and associated powers were Belgium, Bolivia, Brazil, China, Cuba, Czecho-Slovakia, Ecuador, Greece, Guatemala, Haiti, the Hedjaz, Honduras, Liberia, Nicaragua, Panama, Peru, Poland, Portugal, Romania, the Serb-Croat-Slovene State, Siam, and Uruguay. Carnegie Endowment for International Peace, *The Treaties of Peace, 1919–1923* (1924), 3. The additional states,

having a special interest in the matter, met and decided that Belgium, Greece, Poland, Romania, and Serbia should each name a representative to the commission as well. 1919 Commission Report, 20.

55. Paris Peace Conference, vol. 3, 699; Commission on the Responsibility of the Authors of the War and on Enforcement of Penalties, *Report Presented to the Preliminary Peace Conference* (29 March 1919), 23 [hereafter 1919 Commission Report], reprinted in *American Journal of International Law* 14 (1920).

56. The commission completed its report in 1920 and submitted a list of alleged war criminals, who were to be tried by the tribunal. Sources conflict as to the number of alleged war criminals listed for prosecution. See Telford Taylor, *The Anatomy of the Nuremberg Trials: A Personal Memoir* (New York: Knopf, 1992), 17 (stating that the Allies presented a list of 854 individuals, including political and military figures); M. Cherif Bassiouni, *Crimes Against Humanity in International Criminal Law* (Boston: Martinus Nijhoff, 1992), 200 (stating that the Allies submitted a list of 895 named war criminals); Remigiusz Bierzanek, "War Crimes: History and Definition," in *International Criminal* Law, edited M. Cherif Bassiouni, vol. 3 (Dobbs Ferry, NY: Transnational, 1986–1987), 29, 36 (stating that 901 names appeared on the list).

57. Willis, *Prologue to Nuremberg,* 68.

58. Bassiouni, *Crimes Against Humanity.* Pieter Drost, *The Crime of State* (Leyden: A. W. Sythoff, 1959); Schwelb, "Crimes Against Humanity," 178.

59. Convention Respecting the Laws and Customs of War on Land, 18 October 1907, 36 Stat. 2277, preamble, 2779–2780. See also Carnegie Endowment for International Peace, *The Proceedings of the Hague Peace Conferences: Translation of the Original Texts* (New York: Oxford University Press, 1920–1921), 548.

60. 1907 Hague Convention (IV), preamble.

61. Willis, *Prologue to Nuremberg,* 157.

62. Ibid.

63. Commission on the Responsibility of the Authors of the War and on Enforcement of Penalties, *Report Presented to the Preliminary Peace Conference* (29 March 1919), reprinted in *American Journal of International Law* 14 (1920): 113–114.

64. Ibid., 112–117.

65. Ibid., 118–120.

66. Carnegie Endowment for International Peace, *Violations of the Laws and Customs of War: Report of the Majority and Dissenting Reports of the American and Japanese Members of the Commission on Responsibilities at the Conference of Paris, 1919* (pamphlet no. 32). The dissenting U.S. members were Robert Lansing and James Scott, who felt that the words "and the laws of humanity" were "improperly added." Ibid., 64, 73. In their memorandum of reservations, they maintained that the law and principles of humanity were not "a standard certain" to be found in legal treatises of authority and in international law practices. They argued that these laws and principles do vary within different periods of a legal system, between different legal systems, and with different circumstances. In other words, they declared that there is no fixed and universal standard of humanity and that a judicial organ relies only on existing law when administering it.

67. See Her Majesty's Stationery Office, British Foreign Office Papers—FO, FO 608/246, third session, folio 163, 20 February 1919, 20.

68. Commission on the Responsibility of the Authors of the War and on Enforcement of Penalties, *Report,* 121.

69. Ibid.

70. The acts deemed as war crimes are to be found in ibid., 114–115.

71. Ibid., 121–122. At the end of World War I in 1919, the major international instruments relating to the laws of war were the two Hague Conventions on the Laws and Customs of War on Land of 1899 and 1907: Willis, *Prologue to Nuremberg,* 5. Other sources of information on the laws of war included national military manuals and Geneva Conferences beginning in 1864. See Garner, "Punishment of Offenders" (general discussion of laws and customs of war in various states' military regulations at the outbreak of the war in 1914).

72. Commission on the Responsibility of the Authors of the War and on Enforcement of Penalties, *Report,* 121.

73. Ibid., 128.

73. Ibid., 134–135.

75. Ibid., 134.

76. Ibid., 134–135.

77. Ibid., 146.

78. Ibid., 129.

79. Sheldon Glueck, "By What Tribunal Should War Offenders Be Tried?" *Harvard Law Review* 1059 (1943): 1075–1076.

80. For information on the Armenian genocide, see generally Vahakn N. Dadrian, *The History of the Armenian Genocide: Ethnic Conflict from the Balkans to Anatolia to the Caucasus* (Providence, RI: Berghahn Books, 1995); Dadrian, "Genocide as a Problem of National and International Law," 35.

81. Willis, *Prologue to Nuremberg,* 52–62.

82. Memorandum by Miller and Scott, ca. 18 January 1919, published in David Hunter Miller, *My Diary at the Conference of Paris with Documents,* vol. 3 (New York: Printed for the author by the Appeal Printing Company, 1921), 456–457.

83. U.S. Department of State, vol. 11, 93–94; Lansing, "Memorandum of Reservations," 4 April 1919; Lansing to Wilson, in "Wilson Papers," 8 April 1919; Foltz, *The War Crimes Issue,* 135–174; Letter from Lansing to Polk, 14–15 March, 1919, Y.H.C.; Genevieve Tabouis, *The Life of Jules Cambon,* translated by C. F. Atkinson (London: Cape, 1938), 319–320.

84. Wilson had said on the *George Washington* in December that probably the kaiser had been "coerced to an extent" by the general staff: Swern Book ms., chapter 21 at 9, Princeton University Library.

85. Mantoux, *The Deliberations of the Council of Four,* 83.

86. Ibid., 193.

87. Wilson to Lansing, 9 April 1919. Wilson's text with minor changes became part VII of the Peace Treaty of Versailles; see Foltz, *The War Crimes Issue,* 201. A diary letter of Edith Benham from 9 April 1919 records that it was at the suggestion of Mrs. Wilson that the president prepared his compromise formula and secured the signature of his colleagues.

88. *Diary of John W. Davis,* 5 June 1919, Y.H.C.

89. On the anniversary of the Treaty of Vereeniging, General Louis Botha pointedly reminded the British delegation of the incendiary effect upon the Boers of an English proposal that he and General Jan Christiaan Smuts be tried for the crime of causing the Boer War. Ambassador Davis noticed a marked cooling in the eagerness to try the kaiser and a growing disinclination to have the trial staged in London. J. W. Davis to Lansing, 30 July 1919.

90. See Quincy Wright, "The Legal Liability of the Kaiser," *American Political Science Review* 13 (1919): 120.

91. See Taylor, *The Anatomy of the Nuremberg Trials,* 16. The legal grounds for denying the request were that the "offence charged against the Kaiser was

unknown to Dutch law, was not mentioned in any treaties to which Holland was a party, and appeared to be of a political rather than a criminal character." Ibid. See also Wright, "The Legal Liability of the Kaiser." The Netherlands discouraged formal extradition requests because extradition treaties applied only to cases in which a criminal act occurred.

92. The paragraphs above are based on Hankey, *The Supreme Control,* 13, 114, 116, 184, and on Mantoux, *The Deliberations of the Council of Four,* 144–151, and Mantoux, *The Deliberations of the Council of Four,* vol. 2, 524–525.

93. Peace Treaty of Versailles.

94. Ibid., art. 227.

95. Art. 228 states:

The German Government recognizes the right of the Allied and Associated Powers to bring before military tribunals persons accused of having committed acts in violation of the laws and customs of war. Such persons shall, if found guilty, be sentenced to punishments laid down by law. This provision will apply notwithstanding any proceedings or prosecution before a tribunal in Germany or in the territory of her allies.

The German Government shall hand over to the Allied and Associated Powers, or to such one of them as shall so request, all persons accused of having committed an act in violation of the laws and customs of war, who are specified either by name or by the rank, office, or employment which they held under the German authorities.

Art. 229 states:

Persons guilty of criminal acts against the nationals of one of the Allied and Associated Powers will be brought before the military tribunals of that Power. Persons guilty of criminal acts against the nationals of more than one of the Allied and Associated Powers will be brought before military tribunals composed of members of the military tribunals of the Powers concerned. In every case the accused will be entitled to name his own counsel.

96. Willis, *Prologue to Nuremberg,* 52–62.

97. See generally Elizabeth L. Pearl, Note, "Punishing Balkan War Criminals: Could the End of Yugoslavia Provide an End to Victors' Justice?" *American Criminal Law Review* 30 (1993): 1389–1390.

98. M. Cherif Bassiouni, "From Versailles to Rwanda in Seventy-Five Years: The Need to Establish a Permanent International Criminal Court," *Harvard Human Rights Journal* 10 (1997): 18.

99. Peace Treaty of Versailles, art. 227.

100. M. Cherif Bassiouni, "The International Criminal Court in Historical Context," *St. Louis–Warsaw Transatlantic Journal* 99 (1999): 56.

101. Willis, *Prologue to Nuremberg,* 98–101.

102. Division of International Law, Carnegie Endowment for International Peace, pamphlet no. 32 (1919), reprinted in *American Journal of International Law* 14 (Supp. 1920) (the United States, Great Britain, France, Italy, and Japan were to appoint three persons each to the tribunal, and the other countries were to appoint one person each to the tribunal). "Carnegie Report," *American Journal of International Law* 14 (Supp. 1920), annex II, 134, 144.

103. "Carnegie Report," annex II, 14.

104. M. Cherif Bassiouni, "Former Yugoslavia: Investigating Violations of International Humanitarian Law and Establishing an International Criminal Tribunal," *Fordham International Law Journal* 1191 (1995): 1194.

105. Willis, *Prologue to Nuremberg,* 13, 137–139.

106. Ibid., 113.

107. Bassiouni, "The International Criminal Court in Historical Context," 57.

108. Bassiouni, "From Versailles to Rwanda in Seventy-Five Years," 19–20.

109. A. Planzer, *Le crime de genocide* (St. Gallen, Switzerland: F. Scwhald, 1956), 48.

110. Bassiouni, *Crimes Against Humanity in International Criminal Law,* 202.

111. Bassiouni, "From Versailles to Rwanda in Seventy-Five Years," 21.

112. Bassiouni, *International Criminal Law,* 36.

113. See ibid., 36–37.

114. Planzer, *Le crime de genocide,* 51–52.

115. See Willis, *Prologue to Nuremberg,* 126–147.

116. *Times* (London), 9 July 1921; "German War Trials," 628–640, 674–724; see also Mullins, *The Leipzig Trials.*

117. The lists of these suspects were, in part, compiled and transmitted to the Germans by Britain (97), Belgium (334), Poland (57), France (332), Italy (29), and Romania (41). The remaining suspects were fugitives.

118. *German War Crimes: Report of the Proceedings,* British Parliamentary Papers, Cmnd. (1921), 1450.

119. Bassiouni, *Crimes Against Humanity in International Criminal Law,* 202.

120. Taylor, *The Anatomy of the Nuremberg Trials,* 15.

121. Bassiouni, "The International Criminal Court in Historical Context," 58.

122. M. Cherif Bassiouni, "Establishing an International Criminal Court: Historical Survey," *Military Law Review* 149 (1995): 53.

123. Ibid., 55.

124. Churchill, *The World Crisis,* 367.

125. Statement of Minister George Curzon, 4 July 1919, in *Documents on British Foreign Policy, 1919–1939,* edited by W. Woodward and R. Butler, 1st series (London: H.M.S.O., 1952), 661.

126. However, by Wilson's direction the United States was not officially represented at the signing. The United States was already eyeing commercial opportunities in western Asia (Turkey in particular) at the end of the war. Its failure to be represented at the signing was partly prompted by U.S. commercial imperialism and dollar diplomacy, an early indicator that the future of Turkey would be settled not at Paris but rather by requirements of political expedience. The Western Allies' concern about the stability of Turkey and eagerness not to alienate the new Turkish ruling elite that was partial to the Western powers would later result in Turkish officials being given immunity for war crimes.

127. Great Britain Treaty Series no. 11, 1920.

128. Ibid. See also Willis, *Prologue to Nuremberg,* 180.

129. Willis, *Prologue to Nuremberg,* 180–181.

130. Peace Treaty of Sevres, art. 230.

131. Bilal N. Simsir, *Malta Surgunleri* [The Malta Exiles] (Istanbul: Milliyet Yayinlari, 1976), 113. Of these, twenty-six were ordered released by the court-martial itself with the assertion, "There is no case against them." *Spectateur D'orient* (Istanbul), 21 May 1919. Admiral Sir A. Calthorpe informed London regarding the forty-one Turks released from military prison by Ottoman authorities that "there

was every reason to believe [they] were guilty of the most heinous crimes . . . mainly in connection with massacres." British Foreign Office Papers, 72, FO 371/4174/88761, folio 9, 30 May 1919. Referring to the Malta exiles, Foreign Office Near East specialist Sir James Edmonds declared, "There is probably not one of these prisoners who does not deserve a long term of imprisonment if not capital punishment." FO 371/6509/E8745, folios 23–24.

132. Speech delivered by Mustafa Kemal in Ataturk in 1927 (Istanbul, 1963) The speech lasted six days (15–20 October 1927) and was delivered before the deputies and representatives of the Republican Party that was founded by him. The volume containing the speech is published under the auspices of the Turkish Ministry of Education.

133. British Foreign Office Papers, FO 608/244/3749, folio 315 (Rear Admiral Sir Richard Webb's 19 February 1919 telegram to London, quoting from the Turkish minister's 16 February note whose original, full text in French is in British Foreign Office Papers, FO 608/247/4222, folio 177).

134. Ibid., FO 371/4173/47590, folio 89.

135. Dadrian, "Genocide as a Problem of National and International Law," 286.

136. The main tenets of Kemalism are summarized in two documents framed as the party was crystallizing the emergent postwar Turkish nationalism: the Declaration of the Kemalist Congress at Sivas (9 September 1919), and the subsequent National Pact (28 January 1920). See Elliot G. Mears, *Modern Turkey: A Politico-Economic Interpretation, 1908–1923 Inclusive* (New York: Macmillan, 1924), 627–631.

137. David Lloyd George, *Memoirs of The Peace Conference*, vol. 2 (New York: H. Furtig, 1939), 871, 878. Willis summed up the situation as follows:

> During the two years between the armistice and Mudros and the signing of the treaty of Sevres, the Turkish Nationalist movement grew into a major force, and the Allied coalition virtually dissolved. By 1920 most of the victors no longer included among their aims the punishment of Turkish war criminals . . . the Italians evaded a British request for the arrest of former Young Turk leaders then reported as meeting within their territory. The French and Italians hoped to secure concessions in Asia Minor and did not want to antagonize powerful factions in Turkey unnecessarily, particularly. (Willis, *Prologue to Nuremberg*, 63.)

138. This permitted extradition under three conditions: an arrest order, a verdict against the person whose extradition is being sought, or the submission of related judicial documents. As the court-martial had not yet taken place, there was no judicial documentation of a verdict.

139. A. A. Turkei 183/54 A45718. For the protracted exchange on this subject between the German Foreign Office and the Ottoman Foreign Ministry, see British Foreign Office Papers, FO 371/4173/82190, 371/4174/98910, 371/5173/E6949, 618/113/1941, folios 404–415.

140. British Foreign Office Papers, FO 371/4174/156721, folios 523–524.

141. Ibid., FO 371/4174/136069, folio 470.

142. Ibid., FO 371/6500/, W 2178, folios 385–118 and 386–119, Appendix A, 11 August 1920.

143. Ibid. In discussing the evidentiary difficulties, Sir Harry Lamb stated further: "Though none of this information is in itself of strict legal value, still no prosecution could get to work without it." In a report to London on 16 March 1921, High Commissioner Sir H. Rumbold confirmed several of the points that Lamb

made in this memo. Lamb did state in his memorandum that the British High Commission had gathered through its Greek-Armenian section a large mass of information concerning the 118 prisoners on Malta and some 1,000 others, all alleged to have been directly or indirectly guilty of participation in massacres. Despite his concerns, Lamb concluded, "It is safe to say that very few 'dossiers,' as they now stand, would not be marked 'no case' by a practical lawyer." Ibid., FO 371/6500/E3557, folios 385–118.

144. Ibid., FO 371/6500/E3375, folio 284/15.

145. Ibid., FO 371/6509, folio 47 (4 August 1921 summary of the negotiations); Simsir, *Malta Surgunleri,* 447.

146. British Foreign Office Papers, FO 371/7882/E4425 (comment by D. Osborne, 23 May 1922).

147. Ibid., FO 371/7882/E4425, folio 182. This attitude is also evident in the remark General William Campbell inserted in his letter to Lloyd George, whom he was pressuring for the release of his son, Captain James Campbell, from Turkish custody. Captain Campbell had written his father, who repeated it to Lloyd George, "I am more valuable than any of these miserable Turks." Ibid., FO 371/6509/E8562, folio 16. But a major source of pressure was the maneuvering of Winston Churchill, then secretary of state for war, who persuaded the cabinet to adopt a lenient attitude toward "less guilty Turks." Willis, *Prologue to Nuremberg,* 160. It is equally significant that one of the Turkish internees gleefully stated after his release that the British were duped by a "sly trick" of the Ankara government whose "British prisoners" to be exchanged included "six Maltese laborers and their Greek wives and children." Ahmet Emin Yalman, *Turkey in My Time* (Norman: University of Oklahoma Press, 1956), 106.

148. British Foreign Office Papers, FO 371/6509, folio 47. Three months later the interior minister of the Ankara government repeated the same pledge when he informed General Sir Charles Harrington, then the highest military authority at Istanbul, that those Malta exiles implicated in war crimes "will be tried on arrival." Ibid., FO 371/6509/E10411, folio 130. A similar assurance was given by Ankara's Foreign Minister Bekir Sami. Ibid., FO 371/6499/E3110, 190; see also Yalman, *Turkey in My Time,* 106.

149. Sina Aksin, *Istanbul Hukumetleri Ve Milli Mucadele* [The Istanbul Governments and the National Struggle] (Istanbul: Isis, 1983), 140–141; Ismail Hami Danismend, *Izahli Osmanli Tarihi Kronolojisi* [The Annotated Chronology of Ottoman History], 2nd ed. (Istanbul: Kitabevi, 1961), 457.

150. British Foreign Office Papers, FO 371/4173/44216, folio 51 (20 March 1919, report by W. H. Deedes). In folio 50, Deedes explicitly states the official British position of noninterference in Turkey's internal affairs.

151. Dadrian, "Genocide as a Problem of National and International Law," 314.

152. Raphael Lemkin, "Genocide as a Crime Under International Law," *American Journal of International Law* 41 (1947): 150.

153. Treaty with Turkey and Other Instruments, 24 July 1923 (Peace Treaty of Lausanne), reprinted in *American Journal of International Law* 18 (Supp. 1924).

154. Ibid. See also M. Cherif Bassiouni, "The Time Has Come for an International Criminal Court," *Indiana International and Comparative Law Review* 1 (1991): 2–4.

155. K. Bardakjian, *Hitler and the Armenian Genocide* (Cambridge, MA: Zoryan Institute, 1985), 6.

156. M. Cherif Bassiouni and Christopher L. Blakesley, "The Need for an

International Criminal Court in the New International World Order," *Vanderbilt Journal of Transnational Law* 25 (1992): 154.

157. Dadrian, "Genocide as a Problem of National and International Law," 292.

158. Noted international law scholar L. Kuper has explicitly addressed this problem:

> The United Nations remains highly protective of state sovereignty, even where there is overwhelming evidence, not simply of minor violations, but of widespread murder and genocidal massacre. It is no wonder that it may seem to be a conspiracy of governments to deprive their people of their rights. (Kuper, *Genocide,* 182.)

159. Gerry Simpson, "'Throwing a Little Remembering on the Past': The International Criminal Court and the Politics of Sovereignty," *University of California Davis Journal of International Law and Policy* 5 (1999): 142.

3

A New Dawn:
The Birth of the Modern
International Penal Process

In World War I, Germany had defeated Russia and was then itself defeated by a coalition of Western Allied powers. However, Germany's defeat did not extinguish its hopes for global status and influence. On the contrary, it intensified them. With Germany again pursuing an aggressive course, conditions for the second major war of the twentieth century began to ripen. German aggression was fueled in part by resentment of the punitive terms imposed at the 1919 peace conference by the victors (France, Britain, Italy, Japan, and the United States). Under French pressure, the Peace Treaty of Versailles included the destruction of Germany's armed forces, the loss of territory (such as Alsace-Lorraine, absorbed by Germany following the Franco-Prussia war of 1870), and the imposition of heavy reparations to compensate the Western Allies for the damage that German militarism had exacted. Not only was the Peace Treaty of Versailles punitive; more significant and painful, it prevented Germany's reentry into the international system as a coequal member. (Symbolically, Germany was denied membership in the League of Nations until 1926.) As a result of its exclusion, Germany, propelled by nationalistic sentiments and the rise of fascism, sought to recover its rightful status as a European great power by force of arms. The rise of fascism animated this renewed imperialistic push. That ideology glorified the "collective will" of the nation and preached the most extreme version of aggressive nationalism to justify the forceful expansion of the German state.[1]

But German militarism, though a key factor in causing World War II, was not the sole reason.

The collapse of the international economic system during the 1930s was also a major contributor to the war. Great Britain found itself unable to perform the leadership and regulatory roles in the world political economy, as it had before World War I. The United States was the logical successor to Britain as world economic leader, but its refusal to exercise leadership hastened the war. "The Depression of 1929–1931 was followed in 1933 by a world Monetary and Economic Conference whose failures—engineered by the United States—deepened the gloom, accelerated nationalist protectionism and promoted revolution." In this depressed global environment exacerbated by deteriorating economic circumstances at home, Germany and Japan sought solutions through imperialism abroad. The failure of the League of Nations to mount a collective response to the German, Japanese, and Italian acts of aggression [in the interwar years] symbolized the weak institutional barriers to war. So, too, did the preceding collapse of the Disarmament Conference in 1934. When Germany withdrew from the League of Nations in 1933, as did Italy in 1937, war clouds gathered which the League was powerless to dispel.[2]

Psychological forces also played a role in creating World War II. This included "the domination of civilian discourse by military propaganda that primed the world for war," the "great wave of hyper-nationalism [that] swept over Europe" as "each state taught itself a mythical history while denigrating that of others," and the demise of democratic governance.[3] In the final analysis, however, the war would not have been possible without Adolf Hitler and his plans to conquer the world by force. Hence "German responsibility for [World War II] is in a class of its own."[4] Under the mythical claim of German racial superiority (the notion of "master race") and virulent anti-Semitism and anticommunism, Hitler waged war to create an empire that would settle the historic competition and precarious coexistence of the great powers in Europe by eliminating Germany's rivals.

> The broad vision of the Thousand-Year Reich was . . . of a vastly expanded—and continually expanding—German core, extending deep into Russia, with a number of vassal states and regions, including France, the Low Countries, Scandinavia, central Europe and the Balkans, that would provide resources and labor for the core. There was to be no civilizing mission in German imperialism.[5]

Global in scope, World War II pitted a fascist coalition striving for world supremacy—Germany, Japan, and Italy—against an unlikely "Grand Alliance" of great powers that united to prevent world hegemony despite the incompatible ideologies—communism in the case of the Soviet Union and democratic capitalism in the case of Britain, France, and the United States. "The world's fate hinged on the outcome of this massive effort to meet the Axis threat of world conquest and restore the balance of power. Success was achieved, but at a terrible cost over a six-year ordeal: Each day 23,000 lives were lost, as World War II resulted in the death of nearly 17 million soldiers and 34 million civilians."[6]

It was not until World War II that states finally decided to cast off strict Westphalian notions of sovereignty and to embrace the concept of an international penal process. The war crimes committed by the Axis powers during World War II reached dimensions unprecedented in history. The brutal conduct of war by Germany, its treatment of the population of the occupied countries, and its bid to exterminate Jews, Gypsies, and Slavs galvanized into action the Allied powers. The Allies' statesmen had on many occasions during the war solemnly declared their intent to prosecute and punish persons guilty of war crimes and atrocities. A series of denunciations and declarations[7] by the Allied powers culminated in the 1943 Declaration of Moscow,[8] which was preceded by the establishment of the United Nations War Crimes Commission (UNWCC—completely unrelated to the postwar organization) five weeks earlier.[9] The London Agreement of 1945 signed by the Four Powers (France, the Soviet Union, Great Britain, and the United States) brought to life the international military tribunals at Nuremberg and Tokyo. These tribunals marked the first time in the modern era that crimes recognized by the international community were actually enforced through an international penal process.

This chapter discusses the establishment following World War II of the Nuremberg and Tokyo international military tribunals. These tribunals, though in many ways reflecting imperfect forms of international enforcement of international humanitarian law, represented the very first practical manifestation of the international penal process in modern times.[10]

The Breakdown of Collective Security Efforts

The Covenant of the League of Nations adopted as part of Versailles at the end of World War I was based on the ideal of terminating war, through the obligation imposed on all members of the League, to respect the sovereignty and territory of other members, as well as cooperation against aggression by any state against a member. But states developed a popular yet absurd doctrine that the real function of the League of Nations was to afford occasion for international consultation and the creation of international opinion.[11] This was the first event in a series that chiseled away the authority of the League as a supranational entity that provided a mechanism to enforce international obligations.[12]

But even as states were busy interpreting and reinterpreting the scope of the League's authority, France and other vulnerable states recognized that disarmament could be attained only by establishing effective security. The other Western Allies, however, disappointed by the failure of the United States to ratify Versailles, were in no mood to neuter armed forces needed for national security in a world dominated by territorial disputes.

Equally, Germany was not anxious to fulfill promises of disarmament pursuant to Versailles. Hence, while the Permanent Advisory Commission, provided for by article 9 of the League Covenant, was duly set up in May 1920, and the Temporary Mixed Commission was created in 1921, little was done to compile accounts of existing armaments. In 1922 Lord Robert Cecil submitted to the Temporary Mixed Commission views that to be successful any reduction of armaments must be general; that such reduction depended on satisfactory guarantees of security; that such guarantees must be general; and that the provision of such guarantees should be conditioned on an undertaking to reduce armaments. This initiative led to the preparation of a treaty of mutual assistance that was sent in draft to League members and nonmembers for any observations.[13]

The Council of the League was entrusted with the duty of determining aggression, and of allocating to the states the part to be played by each in resisting it. But in view of the slow process, permission was given to form voluntary local alliances with the right of immediate intervention, subject always to penalties for aggression if the council determined that the right had been misused. It was hoped thereby to obviate the risk of a regional association forming for aggressive rather than pacific ends; the very existence of regional associations meant that the chance of outright aggression would be greatly reduced. However, the next several years turned out to be a period of political bickering and diplomatic stonewalling with little progress.

In 1926, the Locarno Pact symbolically confirmed the western borders of Germany and reestablished more or less amicable relationships between the leading powers. In 1928 a symbolic high tide was reached with the adoption of the Kellogg-Briand Pact, renouncing war as an instrument of national policy and thereby attempting to close legal loopholes in the League Covenant; the pact did not contain any sanction. However, it was significant because it reignited interest in the disarmament agenda that had seen little progress. With the Kellogg-Briand Pact, a fresh effort to attain security at the Disarmament Conference in 1932 was made with a French proposal for different degrees of responsibility; all the powers represented at the conference would consult together if there was a breach or threat of a breach of the Kellogg-Briand Pact; abstain from economic and financial relations with an aggressor; and refuse to recognize any international situation brought about by a violation of an international undertaking. The inner circle of members of the League were bound to carry out the effective and loyal application of article 16 of the Covenant.[14]

The disarmament talks seemed to point to the emergence of a new and better system of international relations. This possibility did not materialize: the 1930s saw economic collapse, the rise of dictators, and a series of acts of aggression in Asia, Africa, and Europe that undermined the Covenant and the collective security ideal of the League of Nations. The League powers, led by Britain and France, were unable to develop a coherent policy in response to these events. The first blow was delivered on 18 September 1931, when Japanese forces invaded China, taking control of the whole area of the South Manchurian Railway from Changchun to Port Arthur.[15] This violation of Kellogg-Briand and the League Covenant was patent. The members of the League were under the clear obligation, in light of China's appeal under article 15 of the Covenant, to apply sanctions if Japan continued to defy the League. Yet nothing was done by any power. The foundation of League security was thus directly attacked and defied, and the League powers did not undertake their obligations.

The acid test for the League came in 1935–1936 when circumstances ruled out inaction. Italy was under the most categorical obligation not to employ force against Ethiopia.[16] While Italian dictator Benito Mussolini plotted aggression and conquest, the League played the role of spectator and shirked its responsibilities. The Italians' invasion of Ethiopia destroyed collective security and gutted the political terms of the Covenant. The failure of the League members to stand up meant that public faith in the body could no longer be upheld and that international cooperation pursuant to the Covenant's obligations had been emasculated.

Then the failure of the 1934 Disarmament Conference meant that Germany would rearm; neither Britain nor France would resist by force German rearmament.[17] These powers therefore held discussions in London in February 1935, which recognized the propriety of abrogating the Versailles provisions for disarmament, if Germany would contribute to security by considering adherence to the system of mutual guarantees. Thus freed from the shackles of Versailles, Germany launched its remilitarization. Hitler, emboldened, unilaterally repudiated the Versailles provisions limiting German armaments. The success of Mussolini in Ethiopia and the destruction of Ethiopian sovereignty and territorial integrity, coupled with the lukewarm approach of the divided League of Nations, encouraged Hitler. In March 1936 he sent his troops into the demilitarized Rhineland, thus remilitarizing it in violation of Versailles and Locarno.[18] No action was taken by the League. In the following years the German army was growing in size and power. Rearmament became no secret, and nations turned slowly to face the German threat.

The winter of 1937–1938 was a turning point. Hitler undertook war and aggression. On 12 March 1938 German troops advanced and annexed Austria; Czechoslovakia, with its German population of more than 3 million, was in jeopardy.[19] On 12 September 1938 Hitler accused the Czechoslovakian government of human rights abuses against Germans and of seeking to exterminate them altogether. Hitler then demanded the transfer of predominantly German districts in Czechoslovakia to Germany in order to safeguard their rights as a minority. Thinking that appeasement would halt German expansionism and lead to "peace in our time," Britain and France consented to the dismemberment of Czechoslovakia.[20] Further emboldened, the German army swept through Czechoslovakia in a classic blitzkrieg.

The unilateral absorption of Czechoslovakia led British prime minister Neville Chamberlain to announce on 31 March 1939 that Britain and France would support Poland if invaded.[21] Four months later, on 23 August 1939, Hitler and Joseph Stalin, the Soviet communist dictator, stunned the world with the news that they had signed a nonaggression pact.[22] Eight days after the signing, on the evening of 31 August 1939, German troops moved to the Polish frontier. At dawn on 1 September 1939 German guns opened fire. Hitler's war, its primary aim to expand the sovereign German Reich, had begun. Britain and France declared war on Germany. As Hitler unleashed the German war machine on Europe, the Soviet Union also hastened to carry out its agenda. In the face of German and Russian aggression, the League of Nations and all its principles collapsed. Once again a great war was near.

As German troops marched across Europe, Italy threw in with Germany some weeks after the conquest of Poland, which made Mussolini anxious that he would miss out on the fruits of war. The war expanded as Hitler turned his forces to the Balkans, North Africa, and westward. The powerful, mechanized German troops invaded Norway and marched through Denmark, Belgium, Luxembourg, and the Netherlands.

Even as the German army was beginning its rapid advance through Western Europe in 1939, Japan, which was to enthusiastically throw in with Germany two years later, faced an uncertain future, forcing it to initially stay its hand.[23] The German blitzkrieg of May and June 1940 crashed through Holland and France, leaving Britain, the principal colonial power in Asia, tottering, and also exciting the Japanese, who saw the opportunity that Britain's predicament presented to their expansionist agenda in the Far East. Japan, already disillusioned with Western liberalism and the Paris settlements, had suffered economically from the Great Depression. To end dependency and subordination, and to create the Greater East Asian Co-Prosperity Sphere under its influence, Japan embraced militarism. In the might-makes-right climate that Germany's imperialistic quest for national aggrandizement helped to create, Japan saw a golden opportunity. Japan knew that its political and military hegemony in East Asia was threatened by the formidable United States Navy, leading to Japan's surprise attack on Pearl Harbor on 7 December 1941. This unprovoked Japanese assault, and the German challenge in Europe, pushed U.S. aloofness and isolationism aside, enabling President Franklin D. Roosevelt to forge the so-called Grand Alliance—a coalition with Britain and the Soviet Union to oppose the fascists.

By May 1945 the Thousand-Year Reich lay in ruins. By August 1945, Japan was devastated by the U.S. atomic bombs dropped on Hiroshima and Nagasaki. On 14 August 1945, six years after the start of World War II, with the Axis powers defeated, the war came to an end, closing the darkest chapter in human history. In terms of lives lost, geographical extent, and cities reduced to ashes, the struggle defies rational comprehension. Close to 17 million combatants were killed, 27 million wounded, and nearly 20 million captured or missing. Civilian populations were more affected by this war than any other in the past: How many millions of people not directly involved in the hostilities lost their lives is still controversial. The war marked the first time that bacteriological and atomic weapons were systematically used in war. Material and cultural losses, including destruction of art treasures, are beyond calculation.[24] For all the major belligerent powers, the war was essentially a war of materiel and manpower. Only those nations that had large human reservoirs, as well as superior industrial potential, could compete in this worldwide war of attrition.

World War II witnessed some of the worst atrocities in the history of civilized mankind, perpetrated against both soldiers and civilians. Germany and Japan stood out in this respect; their military commands allowed armies to conduct war with merciless, unrelenting harshness, and they demanded deliberate brutality in dealing with the enemy as a means of ensuring victory and extinguishing resistance in occupied territory. Although a full catalog of the magnitude and extent of violations of the laws of war is beyond the scope of this chapter, the next section paints a vivid picture of the cruel and unsparing nature of the war, which only the combination of modern technology and total disregard for legal and moral standards could produce. The Axis powers were not alone in violating the laws of war (Allied troops committed violations too), but the extent and magnitude of the Axis crimes eclipsed and overshadowed those of the victorious Allies. And fighting a war that Germany had initiated and Japan had spread did leave the victorious Allies on a moral ground of sorts.

Germany and Japan: Emptying the Content of the Laws of War

Germany: The Institutionalization of Fear and Death

Germany's major human rights violations began to occur even before the start of World War II in Germany and continued throughout the war. This was the "incarceration of individuals, both German and foreign, citizens of both friendly and enemy countries, in concentration camps, to which they were sent at the whim of the Gestapo, the SS and the other Nazi organizations."[25]

No judicial proceedings were involved in these actions, either before or during the imprisonment. Extralegal executions were the order of the day. This use of a state's apparatus and its resources for the purpose of spreading terror and death was to prove a macabre precursor to a larger system that was to be perfected as the war continued.

While Hitler was leading Germany into World War II, he ordered the carrying out of the modern world's largest genocide, massacring some 6 million Jews,[26] reflecting the dictator's grim determination to exterminate what he considered the "mortal enemy" of the German people and the universal poisoner of all peoples.[27] The Nazis went about the systematic destruction of Jews (both in Germany and Europe) using two weapons: soldiers and modern technology. The Nazis soon realized that it would be faster and more efficient to organize a system of killing, rather than to have soldiers waste their time shooting Jews one by one. Nazi leaders established the Einsatzgruppen, an arm of the SS, which was part of Hitler's elite storm troopers, to help carry out this task. The second method employed by the Nazi regime was the use of modern technology to torture, overwork, and kill Jewish prisoners.[28] The Nazis arranged six camps with large-scale gassing facilities and crematoria capable of disposing of thousands of bodies.[29] They forced thousands of captured Jews into trains and shipped them to all parts of Europe. The healthy and young were momentarily spared and placed in work camps. However, they became malnourished, and many were eventually worked to death. Older Jews were immediately sent to gassing facilities in Poland. Children too young to work were also killed; as many as 1 million were murdered by the Nazis.[30] Additionally, approximately 500,000 people died in the Eastern European ghettos from hunger, disease, and exhaustion, as well as from anti-Semitic reprisals and random terror.[31]

The story of the Holocaust is often half told. Besides the toll of 6 million Jews, an almost equal number of non-Jews—5 million (predominantly Poles)—perished.[32] Shortly before Germany invaded Poland, Hitler had specifically instructed the army to exterminate every living Polish soul in the land.[33] Street roundups and mass executions quickly were systematized and continued throughout the war. Hundreds of so-called intelligentsia (the Polish leading class—priests, teachers, lawyers, judges, senators, doctors) were sent to concentration camps where they later died.[34] Polish Christians and Catholics were the first victims of Auschwitz, the notorious German death camp. The first Jew arrived at the camp about two years after the first "Polish Gentiles."[35]

Even as Hitler was turning the extermination of Jews and non-Jews into a large-scale industrial operation of terrifying efficiency, he caused the German army to commit violations of the laws of war of great magnitude with his scorn for the belief that war can be waged without resort to terrorism and unsparing brutality. Prisoners of war were subjected to grossly inhumane treatment and conditions. The fate of prisoners of war in German hands was an epic tragedy. For instance, tens of thousands of Soviet prisoners of war in Germany died from starvation and exposure. In the forced marches of prisoners to the camps, those who were unable to keep up were shot dead on the spot by German soldiers, their corpses left to rot in the open. In some camps, no shelter was provided.[36] All this was done with official approval. General Hermann Reinecke, head of the prisoner of war department, had caused the issuance of an order by the Supreme Command of the Armed Forces on 8 September 1941 that rejected long-held principles of international law governing captured enemy soldiers and led to the ruthless and energetic action by use of bayonets, rifle butts, and firearms.[37] The treatment of Soviet prisoners of war was but a reflection of similar practices unleashed on other nationalities as evidenced by the passage of the *Kugel Erlass* (the Bullet Decree), pursuant to which many prisoners of war were turned over to the Gestapo for execution.[38] The war atrocities extended to cover the conduct of war as evidenced by Hitler's top-secret Commando Order of 18 October 1942, which instructed that enemy soldiers captured while on commando missions (i.e., guerrilla or resistance operations) were to be "slaughtered to the last man."[39]

Cruel practices did not stop with the inhumane treatment of prisoners of war or the execution of captured enemy soldiers. The terror affected civilians as well. One of the more extreme measures used against the inhabitants of territories overrun by the German soldiers was the *Nacht und Nebel Erlass* (the Night and Fog Decree), which served as the legal basis for forced disappearances and extrajudicial executions of civilians.[40] "The Night and Fog Decree was a subtly woven fabric of fear cast by Hitler over the territories occupied by his military forces."[41] Augmenting this terror device was the practice of so-called clearing murders. This practice was aimed at breaking the will of occupied territories and of cutting off civilian support for resistance movements. The clearing murders were carried out by the German Gestapo and bands of terrorists acting under the direction of German intelligence officers. Collective punishment through the device of mass execution of innocent civilians was a common practice in occupied territories. Frequently large numbers of civilians would be rounded up and shot dead in revenge for acts of resistance committed against German troops.

The Japanese Imperial Army: Waging a War of Terror

During World War II Japanese soldiers performed extraordinary acts of heroism almost as a matter of routine. Yet along with this fighting spirit, the Imperial Japanese Army also earned a reputation for cruelty and barbarism second to none. Japanese soldiers starved, tortured, and executed Allied prisoners of war. They undertook experiments in biological warfare on thousands of human beings. In *Soldiers of the Sun,* the extreme brutality and scale of Japanese atrocities in the course of World War II is captured in the following words:

> The atrocities committed by the Imperial Japanese Army are impossible to catalogue. The number and the hideous variety of the crimes defy even the most twisted imagination: murder on a scale amounting to genocide; rapes beyond counting; vivisection; cannibalism; torture; American prisoners-of-war allowed to drown in excrement in the "hell ships" taking them back to Japan for use as forced labor; civilian prisoners used as "human sandbags" during air raids; Burmese coolies, dead and dying, stuffed under the sleeping platforms of other laborers on the Burma-Siam Railway.[42]

At a dire disadvantage where operational intelligence was concerned, Japanese commanders regarded prisoners as a crucial source of information, and third-degree methods of interrogation were routine. More than a quarter of all prisoners taken by the Japanese died under interrogation, from starvation and untreated disease, or simply through random brutality.[43] With Japanese culture emphasizing the hierarchical nature of the world and the superiority of Japanese society, all other races were inferior and, therefore, relatively easy to enslave, torture, and murder.[44]

The doctrine of collective responsibility devised in Manchuria and China (and operating in the Japanese homeland) was applied ruthlessly in prisoner-of-war camps. Prisoners were formed into "shooting squads" of between ten and twenty men, all of whom would be shot if one tried to escape. The doctrine of collective punishment extended to civilian prisoners and hostages as well. These atrocities are displayed in captured Japanese documents and recorded in the thousands of files maintained by the United Nations War Crimes Commission and other testimony by victims who survived.[45]

With the Japanese soldier accepting no higher authority than the emperor, represented in practical terms by his superior officers. His only criteria for action were the decree of the emperor and the collective will of those groups to which the soldier belonged. In part this was military conditioning. There were no absolute moral values.[46] This closed moral system governing the Imperial Japanese Army was responsible in large measure for war crimes becoming a part of the army's life and mentality, as the high command acknowledged in a chilling supplement to 16th Army Operation Orders issued in Saigon on 15 January 1942. "The soldiers," stated the directive, must treat the new Western enemies "as *if they were Chinese.* . . . We hear of not few units which have not yet got over the longstanding, regrettable practices of the operations against China."[47] The "regrettable practices" that entailed acts of extreme horror and brutality were employed by the Imperial Japanese Army against Allied troops until the end of the war in the Pacific Theater.

The Japanese code of ethics had its impact on the army's philosophy of total war. There were no constraints on the methods that they might use to secure their ends. Any weapons that they could secure were legitimate, including chemical and bacteriological weapons. Though Japan was a signatory to the 1929 Geneva Convention, cultural and societal factors overrode any constraints on the methods the army might use to secure its ends. Any ploy was acceptable on the battlefield. Wearing enemy uniforms, booby-trapping enemy corpses for stretcher parties, and luring enemy troops into ambushes with the white flag of surrender became routine stratagems. With the Japanese military encouraging a "mental attitude that bordered on psychopathy,"[48] the policy of total war resulted in death and destruction to Japan's enemies on an unlimited scale. The need for the army, including its thousands of pack animals, to live off the land was a permanent menace to civilian supplies—and it also meant that resources were usually lacking to care for prisoners.

The inflation of the army also led to a decline in the caliber of its officers. Indiscipline became more and more noticeable, partly as a by-product of the war developing not necessarily to Japan's advantage, and partly because the policing system was inadequate. Drunkenness was endemic and contributed to the vast majority of excesses, as well as to the fervor of many banzai charges. During the last days, even weeks, of the Japanese occupation of Manila, when Admiral Sanji Iwabuchi's men were running amok, most of them were drunk all the time. The Rape of Manila, though not an authorized orgy of plunder, rape, and murder by the licentious soldiery, as the Rape of Nanking had been, was nonetheless an expression of bewilderment, outrage, and despair by the Imperial Japanese Army.

The atrocities of World War II compelled the need for international prosecutions after the Allied victory. As early as 1942, the Allied powers had signed an agreement at the Palace of St. James,[49] establishing the United Nations War Crimes Commission. The Declaration of St. James was the first step leading to the establishment of the international military tribunals. However, the UNWCC's functions and effectiveness were hamstrung from its inception by political considerations. As late as 1944, neither the British nor the Americans had formulated a policy on the treatment of war criminals. War crimes prosecution continued to be at an impasse.[50] The urgency of resolutions on the issue was accepted by politicians and diplomats only as the end of war was within sight, and both administrations recognized the growing interest of the press and the public in the governments' plans to seize and punish perpetrators of war crimes as more and more German atrocities were revealed. Next we discuss the UNWCC's establishment and the influence that realpolitik considerations had on both its establishment as well as operations.

The United Nations War Crimes Commission

According to Arieh J. Kochavi in *Prelude to Nuremberg:*

> The establishment of the UNWCC in October 1943 constituted the main operative action taken by the Allies to deal with war criminals during the war (mid 1941–43), when the worst of the Axis crimes were committed. Britain played a major role in setting up the commission. The process of establishing this body, though, was characterized by procrastination as well as discord, mainly between Britain and the Soviet Union.[51]

Complications on formation of the UNWCC were based on substantive differences over the war crimes issue, the intrusion of the disputes over West-East cooperation in waging the war against Germany, and Soviet demands relating to their frontiers.[52] At the time, the United States, the third member of the Grand Alliance, was keeping a low profile in regard to war crimes, leaving Britain to handle the details of bringing the UNWCC into being.

> About a year and a half passed from the time the suggestion was first put forth to set up a war crimes commission until this body actually took form. The long process reflected the low priority that the Western Allies then ascribed to the war crimes problem and testified to their willingness to postpone dealing with the issue of punishing war criminals for as long as possible.[53]

The key point of discord between the Soviets and British was Soviet insistence on the immediate trial of war criminals. With the Soviets seemingly inclined to refrain from taking part in the work of the proposed commission, the British foreign minister, Anthony Eden, attributed great importance to preserving good relations with the Soviets. He recommended that Britain should strive to bridge the gap with the Soviets and to do so before additional steps were taken to set up the commission. Commenting on this impasse, Kochavi notes that Eden

> suggested explaining to the Soviets that even war criminals could not be put on trial until the evidence against them had been collected and that the establishment of a United Nations commission constituted an essential preliminary to these trials. . . . Eden recommended that the Americans be informed about British-Soviet contacts but advised that Washington not be asked to concur on the substance of those meetings; otherwise that

might only confirm Soviet suspicions of being confronted with prior decisions agreed on by other Allied governments.[54]

London's objection to the Soviet proposal for the immediate trial of
captured war criminals was derived mainly from fear of Germany's retali-
ating against British POWs. A similar wariness motivated the Americans.[55]
The Soviets, contrarily, wanted action, not resolutions. The cruelty displayed by Germans toward the Soviet population in occupied areas, and in
particular toward Soviet POWs, many of whom were summarily executed,
had neutralized any fears of German retribution.[56] The hesitance of Britain
and the United States upset the Soviet Union, which initially declined to
participate in the establishment of the UNWCC. Britain's persistent efforts
to convince the Soviets to participate seemed at last to bear fruit. On 24
January 1943 Moscow responded to the British appeal, although the Kremlin reiterated that it had not changed its call for an immediate trial before an
international court of justice for captured war criminals. Nonetheless, the
Soviet government acceded to the British point of view. The Soviets' dog-
matic stance was one of the greatest obstacles to establishing the commission.
Though substantive differences over questions of a war criminals policy and
the war were genuine, these did not constitute the main consideration guiding
Soviet action. The Kremlin was incensed that the British had not consulted
with it during the policy formulation process.[57] The Soviets are not entirely
to blame, however. At this stage the Americans exhibited an even worse trait:
nonchalance. This is captured articulately by Kochavi:

> In striving to gain the acceptance of the Americans for establishing the
> Commission, the British Foreign Office found itself forced to contend
> with the foot-dragging of the U.S. State Department. The State Depart-
> ment seemed content, so long as it could, with the [U.S.] president's
> vague declarations on the intention to punish war criminals. The depart-
> ment's rejection of the offer to make its representative the chairman of
> the proposed commission probably emanated from both its lack of enthu-
> siasm at playing a leading role in any Allied effort to punish war crimi-
> nals. . . . Washington, like London, preferred as low a profile as possible
> on the issue for fear of the fate of its own captives. The fact that Ameri-
> cans had not been victims of Nazi atrocities and the lack of any public
> pressure facilitated the adoption of this course. State Department officials,
> furthermore, had never delved very deeply into [the] complexity of pun-
> ishing war criminals.[58]

After about a year and a half of foot-dragging and procrastination, the
representatives of seventeen Allied nations gathered in London on 20 October 1943 to inaugurate the UNWCC. The two principal goals of the commission were: (1) to investigate and record evidence of war crimes and,
where possible, identify the individuals responsible; and (2) to report to the

governments concerned cases in which it appeared that adequate evidence of crimes was forthcoming.[59] As for the arch-villains, Viscount John Simon, the chair of the meeting, expressed the position that British policy considered this to be first and foremost a political question.[60] Officials in both the U.S. State Department and the British Foreign Office viewed the UNWCC as a political necessity and subsequently tried to exploit this body to their own ends, mainly by neutralizing demands by the governments-in-exile for reprisals against Germans and by creating the impression that the war crimes issue was indeed being handled. As powerfully stated by Kochavi, "Officials on both sides of the Atlantic did not want the commission to be a leading organ in formulating a policy toward war criminals; rather they intended it to be a toothless technical committee."[61] This reasoning accounted for the obstacles that were intentionally thrown up in the commission's path.

Shortly after the UNWCC had begun functioning, the British Foreign Office and the U.S. State Department realized that their fears that the commission would take independent initiatives were materializing. The UNWCC was expected to concentrate on investigating and recording war crimes and criminals. Leading members of the commission, however, refused to accept the narrow operating mandate and spurred the UNWCC to prepare a comprehensive plan for trying war criminals and to devise new means to apprehend individuals charged with war crimes.[62] The UNWCC's eagerness to advance preparations for dealing with war criminals soon generated conflict. Given that the UNWCC comprised representatives from seventeen nations, most of which were governments-in-exile possessing only limited powers,[63] and facing an uncertain future, the UNWCC, without British and U.S. goodwill, saw its political influence and support greatly diminish.[64] Despite the UNWCC's onerous mandate, the Allied powers did not provide it with an investigatory staff, adequate support staff, or sufficient funds to conduct its work. In fact, within a few months of the UNWCC's creation, its first chairman, Sir Cecil Hurst, had announced that the commission would be unable to fulfill its mandate.[65]

The UNWCC relied on governments to submit reports but received few cases, and even these contained incomplete or insubstantial information. Even after the UNWCC's exhortations to Allied governments, there were few new government submissions.[66] Troubled by the small number of cases submitted by the various national offices, commission members struggled with the idea of having the international body actively participate in collecting evidence on war crimes and war criminals. They also realized that without direct, close collaboration with Supreme Headquarters, Allied Expeditionary Force (SHAEF), in investigating war crimes and preparing lists of war criminals, the commission would be a failure. However, the commission's bid for closer cooperation with SHAEF at the beginning of

June 1944 resulted only in an unofficial and informal recommendation couched in general terms; it was thought that specific questions regarding formation of a war crimes agency to assist the commission were more suited for decisionmaking by the military authorities themselves.[67] In fact, the commission's proposal for a war crimes agency to liaise with SHAEF was turned down in the face of opposition by representatives of occupied countries who saw this as an infringement on the competence of the national governments in collecting evidence of war crimes.[68]

Still another knotty issue that occupied the UNWCC from its early stages involved the types of courts to try war criminals. Lacking either investigative or executive power, the commission was in a quandary.[69] Nevertheless, the UNWCC members resolved to devote a great deal of time and thought to developing a scheme for the governments to prosecute and punish war criminals as well as methods for their apprehension. "The commission was determined not to repeat the error made during World War I, when no practical plan for prosecuting war criminals was formulated until the cease-fire."[70] The U.S. representative, Herbert Pell, informed the U.S. State Department of the unanimous decision by the commission for establishing an international authority to handle national trials for persons whose offenses were committed in one country, more than one country, or against stateless persons. Pell further suggested that the UNWCC complete the main outlines of such an organization. He cautioned the U.S. secretary of state of the need to prevent the matter of punishing war criminals from descending "into another farce as it did after the last war."[71] The commission's deliberations over the establishment of some machinery of justice that could act rapidly and firmly irritated the British Foreign Office and the U.S. State Department, as the commission was expected to restrict itself to collecting available evidence and assembling proof of guilt, and not to advance the formulation of a policy toward war criminals (a matter considered beyond its jurisdiction).[72]

Only after the Allies liberated German-occupied territories in 1945 did they realize the extent of the atrocities committed. Thereafter, British and U.S. forces began to develop a list of suspected war criminals in order to separate them from other liberated prisoners.[73] At that point, the British government began to press the UNWCC to complete its work.[74] Despite the initial lack of cooperation among various governments, the UNWCC was able to amass 8,178 dossiers on alleged war criminals and would serve as a clearinghouse of information for governments.[75] Although the UNWCC collected information pertaining to allegations of war crimes, it was not institutionally linked to the Nuremberg Tribunal or to the subsequent proceedings by the Allied occupation forces in Germany pursuant to Allied Control Council Law no. 10 (CCL no. 10), each of which had its own investigative teams; nor was it linked to the International Military Tribunal for the Far East (the Tokyo Tribunal) and the Allied military tribunals or commissions in the Far East. However, the information that the UNWCC collected was relied upon by various governments in subsequent national prosecutions.

With the conclusion of the war, political support for the UNWCC waned. As the United States began to dominate the investigation and collection of evidence, U.S. support for the UNWCC evaporated and, with it, any authority it might have enjoyed. Despite high expectations for the UNWCC, for all practical purposes this intergovernmental, treaty-created, investigative body was subordinated to political considerations and ultimately relegated to a role far inferior to that which was expected by the Allies.[76] The UNWCC's moral influence over governments to compel cooperation in pursuing accused war criminals, and to either prosecute or extradite such persons, had thus eroded. This was evident in regard to accused Italian war criminals who were never prosecuted even though Italy was occupied by the United States and Britain subject to a surrender treaty that provided for the prosecution and extradition of war criminals.[77] The goals of that document of surrender, however, were supplanted by the fear of communism that pervaded Europe. The major powers believed that reformed fascists were the best opponents of communism and therefore did not actively pursue their prosecution or extradition for fear of the internal political repercussions.[78]

Next we discuss the establishment of the international military tribunals. The entire international penal process, though fueled by a desire to secure international justice, was affected by the geopolitical interests and national policy considerations of the victorious Allies.

The London International Conference

While the UNWCC was collecting evidence, the four major Allied powers had to reach a decision with respect to the prosecution and punishment of war criminals, particularly the leaders of the Nazi regime, as called for by the Moscow Declaration signed in 1943 by Winston Churchill, Franklin Roosevelt, and Joseph Stalin.[79] There was considerable disagreement from the outset as to the basic purpose of the Nuremberg trials. This was understandable, for there was considerable resistance by some of the participants to the use of the judicial system in the first place. Britain initially favored summary execution of major war criminals, such as Adolf Hitler or Heinrich Himmler on the basis that these evildoers' guilt was "so black" that it was "beyond the scope of any judicial process."[80] By comparison, as early as the discussions at the Palace of St. James in 1942, Stalin advocated a special international tribunal for prosecuting Hitler, his close advisers, and senior military leaders.[81] Similarly, both the United States and France preferred establishing an international tribunal to prosecute war criminals.[82] They wanted the tribunal to record history, educate the world, and serve as a future deterrent. Britain was fearful that fair procedures would allow the accused to use the tribunal as a forum for propaganda and self-justification. Essentially because of the U.S. insistence, through President Harry Truman and Supreme Court Justice Robert Jackson, the international criminal tribunal came into fruition.[83] Even so, conceptual differences persisted. General Ion Timofeevich Nikitchenko, the Soviet representative, for example, seemed to consider the trials essentially as a fulfillment of the political agreements that had been reached at Moscow and Yalta. This was in contrast to the U.S. position that the declarations were an accusation and thus required a judicial finding.[84]

Such conceptual differences were never reconciled, but the Allies went ahead with discussions for establishing the international military tribunal, and all parties were in agreement on prosecuting crimes that were contrary to international law and, more important, the need to convict senior Nazi officials. This had been pointed out in the simultaneous declarations by the United States and Britain issued some three years before the end of the war, on 7 October 1942, when the idea of establishing the UNWCC had been mooted. That announcement stated that it was not the intention of the United Nations (as the victorious Allies had styled themselves even before the birth of the organization that was to bear the name) to resort to mass reprisals but to punish "ringleaders responsible for the organized murder of thousands of innocent persons and the commission of atrocities which [had] violated every tenet of the Christian faith."[85]

Because the four major Allied powers had different national criminal procedures, drafting the Nuremberg Charter was troublesome. Whereas British and U.S. procedures were adversarial and based on common law, France had a civil law system, and the Soviet Union had its own new brand of "socialist justice."[86] The representatives of the Allies sought to reconcile their different legal systems through a mixed process.[87] The drafters also faced the arduous task of defining the crimes for which defendants would be prosecuted. Negotiations in London dragged on for almost six weeks and were characterized by tension and distrust.[88] The proceedings were a matter of substantive arguments and politics. The Nuremberg Charter ultimately provided in article 6 for the prosecution of the following substantive crimes: (a) crimes against peace; (b) war crimes; and (c) crimes against humanity.[89]

Prosecution for crimes against peace was without legal precedent, save for the failed attempt after World War I to prosecute the kaiser under article

227 of the Peace Treaty of Versailles.[90] Article 6(a) of the Nuremberg Charter provided for the prosecution of those who directed or participated in a war of aggression against other nations in violation of treaties and the principles of international law. This was the best legal basis the Allies could devise.[91] The Soviet Union wanted to include the phrase *by the European Axis*[92] in order to make the initiation of a war of aggression a crime limited to the leaders of the European Axis and avoid the application of that same norm to any Soviet conduct.[93] Justice Jackson, the U.S. representative at the London Conference, prevailed in his view that the limiting phrase should not be included. Jackson stated that the U.S. representatives would not draft a law that would be akin to a bill of attainder, which is prohibited by the United States Constitution[94] and that the prohibition against aggression is universal and could also be applied against all states.[95] The United States thus changed from its post–World War I position by deciding to make war of aggression a crime under international law.[96] The Soviet negotiators, apprehensive of the judgment of world opinion upon their own aggressions against Finland and Poland, consistently opposed a broad definition and contended that any definition of crimes against peace should be restricted to aggressive acts committed by the European Axis.

Justice Jackson was fervently determined to punish aggressive war, that "crime which comprehends all lesser crimes."[97] During the London negotiations, he argued that World War II was an illegal war of aggression in violation of the Kellogg-Briand Pact of 1928 and other treaties and was a criminal offense by common law tests at the least.[98] All other Axis atrocities were either preparatory to or done in "execution of this illegal war."[99] Justice Jackson insisted that aggression be either defined in the charter, thus precluding argument at the trial, or defined at the trial, in which case it would be the subject of an argument in which the Germans would participate.[100] Both the French and Soviet delegations flatly disagreed, the French clinging to their centuries-old addiction to the absolute sovereignty of raison d'etat.[101] Soviet general Nikitchenko, noting that neither the League of Nations nor any other international body—despite repeated attempts—had ever been able to define aggression, argued that "the policy of the . . . Axis powers has been defined as . . . aggressive . . . in various Allied . . . and United Nations . . . documents,"[102] to which Jackson sourly responded: "Why do we need a trial at all?"[103]

If Justice Jackson and the U.S. delegation yielded any major point at London, it was in the omission from the charter of any definition of the term *aggression,* leaving it to stand weakened as crimes against peace. No definition of aggression was inserted in the Nuremberg Charter. Thus the crime as set out in article 6(a) of the Nuremberg Charter under the concept of crimes against peace is broader than the concept of war of aggression, the latter being only one element of crimes against peace. The lack of definition would allow the Soviet Union to avoid criminal accountability for its invasion and seizure of a part of Poland in the fall of 1940, pursuant to the secret nonaggression pact between Germany and the Soviet Union, as well as its subsequent invasion of Finland. In this way, the Allies would maintain the principle of individual criminal responsibility for planning and starting the war without actually having to define "war of aggression" in categorical terms—a difficult political task that was to take many years of negotiations and drafting in the UN General Assembly.[104] More than fifty years after the Nuremberg trials, states were still unable to agree on a satisfactory definition to be included in the Rome Statute establishing the International Criminal Court.[105]

In regard to principles of legality, the easiest way to define the three crimes was as "war crimes." War crimes in article 6(b) included customary law as identified, inter alia, by reference to the 1907 Hague Convention (IV)[106] and conventional law as evidenced in the 1929 Geneva Convention Relative to the Treatment of Prisoners of War.[107] The Nuremberg Charter also sought to develop the law of armed conflict in a progressive manner. Article 8 of the Nuremberg Charter removed the defense of obedience to superior orders, making it only a mitigating factor that would not exonerate a defendant. This was contrary to what most military laws provided at the time World War II started.[108] The judgments of the Nuremberg Tribunal did not entirely follow the prescription of article 8, however, and allowed such a defense when the subordinate had no alternative moral choice in refusing to carry out the order.[109]

A more difficult legal issue was whether crimes against humanity under article 6(c) existed under a combination of sources of international law—namely, conventions, custom, and general principles of law.[110] Because crimes against humanity had not been a part of treaty law, the Allies needed to avoid a rigid interpretation of principles so as to avoid enacting ex post facto legislation that could be successfully challenged in court. The rationale for crimes against humanity was predicated on a theory of the jurisdictional extension of war crimes. The reasoning was that war crimes applied to certain protected persons, namely civilians, in time of war between belligerent states, and crimes against humanity merely extended the same war crimes proscriptions to the same category of protected persons within a particular state, provided it is linked to the initiation and conduct of aggressive war or to war crimes.[111] As a result of this interpretation, crimes committed before 1939 were excluded from prosecution. It is evident from the adoption of article 6(c) that the United States radically changed its position from that taken before the 1919 commission that crimes against the laws of humanity did not exist in positive international law. Yet no legal development took place between 1919 and 1945 that could have explained this change. In light of Nazi atrocities, the facts drove the law, and politics was a major consideration.[112]

The formulation of crimes against humanity, as enunciated in article 6(c) of the Nuremberg Charter, was largely the product of historical circumstances. Never before had such atrocities been committed on such a scale and for so long as those that occurred during World War II. The discovery of these atrocities toward the end of the war left little time for deliberate reflections due to the tremendous political and public pressures to bring those responsible to justice quickly.[113] The facts were so horrendously obvious that they spoke for themselves. Indeed, throughout the legislative process that led to the adoption of the Nuremberg and Tokyo Charters, the facts did indeed drive the law.[114] Critics of the formulation of crimes against humanity in the Nuremberg Charter advanced the following three objections: the violation of principles of legality;[115] the setting aside of positive national law through ad hoc promulgation by the victors after the fact; and the double standard of applying the newly enacted norms exclusively to the vanquished.[116] On this basis, critics have concluded that criminal responsibility should not have been extended from war crimes, which existed in positive international law, to crimes against humanity, which did not. By this extension of the law, they argue, the Nuremberg Charter violated the principles of legality known in Western European national criminal law systems, namely, the prohibition against ex post facto laws and the maxims *nullum crimen sine lege* (penal law cannot be enacted retroactively) and *nulla poena sine lege* (no penalty without law).[117]

Besides the controversy over crimes against humanity, one of the more troublesome aspects of the Nuremberg Charter concerns the issue of conspiracy. During the drafting of the Nuremberg Charter, the Allied powers could not agree as to whether criminal responsibility should be enforced on a strictly individual basis or whether the tribunal should be also vested with competence over acts of conspiracy. On the one hand, the violations committed by the Nazis were so massive and systematic that the tribunal proceedings risked appearing artificial, even a mockery of justice, if they were presumed and the burden then shifted to the defendant to prove otherwise. On the other hand, the prosecution of persons based on mere membership in a criminal organization would have constituted a patent violation of the basic presumption of innocence owed to an accused. In the absence of specific evidence to support the charge in each case, one could never be certain that individuals who were not guilty were being prosecuted, tried, and punished purely on the basis that their names appeared on the membership lists of organizations declared criminal by the tribunal.

Together with the fact that the Nuremberg Tribunal seemingly applied law retroactively, the whole idea of conspiracy met with considerable skepticism from some Allied powers. At the London conference, the Soviet and the French representatives viewed the doctrine of conspiracy as unworthy of modern law and inappropriate for insertion into the charter, particularly because Germans were unfamiliar with the legal concept of conspiracy. The Soviet delegation opposed the U.S. plan, arguing that because major criminal Nazi organizations had already been dissolved by the Allies, there was no longer a need to prosecute them. Eventually, however, the differences between the U.S. and Soviet delegations were reduced, and the Allies agreed that organizations should be prosecuted, mainly because without such prosecution it would be quite difficult to assemble evidence against each and every individual. The result is that conspiracy appeared as a crime punishable per se in article 9 of the Nuremberg Charter.[118] A major reason for advancing the conspiracy charge arose from a miscalculation that the chief evidence would have to be elicited from testimony taken in direct and cross-examination. No one anticipated that tons of incriminating Nazi paperwork, much of it signed or initialed by the accused, would fall into Allied hands, obviating much of the need for oral testimony.[119]

Once the procedural and legal issues were resolved, the Nuremberg Charter was appended to the London Agreement of 8 August 1945, which established the International Military Tribunal at Nuremberg.[120] The agreement was signed by the four major Allies and was later acceded to by nineteen states.[121] The four major Allies assembled individual prosecution teams, which also had their own investigators. The U.S. team provided most of the documents that were used as evidence as well as practical and logistical support for the other teams.[122] At the time, more than 1 million Allied troops occupied Germany, with complete access to prisoners of war, civilian witnesses, and government documents. The collection of evidence was made easy by what Telford Taylor has called the "Teutonic penchant for meticulous record keeping."[123]

Arguably, a number of the crimes laid down in the charter were applicable to the Allied and Axis powers alike. For example, the Soviet Union had signed a mutual nonaggression pact with Nazi Germany.[124] Even worse, secret supplementary provisions to the pact established the respective spheres of influence of the two parties, meaning that it was difficult not to conclude that Stalin, like some of the defendants in the dock, had continued to cooperate with Hitler even after he knew of the Nazi attack plans. The position of Britain was also problematic with regard to its plans to invade Norway (officially neutral), which had been elaborated even before the Nazis invaded Norway in 1940.[125]

Next we discuss the trials held at Nuremberg and Tokyo. The proceedings, even though justified to punish the atrocities committed by the Axis powers, nonetheless were one-sided.[126]

The Roar of the Victors:
The International Military Tribunals

The International Military Tribunal at Nuremberg

The scene at Nuremberg following the defeat of Germany existed amid the conspicuous consequences of sovereign excesses: the collapse of the Third Reich, the utter destruction of the war, and the horror of the Holocaust. Nuremberg was selected as the site of the trials for symbolic reasons. The very name—"Nuremberg"—symbolized the Third Reich itself. It was here that the Nazis staged annual mass rallies and here that they promulgated the notorious Nuremberg Laws of 1935, which stripped German Jews of citizenship and made marriage or sexual relations between Jews and Germans a criminal offense.[127] The city was the focal point for the moral disintegration of Germany, with insane and malignant doctrines that Nuremberg spewed forth accounting for the crimes of the defendants and for the terrible fate of Germany under the Third Reich.[128] At Nuremberg, the pageantry and chauvinism of the state was to be replaced by the solemnity and internationalism of an international trial.

The Nuremberg indictment consisted of four counts: conspiracy, crimes against peace, war crimes, and crimes against humanity. Count One (conspiracy) was prosecuted by the United States. The defendants were accused of being "leaders, organizers, instigators, or accomplices" in the crimes defined in the charter.[129] Specifically, these charges included planning and launching aggressive war; ill treatment of civilian populations both at home and abroad; mistreatment of prisoners of war; extermination; enslavement; and other inhumane acts. Justice Jackson, the U.S. chief of counsel for the prosecution, presented the case for conspiracy as a comprehensive history of the Nazi movement, telling of the Nazis' rise to power and their perversion of the authority of government. He revealed the tactics of virulent anti-Semitic propaganda, state terrorism in the streets, and fraud and deceit in foreign diplomacy. The alleged conspiracy covered certain Nazi organizations, three of which were declared to be criminal.[130] Those organizations were instrumental in carrying out the crimes revealed at Nuremberg. They fit into the German government's overall plan to organize and coordinate criminal activities on a massive scale. Hitler could not have carried out these heinous crimes without the aid of both individuals as well as the organizations indicted at Nuremberg. As with individuals, these organizations were not excused merely because their activities were sanctioned by the state.[131]

Count Two (crimes against peace) was prosecuted by Britain. The defendants were charged with direct participation "in the planning, preparation, initiation, and waging of wars of aggression, which were also wars in violation of international treaties, agreements, and assurances."[132] Sir Hartley Shawcross, the British prosecutor, emphasized in his opening statement that the defendants acted in violation of international law and committed substantive crimes, such as murder, which were punishable by any civilized nation. He further pointed out that the accused were not mere agents carrying out the directions of a principal, although that alone would establish guilt. Rather, the defendants were the ones who built up Hitler, made his reign of terror possible, and helped plan and initiate the crimes that the tribunal was prosecuting.[133] Count Two was further proof of the Nuremberg Tribunal's symbol as an international organ applying international standards in adjudging the activities of a state and its officials.[134] The position that aggressive war was a supreme international offense, initially voiced at the end of World War I by the 1919 commission, was judicially dissociated from the sovereign prerogatives of the state at Nuremberg. Count Three (war crimes) and Count Four (crimes against humanity) were prosecuted jointly by France and the Soviet Union and further built on the limits of sovereignty that had been postulated in Count One and Count Two.

The trials revealed instances of horror and depravity too numerous to be recounted, but even a partial list reveals their enormity. The crimes are in themselves shocking, but the cold-blooded and calculated way in which they were woven into comprehensive governmental planning added a frightening dimension. Ironically, that dimension could have shielded some defendants from punishment if the Allied powers had not specified in the charter that acting in an official capacity as governmental functionaries did not relieve defendants of individual responsibility.[135]

The judges at Nuremberg were concerned that the proceedings be seen as the enforcement of legal norms, not simply a process of the victors punishing the vanquished. Thus the Nuremberg decisions devote much attention to the *nullem crimen sine lege* argument.[136] The defendants argued that the old legal system protected them against punishment, an argument that had proven effective in derailing the envisaged war crimes trials at the end of World War I. Although that argument may seem nonsensical to us today, it was not trivial at the time. At the parallel Tokyo trials, which too often are ignored, the Indian judge, Justice Radhabinod Pal, accepted it and dissented from the convictions there.[137] It is important to appreciate that what is factual and uncontested today has not always been so. The decisions at Nuremberg built on and confirmed the growing changes in international law, representing a turning point for individual responsibility and state sovereignty.

It is interesting to note that no industrialists were tried at the Nuremberg Tribunal notwithstanding the fact that they had willingly and knowingly supported the Nazi war effort and had utilized the labor of Jews and other conquered peoples as slave labor.[138] Rather, they were mainly tried under the auspices of CCL no. 10. This was not a coincidence but a calculated, politically motivated move by the United States and Britain. These two powers in their Western zones of occupation had already earmarked Germany as a future ally in the wider scheme to contain communism and were keen to rebuild Germany politically and economically so that it might fulfill that role. All the major German industrialists at the end of the occupation and the Nuremberg trials retained their industries, and even those tried in the United States were handed light sentences, which in time enabled them to go back to Germany and assume control of their industries. This was part of the U.S. idea in early 1946 to create a comprehensive political settlement in hopes of promoting an integrated political and economic order, including Germany. This idea later took the form of the Marshall Plan, the master plan for the reconstruction of Europe geared toward containing the spread of communism.

Before moving to the Tokyo Tribunal, we should note that subsequent to the Nuremberg Charter, the Allies, by virtue of Germany's unconditional surrender, exercised sovereignty over Germany and CCL no. 10. This permitted the Allies to prosecute German nationals in their respective zones of occupation.[139] Prosecutions in the zones of occupation under the auspices of CCL no. 10 could be said to be in the nature of domestic, as opposed to international, prosecutions, because the Allies were exercising sovereign power in Germany as a result of that country's unconditional surrender. CCL no. 10 was, nevertheless, patterned after the Nuremberg Charter. The nature of CCL no. 10 proceedings was different. The U.S. proceedings were held before civilian judges, whereas the British, French, and Russian trials were held before military courts. Although the Americans, British, and French sought to meet minimum requirements of due process, the Russians proceeded summarily, with little or no regard for legalities.[140] Because CCL no. 10 was promulgated by the four major Allies acting as the sovereign authority in Germany, it did not apply to other Axis countries that were also defeated and occupied by the Allies.

Tokyo in the Shadow of Nuremberg

In this section we discuss the Tokyo trials. It should be noted here that the Nuremberg trials were the centerpiece of the international penal process put in place by the Allies. The Tokyo trials were overshadowed, started later, and dragged on for more than two years beginning on 3 May 1946. Tokyo never received the same worldwide attention. Tired of war, the victorious Allies allowed realpolitik to creep into the Tokyo trials. And with General Douglas MacArthur, the American Caesar, as the sole executor of policy, it would appear to some that Tokyo was a product of vengeance, pure and simple.

The Tokyo Tribunal process was also flawed. Part of the problem was MacArthur, whose heavy hand was evident throughout the proceedings. Although the Far Eastern Commission (FEC), under whose auspices the Tokyo Tribunal was constituted was a policy body, MacArthur was the sole executor of that policy. The legal basis for his authority was that Allied Forces in the Far East were still under Allied control, and that included military trials. Though the FEC was used to achieve the overall policy goals of the Allies, it was essentially the body through which the United States sought to isolate its Allies (especially the Soviet Union) and actuate some of its occupational policies.[141]

The International Military Tribunal for the Far East at Tokyo

The history of the Tokyo Tribunal begins with the Far Eastern Commission, which was agreed to in Moscow in December 1945 as a measured response to the request of the Soviet Union.[142] The FEC gave the Soviet Union some element of control over the future of Japan as a reward for its late entry into the war, but control of the FEC remained with the United States. It consisted of eleven states, with the four major Allies having veto power. The FEC, seated in Washington, transmitted its directives to an advisory group known as the Allied Council for Japan, seated in Tokyo. The United States, Britain, China, and the Soviet Union were the only members of the Allied Council for Japan, and they would oversee occupational policies and practices for Japan. The FEC was not an investigative body but a political one; it would establish a policy of occupation for Japan and coordinate Allied policies in the Far East. The FEC played an important role in providing the Allies a political umbrella for prosecution and other policies related to suspected war criminals, trials, sentencing, and release.[143]

With the unconditional surrender of Japan, control over occupational matters rested with MacArthur, a U.S. Army general appointed Supreme Commander for the Allied Powers (SCAP). On 19 January 1946 MacArthur, in his capacity as the SCAP for the Pacific Theater and on behalf of the FEC, unilaterally established the International Military Tribunal for the Far East (the Tokyo Tribunal) through a general military order.[144] There was no treaty and no participation by the defeated party. The Tokyo Tribunal, though modeled after the Nuremberg Tribunal, was not structured like an ordinary criminal court, as was the Nuremberg Tribunal. Rather, the Tokyo Tribunal was similar to a military commission or court-martial. Why the Tokyo Tribunal did not require a treaty for its creation has never been explained, but several political considerations seem relevant. First, the Soviet Union had entered the war against Japan a few weeks before the latter was defeated, and the United States was concerned about Soviet ambitions in the

Far East. Furthermore, the United States did not want the Soviet Union to have any influence over these proceedings, as it was concerned about Japan's post–World War II course of conduct.[145]

The use of different legal mechanisms for establishing the two ad hoc tribunals produced divergent results in substance and procedure. The Tokyo Charter[146] followed the broad outline of the Big Four agreement in London that had established the Nuremberg Tribunal. Like the Nuremberg Charter, it provided for the prosecution and punishment of those accused of committing crimes against peace, war crimes, and crimes against humanity.[147] The respective instruments are substantially the same, with a few exceptions. One exception was that article 5(c) of the Tokyo Charter provided that persecution on political and racial grounds constituted crimes against humanity, whereas article 6(c) of the Nuremberg Charter included religious grounds as well. Such an inclusion was necessary in the Nuremberg Charter because of the Holocaust against the Jewish people.[148] Also with respect to crimes against humanity, the Nuremberg Charter provided that "inhumane acts committed against any civilian population" were subject to prosecution. The Tokyo Charter eliminated the phrase *against any civilian population* from article 5(c), thereby expanding the class of persons beyond civilians only. The definition was broadened "to make punishment possible for large-scale killing of military personnel in an unlawful war."[149] The indictment echoed Nuremberg on an altogether grander scale. The same ideas of conspiracy, the preparation, initiation, and waging of aggressive wars, crimes against peace, responsibility for conventional war crimes, and crimes against humanity that featured at Nuremberg also appeared in Tokyo, though the Tokyo indictment was more extensive, encompassing fifty-five counts rather than four at Nuremberg

Three months after the establishment of the Tokyo Tribunal, on 3 April 1946, the FEC issued a policy decision on the Apprehension, Trial and Punishment of War Criminals in the Far East.[150] Article 6(a) of the FEC decision empowered the SCAP to establish an agency, acting under MacArthur's command, to investigate reports of war crimes, collect and analyze evidence, and arrange for the apprehension of suspects. Article 6(a) also gave the SCAP the power to decide what individuals or organizations would be prosecuted and before which court they would appear.[151] Participants in the FEC, and later in the Tokyo Tribunal, were chosen on a representational basis. Each individual member acted as a representative of his country's government, not in an individual capacity.[152] This led to a politicization of the FEC and the Tokyo Tribunal and affected the internal workings of these bodies as well as the quality of justice they administered. Almost everything that was done by the FEC and the Tokyo Tribunal was guided by MacArthur's wishes, as were the U.S. military commissions to try Japanese military personnel in the Philippines and other areas of the Far East Military Theater of Operations, which he subsequently established pursuant to his authority as the SCAP.

The proceedings at Tokyo were fraught with procedural irregularities and marred by abuses of judicial discretion.[153] The defendants were chosen on the basis of political criteria, and their trials were generally unfair.[154] The execution of sentences was also inconsistent, controlled by the political whims of General MacArthur, who had the power to grant clemency, reduce sentences, and release convicted war criminals on parole.[155] The prosecution, conviction, and execution of General Tomoyuki Yamashita in the Philippines (though occurring under the auspices of U.S. national proceedings) exemplifies the domineering influence of MacArthur over the judicial process in the Far East. It demonstrates the condemnation of an individual whose role in the atrocities was negligible or nonexistent at his personal instigation. General Yamashita was the last Japanese commander in the Philippines before Allied forces landed.[156] MacArthur, who had fled the Philippines before it fell to Japanese forces, had vowed "I shall return" and punish the Japanese for their brutal occupational practices and for war crimes. MacArthur ordered the trial of Yamashita even though he had not ordered or even been aware of any war crimes; Yamashita had been in command in the Philippines for less than a month before it was retaken by Allied forces.[157]

At Tokyo, the prosecution's argument centered on the principle of individual responsibility. In rebuttal one of the defense counsels, Takayanagi Kenzo, called the concept of individual responsibility for crimes against peace "perfectly revolutionary," arguing that under general principles of international law duties and responsibilities are placed on states and nations and not on individuals, also noting that individuals' immunity was a legal principle and a practical necessity of statecraft.[158] This argument found favor with Justice Pal of India, who agreed with the defense that individuals were not liable to prosecution for acts of the state unless the nations involved agreed to a principle of sovereign limitation.[159] The defense harped on a number of other grounds, focusing on the fact that Japan's military decisions of the 1930s and early 1940s, when the Japanese political mandarins on trial were at the helm of government, should be considered as pursuant to the interest of national survival and international respect.[160] Argument was further raised over the demonization of the entire Japanese leadership on trial by the victorious Allies. Warming up to the defense, Ichiro Kiyose, another defense counsel, argued that the crimes against peace and humanity "overstepped the bounds of international law."[161]

With the exception of Justice Pal, the defense's argument against individual responsibility was rejected by the tribunal, which applied the principle of individual responsibility already articulated at Nuremberg that crimes can be committed only by real people. The majority judgment held that individuals could be held responsible for acts of state. The subsequent convictions of the defendants represented the second time in modern history that political and military leaders had been tried and convicted for acts done in the name of the state. In applying the principle of individual responsibility, the Tokyo trials reemphasized that individuals have international duties transcending the domestic system. Though states are entitled to interpret the rules of international law, they must do so in good faith. Even if a national law or a national authority orders an individual to do something, it does not end there. There are provisions that transcend national obligations of obedience; this means that in some cases individuals are required to shun orders and duties imposed by the state if they contravene international law.

The influence of politics on the selection of defendants was evident in the FEC policy decision of 3 February 1950 not to prosecute Emperor Hirohito of Japan as a war criminal.[162] The decision was based on a need to preserve the image of the emperor, who had agreed to the unconditional surrender of Japan, as a means of ensuring better political cooperation by the post–World War II Japanese ruling elite and to obtain support for the administration of the occupied Japanese territories.[163] Others, such as Allied military personnel, were conspicuously absent from the list of defendants. None of the Allies was prosecuted for war crimes. In addition, the application of the law was dubious, if not erroneous.[164] Whether Emperor Hirohito, under whose name the war was waged, offered wartime leaders encouragement, or whether his name was invoked only to justify policies, is subject to controversy. There was strong argument in favor of the emperor's innocence: although he was the symbol and essence of the nation unlike Hitler, who consolidated governmental and military power in one person, the emperor held a constitutional position and the government simply spoke through him.[165] But this argument did not find favor with Justice Henry Bernard of France, who held that the failure to indict the emperor was a serious defect, strong enough to nullify the trial. He was of the view that the emperor was not merely a suspect but a principal defendant missing from the trial.[166] Whether the emperor was a puppet or puppeteer was a question that only his trial would have answered. Even as the emperor's absence continued to rankle many, before the Tokyo Tribunal the defense argued with a degree of success that the Kellogg-Briand Pact, a keystone of the prosecution's argument that aggressive war was illegal, did not limit the right of the state to its interpretation of obligations, especially in self-defense. This was buttressed further by Major Ben Bruce Blakeney, appearing for the defense, who argued that war was not a crime, as the very concept of war implied the legal right to use force, thus eliminating the argument that killing in war would be murder. This line of argument impressed four justices, three of whom rejected the prosecution's reading of the pact and supplied alternative routes to the conclusion that an aggressive war was illegal; one justice rejected outright the contention that aggressive war was illegal, arguing in favor of the state's right of action.[167]

In the Tokyo trials, arguments were raised as to the ambiguity and injustice of the judicial process. One of the many grounds on which Justice Pal registered dissent was that the legal concept of conspiracy, derived from Anglo-Saxon law, was foreign to Asia. In Justice Pal's view, it was not acceptable for a court to conclude guilt on a conspiracy theory, then work backward to construct the involvement of the accused. Justice Pal further assailed the majority judgment for applying one standard to Japan and another to the Allies. He called into question the objectivity of the majority judgment, arguing that it confused moral wrong with legal wrong. In his view, moral wrongfulness did not necessarily give rise to legal responsibility or criminal responsibility, despite any general consensus on what is morally wrong.[168] And even though the overall tenor of Justice Pal's dissent was critical, it illuminated other legal aspects of the process. He was of the view that the right of the victorious Allies to set up the Tokyo Tribunal was derivative not of their individual sovereignties, but rather as a consequence of rights conferred on them as members of the international society by international law. In other words, the Tokyo Tribunal, as a creature of international law, had standing over and above that of the sovereigns who had brought it into existence.[169]

Even as the Tokyo trials were proceeding, the Allies were losing their appetite for the process and the expense it entailed; political considerations increasingly dominated the scene. In 1949 the FEC issued a formal advisory to all nineteen Allied powers in the Far East that Japanese war crimes trials should be held no later than 30 September 1949.[170] Subsequently, the Treaty of Peace with Japan, signed at San Francisco on 8 September 1951 by forty-eight states, provided in article II that all convicted war criminals should be transferred to Japan to serve the remainder of their sentences under the SCAP's control.[171] This was done to effectuate early releases, and between 1951 and 1957 all convicted war criminals in the Far East were released on parole or had their sentences commuted.[172] Previously, on 3 November 1946, Emperor Hirohito, on the occasion of the promulgation of Japan's new U.S.-inspired constitution, signed an imperial rescript (or edict) pardoning all members of the Japanese armed forces who may have committed offenses during the war.[173] The edict was tacitly approved by General MacArthur, but it was not publicized to avoid opposition from public opinion in Allied countries. Subsequently, Japan passed Law no. 103 of 1952, establishing a commission to oversee the repatriation and release of convicted Japanese war criminals.[174] This Japanese commission acted in

reliance on article II.[175] "Unlike in Germany, where those accused and convicted of war crimes became, for the most, pariahs in their society, the
Japanese did not view such persons as criminals but as victims. For the
Japanese, the trials were victors' vengeance couched in terms of victors'
justice, a grim reminder that no state is willing to have its actions held to
external judicial scrutiny and accountability."[176]

With Japan having successfully negotiated an agreement whereby all
convicted Japanese prisoners were allowed to return to Tokyo to serve their
sentences, ultimately not one of the twenty-five convicted and sentenced
to prison remained incarcerated for the full term. By the end of 1953, Japan
had released almost all of the convicted prisoners, even though many had
not finished serving their sentences. Most telling is the fact that by 1954
two of the major war criminals convicted by the Tokyo Tribunal subsequently became the prime minister and the minister of foreign affairs of
Japan.[177] By that time, however, the United States, the prime force behind
the Tokyo Tribunal, had based its future Southeast Asia policy on Japan's
stability and strength, and it was important that the Japanese not feel humiliated by the consequences of World War II. Their culture made them more
susceptible to humiliation, and the United States was careful to avoid placing them in that situation, evidenced most vividly by the U.S. decision not
to prosecute the emperor.[178] In return, Japan became a strong U.S. ally.
Thus, political considerations overshadowed the need to provide effective
accountability.

Conclusion

The trials of major war criminals at Nuremberg and Tokyo were an attempt
to unravel the factual complexity of the crimes committed by Nazi and
Japanese forces. That the crimes were cruel and inhuman to a degree not
previously known to humanity was exceptionally well documented by the
Nazis themselves.[179] Millions of innocent civilians were murdered as part
of a systematic, cold-blooded plan or series of plans. Chief among the
Nazis' victims were the Jewish people, but by no means did the Nazis limit
their victims to Jews alone.[180] Both major Axis powers carried out crimes
against political enemies[181] and terrorized the populations of countries that
they occupied.[182] Entire towns were destroyed, inhabitants murdered, build-
ings razed.[183] The list of crimes is virtually endless.

The principles by which these tribunals were guided were recognized
in 1946 by the United Nations General Assembly as principles of substantive and procedural international criminal law.[184] The Nuremberg and
Tokyo Tribunals were not created merely to establish that the rules of public

international law should and do apply to individuals; they also demonstrated that the protection of human rights was too important to be left to states, a proposition already enunciated in the preamble and in article 55 of the UN Charter.

The Nuremberg and Tokyo Tribunals are commonly regarded as archetypes of modern international humanitarian law implementation. However, these tribunals represent only imperfect examples, particularly in regard to their international facet. On the one hand, the Nuremberg and Tokyo Charters specified that the tribunals would enforce criminal responsibility for crimes against peace, war crimes, and crimes against humanity, thus empowering them to apply international law. Also, the judges were drawn from more than one country, making them internationally constituted in that sense. The seemingly international character of the tribunals was further reinforced by article 2 of the Agreement for the Establishment of an International Military Tribunal, which stated that the Nuremberg Tribunal was constituted "for the trials of war criminals whose offences have no particular geographical location."[185] Even their official names—as "International Military Tribunals"—tend to confirm their stature. However, certain aspects of the Nuremberg and Tokyo Tribunals indicate that they more closely resemble products of joint municipal jurisdiction.

In principle, the crimes enunciated in the Nuremberg Charter are breaches of international law, but certain aspects of the crimes were not clear and specific at that time. For instance, while drafting the Nuremberg Charter, the U.S. government insisted that the charter include the new category of "crimes against humanity" because norms prohibiting war crimes covered enemy soldiers only and not acts committed by the government of Germany against its own nationals. Unfortunately, the Nuremberg Charter made "crimes against humanity" overlap with "war crimes" in that an act could only qualify as a "crime against peace" or a "war crime" coming within the jurisdiction of the Nuremberg Tribunal. Thus the charter cast the norm prohibiting crimes against humanity as necessarily tied to the events of World War II, giving the Allies the necessary legal alibi to prosecute the Germans and subsequently the Japanese.

The judgment at Nuremberg remains controversial not only because it failed to establish that norms prohibiting aggression were grounded in *lex lata* (what the law is); it also construed norms providing for individual criminal responsibility from instruments that made no such mention, seemingly offending the principles of *nullum crimen sine lege* and *nulla poena sine lege.*[186] Nevertheless, the evidence overshadowed anything that the defendants or their lawyers could say in defense. Ultimately, the higher values and goals sought to be achieved by the United States, France, and Britain prevailed. The partisan proceedings in effect deprived the principles of the charter a large measure of fairness. Aside from the trial process itself, larger questions of procedural fairness arose from the fact that both smacked of victor's justice. In the words of M. C. Bassiouni:

> The Charter and related post-Charter instruments were designed to facilitate their ultimate enforcement rather than to provide a clear guide to conduct. It appears from the insufficiency of the general requirements and specific proscriptions of these instruments that they were not intended to provide the public at large with a framework for permissible behavior, as required by the "principles of legality" of the world's major criminal justice systems. Rather, they inform prosecutors and judges how to proceed. This approach was ultimately intended to deter through fear of potential enforcement. The Charter and related instruments arguably legitimize the selective application of decision rules by the occasional enforcer, thereby undermining the normative expectations of the public at large. Selective and occasional enforcement of decision rules does not contribute to a viable and equitable international criminal justice policy. Indeed, if prevention and deterrence are genuinely sought then both the normative standards of behavior and the methods of enforcement have to be explicit and widely diffused.[187]

As part of the universal determination to avoid the scourge of war, the post–World War II tribunals created legal precedents that outlawed wars of aggression, war crimes, and crimes against humanity. The implied promise held forth to the world was that such crimes would be condemned in the future wherever they occurred and that no person or nation would be above the law. Out of the tragedies of war came the hope and expectation that lawyers and statesmen could fashion a new legal system to help curb ancient habits of cruelty and killing. People who had seen suffering were reaching toward a more tranquil world in which persons could feel more secure under the mantle of international legal protection against the worst forms of violence and abuse. Nuremberg and similar proceedings were part of a process that reflected humankind's slow, difficult movement toward a more humane civilization.

Despite the hope that sovereign excesses were now subject to international law, and that international justice was now a practical concept, the excesses of World War II failed to deter resumption of great power rivalry. Another system transforming hegemonic struggle—the Cold War—was on the horizon even before the ashes of World War II had cooled. Committees of distinguished jurists from many nations began to codify international penal law and to consider establishing an international criminal court. However, the Cold War was to stymie progress and prevent consensus. It led to a turbulent world political order that spawned, perpetuated, and propagated interstate wars, regional instability, and civil strife. Only with the end of the

Cold War did pragmatic international cooperation resume, leading to a spurt of international activity, evidenced by the establishment of the ad hoc tribunals for Rwanda and Yugoslavia, which signified a return to the Nuremberg precedent. We now turn to the Cold War and the landmark ad hoc tribunals that ushered in the post–Cold War world.

Notes

1. Charles W. Kegley Jr. and Eugene R. Wittkopf, *World Politics: Trend and Transformations* (New York: St. Martin's, 1995), 82.

2. Ibid., 83.

3. Stephen Van Evera, "Primed for Peace: Europe After the Cold War," *International Security* 15 (1990–1991): 7–57.

4. Peter Calvocoressi, et al., *Total War: Causes and Courses of the Second World War,* 2nd rev. ed. (London: Penguin, 1972).

5. Kalevi J. Holsti, *Peace and War: Armed Conflicts and International Order, 1648–1989* (Cambridge: Cambridge University Press, 1991).

6. Kegley and Wittkopf, *World Politics,* 81–82.

7. For a detailed presentation of these denunciations and declarations, see M. Cherif Bassiouni and Ved P. Nanda, eds., *A Treatise on International Criminal Law: Crimes and Punishment,* vol. 1 (Springfield, IL: Thomas, 1973), 571–573.

8. Declaration on Security (Moscow Declaration), 1 November 1943, *Department of State of Bulletin* 9 (1943): 308, reprinted in *American Journal of International Law* 38 (1944): 5.

9. Even though this commission's name was preceded by "United Nations," it was unrelated to the world body founded in San Francisco in 1945.

10. The Law of Nuremberg, confirmed by the UN General Assembly at its first session with Resolution 95(1) of 11 December 1946, was declared part of general international law. The international community at that time (nineteen members of the United Nations) approved *a posteriori* the legitimacy of the military courts created by the Allies to prosecute and punish the major war criminals of the Axis forces. The General Assembly in 1947 adopted two resolutions, one that created the International Law Commission (ILC), whose objectives were to promote "the progressive development of international law and its codification" (UN G.A. Res. 174 [II], 21 November 1941), while the other directed the ILC to "formulate the principles of international law recognized in the Charter of the Nuremberg Tribunal and in the judgment of the Tribunal" (UN G.A. Res. 177 [II], 21 November 1947).

11. The doctrine was popular in the United States, where a wholly disproportionate importance was always attached to words, and it encouraged the fatal delusion that the machinery against aggression contained in the League Covenant was in itself undesirable. It was forgotten that the United States could, if it pleased, wipe its hands of responsibility for peace in Europe, but that for Britain collective security was real and urgent. See Arthur Berriedale Keith, *The Causes of War* (London: Nelson, 1940), 195–197; cf. Arthur Berriedale Keith, *War Government of the British Dominions* (Oxford: Clarendon, 1921), 161ff.

12. As early as 1923, shortly after Benito Mussolini established his power, Italy (which was destined to administer the fatal blow to the League Covenant by the

destruction of Ethiopian independence) set an example of defiance of the Covenant and international law. Italy occupied Corfu. Subsequently, the Italian representative at Geneva refused to consent to League action. This refusal was absurdly insolent, as League Covenant articles 10, 12, and 15 relating to nonaggression and the role of the League in the peaceful settlement of disputes were at stake with Italy threatening an indefinite occupation. It was from this time that opinion generally, which had regarded the League as indicating a new orientation in public morality, began to stress the view that the League had been adapted by the great powers as a means of furthering purely selfish ends by clothing their private interests in the guise of international justice.

13. It was made clear that all states that signed the treaty were to be under a joint and several obligation to aid any other state that signed against a war of aggression, declared formally to constitute an international crime; military, aerial, or naval action was to be required only from those states situated in the continent wherein arose the aggression.

14. Keith, *The Causes of War,* 210–218.

15. To Japan, Manchuria presented special interest because in Japanese hands it would serve to separate the Communist doctrines of Russia from the anti-Japanese propaganda of the Kuomintang (National Party) in the south. Moreover, the country could supply large amounts of soya bean, coal, and iron, and oil shale was present in large quantities.

16. On 2 September 1928, discussions had led to a compact between Ethiopia and Italy that neither should take action detrimental to the independence of the other and that disputes should be submitted to conciliation and arbitration without resort to armed force.

17. Keith, *The Causes of War.*

18. See G. Pearson, *Towards One World: An Outline of World History from 1600 to 1960* (Cambridge: Cambridge University Press, 1962).

19. Alan Bullock, *Hitler: A Study in Tyranny* (London: Odhams, 1952), 442.

20. See Keith, *The Causes of War,* 343–352.

21. A formal pact was signed between Britain, France, and Poland on 25 August 1939.

22. This accord was the crucial factor in Hitler's decision to resort to war. Hitler was now certain that Britain and France would not intervene. He was convinced that the Western powers had given their support to Poland on the belief that they could rely on Russian cooperation and their will to war would quail before his fait accompli.

23. Two years of conflict in China and half a million casualties had brought not victory to the Imperial Japanese Army but the prospect of unending war, with the empire's economy floundering under the strain.

24. For a German estimate of the human and material losses of the war, see Gerhard Stalling Verlag, *Bilanz Des Zweitan Weltkreiges Erkenntinisse und Verpflichtungen Fur Die Zukunf* [Balance of World War II: Insights and Duties for the Future] (Oldenburg: Stalling, 1953).

25. Lieutenant Commander Gregory P. Noone, "The History and Evolution of the Law of War Prior to World War II," *Naval Law Review* 47 (2000): 176.

26. This number includes Jewish men, women, and children, the latter group numbering as many as 1 million, who were slaughtered in the Nazi concentration camps and systematically killed in other parts of Europe and parts of the Soviet Union. Raul Hilberg, *The Destruction of the European Jews,* rev. ed., vol. 3 (New York: Holmes and Meier, 1985), 1202.

27. Lucy S. Dawidowicz, *The Holocaust and the Historians* (Cambridge, MA: Harvard University Press, 1981), 9; Hilberg, *The Destruction of the European Jews,* 31–36.

28. Alan C. Laifer, "Never Again? The 'Concentration Camps' in Bosnia-Herzegovina: A Legal Analysis of Human Rights Abuses," *New Europe Law Review* 2 (1994): 159.

29. The gassing facilities were located on Polish-controlled territory: Oswiecim (Auschwitz), Belzec, Chelmo, Majdanek, Sobibor, and Treblinka. Dawidowicz, *The Holocaust and the Historians,* 12.

30. Hilberg, *The Destruction of the European Jews,* 1202.

31. The Jewish people were not the only victims of Nazi terror. The Nazis considered homosexuals, Gypsies, and Christians to be enemies of the Aryan state. Dawidowicz, *The Holocaust and the Historians,* 13.

32. Richard C. Lukas, *The Forgotten Holocaust: The Poles Under German Occupation, 1939–1944* (New York: Hippocrene Books, 2001); Stefan Korbonski, *The Jews and the Poles in World War II* (New York: Hippocrene Books, 1989).

33. On 22 August 1939, a few days before the official start of World War II, Hitler authorized his commanders, with these infamous words, to kill "without pity or mercy, all men, women, and children of Polish descent or language. Only in this way can we obtain the living space [*lebensraum*] we need." Heinrich Himmler echoed Hitler's decree: "All Poles will disappear from the world. . . . It is essential that the great German people should consider it as its major task to destroy all Poles." See the Holocaust Forgotten website at www.holocaustforgotten.com/poland.htm.

34. Poland's educated class was purposely targeted because the Nazis knew that this would make it easier to control the country.

35. For detailed information, see Lukas, *The Forgotten Holocaust.*

36. Harris R. Whitney, *Tyranny on Trial: The Trial of the Major German War Criminals at the End of World War II at Nuremberg Germany, 1945–1946,* rev. ed. (Dallas, TX: Southern Methodist University Press, 1999), 179–180.

37. Ibid., 177.

38. Ibid., 246–250.

39. Ibid., 226.

40. Ibid., 220–224.

41. Ibid., 226.

42. Meirion Harries and Susie Harries, *Soldiers of the Sun: The Rise and Fall of the Imperial Japanese Army* (New York: Random House, 1991), 405.

43. Ibid., 404–405.

44. Ibid., 409.

45. Ibid., 406.

46. As noted in Harries and Harries in *Soldiers of the Sun,* the Japanese did of course distinguish between "right" and "wrong" along the same lines as Western cultures, but the distinction could more easily be overridden according to the demands of the particular situation. "Right" tended to be what was deemed right by the group in a particular situation. In this context, individual conscience was a meaningless concept. *Soldiers of the Sun,* 408.

47. Ibid., 409.

48. Fred L. Borch, "Soldiers of the Sun," *Military Law Review* 137 (1992): 241, 243.

49. The Inter-Allied Declaration, 13 January 1942, reprinted in *Punishment for War Crimes: The Inter-Allied Declaration Signed at St. James' Palace, London, on*

13 January 1942, and Relative Documents, Inter-Allied Information Committee, London (undated). See also United Nations War Crimes Commission, *History of the United Nations War Crimes Commission and the Development of the Laws of War* (London: H.M.S.O., 1948), 89–92.

50. United Nations War Crimes Commission, *History,* 34. President Roosevelt, dissatisfied with the events of a meeting in Quebec with Churchill where they initiated the Morgenthau Plan, told the State Department that he left Washington with "no presidential guidance on war crimes policy formulation"; see also Bradley F. Smith, *The American Road to Nuremberg: The Documentary Record, 1944–1945* (Stanford: Hoover Institution Press, 1982), n. 97, 10 (discussing Roosevelt's reaction to Morgenthau's political victory in Quebec, which threw war crimes policy "wide open").

51. Arieh J. Kochavi, *Prelude to Nuremberg: Allied War Crimes Policy and the Question of Punishment* (Chapel Hill: University of North Carolina Press, 1998), 27.

52. Ibid.

53. Ibid.

54. Ibid., 37.

55. Ibid., 44.

56. Of the 3.3 million Soviet POWs held by the Germans in 1941, approximately 2 million had perished by the beginning of 1942.

57. This act of neglect was perceived as still another expression of Britain's deliberate avoidance of Moscow's views and needs. At the time Moscow was not satisfied with the cooperation of its Western allies in the conduct of the war. The Kremlin did not need a United Nations commission, which could be expected to limit its freedom of action on implementing a policy calling for the immediate trial of war criminals upon their arrest.

58. Kochavi, *Prelude to Nuremberg,* 60.

59. Ibid., 54.

60. Ibid.

61. Ibid., 134.

62. Cecil Hurst and particularly Herbert Pell, the British and the U.S. representatives, failed to follow Foreign Office and State Department objectives and in fact stimulated the commission to follow its own path and to formulate its own proposals for policy and action. For a discussion of the obstruction of the UNWCC, see Kochavi, *Prelude to Nuremberg,* chap. 4.

63. Ann Tusa and John Tusa, *The Nuremberg Trial* (New York: Atheneum, 1984), 22.

64. See Telford Taylor, *The Anatomy of the Nuremberg Trials: A Personal Memoir* (New York: Knopf, 1992), 26–27.

65. United Nations War Crimes Commission, *History*; Tusa and Tusa, *The Nuremberg Trial,* 22.

66. Tusa and Tusa, *The Nuremberg Trial,* 70.

67. United Nations War Crimes Commission, *History,* 346–349.

68. Kochavi, *Prelude to Nuremberg,* 106.

69. It should be noted that objective difficulties, particularly during 1944, played a role in preventing the various national offices from presenting the commission with reports on war criminals and crimes perpetrated in the occupied countries.

70. Kochavi, *Prelude to Nuremberg,* 133.

71. Correspondence from Pell to Winant, 28 January 1944, and Reports and Printed Matters from Laurence Preuss (Pell's assistant) to Durward V. Sandifer

(Division of Political Studies, State Department), Franklin D. Roosevelt Library, Hyde Park, NY, Pell Papers, box 28, 20 January 1944.

72. Kochavi, *Prelude to Nuremberg,* 110–111.

73. Ibid., 29.

74. Ibid.

75. The UNWCC examined the 8,178 dossiers submitted by governments and, if satisfied with the contents, recommended prosecution of the individual. The dossiers amounted to 24,453 accused, 9,520 suspects, and 2,556 material witnesses. United Nations War Crimes Commission, *History,* 508–509.

76. The UNWCC indeed continued to operate until 31 March 1948. In the course of its four and a half years of operation a total of 8,178 files, involving 36,810 individuals and groups, were opened. The commission ultimately presented eighty lists containing 36,529 names of suspected war criminals, of whom the overwhelming majority (34,270) were Germans. Most of the lists, however, were compiled after the end of the war. See for example United Nations War Crimes Commission, *History,* 350–366.

77. The Instrument of Surrender of Italy (29 September 1943), art. 29. The United States and Britain prosecuted a small number of Italian war criminals, mostly those accused of committing crimes against their respective military personnel. Eighty-one defendants were tried in forty proceedings by the British in Italy. See R. John Pritchard and Jane L. Garwood-Cutler, *The Allied War Crimes Trials of Suspected Italian War Criminals, 1945–1949: A Forgotten Legacy with Vital Lessons for the Present Day* (New York: Garland, 1994).

78. The UNWCC had listed 750 Italian war criminals whose different charges included the following: illegal use of poisonous gas in violation of the 1925 Geneva Protocol against Ethiopian civilians and combatants; killing of innocent civilians and POWs; torture and mistreatment of prisoners; bombing ambulances; destruction of cultural property; and other violations of the laws of armed conflicts during the Italo-Abyssinian war. See M. Cherif Bassiouni, *Crimes Against Humanity in International Criminal Law* (Boston: M. Nijhoff, 1992), 85, 227. Various governments submitted to the UNWCC charges against Italians. The total number of charged and listed Italian war criminals equaled 1,204. See United Nations War Crimes Commission, *History,* 68, 189–190, 511. In addition, the UNWCC had extensive evidence of crimes committed by the Italian military personnel in Greece, Libya, and Yugoslavia during World War II. The governments of Ethiopia, Greece, Libya, and Yugoslavia requested extradition of the war criminals pursuant to article 29 of the instrument of surrender of Italy, but the occupying forces of Italy, the United States, and the United Kingdom did not act on their requests, with the effect that no Italian troops were prosecuted. With the Italian government denial of requests for extradition in 1946, political views prevailed over justice considerations. See Bassiouni, *Crimes Against Humanity,* 228.

79. Joint Four-Nation Declaration, Moscow Conference, October 1943 (Moscow Declaration). One of the most influential steps toward the establishment of the military tribunal at Nuremberg was the convening of an ostensibly private group of statesmen, scholars, and public officials as the London International Assembly. That group developed many of the concepts and some of the norms that went into the Statute of the Nuremberg Tribunal. See Report of Commission, vol. 1, *The Punishment of War Criminals: Recommendations of the London International Assembly,* 1944.

80. Taylor, *The Anatomy of the Nuremberg Trials,* 29.

81. Ibid., 26. See also Aron N. Trainin, *Hitlerite Responsibility Under Criminal Law,* translated by Rothstein (London: Hutchinson, 1945). In 1946, Trainin

recalled his contribution to the prosecutions of German war criminals in A. N. Trainin, "Le tribunal militaire international et le proces de Nuremberg," *Revue Internationale de Droit Penal* 17 (1946): 263. The Soviet Union was, however, dealing with alleged war criminals within its territory by summary execution. Taylor, *The Anatomy of the Nuremberg Trials*, 52.

82. Taylor, *The Anatomy of the Nuremberg Trials*, 32.

83. President Roosevelt (prior to his death and Truman's ascension to the presidency) had preferred a military court. In a letter to Herbert Pell, the U.S. representative on the UNWCC, Roosevelt expressed his fear that an international tribunal composed of civil jurists would move very cautiously and "might more readily lend itself to resort by the accused and his counsel to legalistic and dilatory tactics." Although Roosevelt did not rule out such a tribunal, he thought that more expeditious results would be obtained if military men staffed the special courts: Roosevelt to Pell, 12 February 1944, Franklin D. Roosevelt Library, Hyde Park, NY, Pell Papers, box 25, file: Roosevelt, Foreign Office, 1936–1945.

84. Harris Whitney, *Tyranny on Trial: The Evidence at Nuremberg* (Dallas, TX: Southern Methodist University Press, 1954), 16–19.

85. Ibid., 18.

86. See for example M. Cherif Bassiouni and Valeri M. Savitsky, eds., *The Criminal Justice System of the U.S.S.R.* (Springfield, IL: Thomas, 1979); Russian S.F.S.R., *Soviet Criminal Law and Procedure*, translated by Harold Berman, 2nd ed. (Cambridge, MA: Harvard University Press, 1972); Harold Berman, *Justice in the U.S.S.R.: An Interpretation of Soviet Law* (New York: Vintage Books, 1963).

87. See John F. Murphy, "Norms of Criminal Procedure at the International Military Tribunal," in *The Nuremberg Trial and International Law*, edited by George Ginsburgs and Vladimir N. Kudriavtsev (Boston: Martinus Nijhoff, 1990), 61.

88. See for example Kochavi, *Prelude to Nuremberg*, 22–240.

89. Charter of the International Military Tribunal (Nuremberg Charter), art. 6; Agreement for the Prosecution and Punishment of the Major War Criminals of the European Axis (London Agreement), 8 August 1945, 58 Stat. 1544, E. A. S. no. 472, 82 UNTS 280.

90. The Netherlands discouraged formal extradition requests because extradition treaties applied only to cases in which a criminal act occurred. The Netherlands viewed the charge against the kaiser as a "political offense" because a head of state's decision to go to war was within the prerogative of national sovereignty and, therefore, not a crime under Dutch law. See James W. Garner, "Punishment of Offenders Against the Laws and Customs of War," *American Journal of International Law* 14 (1920): 70, 91; See also Quincy Wright, "The Legality of the Kaiser," *American Political Science Review* 13 (1919): 121.

91. The Allies particularly relied on the 1928 General Treaty for the Renunciation of War as an Instrument of National Policy (Kellogg-Briand Pact) of 27 August 1928 as a legal justification for "crimes against peace." 94 L.N.T.S. 57, 46 Stat. 2343, reprinted in *American Journal of International Law* 22 (Supp. 1928).

92. See "Memorandum of Reservations Presented by the Representatives of the United States to the Report of the Commission on Responsibilities," 4 April 1919, Annex II, reprinted in *American Journal of International Law* 14 (1920): 127, 144, annex II, 65.

93. See U.S. Department of State, Pub. no. 3080, *Report of Robert H. Jackson, United States Representative to the International Conference on Military Trials* (Washington, DC: U.S. Government Printing Office, 1949), vii–viii. It is likely that

the Soviet Union desired to avoid codifying a broad definition of crimes against peace that could be used again in the future. Without such a definition, the Soviet Union would be free to act as it wished without repercussions.

94. U.S. Constitution, art. I, sec. 10, cl. 3; art. I, sec. 10, cl. 1.

95. U.S. Department of State, *Report of Robert H. Jackson*, vii–viii.

96. See for example M. Cherif Bassiouni and Benjamin Ferencz, "The Crime Against Peace," in *International Criminal Law*, edited by M. Cherif Bassiouni, vol. 1 (Dobbs Ferry, NY: Transnational, 1987), 174–176; Benjamin Ferencz, *Defining International Aggression, the Search for World Peace: A Documentary History and Analysis* (Dobbs Ferry, NY: Oceana, 1975). The UN Charter prohibits aggression, and the Security Council has the power under Chapter VII to take measures, including sanctions, to preserve and maintain peace: UN Charter, arts. 2(3), 2(4), 39–51. See generally Bruno Simma, ed., *The Charter of the United Nations: A Commentary,* 2nd ed. (Oxford: Oxford University Press, 2002). It is noteworthy that there has never been an international convention explicitly making aggression an international crime. Other than the General Assembly's 1974 Resolution (G.A. Res. 3314, UN GAOR, 29th sess., Supp. no. 31, UN Doc. A/9631, 1974, 143), defining aggression and adopted by consensus, there is no definition of that crime.

97. Taylor, *The Anatomy of the Nuremberg Trials,* 54.

98. See for example Taylor, *The Anatomy of the Nuremberg Trials,* 20; Smith, *The American Road to Nuremberg,* 78–79.

99. U.S. Department of State, *Report of Robert H. Jackson,* 299.

100. Ibid., 302; Taylor, *The Anatomy of the Nuremberg Trials,* 54 (Jackson believed the charge of "invasion of other countries and initiation of wars of aggression in violation of international laws or treaties" was the most important charge). Jackson warned that if aggression was not defined, defendants would respond to the charge by accusing the British and French of grievously injuring Germany after World War I, through the terms of the Versailles Treaty, politically and economically: Taylor, *The Anatomy of the Nuremberg Trials,* 51.

101. See for example Taylor, *The Anatomy of the Nuremberg Trials,* 65–66 (stating that the French clearly did not consider it a criminal violation to launch a war of aggression).

102. Ibid., 65. In a revision to the U.S. draft proposal, the Soviets sought to try all persons who participated in aggression against other nations in violation of the principles of international law and treaties. However, the Soviets only wanted this to apply to aggressions that were carried out by the European Axis. Ibid.

103. U.S. Department of State, *Report of Robert H. Jackson,* 303; see Taylor, *The Anatomy of the Nuremberg Trials,* 66 (Jackson publicly stated that the prime purpose of the London Charter negotiations was to establish the criminality of aggressive war).

104. General Assembly Resolution 3314 (XXIX) of 14 December 1974 on the definition of aggression.

105. Rome Statute of the International Criminal Court, opened for signature 17 July 1998, adopted by the United Nations Diplomatic Conference of Plenipotentiaries on the Establishment of an International Criminal Court on 17 July 1998. The final vote recorded was 120 in favor, seven against, and twenty abstentions. Article 5(2) provides that "the Court shall exercise jurisdiction over the crime of aggression once a provision is adopted in accordance with arts. 121 and 123 defining the crime and setting out the conditions under which the Court shall exercise jurisdiction with respect to this crime. Such a provision shall be consistent with the relevant provisions of the charter of the United Nations."

106. Convention Respecting the Laws and Customs of War on Land, 18 October 1907, preamble.

107. The 1929 Geneva Convention Relative to the Treatment of Prisoners of War, 27 July 1929.

108. Lassa Oppenheim, *International Law*, 1st ed. (London and New York: Longmans, Green, 1906), 264–265. The *British Manual of Military Law*, no. 443 (1914), relied upon Oppenheim in its formulation. Oppenheim's recognition of the defense remained in the first five editions up to 1940, when it changed to become the basis for the Nuremberg Tribunal's art. 8, which denied the defense. U.S. Department of the Army, *Field Manual* (1940), 27–10, reflected the same position in sec. 345(1). On 15 November 1944, a revision of sec. 345(1) limited, but retained, a qualified defense. But see U.S. Department of the Army, *Field Manual* 27–10. For a historical evolution of the question, see Leslie C. Green, "Superior Orders and Command Responsibility," *Canadian Yearbook of International Law* 27 (1989): 167; Major William H. Parks, "Command Responsibility for War Crimes," *Military Law Review* 62 (1973): 1.

109. See generally Nico Keijzer, *Military Obedience* (Alphen aan den Rijn: Sijthoff and Noordhoff [International Publishers], 1978); Leslie C. Green, *Superior Orders in National and International Law* (Leyden: A. W. Sijthoff, 1976); Yoram Dinstein, *The Defence of "Obedience to Superior Orders" in International Law* (Leyden: A. W. Sijthoff, 1965); Ekkehart Muller-Rappard, *L'ordre superieur militaire et la responsibilite penale du subordonne* (Paris: A. Pedone, 1965).

110. Bassiouni, *Crimes Against Humanity in International Criminal Law*, 18–32; Egon Schwelb, "Crimes Against Humanity," *British Yearbook of International Law* 23 (1946): 178.

111. See Bassiouni, *Crimes Against Humanity in International Criminal Law*, 18–47; M. Cherif Bassiouni, "International Law and the Holocaust," *California Western International Law Journal* 9 (1979): 201. See also Leila Sadat Wexler, "The Interpretation of the Nuremberg Principles by the French Court of Cassation," *Columbia Journal of Transnational Law* 32 (1994): 289; Schwelb, "Crimes Against Humanity."

112. "Memorandum of Reservations Presented by the Representatives of the United States to the Report of the Commission on Responsibilities," reproduced in fourteen *American Journal of International Law* 95, Annex II at pp. 127–151.

113. See Bassiouni, *Crimes Against Humanity in International Criminal Law*, 1–17. See generally Bradley F. Smith, *Reaching Judgment at Nuremberg* (New York: Basic Books, 1977), xvii; Taylor, *The Anatomy of the Nuremberg Trials*; U.S. Department of State, *Report of Robert H. Jackson*.

114. Bassiouni, *Crimes Against Humanity in International Criminal Law*, 1–17.

115. For the positivist view, see John Austin, *The Province of Jurisprudence Determined*, 2nd ed. (New York: B. Franklin, 1970); H. L. A. Hart, *The Concept of Law* (New York: Oxford University Press, 1961); H. L. A. Hart, "Positivism and the Separation of Law and Morals," *Harvard Law Review* (1958): 593. Compare Anthony A. D'Amato, "The Moral Dilemma of Positivism," *Valparaiso University Law Review* 20 (1985): 43, which states: "Not only do positivists insist upon separating law from morality, but they also appear to be unable to deal with moral questions raised by law once the two are separated. This inability stems, I believe, from their simultaneous attempt to assert and to prove that law and morality are separate; the argument reduces to a vicious circle." See also Anthony A. D'Amato, *Jurisprudence: A Descriptive and Normative Analysis of Law* (Dordrecht, Netherlands, and

Boston: M. Nijhoff, 1984), 294–302; Lon L. Fuller, "Positivism and Fidelity to Law—A Reply to Professor Hart," *Harvard Law Review* 71 (1958): 630.

116. See for example August Von Knieriem, *The Nuremberg Trials,* translated by E. D. Schmitt (Chicago: H. Regnery, 1959); Hans Ehard, "The Nuremberg Trial Against the Major War Criminals and International Law," *American Journal of International Law* 43 (1949): 223; Gordon Ireland, "Ex Post Facto from Rome to Tokyo," *Temple Law Quarterly* (1947): 27. But see A. Frederick Mignone, "After Nuremberg, Tokyo," *Texas Law Review* 25 (1947): 475; Georg Schwarzenberger, "The Judgment of Nuremberg," *Tulane Law Review* 21 (1947): 329.

117. For a survey of these "principles of legality," see Stefan Glaser, "Le principe de la legalite en matiere penale, notamment en droit codifie et en droit coutumier," *Revue de Droit Penal et de Criminologie* 46 (1966): 899; Jerome Hall, "Nulla Poena Sine Lege," *Yale Law Journal* 47 (1937): 165. For national approaches, see Roger Merle and Andre Vitu, *Traité de droit criminel: Problèmes généraux de la législation criminelle, droit pénal général, procédure pénale* (Paris: Editions Cujas, 1967), 108, which documents the historical right of the judge in the French criminal justice system to interpret principles of law and that, at 113, acknowledges the decline in the twentieth century of the rigid positivist approach to "principles of legality."

118. Article 10 provides that once the Nuremberg Tribunal declares a particular group or organization criminal, competent national authorities may prosecute individuals for having been members of such entities, and that in such cases "the criminal nature of the group or organization is considered proved and shall not be questioned." The result was that six organizations were indicted at the Nuremberg trials, of which three were declared criminal, namely the SS, the Gestapo, and the Leadership Corps. The High Command, the Reich Cabinet, and the SA were not declared to be criminal organizations.

119. See for example Taylor, *The Anatomy of the Nuremberg Trials,* 35.

120. See Agreement for the Prosecution and Punishment of the Major War Criminals of the European Axis (London Agreement); Nuremberg Charter.

121. London Agreement.

122. There was no reliance on the work of the UNWCC.

123. Taylor, *The Anatomy of the Nuremberg Trials,* 57.

124. Signed on 23 August 1939 in Moscow.

125. Lyal S. Sunga, *The Emerging System of International Criminal Law: Developments in Codification and Implementation* (The Hague and Boston: Kluwer Law International, 1997), 42.

126. For a critical perspective of the Nuremberg Tribunal, see Hans Ehard, "The Nuremberg Trial Against the Major War Criminals and International Law," *American Journal of International Law* 43 (1949): 223; Mignone, "After Nuremberg, Tokyo"; Gordon Ireland, "Ex Post Facto from Rome to Tokyo," *Temple Law Quarterly* 21 (1985): 27. Many of the concerns raised by the authors cited above are also present in the following: Georg Schwarzenberger, "The Judgment of Nuremberg"; Hans Kelsen, "Will the Judgment in the Nuremberg Trial Constitute a Precedent in International Law?" *International Law Quarterly* 1 (1947): 153; Gordon W. Forbes, "Some Legal Aspects of the Nuremberg Trial," *Canadian Bar Review* 24 (1946): 584; A. L. Goodhart, "The Legality of the Nuremberg Trials," *Juridical Review* 58 (1946): 1. For the views of four defense counsels at the Nuremberg Tribunal, see Herbert Kraus, "The Nuremberg Trials of the Major War Criminals: Reflections After Seventeen Years," *DePaul Law Review* 13 (1964): 23 (chief counsel for

Schacht); Carl Haensel, "The Nuremberg Trials Revisited," *DePaul Law Review* 13 (1964): 248 (chief counsel for the SS and SA); Otto Kranzbuhler, "Nuremberg Eighteen Years Afterwards," *DePaul Law Review* 14 (1965): 333 (chief counsel for Admiral Karl Donitz); Otto Pannenbecker, "The Nuremberg War Crimes Trial," *DePaul Law Review* 14 (1965): 348 (chief counsel for Wilhelm Frick). For two other authors who address the question of Allied violations, see James Bacque, *Other Losses: The Shocking Truth Behind the Mass Deaths of Disarmed German Soldiers and Civilians Under General Eisenhower's Command* (Bolton, Ontario: Little, Brown, Canada, 1991), and Alfred M. De Zayas, *The Wehrmacht War Crimes Bureau: 1939–1945* (Lincoln: University of Nebraska Press, 1989). In the latter book, the author reveals that the German Army established a bureau to record war crimes committed by the Allies against German military personnel. These apparently uncontroverted violations were never pursued by the Allies.

127. Law for the Protection of German Blood and Honor (15 September 1935) and First Ordinance to the Reich Citizenship Law (14 November 1935), reprinted in Raul Hilberg, *Documents of Destruction, Germany, and Jewry 1933–1945* (Chicago: Quadrangle Books, 1971), 18–21; Richard Lawrence, *Nazi Justice: Law of the Holocaust* (Westport, CT: Praeger, 1995), 145–148.

128. Opening statement of Brigadier General Telford Taylor, chief prosecutor of the series of trials that followed the Major War Crimes Tribunal: International Military Tribunal, *Trial of the Major War Criminals Before the International Military Tribunal*, vol. 1 (Nuremburg: The Tribunal, 1947–1949), 29.

129. International Military Tribunal, *Trial of the Major War Criminals*, vol. 1, 29.

130. See text accompanying n. 118 above.

131. International Military Tribunal, *Trial of the Major War Criminals*, vol. 1, 12 (arts. 7 and 8).

132. Ibid., 42.

133. Steven Fogelson, "The Nuremberg Legacy: An Unfulfilled Promise," *Southern California Law Review* 63 (1990): 833, 850–851.

134. Crimes against peace, including planning and launching a war, were generally considered to be within a sovereign's legitimate powers by the international legal community at the time of the Nuremberg trials. Thomas Joseph Lawrence, *The Principles of International Law*, 7th ed., vol. 1 (Boston: D. C. Heath, 1923), 311; Lassa Oppenheim, *International Law*, 6th ed. (London: Longmans, Green, 1944), 144–145; John Westlake, *International Law*, 2nd ed., vol. 2 (Cambridge: Cambridge University Press, 1910–1913), 4; Henry Wheaton, *Elements of International Law*, edited by Richard Henry Dana Jr., 8th ed., vol. 1 (Buffalo, NY: Willian S. Hein, 1986), 368, 373–374. However, as Justice Jackson noted in his report to the president of 6 June 1945, this nineteenth-century doctrine itself was a departure from earlier international legal principles as taught by Hugo Grotius. U.S. Department of State, *Report of Robert H. Jackson*, 129–132.

135. Nuremberg Charter, 12 (art. 7).

136. Tusa and Tusa, *The Nuremberg Trial*.

137. R. B. Pal, *Dissentient Judgment of Justice R. B. Pal* (Calcutta: Sanval, 1953).

138. See Benjamin Ferencz, *Less Than Slaves: Jewish Forced Labor and the Quest for Compensation* (Cambridge, MA: Harvard University Press, 1979).

139. Allied Control Council Law no. 10, Punishment of Persons Guilty of War Crimes, Crimes Against Peace and Against Humanity, 20 December 1945, *Official Gazette of the Control Council for Germany* (Berlin), no. 3, 31 January 1946,

reprinted in Benjamin B. Ferencz, *An International Criminal Court, a Step Toward World Peace: A Documentary History and Analysis* (Dobbs Ferry, NY: Oceana, 1980), 488.

140. With respect to prosecutions in certain Eastern and Central European countries as well as extrajudicial execution, see Istvan Deak, "Post World War II Political Justice in a Historical Perspective," *Military Law Review* 149 (1995): 137.

141. This was evident in the FEC's decision to end prosecutions by 1950 and to repatriate to Japan by 1953 all those who were convicted.

142. See generally FEC report, *Activities of the Far Eastern Commission, Report by the Secretary General, 26 February to 10 July 1947, Department of State Bulletin* 16 (1947): 804–806.

143. Ultimately, however, "the Far Eastern Commission became little more than a debating society, and when a peace treaty was finally signed with Japan, it died a quiet death." Bassiouni, *Crimes Against Humanity in International Criminal Law,* 293.

144. Special Proclamation by the Supreme Commander for the Allied Powers at Tokyo, 19 January 1946; Charter dated 19 January 1946; Amended Charter dated 26 April 1946, 28. Even though MacArthur established the International Military Tribunal for the Far East (IMFTE), the U.S. Supreme Court held that the tribunal was not a U.S. court. Rather, the Supreme Court maintained that the tribunal was merely created by an "agent of the Allied Powers." This method of establishing the IMFTE was determined to be constitutional under U.S. law in *Hirota v. MacArthur* 338 U.S. 197 (1948), 198.

145. The political and military tensions between the United States and the Soviet Union affected the proceedings in many ways. For instance, all information related to the existence of a bacteriological weapons research lab located in Manchuria was purposely kept from the tribunal. Bernard Roling believed that this information was withheld by U.S. military authorities who wanted to reap the benefits of the research and keep the information from the Soviets. Howard Levie has a differing view, however, believing that the information was withheld by both the Americans and the Soviets because both countries had access to the information and wanted to prevent the other from obtaining research results. See Howard Levie, *Terrorism in War: The Law of War Crimes* (Dobbs Ferry, NY: Oceana, 1993), 141. Levie highlights Soviet criticisms of the Tokyo Tribunal, including accusations that the tribunal displayed anti-Soviet tendencies and was influenced by the overwhelming U.S. presence in its administration. Ibid., 145.

146. U.S. Department of State, *Trial of the Japanese War Criminals* (Washington, DC: U.S. Government Printing Office, 1946), 39–44.

147. Nuremberg Charter; Tokyo Charter.

148. See Bassiouni, "International Law and the Holocaust"; Bassiouni, *Crimes Against Humanity in International Criminal Law*, 34.

149. B. V. A. Roling, *The Tokyo Trial and Beyond: Reflections of a Peacemonger,* edited by Antonio Cassese (Cambridge: Polity, 1993), 3. See also B. V. A. Roling, "The Nuremberg and Tokyo Trials in Retrospect," in *A Treatise on International Criminal Law,* edited by M. Cherif Bassiouni and Ved P. Nanda (Springfield, IL: Thomas, 1973), 590.

150. See FEC report, *Activities of the Far Eastern Commission.*

151. See Tokyo charter, art. 6(a). Accused war criminals were divided into Class A, B, and C. The first Tokyo proceedings were against twenty-eight senior Japanese officials considered Class A suspected war criminals, though clearly some of them did not deserve being placed in that category, according to most experts on

the subject. For an early appraisal, see Solis Horwitz, "The Tokyo Trial," *International Reconciliation* 465 (1950): 473. For a more recent appraisal, see Levie, *Terrorism in War,* 141.

152. While the choice of judges at the Nuremberg Tribunal was made by the respective four major powers, the U.S., British, and French judges and their alternates were highly qualified and known for their personal integrity and independence. The judges from the Soviet Union, who were military officers, were believed to be less knowledgeable and subject to their government's directives, though their performance on the bench paralleled that of their Western counterparts. This was not the case at Tokyo, however. With the exception of Roling (Netherlands), Pal (India), and Bernard (France), many of the judges appeared politically motivated, especially the president, and General MacArthur's influence seemed rampant. See John A. Appleman, *Military Tribunals and International Crimes* (Westport, CT: Greenwood Press, 1954), 239–244 (referring to page numbers in the transcript evidencing prejudice and unfairness, particularly by Presiding Judge Sir William Webb of Australia). Levie is equally critical.

153. See Appleman, *Military Tribunals and International Crimes,* 239–258.

154. See Bassiouni, *Crimes Against Humanity in International Criminal Law,* 211–212.

155. See Levie, *Terrorism in War.*

156. A. Frank Reel, *The Case of General Yamashita* (New York: Octagon Books, 1971). Reel was a JAG captain who was one of Yamashita's defense counsels at these proceedings. For other military trials, see Lawrence Taylor, *A Trial of Generals: Homma, Yamashita, MacArthur* (South Bend, IN: Icarus, 1981).

157. In December 1945 MacArthur set up a special military commission to prosecute Japanese war criminals in the Philippines. MacArthur influenced the military judges who applied an inappropriate legal standard that has not been applied since in cases of command responsibility: Yamashita was held responsible for acts of his subordinates that he had not ordered and of which he was unaware. The U.S. Supreme Court denied Yamashita's petition for a writ of habeas corpus, but two justices wrote compelling dissents. See *Re Yamashita,* 327 U.S. 1 (1946), 26–81 for a discussion of the trial. See Parks, "Command Responsibility for War Crimes," 1; Telford Taylor, *Nuremberg and Vietnam: An American Tragedy* (Chicago: Quadrangle Books, 1970).

158. Takayanagi Kenzo, *The Tokyo Trials and International Law* (Tokyo: Yahikaku Showa, 1948): 59, 60, 63.

159. Pal, *Dissentient Judgment,* 71.

160. Timothy P. Maga, *Judgment at Tokyo: The Japanese War Crimes Trials* (Lexington: University Press of Kentucky, 2001), 48.

161. Arnold C. Brackman, *The Other Nuremberg: The Untold Story of the Tokyo War Crimes Trials* (London: Collins, 1989), 106.

162. *Department of State Bulletin* 22 (1950): 244. MacArthur reportedly instigated the decision because he felt that prosecuting the emperor would make pacification of Japan a difficult task, costing the United States many casualties at the hands of Japanese guerrillas.

163. William Manchester, *American Caesar: Douglas MacArthur, 1880–1964* (London: Arrow Books, 1978), 484–491.

164. Bernard V. A. Roling, "The Nuremberg and the Tokyo Trials in Retrospect," in Bassiouni and Nanda, eds., *A Treatise on International Criminal Law,* 600–601, 605–607.

165. John L. Ginn, *Sugamo Prison, Tokyo: An Account of the Trial and Sentencing of Japanese War Criminals in 1948 by a U.S. Participant* (Jefferson, N.C.: McFarland, 1992), 54; Roling, *Reflections of a Peacemonger,* 39.

166. Richard H. Minear, *Victors' Justice: The Tokyo War Crimes Trials* (Princeton, NJ: Princeton University Press, 1972), 117.

167. Ibid., 53–54.

168. Elizabeth S. Kopelman, "Ideology and International Law: The Dissent of the Indian Justice at the Tokyo War Crimes Trial," *New York University Journal of International Law and Politics* 23 (1991): 413.

169. Pal, *Dissentient Judgment.*

170. R. John Pritchard, "The Gift of Clemency Following British War Crimes Trials in the Far East, 1946–1947," *Criminal Law Review* 7 (1996): 15, 18.

171. Ibid., 37.

172. Ibid., 37–49.

173. Ibid., 24.

174. Ibid., 38.

175. Ibid., 37.

176. See for example M. Cherif Bassiouni, "From Versailles to Rwanda in Seventy-Five Years: The Need to Establish a Permanent Criminal Court," *Harvard Human Rights Journal* (1997): 1, 34–35.

177. Ibid., n. 109.

178. The Japanese treated the emperor with extreme reverence, as he was to them a semidivine being under the prewar Japan climate in which nationalists used state Shintoism with its support for a divine and unbroken emperor to push the nation into military excursions abroad. Thus the United States decided not to prosecute him, as this would have been a crushing humiliation for the Japanese and would likely have prolonged the war and made administration of occupied Japan a nightmare in the face of a hostile populace incensed by this affront to the honor and dignity of their nation.

179. See International Military Tribunal, *Trial of the Major War Criminals,* 22–42 (documents in evidence at Nuremberg); Office of United States Chief of Counsel for the Prosecution of Axis Criminality, *Nazi Conspiracy and Aggression* (Washington, DC: U.S. Government Printing Office, 1946) (ten volumes of German documents collected by the U.S. and British staffs at Nuremberg); see also R. Conot, *Justice at Nuremberg* (New York: Harper and Row, 1983), 24–25 (describing the daunting task of assimilating the wealth of German documents available to the tribunal); Robert H. Jackson, *The Nuremberg Case* (Washington, DC: U.S. Government Printing Office, 1947), 433 ("in preparation for the trial over 100,000 captured German documents were screened or examined").

180. Lucy S. Dawidowicz, *The War Against the Jews, 1933–1945* (London: Weidenfeld and Nicolson, 1975), 148; K. Feig, *Hitler's Death Camps: The Sanity of Madness* (New York: Holmes and Meier, 1979), 24.

181. See for example International Military Tribunal, *Trial of the Major War Criminals*, vol. 2, 192; see also W. L. Shirer, *The Rise and Fall of the Third Reich: A History of Nazi Germany* (London: Pan Books, 1979), 305–314 (discussing the arrest and execution of the Nazis' political opponents in late June and early July 1934).

182. See for example International Military Tribunal, *Trial of the Major War Criminals,* vol. 1, 226–228, 232–243; see also "Decree for the Conduct of Courts Martial in the District of Barbarossa," 13 May 1941, in Office of United States Chief of Counsel for the Prosecution of Axis Criminality, vol. 3, 637 (a decree from Hitler and signed by Keitel that provides for, inter alia, collective punishment of civilians and discourages prosecution of offenses committed by German soldiers against civilians).

183. See for example International Military Tribunal, *Trial of the Major War Criminals,* vol. 1, 62, 234, 270; Conot, *Justice at Nuremberg,* 277.

184. The resolution of the 51st plenary session of the UN General Assembly of 11 December 1946, cited in Bassiouni and Nanda, eds., *A Treatise on International Criminal Law,* 43.

185. See Nuremberg Charter.

186. Sunga, *The Emerging System of International Criminal Law,* 42.

187. M. Cherif Bassiouni, "Crimes Against Humanity: The Need for a Specialized Convention," *Columbia Journal of Transnational Law* (1994): 457.

PART 2

The Cold War and the 1990s

4

Cold War: International Justice in the Shadow of Realpolitik

At the end of World War II, the Big Three (the United States, the Soviet Union, and Great Britain) sought to design a new world order, but the vague compromises reached concealed the differences percolating below the surface. As noted by Charles W. Kegley Jr. and Eugene Wittkopf,

> the end of World War II generated uncertainty and mistrust. The agreements governing goals, strategy, and obligations that guided the collective Allied effort to defeat the common enemy began to erode even as victory neared. Victory only magnified the growing distrust that each great power harbored about the others' intentions in an environment of ill-defined borders, altered allegiances, power vacuums, and economic ruin.[1]

With the defeat of Germany and Japan, the façade of Allied unity began to erode. Perhaps the most certain feature of the otherwise uncertain post–World War II geopolitical environment was the ascendancy of the United States and the Soviet Union as dominant world powers. The other major power victors, Great Britain and France, had exhausted themselves during the war and fell from the apex of the world power hierarchy. Germany and Japan, defeated in war and now in ruins, also fell from the ranks, excluded from the game of great power politics that they had pursued in seeking world domination through force of arms.[2] Unparalleled in scope and unprecedented in destructiveness, World War II transformed the world into a new system dominated by two super-states, the United States and the Soviet Union, whose combined resources surpassed all others. Their preeminent status made each naturally suspicious of the other; rivalry was inescapable. It also speeded the disintegration of the great colonial empires assembled by imperialist nations during previous centuries, thereby hastening the emancipation of many peoples from foreign rule. Unlike earlier international systems, the emergent one featured a distribution of power consisting of many sovereign states outside the European core. The advent of nuclear weapons also added a new twist, for they radically changed the role that threats of warfare would henceforth play in world politics.

Determining the origins of the Cold War—the twentieth century's third hegemonic struggle for domination—is difficult because the historical evidence is amenable to different interpretations.[3] Despite this, the principal cause of the Cold War was the essential duopoly of power (resting with the two superpowers) left by World War II, a duopoly that quite naturally resulted in the filling of a vacuum (Europe) that had once been the center of the international system. Control of Europe would confer a great, and perhaps decisive, power advantage to the possessor. The root cause of the Cold War was to be found in the structural circumstances that characterized the international system at the close of World War II.[4] These circumstances gave each superpower reasons to fear and to combat the other's potential global leadership.[5]

In practice, the United States and the Soviet Union mattered most. They were to subsequently use the fledgling United Nations not to keep the peace but to pursue competition with one another. Out of these circumstances grew the superpower competition. Once their shared interests in World War II disappeared, ideology became the chief means to differentiate friend from foe.[6] Rules that were written into the UN Charter, which obligated the United States and the Soviet Union to share (through the United Nations Security Council) responsibility for preserving world peace, were to fail miserably through misuse and abuse.

The fallout had a disastrous impact on the international system and its operation. One of the casualties was the concept of international justice. Ironically, this had provided common ground in the face of Nazi and Japanese aggression. The precedent and promise that the post–World War II trials represented—that never again would atrocities be carried out with impunity and that individuals who carried out atrocities against enemies and civilians would be called to the bar of justice—was washed away by mistrust and hostility that engulfed the rest of the world as other states took up sides.

The idea that individual human rights can be protected by the international community was one of the great practical achievements of Nuremberg and Tokyo, which gave tangible expression to the principle that human dignity transcends national boundaries and national distinctions. Unfortunately, despite post–World War II international human rights and humanitarian law instruments, important steps to limiting sovereignty, the Cold War tied the issue of sovereignty to ideological and revolutionary agendas. The Soviet Union increasingly saw "restriction of sovereignty" and the concepts of "common interest" and "common good" as nothing more than a diplomatic screen hiding the avaricious and predatory aims of the imperialist powers.[7] The effect was to strengthen sovereignty considerations, as the UN became a ground for cultivating the agenda of nationalism brought to the fore by the rise of the third world. Sadly, half a century was to elapse before the next international criminal trials were held, despite many conflicts leading to gross and systematic violations. Notwithstanding the strengthening of international humanitarian law during the Cold War era,[8] accountability to the law was not the rule; it was the exception. Superpower hostility and competition bred conflict, and mutual mistrust between the East-West blocs forestalled meaningful cooperation that would have resulted in the creation of an international penal process to enforce humanitarian law.

With sovereignty viewed as a vital element of global international society, Cold War power politics curtailed the expected benefits of limiting sovereignty articulated at the post–World War II trials. No prosecutions were to occur at the international level during the Cold War. Principally, this was due to the absence of UN-authorized actions to bring justice to those responsible for aggression, crimes against humanity, and violations of international humanitarian law. Instead of following the Nuremberg principle (punishing only the guilty after a fair trial), economic sanctions and other curbs imposed on civilian populations—many of which disagreed with the aggressive policies of their governments—became the sole means of censuring rogue governments. With the failure at the international level, the key juridical moments of international criminal law were confined to the domestic circuit. One calls to mind the trials of Eichmann, Demajanjuk, Barbie, Polyukhovich, Preibke, Touvier, and others.[9] Few, if any, of these trials were satisfactory from a strictly legal perspective. Cases of mistaken identity, failing memory, and dubious assertions of jurisdiction would undercut all that.

Although no international prosecutions occurred from 1951 until 1992, several UN efforts were made to draft a code of crimes and to establish a statute for an international criminal court. However, all were blocked in one way or another. See Chapter 7, which includes a discussion of the permanent International Criminal Court. The next section looks at the groundbreaking developments in international humanitarian law and human rights during the Cold War era. Great advances were made, but wars large and small continued during this period of history.

People First, Nations Second:
Developments in the International Law Regime

The renaissance of the law of war in the post–World War II era was triggered by the emerging centrality of human rights in the aftermath of the war. In various Charter provisions, the founders of the United Nations paid tribute to the idea of international human rights.[10] Active discourse at the international level furthered the humanitarian agenda, evidenced by UN reports on respect for human rights in armed conflict,[11] the Tehran conference on human rights of 1968, and numerous other initiatives by non-governmental actors. "Law of war experts have recognized that the development of international humanitarian law had approached stagnation before the influence of the human rights movement was brought to bear."[12] World events called attention to other deficiencies with respect to humanitarian norms and the need to expand international norms. From the 1970s, the United Nations regularly concerned itself with important aspects of international humanitarian law in human rights contexts. Thematic rapporteurs were appointed to analyze issues surrounding armed conflicts, resulting in special reports. Country rapporteurs made extensive reference to humanitarian law norms in their reports. Although most human rights bodies lack explicit mandates to apply international humanitarian law, violations during armed conflicts often led to investigations of abuses in light of humanitarian law.[13] Many measures were used to coerce compliance with human rights law, including protest, diplomacy, reprisals, and sanctions. However, coercive tactics proved to be selective and ineffective, largely due to external political considerations.

With the ascendance of the UN as a key player in the international system, the United Nations Charter, with its stature as a "world constitution" of sorts, became the focus of international initiatives. The Charter provisions promoting human rights as a basic purpose of the UN Organization were singled out as particularly important in crafting an international system that would redeem the failures that led to World War II. The recognition of crimes against humanity as an international crime, the conclusion of the 1948 Genocide Convention, and the regulation by a multilateral treaty of international and noninternational armed conflicts were important milestones.[14] The establishment of mechanisms for universal criminal jurisdiction and the move to repress grave breaches revealed the intent "to go beyond the interstate level and to reach for the level of the real (or ultimate) beneficiaries of humanitarian protection, i.e. individuals and groups of individuals."[15] The greatest impetus toward an international rule of law arose from international human rights instruments adopted in the post–UN Charter period and the creation of international processes of state accountability. Protection of individuals assumed a prominent element of the law of war, with the interests of states and sovereignty being recognized as antagonistic to the ideals of human rights.

Three post–World War II documents—the Universal Declaration of Human Rights (UDHR),[16] the International Covenant on Civil and Political Rights (ICCPR),[17] and the International Covenant on Economic, Social, and Cultural Rights (ICESCR)[18]—articulate basic human rights entitlements and laid the bedrock for subsequent developments in international humanitarian law as well as in human rights. Post–World War II international instruments stimulated the development of human rights at the universal level and within regions.

The UDHR was adopted in 1948, seven months after the American Declaration of the Rights and Duties of Man was signed at the Inter-American Conference in Bogotá.[19] Two years later, the European Convention on the Protection of Human Rights and Fundamental Freedoms was signed by member states of the Council of Europe.[20] Two decades later, the Organization of American States adopted the American Convention on Human Rights, signed in 1969.[21] Despite the flurry of activity in other regions of the world, Africa lagged behind, still caught in an intoxicating mixture of newfound independence and the power of the sovereignty doctrine, which was routinely used but more often abused. It was not until the 1980s that African states shook off some of their early ultranationalism that had followed emancipation from imperial domination. In 1981 the African Charter on Human and Peoples' Rights was signed during a summit of the Organization of African Unity in Nairobi.[22]

Amid the groundswell of international and regional support for the centrality of human rights, in 1982 the UN General Assembly urged "states in areas where regional arrangements in the field of human rights do not yet exist to consider agreements with a view to the establishment within their respective regions of suitable regional machinery for the protection and promotion of human rights."[23] Matters such as the prohibition of torture and cruel, inhuman, or degrading treatment and punishment, arbitrary arrest and detention, and discrimination, as well as the guarantees of due process of law, became the focus of human rights and exercise vast influence on instruments of international humanitarian law.

The UDHR and other post-Charter human rights treaties and declarations created fertile ground for the Geneva Conventions adopted in 1949, which were reinforced by two Additional Protocols about three decades later in 1977. These key international humanitarian law instruments, later co-opted into international customary law, addressed the rights of individuals and populations. The Geneva Conventions represented a shift from the methods of warfare to the protection of the victims of war, leading to a preference for standards rather than rules. The reason for this change was largely pragmatic: the technology of war outpaced the ability of legislators to author effective prohibitions. Generalized standards that focused on the rights of classes of individuals (namely, civilians, prisoners of war, and sick or wounded combatants), rather than prophylactic prohibitions aimed at actions that are likely to cause excessive harm, were seen as less likely to become outdated as military technology rushed ahead.

The four Geneva Conventions marked a redefining moment in international humanitarian law, which was still dominated by the state-centric Hague Laws of the nineteenth century, whose deficiencies had been exposed by the two world wars. The 1949 Geneva Conventions mirrored international developments in the twentieth century. The significant developments were the shift of some state-to-state aspects of international humanitarian law to individual criminal responsibility, and a move away from the interests of states to the rights of individuals and populations—the primary victims of the world wars and a profusion of others. The Geneva Conventions and their subsequent Additional Protocols aimed to protect classes of war victims—wounded soldiers, prisoners of war, and civilians. "They did so not through bright-line identifications of prohibited actions, but through generalized standards designed to be flexible as to the context of the combat."[24] The focus of the Geneva Conventions is on groups of individuals, rather than on the conduct in which states may or may not engage. In practice, Geneva law guides the behavior of individual combatants, rather than the decisionmaking of heads of state and military commanders, and is more flexible across varying combat situations.

The article 1 common to the 1949 Geneva Conventions derived from the rejection of the classic doctrine of reciprocity and goes to the heart of accountability for violations of international humanitarian law. Although it may have been intended to address the obligations of a party to comply with and ensure respect for the Geneva Conventions by its entire civilian and military apparatus, and perhaps even by its entire population, article 1 has been interpreted as creating standing for states parties vis-à-vis violating states. Parties could therefore endeavor to bring a violating party back into compliance and thus promote universal application. To a large extent, these interpretations were triggered by the International Committee of the Red Cross's commentaries to the Geneva Conventions and the supportive literature generated by them.[25] Whether the parties must act jointly, or possibly take individual measures with respect to a violating state, is uncertain, as are the actions taken. Common article 2(3), also derived from the rejection of reciprocity, and providing for the application of the Geneva Conventions between parties, even if one of the belligerents is not a party to them, specifies that belligerents shall be bound by the Geneva Conventions in relation to the said power, if the latter accepts and applies the provisions thereof—that is, if that power accepts the Geneva Conventions only for that specific conflict.

The Geneva Conventions distinguish between international conflicts, as defined in common article 2, and conflicts not of an international character, under common article 3. Lower-intensity violence that does not rise to armed conflict is distinguished from noninternational armed conflicts to which the provisions of that article are applicable. The applicable thresholds, however, continually evolved in light of the conflicts being waged throughout the world. Guerrilla warfare became an important development. Civil wars proliferated, as did wars of liberation. What soon became apparent to the international community, as well as to the ICRC, was that humanitarian law had to be adapted to new and developing situations. Therefore, after much preparation on expert levels, the Swiss government, acting on a proposal by the ICRC, in 1974 convened a diplomatic conference for the reaffirmation and development of international humanitarian law, leading to the adoption of two Additional Protocols in 1977 to the 1949 Geneva Conventions. The Additional Protocols distinguish between international armed conflicts as defined in article 1 of Protocol I, noninternational armed conflicts[26] as defined in article 1 of Protocol II, and "situations of internal disturbances and tensions," which fall below the threshold of applicability of Protocol II.

The adoption of the Additional Protocols was an important stage in the codification of international humanitarian law. They completed the provisions of the Geneva Conventions and adapted humanitarian standards to present-day realities. They better protected individuals during armed conflicts by taking into account new battlefield realities, in particular the emergence of guerrilla warfare and technical advances in weapons technology. Such developments made it possible to extend the battlefield ad infinitum, causing tremendous risks to civilian populations.

The major breakthrough of Additional Protocol I was the progress achieved in rules for the conduct of hostilities. Contrary to the treatment of civilians in enemy hands, the authorized methods and means of warfare and the protection of the civilian population against the effects of hostilities had remained untouched since the Hague Conventions of 1907. The cornerstone, which stands for Protocol I's aim of better protecting the civilian population, is the principle of *distinction*.[27] In addition, Protocol I reaffirms and defines for the first time in a treaty the customary principle of *proportionality* in the conduct of hostilities.[28] It should be emphasized that there are other rules relating to methods and means of warfare, such as the prohibition of weapons and methods of warfare of a nature to cause superfluous injury, which protect not only civilian populations but also combatants.

Additional Protocol II is the first-ever universal treaty devoted exclusively to protecting the individual and restricting the use of force in noninternational armed conflicts, which constitute the majority of conflicts today. In this sense, Protocol II is a remarkable complement to common article 3 (common to all four Geneva Conventions), then the only provision applicable to such situations. Protocol II thus represents an important step in protecting the victims of civil wars.

The Geneva Conventions are often contrasted with the Hague Laws.[29] World War I saw many violations of the Hague Laws, including killing among civilian populations, bombing of nonmilitary targets, unnecessary destruction of private industry, sinking of merchant ships, and looting. The founding of the League of Nations, however, had shifted the focus of the international community from striving to regulate the conduct of war to more absolute prohibitions on waging war. Thus it was not until World War II that it was demonstrated that outright prohibitions on warfare were inadequate; the international community returned to regulating the conduct of war, regardless of the morality of the war itself. The nature of that regulation, however, began to diverge from Hague prohibitions.

The law of war has always operated on the assumption that its rules bind not only states but also their nationals.[30] Traditionally, violations of the laws and customs of war by soldiers could be prosecuted only by their national state or the captor state. Increasingly, violations of the laws and customs of war, genocide, and crimes against humanity are recognized as justifying third-country prosecution in accordance with the principle of *universal jurisdiction*.[31] Under the Geneva Conventions, all contracting parties have the duty either to prosecute or to extradite persons alleged to have committed or ordered grave breaches.

The traditional alternative to state-level enforcement of human rights and humanitarian norms has been the prosecution of individual violators within the national court systems. To the extent that actions were also a crime in the country where they occurred (e.g., murder), criminal as well as civil trials are, at least in theory, available remedies. But given the unwillingness of states to allow prosecution of their own for violations committed pursuant to state policy, national enforcement continues to be elusive.[32] This is aggravated by inadequacies inherent in many countries' judicial systems. Therefore, international enforcement of human rights through prosecution of individuals is a necessary response to the failings of state and national enforcement.

But international enforcement looked to creative means, including national prosecutions of offenders and the formation of permanent regional human rights courts. Regarding the first, given universal jurisdiction over human rights violations and personal jurisdiction through extradition or other means, violators may be prosecuted in the national criminal systems of third-party countries. (The case of Augusto Pinochet is a good example. The Chilean senator-for-life faced extradition from Great Britain to Spain for human rights abuses committed during his term as president.[33]) The increased prominence of international criminal law changed the focus in the enforcement of the law of war from scrutiny of state compliance to scrutiny of individual compliance. This trend began with the trial of war criminals at Nuremberg, continued in Tokyo, and remains today in international tribunals and permanent human rights courts. This scheme of individual criminalization has added a new layer to the deterrence of war crimes. The authors of humanitarian norms have geared rules toward individual compliance. Individuals who orchestrate massacres of civilian populations are indeed blameworthy, and such behavior can be more readily deterred. Such crimes are already criminal under national codes, and as the body of case law from international tribunals grows, individuals will be on notice regarding the types of actions that are prosecutable at the international level.

The creation of the two ad hoc international criminal tribunals and the adoption, in July 1998, of the Rome Statute of the International Criminal Court cemented this important change: individuals can be subject to international law. Violations of the laws of war, and of certain fundamental human rights, including those in the Geneva Conventions and other instruments, can now be prosecuted directly before international tribunals without the interposition of national law. This is an important advance, especially given the high standards of due process applied by international courts. The influence of international human rights in giving international humanitarian law content and contour is apparent: the norms that define crimes against humanity, as well as those stated in common article 3 of the 1949 Geneva Conventions, and some rules incorporated in the Rome Statute for noninternational armed conflicts, are indistinguishable from fundamental human rights. International humanitarian law/law of war and the corresponding institutions have thus become central to the protection of human rights.

A New Plank in International Enforcement: The Rise of NGOs

When governments met in 1945 to create the United Nations, human rights was a foremost concern. But even as human rights were elevated, UN governments faced the reality that individuals and private groups would have a role in addressing such a sensitive issue. The creation of the United Nations, with the explicit commitment to promoting human rights internationally, provided the environment to enable the NGO human rights movement to develop.

World War II changed state sovereignty, and support for international human rights laid the groundwork for a crucial shift. The drafting subcommittee at the San Francisco Conference in 1945 drafted a provision that eventually became article 71 of the United Nations Charter. This article authorizes the UN Economic and Social Council (ECOSOC) to establish an official relationship with NGOs, international and national, regarding all matters that have been entrusted to ECOSOC.[34]

The adoption of two international covenants, one on economic, social, and cultural rights, and one on civil and political rights, provided a common framework within which nongovernmental advocates could operate.

With the United Nations establishing international enforcement mechanisms and procedures, a forum emerged for independent human rights
advocates to present information about violations and to make the case for
stronger international action. Gradually, various United Nations bodies
stressed the need for the development of effective national institutions,
including nongovernmental advocacy groups, to advance human rights.

In the post–World War II era, the role of NGOs in promoting and protecting human rights expanded.[35] Empowerment within and outside the UN
system, especially in the field of human rights, paved the way for NGOs to
participate in the process of shaping human rights at the regional and universal levels. NGOs contribute to the evolution and efficacy of human
rights systems. In 1993 the international community yet again recognized
and confirmed the importance of NGOs at the Vienna World Conference on
Human Rights.[36]

This formal recognition, as well as the development of a dynamic international human rights regime, opened the international arena for NGOs.
First, NGOs are beneficiaries of rights granted by international instruments,
such as freedom of expression and freedom of association. Second, states
and intergovernmental organizations have invited NGOs to participate in
the implementation of human rights, and therefore they can defend the
rights of every individual. Even though states remain the main actors in
international affairs, the existence of an international movement for human
rights is evidence that the international community now has a private sec-
tor with legal recognition and international legitimacy.

States entering human rights agreements are obligated to enforce their
terms within their jurisdictions. Most international agreements containing
human rights standards provide for a mechanism to supervise the implementation of those standards.[37] Human rights treaties often contain a
reporting requirement, which means that states must report their progress in
implementing the agreement. State reports can be due periodically, or after
an ad hoc request of a treaty body. The degree of NGO involvement in state
reporting procedures is determined by the following variables: (1) the willingness of states to inform NGOs of their reporting activities and to let
them participate in the process; (2) the availability of state reports to
NGOs;[38] and (3) the extent to which the respective treaty body accepts
"alternative" reports presented by NGOs and makes use of information
provided by NGOs. The inclusion of NGOs in the process can be based on
explicit treaty language, or on the established practice of a treaty body.

NGO activities have been pivotal in protecting human rights, giving rise
to "soft control" of international human rights norms.[39] Rather than using a
formal mechanism under international law, international standards are used
as a tool to fight human rights abuses. Relying on the UDHR and other
instruments, such as the ICCPR and regional human rights conventions,

NGOs frequently remind states of their obligations and seek to hold them responsible by publicly disclosing human rights violations. Rising public awareness, fact-finding missions,[40] reporting, human rights education and publication, lobbying decisionmakers on the domestic and international level, legal assistance, and domestic human rights litigation—all are examples of this category.[41]

Nowhere is the centrality of nonstate entities more clear than in the International Committee of the Red Cross. The ICRC can be described as the "custodian" of the Geneva Conventions. It is mentioned approximately 100 times in the Geneva Conventions and Additional Protocols. The ICRC is obliged to exercise a range of tasks and functions; others are left to the discretion of the ICRC. The three categories of functions include: inspection; operation of an information and tracing agency; and cooperation in various domains, such as the designation of protecting powers, dissemination, and repatriation of wounded persons. The ICRC is specifically charged under the Geneva Conventions with controlling the way in which protected persons are treated. In carrying this out, the ICRC enjoys the same prerogatives as a protecting power, including the right to enter places where protected persons are held, whether they are at liberty or imprisoned, and to interview them without witnesses. Protected persons also have the right to address the ICRC directly. The ICRC can exercise supervision over the distribution of relief materials, regardless of the existence of a protecting power.

As for the evolution of nongovernmental human rights advocacy, we have seen creation and development of internationally focused NGOs.[42] The largest and most influential is Amnesty International, created in 1961. Amnesty International is respected and relied upon for information and leadership in the human rights field.[43] In 1977, barely two decades after its formation, Amnesty International was awarded the Nobel Prize.[44] Amnesty's ascendance reflected the influence and proliferation of NGOs focusing on humanitarian issues. Since its founding, Amnesty International has been joined by many other human rights NGOs, as well as monitoring and advocacy groups, in all regions.

Since the 1970s, many internationally focused NGOs have added their voices to the debate. These include the Lawyers Committee for Human Rights and Human Rights Watch, based in the United States, and Article 19 and Interights, based in England. Together with Amnesty International, these and other NGOs (e.g., the International Commission of Jurists, the Minority Rights Group, Index on Censorship, Physicians for Human Rights, and the International Federation for Human Rights) have focused international attention on human rights violations around the world. They also helped to shape and to invigorate the work of the United Nations and other intergovernmental bodies. By providing accurate, up-to-date information, and by being aggressive, creative, and ever-present advocates, they have helped to generate a more urgent and real confrontation of ongoing crises.[45]

The effective domestic implementation of humanitarian norms depends in large part on the development, institutional strength, and independence of human rights organizations. Their development is a key to orderly civil society, particularly for societies transitioning from authoritarian to participatory governments. NGOs frequently provide evidence to international monitoring organs and investigative commissions and appear before ad hoc international criminal tribunals. NGOs are thus an essential component in the drive to effective international enforcement of humanitarian norms. Their future in the process is assured with the recognition of their role in the Rome Statute. NGOs in the humanitarian field seek to hold governmental authorities accountable for their actions and serve as a source of support and protection for victims. They also serve an important educational function, informing communities of their rights and of the government's obligation to respect them.[46]

Conclusion

The Cold War era was a mixed bag for international humanitarian law. Advances were made in the codification and broadening of international humanitarian law, but East-West rivalries prevented real enforcement at the international level. States did not achieve much in this context as they came to view international humanitarian law with some cynicism. The East-West rivalry cast a shadow over the application of international humanitarian law in conflicts. International criminal prosecutions did not occur between 1946 and 1993, largely because the structure of the international system after 1945 made consensus impossible on the prosecution of criminal acts by any party. In that bipolar international system, either the United States or the Soviet Union was bound to object to attempts to impose criminal liabilities and even block such attempts through the veto in the UN Security Council.

Fundamentally, international law affects the jurisdiction of states, but there is also an interest in the conduct of the state toward individuals. The internationalization of the legal status of the human being, begun after World War I, became one of the most prominent features of the post–World War II period.[47] A contradiction in the Cold War thus appeared. International law continued to pursue its original, and still topical, ambition: to regulate relations among states in international affairs while tending to defer more and more to states in domestic affairs. This interpenetration between international and national affairs, against the background of superpower rivalry, is a characteristic feature of contemporary international law.

The end of the Cold War led to more vigorous activity within the United Nations. States, chastened by past failures to enforce international humanitarian law, conscious of public revulsion toward gross violations, and seeing the inability of the international community to rectify human rights atrocities, were more responsive to initiatives. The breakdown of bipolarity, and the emerging importance of multilateralism, led the UN Security Council to create the criminal tribunals for the former Yugoslavia and Rwanda under Chapter VII powers.[48] This international consensus sought to legitimize the international exercise of adjudicative power and strengthen deterrence, both sorely lacking during the Cold War.

Next we look at the post–Cold War era and analyze in depth the ad hoc tribunals, important milestones in the international system. They have and will continue to make important contributions to the structure of the international system and to the substance of international humanitarian law. Nevertheless, the reality is that the tribunals symbolized the failures of the international community.

Notes

1. Charles W. Kegley Jr. and Eugene Wittkopf, *World Politics: Trend and Transformation*, 5th ed. (New York: St. Martin's, 1995), 87.

2. Commenting on the genesis of the Cold War, Kegley Jr. and Wittkopf (ibid.) note that:

> As World War II drew to a close in 1945, it became increasingly apparent that a new era of international politics was dawning. World War II, like all previous great-power wars, paved the way for a New World Order. Planning by the Allies for a new postwar structure of peace had begun even as the war raged. As early as 1943 the Four-Power Declaration advanced principles for allied collaboration in "the period following the end of hostilities." The product of the Allies' determination to create a new international organization to manage the postwar international order—the United Nations—was conceived in this and other wartime agreements. Consistent with the expectation that the great powers would cooperate to manage world affairs, China was promised a seat on the United Nations Security Council along with France and the Big Three. The purpose was to guarantee that all of the dominant States would share responsibility for keeping the peace.

3. J. H. Gaddis, *The United States and the Origins of the Cold War* (New York: Columbia University Press, 1972); Arthur Schlesinger Jr., *The Cycles of American History* (London: Penguin Books, 1986); Richard A. Melanson, *Writing History and Making Policy: The Cold War, Vietnam, and Revisionism* (Lanham, MD: University Press of America, 1983).

4. Robert W. Tucker, "1989 and All That," *Foreign Affairs* 69 (1990): 93–114.

5. The Cold War was in part an extension of the superpowers' mutual disdain for the other's political system and way of life. These ideological differences were to translate into political disputes. The Cold War was a conflict not only between

two powerful states but also between two different social systems. Whether real or imagined, U.S. fears of Marxism stimulated the emergence of anticommunism as a U.S. counterideology. Accordingly, the United States embarked on a missionary crusade of its own, dedicated to containing and expunging the despised atheistic communist menace from the face of the earth. Similarly, Soviet policy was fueled by the belief that capitalism could not coexist in the long run with communism since the two systems were incompatible. See for example Robert Jervis, "Will the World Be Better?" in *Soviet-American Relations After the Cold War,* edited by Robert Jervis and Seweryn Bialer (Durham, NC: Duke University Press, 1991), 10; Henry S. Commager, "Misconceptions Governing American Foreign Policy," in *Perspectives on American Foreign Policy,* edited by Charles W. Kegley Jr. and Eugene R. Wittkopf (New York: St. Martin's, 1989), 10; Lloyd C. Gardner, *Architects of Illusion: Men and Ideas in American Foreign Policy* (Chicago: Quadrangle Books, 1970); Michael Parenti, *The Anti-Communist Impulse* (New York: Random House, 1969); Kegley Jr. and Wittkopf, *World Politics: Trends and Transformation,* 89.

6. J. H. Gaddis, "Containment: Its Past and Future," in Kegley Jr. and Wittkopf, *Perspectives on American Foreign Policy,* 16–31.

7. See for example I. E. Korovin, "Respect for Sovereignty: An Unchanging Principle of Soviet Foreign Policy," *International Affairs* (Moscow) (1956): 11, 32, 37–39.

8. See Geneva Convention for the Amelioration of the Condition of the Wounded and Sick in Armed Forces in the Field, 12 August 1949, 75 U.N.T.S. 31 (Geneva Convention I); Geneva Convention for the Amelioration of the Condition of Wounded, Sick and Shipwrecked Members of Armed Forces at Sea, 12 August 1949, 75 U.N.T.S. 85 (Geneva Convention II); Geneva Convention Relative to the Treatment of Prisoners of War, 12 August 1949, 75 U.N.T.S. 135 (Geneva Convention III); Geneva Convention Relative to the Treatment of Prisoners of War, 12 August 1949, 75 U.N.T.S. 287 (Geneva Convention IV).

9. For a general overview of these cases, see Gerry Simpson, "Didactic and Dissident Stories in War Crimes Trials," *Alberta Law Review* 60 (1997): 801.

10. UN Charter, preamble, arts. 1(3), 13(1)(b), 55(c), 62(2), 68, and 17(c).

11. See for example *Report of the Secretary-General on Respect for Human Rights in Armed Conflicts,* UN Doc. A/7720 (1969).

12. Theodor Meron, "The Humanization of Humanitarian Law," *American Journal of International Law* 94 (2000): 239, 247.

13. See Daniel O'Donnell, "Trends in the Application of International Humanitarian Law by United Nations Human Rights Mechanisms," *International Review of the Red Cross* 324 (September 1998): 481, 482–483 (citing UN Doc. E/CN4/1993/45, para. 113; UN Doc. E/CN.4/1994/58, paras. 112–116).

14. See Louise Doswald-Beck, "Implementation of International Humanitarian Law in Future Wars," *Naval War College Review* 52 (1998): 24, 32–33.

15. Georges Abi-Saab, "The Specificities of Humanitarian Law," in *Studies and Essays on International Humanitarian Law and Red Cross Principles in Honour of Jean Pictet,* edited by Christophe Swinarski (Genève: Comité international de la Croix-Rouge; La Haye: Nijhoff, 1984), 265, 269.

16. GA Res. 217, UN GAOR, 3rd sess., part 1, UN Doc. A/810 (1948).

17. International Covenant on Civil and Political Rights, 16 December 1966, 999 U.N.T.S. 171.

18. International Covenant on Economic, Social, and Cultural Rights, 16 December 1966, 993 U.N.T.S. 3.

19. See generally Philip Alston, ed., *The United Nations and Human Rights: A Critical Appraisal* (Oxford: Clarendon, 1992).

20. The European Convention on the Protection of Human Rights and Fundamental Freedoms, 4 November 1950, 213 U.N.T.S. 221, ETS no. 5 (European Convention).

21. The American Convention on Human Rights (Pact of San José), OAS Off. Rec. OEA/Ser.K/XVI/1.1, doc.65, rev1, corr. 2 (1970), reprinted in 9 I.L.M. 673.

22. African Charter on Human and Peoples' Rights, 27 June 1981, O.A.U. Doc. CAB/LEG/67/3/Rev5 (1981), reprinted in 21 I.L.M. 59, entered into force 21 October 1986 (African Charter; also referred to as the "Banjul Charter," because the ministers of justice of the Organization of African Unity had agreed on the text of the charter during two meetings in Banjul, Gambia, prior to the Nairobi summit in 1981).

23. G. A. Res. 32/127 of 15 December 1977, quoted in Henry J. Steiner and Philip Alston, *International Human Rights in Context* (Oxford: Oxford University Press, 1996), 564. The international community has recently reaffirmed its esteem for the protection of human rights on the regional level in para. 37 of the Vienna Declaration and Programme of Action, UN Doc. A/CONF157/24 (1993), reprinted in 31 I.L.M. 1661:

> Regional arrangements play a fundamental role in promoting and protecting human rights. They should reinforce universal human rights standards, as contained in international human rights instruments, and their protection. The World Conference on Human Rights endorses efforts under way to strengthen these arrangements and to increase their effectiveness, while in the same time stressing the importance of cooperation with the United Nations human rights activities. The World Conference on Human Rights reiterates the need to consider the possibility of establishing regional and sub-regional arrangements for the promotion and protection of human rights where they do not already exist.

24. Meron, "The Humanization of Humanitarian Law."

25. See Oscar M. Uhler and Henri Coursier, eds., *ICRC Commentary on the Geneva Convention (IV) Relative to the Protection of Civilian Persons in Time of War* (Geneva: International Committee of the Red Cross, 1958), 16; see also Jean S. Pictet, ed., *ICRC Commentary on the Geneva Convention (I) for the Amelioration of the Condition of the Wounded and Sick in Armed Forces in the Field* (Geneva: International Committee of the Red Cross, 1952), 26; Theodor Meron, *Human Rights and Humanitarian Norms as Customary Law* (Oxford: Clarendon, 1989), 27–30. For influential supportive literature, see especially Luigi Condorelli and Laurence Boisson de Chazournes, Quelques, "Remarques à propos de l'obligation des Etats de 'respecter et faire respecter' le droit international humanitaire 'en toutes circonstances,'" in Swinarski, ed., *Studies and Essays;* and Georges Abi-Saab, "The Specificities of Humanitarian Law," in Swinarski, ed., *Studies and Essays.*

26. Article 1 of Protocol II defines such conflicts as those "which take place in the territory of a [state] between its armed forces and dissident armed forces or other organized armed groups which, under responsible command, exercise such control over a part of its territory as to enable them to carry out sustained and concerted military operations and to implement this Protocol."

27. This principle requires that the parties to the conflict distinguish at all times between the civilian population and combatants and between civilian objectives and military objectives.

28. By this principle attacks on lawful targets remain lawful only if the incidental casualties or damages are not excessive.

29. 1949 Geneva Conventions; see also Protocol Additional (I) to the Geneva Conventions of 12 August 1949, and Relating to the Protection of Victims of International Armed Conflicts, 8 June 1977, 1125 U.N.T.S. 3; Protocol Additional (II) to the Geneva Conventions of 12 August 1949, and Relating to the Protection of Victims of Non-International Armed Conflicts, 8 June 1977, 1125 U.N.T.S. 609.

30. See Lassa Oppenheim, *International Law: A Treatise*, edited by Hersch Lauterpacht, 8th ed., vol. 1 (London: Longman, 1955), 341.

31. See Theodor Meron, *War Crimes Law Comes of Age: Essays* (Oxford: Clarendon, 1998), chap. 13.

32. See Steven R. Ratner, "New Democracies, Old Atrocities: An Inquiry in International Law," *Georgia Law Journal* 87 (1999): 707, 727. Problematic in this area has been the adoption of amnesty laws by many countries, including Uruguay, Chile, Argentina, Mozambique, Brazil, Peru, Honduras, Nicaragua, Haiti, Ivory Coast, Angola, Togo, and Cambodia, in an attempt to secure governmental stability during the transition to democracy. States like these, with dubious human rights pasts, have chosen to forgo domestic prosecution of human rights violations in the trade of peace for amnesty. See ibid.

33. See *Regina v. Bartle and the Commissioner of Police for the Metropolis and Others Ex Parte Pinochet, Regina v. Evans and the Commissioner of Police for the Metropolis and others Ex Parte Pinochet,* House of Lords, 25 November 1998.

34. See Bruno Simma, *The Charter of the United Nations: A Commentary* (Oxford: Oxford University Press, 1995), 902–904.

35. See generally Steiner and Alston, *International Human Rights in Context,* 456–499; Asbjorn Eide, *The Human Rights Movement and the Transformation of the International Order, XI Alternatives* (Oslo: Norwegian University Press, 1986), 367; Felix Ermacora, *"Non-Governmental Organizations as Promoters of Human Rights,"* in *Protecting Human Rights: The European Dimension,* edited by Franz Matscher and Herbert Petzold (Köln: Heymanns, 1988), 171; Hurst Hannum, "Implementing Human Rights: An Overview of Strategies and Procedures," in *Guide to International Human Rights Practice,* edited by Hurst Hannum, 2nd ed. (Philadelphia: University of Pennsylvania Press, 1992), 19; Nigel S. Rodley, "The Work of Non-Governmental Organizations in the World-wide Promotion and Protection of Human Rights," *UN Bulletin of Human Rights* 90/1 (1991): 84.

36. See generally Manfred Nowak, ed., *World Conference on Human Rights, Vienna, June 1993: The Contributions of NGOs; Reports and Documents* (Wien: Manzsche Verlags-und Universitätsbuchhandlung, 1994). See also the "Vienna Declaration and Programme of Action," UN Doc. A/CONF157/24 (1993), reprinted in 32 I.L.M. 1661.

37. ECOSOC Res. 1996/31, UN Doc. E/1996/L.25, was adopted at the 49th plenary meeting of the Council on 25 July 1996. ECOSOC Res. 1296 (XLIV) of 23 May 1968, "Arrangements for Consultation with Non-Governmental Organizations," ESCOR (XLIV), Supp. no. 1, 21.

38. For example, the Convention on the Rights of the Child, UN G.A. Doc. A/Res/44/25 (1989), contains provisions giving NGOs a role in its implementation. Article 44(6) of the convention obliges states parties to make their periodic report under the convention "widely available to the public in their own countries." Another example is Article 23(2) of the ILO Constitution, which requires states to send copies of their reports to the most representative employers' and workers' organizations.

39. Mario Bettati, "La contribution des organisations non-gouvernementales à la formation et à l'application des normes internationales," in *Les O.N.G. et le Droit International*, edited by Mario Bettati and Pierre-Marie Dupuy (Paris: Economica, 1986), 64.

40. See generally Diane Orentlicher, "Bearing Witness: The Art and Science of Human Rights Fact-Finding," *Harvard Human Rights Journal* 3 (1990): 83.

41. See generally David Weissbrodt, "The Contribution of International Non-governmental Organisations to the Protection of Human Rights," in *Human Rights in International Law*, edited by Theodor Meron (Oxford: Clarendon, 1984).

42. Jerome J. Shestack, "Sisyphus Endures: The International Human Rights NGO," *New York Law School Law Review* 24 (1978): 89, 90.

43. See Harry M. Scoble and Laurie S. Wiseberg, "Human Rights and Amnesty International," in *Annals of the American Academy of Political and Social Science* (1974): 11.

44. See Amnesty International, *The Amnesty International Handbook*, 7th ed. (Claremont, CA: Hunter House, 1991), 115.

45. David Weissbrodt, "The Contribution of International Nongovernmental Organizations to the Protection of Human Rights," in *Human Rights in International Law: Legal and Policy Issues*, edited by Theodor Meron (Oxford: Clarendon Press, 1984), 403; David Weissbrodt, "The Role of International Nongovernmental Organizations in the Implementation of Human Rights," *Texas International Law Journal* 12 (1977): 279, 293.

46. Lawyers Committee for Human Rights, *Shackling the Defenders: Legal Restrictions on Independent Human Rights Advocacy* (New York: Lawyers Committee for Human Rights, 1994).

47. Mohammed Bedjaoui, *International Law: Achievements and Prospects* (Paris: UNESCO, 1991), 13.

48. UN Charter, art. 39 ("the Security Council shall determine the existence of any threat to the peace, breach of the peace or act of aggression and shall make recommendations, or decide what measures shall be taken to maintain or restore international peace and security").

5

Crisis in the Balkans:
Raising the Nuremberg Precedent

The end of the Cold War, a conflict that had paralyzed the United Nations from its inception, was cause for celebration and hope. In the early 1990s, while Western leaders were still congratulating themselves over the end of communism and the fall of the Soviet empire, the security structure that helped bring about those events began to fall apart. Less than two years after the fall of the Berlin Wall, the structure of international law seemed to be crumbling. Following the historic January 1992 summit meeting of the Security Council, then–Secretary-General Boutros Boutros-Ghali spoke of a growing conviction "among nations large and small, that an opportunity has been regained to achieve the great objectives of the UN Charter—a United Nations capable of maintaining international peace and security, of securing justice and human rights and of promoting, in the words of the Charter, 'social progress and better standards of life in larger freedom.'"[1] Even as this optimistic mission statement was being made, the Balkans had erupted into a theater of war, and Rwanda's genocide was in the offing. It took a war in Europe—Croatia 1991—to stir public interest. The war in Bosnia-Herzegovina (1992) and the Rwandan genocide (1994) amplified the alarm, though it had been sounded earlier.[2]

The International Criminal Tribunal for the Former Yugoslavia (officially, the International Tribunal for the Prosecution of Persons Responsible for Serious Violations of International Humanitarian Law Committed in the Territory of the Former Yugoslavia Since 1991) was established by the UN Security Council in May 1993. In an unprecedented decision by the Security Council, the ICTY was established as an enforcement measure pursuant to Chapter VII of the UN Charter.[3] Its creation was prompted by two considerations. First, by 1993 it had become obvious that the parties to the Yugoslav conflict were unwilling, and in the case of Bosnia-Herzegovina unable, to bring to justice persons responsible for the crimes that were taking place. Second, by establishing the tribunal, the Security Council hoped to deflect criticism for its reluctance to take more decisive action to stop the bloodshed in the former Yugoslavia. In political and legal terms, the Council's action was groundbreaking. With the Cold War over, and with it the crumbling of the ideological barrier between East and West, it became possible for the Security Council to reach agreement on a measure that would have been unthinkable only four years earlier.[4]

Brutal wars are, of course, not new, and there were conflicts prior to Yugoslavia's dissolution that could have as equally justified the establishment of war crimes tribunals. The persecutions committed in Cambodia under Pol Pot, to cite one example, did inspire talk of establishing a criminal tribunal, but not until the summer of 1997.[5] Similarly, in the aftermath of the Gulf War world leaders clamored for Saddam Hussein's trial by an international war crimes tribunal. But that chance was lost when the Coalition chose not to pursue Saddam and his henchmen in Baghdad for the Iraqi violations of human rights in Kuwait.

Anne Bodley poses the question, "Why, then, did the international community react so strongly to the conflict in the former Yugoslavia?"[6] In answering this critical question she sets out the following premises:

> There are various possible reasons for the reaction. First, there is the resemblance of the Serb-run detention camps to Nazi Germany, with recollections of establishing the Nuremberg Tribunal following the war. Second, widespread media coverage focused attention on the atrocities being committed in the region and the repeated failure of the international community to induce a negotiated peace between the warring parties. A third possible reason is political—with the collapse of the Cold War and renewed interaction among the Security Council members individually, there was new willpower, as well as the ability to effect political change [by a United Nations keen to carve out a much broader role by acting as a watchdog over international disputes, peacemaker, and peacekeeper].[7]

Not without controversy, the international community, with the Security Council in the lead, decided that establishing a tribunal to prosecute crimes committed in the former Yugoslavia was a worthy precedent, even if doing so subjugated the sovereignty of states involved. Although the ICTY was welcomed, its legal basis was not, owing to considerations of state sovereignty. But in the end the international outrage generated by the Balkan conflict prevailed, with no state (except the Yugoslav republics) bold enough to object.

The ICTY marks the beginning of genuine implementation of international humanitarian law and the return to the model of Nuremberg. In the Cold War era, national prosecutions supplanted this model. This chapter seeks to show that even this ad hoc tribunal was the by-product of international realpolitik. It was born out of a political desire to redeem the international community's conscience rather than the primary commitment of the international community to guarantee international justice. The ICTY was not established because of the intrinsic value of punishing war criminals or of upholding the rule of law; rather, it came about as a result of the mobilization of NGOs.[8]

To appreciate the significance of realpolitik in the run-up to the ICTY's establishment, the next section reviews the Balkans' transformation into a theater of war and the subsequent establishment of the first international criminal tribunal since Nuremberg and Tokyo.

Death of a State:
The Dissolution of the Yugoslav Federation

Prior to its dissolution in 1991, Yugoslavia was not so much a melting pot as a boiling cauldron of ethnic tension with a deep history.[9] Yugoslavia's troubled history stretches back to 1918, when it was created as a state from the kingdoms of Serbia and Montenegro, as well as portions of the defunct Austro-Hungarian Empire. It was known as the State of Serbs, Croats, and Slovenes until it was renamed Yugoslavia in 1929 and, in 1974, the Socialist Federal Republic of Yugoslavia.[10]

The rebirth of Yugoslavia as a federal state, including its structure and composition prior to dissolution in 1991, dates to World War II. During that war, resistance to the Axis occupation of Yugoslavia came from the Communist partisan forces, led by Croatian-born Josip Broz Tito. With the support of the Allies, Tito's partisans eventually triumphed. Tito suppressed resurgent nationalist ambitions of ethnic groups consistently during his rule from 1946 until his death. Tito's death on 4 May 1980 and the collapse of the Soviet threat in the late 1980s unleashed the festering forces that would lead to Yugoslavia's disintegration.[11]

With Tito's demise, the country was now ruled by a hopelessly inefficient collective presidency that Tito had devised, comprising representatives from each of the six republics and the two autonomous regions. With no leader possessed of Tito's charismatic authoritarianism, Serb nationalists, many of them Communist Party members, began grumbling forcefully that Tito's national policy was designed to fragment Yugoslavia, dilute Serb dominance, and make it easier for Tito to rule unchallenged.[12] Not long after Serb nationalistic sentiment gathered momentum, individual republics, ever resentful of the might of Serbia, began to agitate for greater autonomy from the central government, heralding the beginning of virulent nationalism.

In 1987 Slobodan Milosevic rose to power in Serbia on a wave of crude, nationalistic rhetoric.[13] Though possessing Tito's determination to rule unchallenged, he lacked Tito's personal authority and mastery at balancing ethnic interests and thus maintaining the delicate ethnic balance in the federation. His initial goal of taking over Tito's creation appeared increasingly impossible as the cauldron of ethnic hatreds among Croats, Serbs, Bosnian Muslims, and Slovenes transformed into nationalistic fervor among the respective republics. Late in 1989, with growing nationalism in the various Yugoslav republics, Milosevic decided that in the event of the breakup of Yugoslavia he would endeavor to win most of it for himself. Thus was born the idea of Greater Serbia.[14]

Slovenia delivered the first blow to the federation. In a referendum on the question of secession from Yugoslavia, held in December 1990, an overwhelming majority of Slovenian voters opted for independence. A declaration of independence was announced on 8 May 1991, followed by the necessary amendments to the operative constitutional law on 25 June. In a bid to force the Slovenes to rescind the declaration of independence, Milosevic, the Serb president, ordered the invasion of Slovenia by the Yugoslav National Army (JNA).[15] The Yugoslav-Slovene war, the first in a series in the crumbling federation of Yugoslavian states, started on 27 June. Within seventy-two hours, a "troika" of European Community (EC) foreign ministers (from Italy, Luxembourg, and the Netherlands) mounted two missions to Yugoslavia.[16] The EC negotiators received repeated promises of cease-fires, but violence continued as federal troops consolidated their positions in Slovenia. After several failed cease-fires, a political settlement was reached via the so-called Brioni Agreement effectively awarding Slovenia its independence. The Yugoslav-Slovene war was short, even negligible compared to what came next.[17] Within ten days, after light casualties and the negotiation of the Brioni Agreement, Milosevic ordered the JNA to withdraw. The secession of Slovenia from the Federal Republic of Yugoslavia opened the door to other secessionist claims, leading to territorial disputes among the ethnic and religious groups of Yugoslavia and reviving determination to settle old scores.[18]

Amid the unfolding drama in Slovenia, Croats living in the Republic of Croatia declared independence from the rump Federation of Yugoslavia on 16 March 1991. Shortly after Croatia's declaration, the Serb-dominated JNA stormed Croatian territory in an attempt to crush the Croats' bid for independence. This act of aggression, spurred by Communist-run Serbia's quest for all of Yugoslavia's 8.3 million Serbs to live in a Greater Serbia,[19] launched the Serb-Croat war, the second in the series of conflicts that would decimate the Balkans. Unlike Slovenia, which had almost no Serbs, Croatia had a large Serb population, and Milosevic was determined to secure all territory inhabited by Serbs for Greater Serbia, hence the invasion by a Yugoslav National Army that had now become a Serb army fighting for Serbs.

Neither the EC nor the Council for Co-operation and Security in Europe (CSCE, the security arm of the EC) was prepared for the crisis resulting from the Serb invasion of Croatia. Members of the EC were about to start the final phase of negotiations leading up to the Maastricht summit of December 1991. The strengthening of EC cooperation in foreign policy and the transformation of cooperation into a common foreign policy led to controversy over what sort of international response was permissible with or without consent of the parties involved in the conflict. Milosevic insisted on noninterference as Europe discussed military intervention in the summer of 1991, and he had considerable support among, for example, many third world countries.[20] A rather confusing debate concerning the meaning of article 2(7) of the UN Charter—the principle of nonintervention—delayed and weakened the initial response. Couple this with the fact that the CSCE was transforming from a mechanism to maintain crisis stability in Cold War Europe to a standing organization offering procedures akin to collective security within Europe. This meant that the regional effort was hamstrung by lack of concrete ideas on how best to react.[21] The Soviet Union, concerned about the precedent that UN intervention would set for future conflicts in Yugoslavia, insisted on noninterference. Even the UN Secretary-General was skeptical; he argued that this was an internal matter. At this time many officials were suggesting that the violence could degenerate into civil war if not immediately suppressed, and that establishing a peacekeeping force in the region was the best chance to prevent open war.[22] Despite these warnings, the Secretary-General's hands-off decision was likely prompted by the belief that UN action in this vein would be vetoed by the Soviet Union.[23]

As violence in Croatia escalated over the next several months, the European Community assumed a monitoring and negotiating role in an effort to bring peace to the region and prevent all-out war in the Yugoslav federation.[24] The European Community Monitor Mission (ECMM), comprising personnel from the twelve EC members, was a channel of communication between the opposing forces to arrange cease-fires.[25] However, the attempt proved futile;[26] cease-fires failed to take hold, and violence increased in Croatia due to active support of the Croatian-Serb militia by the JNA.[27] The EC's efforts were plagued by irreconcilable demands, conflicting chains of command, dissension over the withdrawal of armed forces, and security considerations with respect to the nonmilitary, unarmed ECMM.[28] As regional negotiations undertaken in conformity with Chapter VIII of the UN Charter[29] failed to restore peace, the UN Security Council responded to calls for reinforcement of the ECMM by convening its first meeting to assess the situation on 25 September 1991, four months after Croatia's declaration of independence.[30]

International Response Through Political Process: Fudging the Problem

There were never any easy options for the former Yugoslavia. The war challenged norms and principles among concerned governments outside the bounds of the classic, strategic threat. The use of armed force, even collectively, to influence the conflict was therefore likely to generate contradictory pressures and unsatisfactory results. From the initial stages, the major actors had varying inclinations or interests, and this created tensions in the regional organizations as well as in the UN.[31] The result was disaster. Support for maintaining the unity and territorial integrity of Yugoslavia worsened the situation, delaying international pressure on the Serbs "to undertake timely reform toward a loose confederation while intensifying internal pressures for a complete break-up."[32]

As the EC was the only organization involved firsthand in the developing crisis, it should have apprised the international community that the dissolution of Yugoslavia was inevitable, and that appeals to preserve unity were reinforcing the Serb-dominated government and army's efforts to quash the republics' independence.[33] The initial EC policy, keeping Yugoslavia together, was replaced by attempts at compromise solutions, which meant redrawing frontiers. But that approach failed in light of the parties' unwillingness to compromise on territory.[34] Adding to the problem was that some European states prematurely recognized the independence of some of the breakaway states, and Europeans kept the UN out of Yugoslavia during the early stages. The EC's year-long solo efforts proved inadequate to negotiate a political settlement. And though the commitment of the EC to handle the crisis was meritorious, it was not realistic. The nature of the dispute simply did not lend itself to simple negotiation of a solution.[35] The United States, still involved in the Persian Gulf, insisted on the logic of the UN Charter and thus felt that the UN had no role to play unless regional attempts failed.

The initial, ambivalent Security Council resolutions, which sided with or punished the Serbs, also undermined any efforts that depended on cooperation.[36] In its first action, the Security Council displayed an incomplete understanding of the crisis. At its first meeting to address the crisis, the Council unanimously adopted Resolution 713, expressing "deep concern" over the fighting in Yugoslavia, the heavy loss of life, and in particular the consequences for the border areas of neighboring countries.[37] As a remedy, the resolution called for the immediate implementation of a complete embargo on all deliveries of weapons and military equipment to Yugoslavia.[38] Although meant to curb the escalating violence and to cut off weapons supply to the factions, the Council's action instead tipped the balance of power. It solidified the Serbs' military advantage, with control over most of the country's armaments and the federal army, as well as its position as the world's tenth largest arms producer.[39] This exacerbated the crisis, enabling the Serbs to overpower Croats and Muslims. The arms embargo neither deterred the fighting nor quenched animosity; rather, it fueled Bosnian Muslims' resentment toward the UN's approach, for they saw it as removing their ability to defend themselves.

After the EC-brokered cease-fires collapsed one after another, the UN appointed Cyrus R. Vance, former U.S. secretary of state, as the Secretary-General's personal envoy to Yugoslavia.[40] Stepping in amid the EC-sponsored peace process and the tenth failed cease-fire in three months, Vance commenced a fact-finding mission in Yugoslavia to sound out the parties on prospects for future negotiations.[41] Although the Security Council did not act during the next two months, Vance maintained an active role at the request of the Secretary-General.[42] Embarking on two subsequent missions to Yugoslavia in October and November 1991, Vance evaluated the feasibility of deploying a UN peacekeeping operation in Yugoslavia and arranged yet another cease-fire.[43] In Resolution 721, the Council endorsed Vance's efforts, although it would not consider a peacekeeping operation until the warring parties complied with previous agreements.[44] Vance's efforts were targeted exclusively at ending the Serb-Croat war, despite signs that the theater of war was likely to expand as other states clamored for independence.

In response to the so-called Vance Plan, the UN in January 1992 passed Resolution 749, which authorized the full deployment of the United Nations Protection Force (UNPROFOR), which was to be deployed in three UN Protected Areas. The Vance Plan defined UN peacekeeping in Yugoslavia as an interim operation to create conditions for the negotiation of an overall settlement. With UNPROFOR's establishment, the Security Council primarily focused its efforts on the ground, enforcing, expanding, and reinforcing UNPROFOR's mandate to create the right conditions for peace and security. The UN made no attempts to coordinate with the EC's mediation efforts. This disjointed approach, with the UN concentrating on peacekeeping while the EC struggled toward peacemaking, resulted in "a host of mutually incompatible and haphazardly constructed policies," which doomed both operations to failure.[45]

On 3 March 1992, about two months after the deployment of UNPROFOR in Croatia, Bosnia declared itself an independent nation after a referendum in which 63 percent voted for an independent republic. Backed by Belgrade, Bosnian Serbs demanded that the Bosnian government, headed by President Alija Izetbegovic, withdraw its declaration of independence. Within a few days of the demand and refusal of the Bosnian government to withdraw the declaration, the Bosnian-Serb nationalist militia, including some soldiers from the JNA, invaded parts of Bosnia-Herzegovina. Under Serbian Democratic

Party leader Radovan Karadzic,[46] the Serb Republic was proclaimed, with its administrative center in Pale. Well-armed Serbian militias were able to occupy, at some points, 70 percent of Bosnian territory. The Serb leaders carried out a policy of ethnic cleansing in an attempt to rid the occupied territories of Bosnian Muslims; this included widespread massacres, other serious violations of human rights and humanitarian law, and mass deportations of Muslim civilians.[47]

In June 1992, as the conflict intensified, the Security Council attempted to stem the escalating violence and facilitate humanitarian assistance,[48] enlarging UNPROFOR's mandate and strength to secure the airport at Sarajevo and to deliver humanitarian assistance to that city and its environs. However, the Council deferred to the European Community, urging the three communities in Bosnia to participate in its ongoing discussions.[49] Thus, the EC, acting under the auspices of the Conference on Yugoslavia since September 1991, continued talks with the three factions to achieve a settlement and negotiate constitutional arrangements for Bosnia-Herzegovina. Because the Vance Plan, proposed in the midst of the Serb-Croat conflict, primarily dealt with the facilitation of UNPROFOR for Croatia, the Council made only sporadic mention of the plan in the months following its endorsement.[50] U.S. and EC recognition of the republic's independence deepened mistrust and animosity, complicating the scenario even further.

Over a year after conflict erupted in the former Yugoslavia, the International Conference on the Former Yugoslavia (the London Conference), successor to the Conference on Yugoslavia, refreshed the peace process by building new diplomatic machinery. Secretary-General Boutros Boutros-Ghali, anticipating that the London Conference would "create a new momentum,"[51] remained in continuous sessions until a final settlement was reached.[52] The London Conference combined an unprecedented coalition of the United Nations and the European Community "to deal with a situation fraught with danger for international peace and security."[53] EC envoy Lord David Owen entered the negotiating scene as cochair of the Steering Committee of the London Conference,[54] forming a joint effort with UN representative Cyrus Vance. Owen was charged with forging the EC's efforts through the Conference on Yugoslavia and heading up the UN activities to prepare the basis for a general settlement.[55]

Vance and Owen's assignment was reconciling the views of the Muslims, Croats, and Serbs on the future of Bosnia-Herzegovina.[56] Thus, Vance and Owen embarked on achieving a comprehensive list of demands that seemed unrealistic. Widespread support for the Vance-Owen Plan for Bosnia-Herzegovina rose from the ashes of the failed EC-UN efforts. As the situation spiraled out of control, the UN defended the Vance-Owen agenda of diplomacy and conciliation as the best hope. The UN thus allowed the peace process to become the scapegoat, hoping to divert attention from its own mishandling of this major threat to peace on the European continent.

Beyond Politics?
Reawakening the International Penal Process

Over the next several months, the situation in Bosnia-Herzegovina deteriorated. The Security Council's already shaky peacekeeping and humanitarian efforts were threatened by reports of widespread violations of international humanitarian law, the Serbs' continued mass forcible expulsion and deportation of Bosnian Muslims in the region,[57] the imprisonment and abuse of civilians in detention centers, and the wanton devastation and destruction of property.[58] The full extent of the atrocities had yet to unfold:

> In the summer of 1992 . . . the world learned of mass forced population transfers of Muslims in convoys of cattle trucks; of organized massacres and the physical destruction of whole towns, including more than one thousand major historical, religious and cultural monuments throughout Bosnia and Croatia; of the systematic and repeated rape of as many as 20,000 Muslim women and young girls; and of the existence of over four hundred Serb-run detention centers where tens of thousands of Bosnian Muslims were being tortured and killed in a manner reminiscent of the Nazi-run concentration camps of World War II. While most of these atrocities were being committed by Serb forces, the reports clearly indicated that all parties to the conflict had committed abuses against other ethnic groups.[59]

In response to the deteriorating human rights situation, the UN Commission on Human Rights was called into its first-ever special session, during which it adopted resolution 1992/S-1/1 on 14 August 1992, requesting the chairman of the commission to appoint a special rapporteur "to investigate first hand the human rights situation in the territory of the former Yugoslavia, in particular within Bosnia and Herzegovina."[60] The first report of the special rapporteur, Tadeusz Mazowiecki, concerned, inter alia, the policy of ethnic cleansing and other serious human rights violations committed in the territory of the former Yugoslavia. The report stated that "the need to prosecute those responsible for mass and flagrant human rights violations and for breaches of international humanitarian law and to deter future violators requires the systematic collection of documentation on such crimes and of personal data concerning those responsible."[61] The special rapporteur then recommended that a "commission should be created to assess and further investigate specific cases in which prosecution may be warranted. This information should include data already collected by various entities within the United Nations system, by other inter-governmental organizations and by non-governmental organizations."[62]

Subsequently, a number of reports called for criminal investigations into war crimes and serious violations of humanitarian law, as well as for the timely collection of information and evidence to support such investigations.[63] Various governments, international organizations, and NGOs also urged that international prosecutions be carried out. But the Security Council was reluctant to face the Herculean tasks an international penal process would entail, and it was hesitant to undercut any efforts at political settlement by the EC and the UN. The Security Council was, however, keen on deflecting international criticism; on 13 August 1992 it adopted Resolution 771, requiring UN member states to submit reports on violations of humanitarian law in the former Yugoslavia. Finally, in response to sustained internal and external criticism, action by the UN came in the form of a war crimes commission, established to assimilate the information and evidence regarding alleged war crimes being turned over to the UN. On 6 October 1992, the Security Council adopted Resolution 780, which requested the Secretary-General

> to establish, as a matter of urgency, an impartial Commission of Experts to examine and analyze the information submitted pursuant to resolution 771 (1992) and the present resolution, together with such further information as the Commission of Experts may obtain through its own investigation or efforts, of other persons or bodies pursuant to resolution 771 (1992), with a view to providing the Secretary-General with its conclusions on the evidence of grave breaches of the Geneva Conventions and other violations of international humanitarian law committed in the territory of the former Yugoslavia.[64]

The Secretary-General duly constituted the five-member Commission of Experts to determine whether there were grave breaches of the 1949 Geneva Conventions.[65] The commission interpreted its mandate as requiring the collection of all relevant information and evidence concerning violations of international humanitarian law that it could given its resources and capabilities. The commission collected information from various sources, carried out investigations, and submitted three reports to the Secretary-General, referring to widespread patterns of willful killing, ethnic cleansing, mass killings, torture, rape, pillage and destruction of civilian property, destruction of cultural and religious property, and arbitrary arrests.[66]

With international pressure mounting due to media coverage, the Security Council on 22 February 1993 unanimously adopted Resolution 808, which underlined the Council's intention to create an international tribunal to prosecute individuals responsible for serious violations of international humanitarian law and requested the Secretary-General to report on all aspects and to make proposals on the resolution's implementation.[67] Not all of the Security Council's permanent members supported the tribunal, seen as potentially disruptive to the negotiations for a political settlement. Some Security Council members, as well as other member states, felt that such a judicial organ should be established by the General Assembly or by multi-lateral treaty. Other members urged that this was an opportunity to establish a permanent international criminal court. The political advantages of controlling an ad hoc institution prevailed.

Arguably the Vance-Owen peace negotiations were not helped by the formation of the war crimes commission. The political climate and the intensity of the conflict meant that the pursuit of a political settlement was the priority. The alleged criminals were the very same leaders of the Yugoslav factions that Vance and Owen were assigned to pressure and cajole. Certainly, the last thing they needed was a war crimes commission revealing the criminality of Serbian leaders, including Milosevic, and the victimization of the Bosnians. If that happened, world public opinion would clamor for justice. Milosevic and other Serbian leaders would not, under these circumstances, agree to a negotiated settlement if they were the targets of the investigation. Owen thought that a climate of equal moral blameworthiness was needed to convince the Bosnians to accept whatever the Serbians dictated—and to avoid focusing on the prosecution of Serbian leaders.

The pursuit of justice was a response to international humanitarian concerns and to the extensive media coverage of the atrocities. But because the major powers did not want to intervene militarily, the UN and EC mediators had neither stick nor carrot to end the violence. Establishing an international investigative body with the broadest possible mandate since Nuremberg was just the sort of stick that the UN and EC mediators needed to pressure the Serbian leadership. However, negotiations could not be conducted while prospects for a criminal investigation and prosecution existed. In the face of this dilemma, the choice made was to favor politics over justice. As a result, the Commission of Experts never received adequate funding from the UN to conduct its field investigations. The limited resources provided by the UN covered the bare minimum of administration costs for a short period. Moreover, the UN erected bureaucratic and financial hurdles. Consequently, the Commission of Experts resorted to external funding sources and accepted the aid of volunteers and personnel contributed by certain governments.[68] It is difficult to understand why no resources were made available by the General Assembly and why so few voluntary contributions were obtained from governments. "If the Iran-contra investigation in the United States cost over $40 million, how could a $1.3 million trust fund be sufficient in the context of such large-scale victimization as has occurred in the former Yugoslavia?"[69]

As the database grew to substantiate patterns of criminality by design and involving senior political and military leadership, the work of the

Commission of Experts threatened the political process.[70] Consequently, it became necessary to terminate the work of the commission while attempting to avoid the negative consequences of such a direct action. The Commission of Experts was arbitrarily terminated on 30 April 1993 by a decision of the United Nations Office of Legal Affairs (OLA), contrary to the Security Council's mandate in Resolution 827, which requested that the commission continue work pending the appointment of a prosecutor for the tribunal; however, the prosecutor did not take office until 15 August 1994, almost eight months after the OLA told the commission to terminate activities. As eminent international law scholar M. C. Bassiouni (chairperson of the Commission of Experts) observed:

> By employing bureaucratic measures, an obstruction of justice was carried out quietly. An administrative decision was taken—probably at the behest, but certainly with the support of, some of the Permanent Members—leaving no legal trace of the deed. The reasons for this action were not explained and the Security Council did not take a position on the termination of the Commission of Experts. Nevertheless, the Secretary-General, in a 1995 report to the Commission of Human Rights, incorrectly stated that the Commission of Experts concluded its work by 30 April 1994 in accordance with the decision under the terms of the SC resolution 827 (1993).[71]

In a further broadside, Bassiouni stated:

> The premature termination of the Commission cannot be explained. Could it have been a purposeful political action to prevent the further discovery of the truth? Or was it simply an unwise administrative decision? Or perhaps it is the nature of the UN beast—part political, part bureaucratic—that accounts for what I believe to be an unconscionable outcome, no matter what the reason.[72]

Notwithstanding the political and bureaucratic muddles that surrounded the Commission of Experts, dedication and commitment enabled it to unearth hard evidence that implicated senior government officials, personnel, and state organs. The Rubicon had been crossed, and the United Nations had to act, whether it was willing or not. Drawing on the commission's work, the Secretary-General on 3 May 1993 duly submitted his report to the Security Council as requested.[73] The report: explained the legal basis for the tribunal's establishment, its competence and organization, investigation and pretrial proceedings, trial and posttrial proceedings (including those relating to the rights of the accused, witness protection, judgment and penalties, appeal, review, and the enforcement of sentences); and provided for the cooperation of and judicial assistance from states. The Statute of the International Criminal Tribunal for the Former Yugoslavia, as proposed by the Committee of Experts to the Secretary-General, formed the appendix to this report.

The Security Council was presented with a difficult choice. It could either rigidly uphold the sanctity of state sovereignty, even at the risk of allowing horrific acts of war to go untried and unpunished; or it could undermine state sovereignty to override the wishes of the states involved by creating an international criminal tribunal. That tribunal would demand the extradition of those states' nationals for public trial; make incursions into their demarcated territories for the purpose of collecting evidence by which to prosecute their nationals; exhume mass gravesites; and deepen the sense of subjugation in states already angered by a perceived prejudice against them. The Security Council opted to invoke Chapter VII. On 25 May 1993, the Security Council adopted Resolution 827 and unanimously approved the report of the Secretary-General, deciding

> to establish an international tribunal for the sole purpose of prosecuting persons responsible for serious violations of international humanitarian law committed in the territory of former Yugoslavia between 1 January 1991 and a date to be determined by the Security Council upon the restoration of peace and to this end to adopt the statute of the International Tribunal annexed to the report of the Secretary-General.[74]

The creation of an international criminal tribunal established under the auspices of the United Nations led to surprisingly little dissent among the international community. Although several countries offered draft statutes that differed in jurisdictional scope and other powers from the final statute,[75] only one country actually denied the power of the Security Council to establish a tribunal at all. Not surprisingly, this was the Federal Republic of Yugoslavia, which argued that its state sovereignty would be unacceptably violated by a tribunal prosecuting Serbs.[76] Yugoslavia voiced its objections in a letter addressed to the Secretary-General, stating that while "Yugoslavia considers that all perpetrators of war crimes committed in the territory of the former Yugoslavia should be prosecuted and punished,"[77] this was the proper mandate for national, as opposed to international, laws and tribunals. The international community was not deaf to such arguments. Even the CSCE, as Yugoslavia rightly pointed out, had concerns about respecting the internal sovereignty of the states involved.[78] In recognition of this concern, some states suggested that the General Assembly play a role in creating the tribunal, such as reviewing or even redrafting the statute.[79]

Enemies of Promise: NATO and the Security Council

The Dayton Accords that settled the violence in Bosnia were negotiated at Wright Patterson Air Force Base in Dayton, Ohio.[80] They were signed by the negotiating parties and a group of guarantor states, which were prepared to endorse and materially support a peace settlement for the Bosnian war in Paris on 14 December 1995. The peace agreement was reached after three weeks of intense negotiations. It was intended to end more than three years of war in Bosnia, after numerous failed prior diplomatic attempts by Western mediators to secure an end to the violence.[81] The Dayton Accords are a complex package of interrelated texts augmented by Security Council resolutions that establish the international forces and organs that support the accords.[82]

In the Western guarantor states Dayton was heralded as a triumph of diplomacy over chaos, reasoned agreement over crude warfare, a multilateral agreement that forced the affirmation, by all parties to the conflict, of the legal existence and viability of the Bosnian state. Despite ending mass fratricidal violence on Bosnian territory, Dayton is a paradox of substance and implementation.[83] In the accords, the Republics of Bosnia and Herzegovina, Croatia, and the Federal Republic of Yugoslavia (representing the Republika Srpska) agreed to "welcome and endorse the arrangements that were made concerning the establishment of an arbitration tribunal . . . [and] fully respect and promote fulfillment of the commitments made therein."[84] The Dayton Accords contained several provisions requiring the parties to cooperate with the ICTY. Article IX of the General Framework Agreement and article XIII (4) of the Agreement on Human Rights required the parties thereto (Bosnia, Croatia, and the FRY) to cooperate fully with and give unrestricted access to the ICTY; this requirement was extended to the Republika Srpska by article IV of the Agreement on Civilian Implementation.

The Dayton Accords provided for the deployment of the multinational Implementation Force (IFOR)[85] to oversee implementation of the military aspects of the peace agreement: bringing about and maintaining an end to hostilities; separating the armed forces of Bosnia's two newly created entities, the Federation of Bosnia and Herzegovina and Republika Srpska; transferring territory between the two entities according to the peace agreement; and moving the parties' forces and heavy weapons into approved storage sites. The day the Dayton Accords were signed by the parties in Paris, the president and the prosecutor of the ICTY issued a joint statement underscoring "the authority of IFOR to arrest indicted war criminals" and concluded that "this Agreement promises that those who have committed crimes which threaten international peace and security—genocide, crimes against humanity and war crimes—will be brought to justice." But this optimistic public assessment of IFOR's role in apprehending indicted war criminals was not shared behind the scenes by the North Atlantic Treaty Organization (NATO, the overall command body and main provider of the units comprising IFOR)[86] or the Security Council. Though the tribunal called upon the Security Council and NATO to insist on the cooperation of the Balkan states, it is well known that in practice the parties' commitment to "welcoming"[87] or "cooperating" with[88] the tribunal fell short of this pledge.

The former Yugoslav republics were not alone in their initial hostility and later extreme reluctance toward cooperating with the ICTY. Even after the ICTY was established, few prosecutions occurred initially because the massive NATO forces deployed in Bosnia were reluctant to apprehend indicted criminals for fear of retaliation. Most shocking was the initial refusal by NATO to arrest war crimes suspects following the U.S.-brokered Dayton Accords and the deployment of 60,000 troops in Bosnia.[89] Perhaps the reason lies in the U.S. reliance on Milosevic—the Serbian president many viewed as the architect of the genocidal war—to broker the agreement.[90] In any event, the Dayton Accords largely ratified the gains of the Serbs, leaving the Bosnian Muslims with only 51 percent of Bosnia-Herzegovina, a Muslim-Croat federation; the rest became Republika Srpska, a separate and autonomous Serb republic, and a haven for Karadzic and Ratko Mladic, two of the most senior Serbs indicted by the ICTY.[91]

Despite the creation of the ICTY and the Western countries' repeated promises to support the tribunal's mandate, it is no secret that implementation of the Dayton Accords was a problem. However, there were two initial successes: military confrontation and the slaughter of civilians came to a halt; and, later, NATO troops managed to nudge the armies of the parties to the boundaries prescribed by the Dayton Accords.[92] The failures were many, the most significant being that the principal and other war criminals remained at large, for the most part in plain sight; in spite of explicit prohibitions in the U.S.-inspired constitution for Bosnia, many of these criminals were running their respective fiefdoms contrary to the provisions of the Dayton Accords.[93] NATO, through its policy of "monitor, but don't touch," largely declined to use force to apprehend indicted war criminals in its area of operations, despite its massive military presence. To justify such inaction, NATO commanders initially claimed that NATO's mandate in Bosnia did not permit use of force in aid of international criminal justice, except under extremely limited circumstances (i.e., when indicted war criminals are "encountered in the course of its duties and if the tactical situation permits").[94]

Initially, the ICTY remained a symbolic gesture without the wherewithal to discharge its mission. The United States feared that going after suspects would upset the Dayton Accords.[95] In any event, both the United States and NATO forces initially carried out a policy of appeasement toward indicted war criminals.[96] NATO forces were keen to discharge the official policy ("monitor, but don't touch") but subsequently undertook limited, case-by-case arrests,[97] arguably to deflect international criticism and condemnation. Clearly, in its early days, the Dayton Accords were not being carried out in good faith by anyone, including Bosnia, the General Framework Agreement (GFA) parties, and the sponsoring powers.[98]

It was to take many months before NATO commanders abandoned their hands-off policy, which had guaranteed war criminals freedom of movement even in NATO-controlled enclaves. Surprisingly, it was the UN peacekeeping force in Croatia, and not the NATO force, that made the first arrest in June 1997.[99] Encouraged by the success of the UN operation, a month later, on 10 July 1997, British Stabilization Force (SFOR) troops swung into action.[100] In the following months, other NATO national contingents, smarting from repeated criticisms of their passivity and complacency, hastened to follow the precedent set by others.[101]

In view of its envisaged role in the Dayton Accords, NATO's role as an enforcer was disheartening. However, NATO's reluctance was mirrored by the Security Council itself, on which fell the full and direct burden of enforcing the will of the tribunal; the attitude of the Security Council was merely indifferent. The ICTY Statute provided that if the Trial Chamber is satisfied that the failure to serve an arrest warrant "was due in whole or in part to a failure or refusal of a state to cooperate with the tribunal in accordance with Article 29 of the Statute," the president must notify the Security Council. The rules, though silent on what happens next, envisaged that the Security Council would take enforcement action to compel compliance, including economic sanctions and military action. No such action was forthcoming from the Security Council.

Despite the fact that the preamble of Security Council Resolution 1022 noted that "compliance with the requests and orders of the international tribunal for the former Yugoslavia constitutes an essential aspect of implementing the Peace Agreement," neither Carl Bildt, the UN high representative for civilian implementation, nor Admiral Leighton Smith, the IFOR commander, viewed the refusal to arrest or transfer indicted persons to the tribunal, or the continued presence of such persons in official positions in the Republika Srpska, as a "significant failure" to meet obligations under the Dayton Accords within the meaning of Resolution 1022.[102] Thus, no triggering report to the Security Council was forthcoming from either Bildt or Smith when the tribunal informed them that the Federal Republic of Yugoslavia (FRY) and Republika Srpska had refused to comply with the tribunal's arrest warrants and that a number of persons indicted by the tribunal continued to hold official positions in Prijedor and Foca.[103]

Any hopes for a change of heart and decisive action by the Security Council were effectively buried when the Security Council adopted Resolution 1074, permanently terminating the Yugoslav sanctions and disbanding the sanctions committee,[104] thus giving away an effective mechanism to pressure the Serbs to surrender indicted persons to the ICTY. Thus it was no surprise, when the ICTY reported that the FRY had repeatedly refused to comply with the orders of the tribunal,[105] that the Security Council condemned the failure to arrest and transfer the individuals involved but declined to reimpose any sort of sanctions to enforce compliance.[106] By then, it would appear that the Security Council was more interested in wider political goals than the necessities of international justice, a stand-offish position that continues to prevail today.

The first high-profile broadside against the Security Council's recalcitrance was fired by none other than Gabrielle Kirk McDonald, the ICTY's outgoing chief judge. In 1999 she derided the Security Council for ignoring its responsibility to compel Serbia and Croatia to turn over suspected war criminals. McDonald explained how she had made two personal appeals and four more in writing to the Security Council to compel the Serbian leadership to turn over three Serbs, known as the "Vukovar Three," who were wanted in Croatia. In response, she said, "the Council [had] done nothing."[107] The Security Council's failure in this instance was a reflection of its failure to react meaningfully to the Balkan republics' noncooperation. The Council was content to issue statements of displeasure and resolutions carrying hollow threats of action.

Because of the lack of cooperation and the Security Council's reluctance, it is to the credit of the tribunal that it developed other means to enforce its authority. It has experimented with "indirect" or "soft" enforcement methods,[108] based on the provisions of the ICTY Statute as well as direct appeals to the international community and its institutions. Measures adopted have been derived from the tribunal's cooperation with the UN, other international organizations, and various states outside the former Yugoslavia. These measures have included political pressure through condemnation by UN organs, the use of economic sanctions, and offers of monetary rewards.

Fulfilling a Mandate: Developments in the ICTY

On 4 November 1994, Dragan Nikolic became the first person to be indicted by the ICTY.[109] However, it was not until early 1995, two years after its creation, that the ICTY secured custody of an accused: Dusko Tadic. As his case proceeded to court, it triggered the development of the ICTY's institutional structure: a detention unit to hold the accused, monitored by the ICRC; detention regulations; and an international legal aid system. Notwithstanding these important milestones, the ICTY was bedeviled by the refusal of some states (especially in the former Yugoslavia) to cooperate, a recalcitrance that continues to some extent to date. By way of example, whereas more than seventy people had been indicted by mid-1997, only eight were in custody. States were reluctant to provide staff or funds, declined to order the 60,000 peacekeepers in Bosnia to assist what few investigators the prosecutor had, and refused to provide intelligence information that would have allowed the investigation of indictees. The situation was so bad that Ted Meron, a leading international human rights scholar (subsequently appointed a judge of the tribunal) and one of the tribunal's biggest supporters, suggested that the international community should support the ICTY or shut it down.[110]

In the early years, the ICTY was a victim of the tension between the perceived demands of peace and justice. The ICTY's creation was simultaneously an act of hope, desperation, and cynicism by an international community lacking a coherent policy to respond to the carnage inflicted in the former Yugoslavia. Its mandate was to help restore international peace and security, but the logical implication of this—the indictment and trial of the most senior officials considered to be the primary perpetrators—was also seen as an unacceptable risk to the peace process. In mid-1997, the ICTY was finally given the enforcement support it lacked. At that time, a small but influential group of states pushed for the arrest of indictees. The UN force in Croatia, and then NATO in Bosnia, began detaining indictees,[111] and the United States assisted in securing the surrender of ten accused from Croatia. In the final six months of 1997, the population of the ICTY's detention unit jumped from eight to twenty-two. By 1998 several governments were providing additional staff and funding. Although obviously welcome, the generosity was limited to a handful of members of the international community. Not only was their largesse finite; the nature of the tribunal itself required all states to cooperate.

The new spirit of state cooperation was reflected in a steady rise of arrests and surrenders. By the end of 2000, the ICTY had publicly indicted ninety-seven individuals.[112] Thirty-five of the accused were in custody in the ICTY detention unit, four had been provisionally released, and twenty-seven arrest warrants remained outstanding.[113] Proceedings against five accused had been completed.[114] Eleven accused were before the Appeals Chamber; twelve were before the Trial Chamber; and sixteen were in pretrial stages. In the same year, two trials were concluded. In *Prosecutor v. Kupreskic and Others,* five members of the Croatian Defense Council (HVO) were found guilty of crimes against humanity and violations of the laws or customs of war connected to their role in the attack on the village of Ahmici in central Bosnia.[115] A sixth defendant, Dragan Papic, was acquitted on insufficient evidence to establish guilt beyond a reasonable doubt.[116] In *Prosecutor v. Blaskic,* Tihomir Blaskic, a general in the HVO, was found guilty by virtue of individual and superior responsibility on three counts of crimes against humanity, six counts of grave breaches of the Geneva Conventions, and ten counts of violations of the laws of war.[117] Blaskic received a lengthy incarceration of forty-five years.[118]

Several ICTY firsts occurred in 2000. Besides the active pursuit of suspects, success in securing them, and an active court docket, two defendants were released pending trial.[119] The defendants, Simo Zaric and Miroslav Tadic, had surrendered voluntarily to the tribunal.[120] They are each charged with two counts of crimes against humanity and one count of grave breaches of the Geneva Conventions.[121] The rules of procedure and evidence regarding release pending trial had been amended in November 1999, so that exceptional circumstances were no longer among the criteria required for release.[122]

The ICTY steadily made progress in fulfilling its mandate. Included in the thirty-seven persons in custody in The Hague were: Radovan Karadzic's[123] deputy and the former Bosnian Serb member of the postwar national presidency of Bosnia (Momcilo Krajisnik); a major political representative for Bosnian Croats (Dario Kordic); the generals allegedly responsible for organizing Serb military operations against Sarajevo and against Srebrenica (Stanislav Galic and Radislav Krstic); the commanders of detention camps in northwestern Bosnia; and three men accused of controlling detention facilities and widespread sexual slavery and other torture in Foca. Fifteen persons were tried in seven completed trials, four cases were on appeal, four more were ongoing, and nine were in the pretrial stage. Four individuals had exhausted appeals and were serving or had served their sentences, and ten others appealed theirs. Two individuals were acquitted and released.[124]

The turn of the century witnessed a fully functioning ICTY, holding trials and appellate proceedings on a regular basis. More than 1,000 people from seventy-five countries are involved in prosecuting and trying crimes committed across the region. International lawyers locate and interview witnesses, police and forensics experts exhume gravesites. A coalition of NATO forces from other states identify, track, and detain persons indicted by the tribunal and transfer them hundreds of miles to The Hague. Thus, the ICTY has proved that in practice perpetrators of horrific crimes can be held accountable and that it is possible to operate a system of international criminal justice.

The year 2001 marked a watershed in the history and development of the ICTY. That year, Slobodan Milosevic, the former president of Serbia and Montenegro, was arrested by officials of the FRY; he was transferred to the ICTY, and trial proceedings against him on charges of genocide, crimes against humanity, and other violations of international law were initiated in early 2002. The charges against Milosevic stem from three different indictments—two for events in Bosnia-Herzegovina and Croatia during the early 1990s, and a third covering the more recent events in Kosovo.[125] Regrettably, it was the dictates of politics and not justice that played a central role in this historic event.[126] The arrest of Milosevic represented the most important step to date toward a major goal of the ICTY: to hold trials for and pass judgment on the highest-ranking civilian and military leaders under indictment. Milosevic consistently refuses to recognize the legitimacy of the ICTY and its right to try him, just as he did when he was president; the difference is that he is now on trial. As a result, court-appointed amici curiae (friends of the court) filed a motion on his behalf to dismiss the charges, raising several legal objections to the ICTY proceedings against Milosevic, all of which were rejected by the Trial Chamber.[127] Subsequently, the three indictments against him were joined for the purpose of holding a single trial, which began on 12 February 2002.[128]

Since the ICTY's inception, sixty-seven indictees have appeared in proceedings before it; thirty-one have been tried.[129] Eighty outstanding public indictments have been issued, with thirty indictees still at large. The remaining fifty faced proceedings before the ICTY.[130] Forty-two of those in proceedings are held in the detention facilities, and eight have been provisionally released.[131] During 2001, seven sentencing judgments and five dispositive judgments on appeal were handed down. This was a large increase compared to the year before, attesting to the increased state cooperation as well as the effect of streamlining the procedural and structural aspects of the tribunal.[132] In addition to the judgments in the *Kunarac* and *Krstic* cases, the ICTY Trial Chamber issued judgments in five other cases, involving, inter alia, Croatian intervention in the armed conflict;[133] a former chief of police for the municipality of Bosanski Samac who pled guilty to one count of persecution as a crime against humanity as part of a plea bargain with the prosecutor;[134] resentencing of previously convicted individuals as per an Appeals Chamber judgment;[135] and crimes against humanity and war crimes committed against non-Serb Bosnians within the Omarska, Keraterm, and Trnopolje detention camps after Serb forces took control of the Prijedor region.[136]

There is a burgeoning of the Appeals Chamber's docket. The judges of the Appeals Chamber also form the appellate court of the ICTR. Due to the low number of accused in custody and the narrow grounds of appeal,[137] the first ICTY appeal was not submitted until mid-1995,[138] and the ICTR Appeals Chamber was first called to consider a matter three years later, in mid-1998.[139] By March 2000, however, the appellate judges had a docket of more than forty ICTY and ICTR matters. This growth was fueled by the addition of one Trial Chamber, which resulted in an increase in the proceedings being conducted, as well as the steady expansion of grounds of appeal. Although this figure represents a normal, or even light, workload for a national court, it swamped the ICTY. This carried through to 2001. Among other cases decided in 2001, it addressed for the first time the permissibility of cumulative convictions on several charges that are based on the same conduct.[140] The ICTY Appeals Chamber held that cumulative convictions are "permissible only if each statutory provision involved has a materially distinct element not contained in the other."[141] It also reversed a 2000 trial judgment that found five individuals guilty of crimes against humanity and violations of the laws or customs of war during an attack on the village of Ahmici in central Bosnia.[142] Three of the convictions were reversed in their entirety, and two others were partially reversed, primarily because the evidentiary basis for the convictions—largely the testimony of a single eyewitness—was inadequate. The decision was also based on the additional finding that some indictments were defective, insofar as they failed to plead the material facts of the prosecutor's case with the requisite amount of specificity.[143] The judgment represented the first time that the Appeals Chamber had overturned convictions from the Trial Chamber.[144]

Between 1 August 2001 and 1 July 2002, there were twenty-three accused who either surrendered voluntarily or were arrested—almost three times the number during the previous period.[145] Twelve accused surrendered voluntarily, whereas eleven were arrested, mainly by Bosnian and FRY authorities. Further, the prosecutor signed the indictments concerning Hadzihasanovic, Mrdja, and Deronjic on 5 July 2001, 16 April 2002, and 3 July 2002, respectively. There are a number of other accused in indictments that remain sealed; however, the number is not high. These indictments remain sealed to provide an opportunity for SFOR to apprehend the accused, following the complete failure of the Republika Srpska to apprehend and surrender one single accused, including Radovan Karadzic.[146]

The ICTY expects to complete the investigations in 2004. In fact, the prosecutor envisages that by 2004, about twenty-five new investigations should be completed and thirty-three new indictments issued, covering an additional 100 accused.[147] These investigations correspond to seventeen indictments representing fifty potential intermediate-level accused. Discounting ongoing cases and existing indictments, the ICTY would thus have to rule on only sixteen new indictments involving fifty individuals. In addition, assuming that all those persons are indicted and transferred to the ICTY, it would have to organize only sixteen new trials.[148] According to the ICTY's annual report published in 2002:

> The Prosecutor's investigative strategy continues to be to prosecute the high-level leaders and notorious offenders responsible for the most serious crimes committed during the conflicts. Lower- and mid-level perpetrators should continue to be subject to local/domestic prosecutions. With appropriate judicial reform and adequate witness protection facilities, it may be possible in the future for the Tribunal to remit some of its cases to such local/domestic courts.[149]

Conclusion

The political and legal processes aimed at addressing the Balkan crisis were dogged by realpolitik considerations. Once the ICTY was formed, the lackluster approach by states dissipated as the international community was pressured to meet the dictates of international law. However, the ICTY was foremost a symbol of the failure of the international community to react as the Balkan crisis unfolded. No doubt the ICTY contributed to respect for international humanitarian law and human rights through its indictments and trials, and it has proven the practicability of trying those responsible for shocking crimes and that the international penal process can create positive social change.

With political settlement out of the question, the idea of an international criminal tribunal gained support and momentum. The civil war in the Balkans and the inept efforts at political settlement generated urgency in the West to do *something* to mask the disorder and moral collapse. With the United States as lead lobbyist and financier, the idea of an ad hoc international criminal tribunal gained currency.

Charged with the maintenance of international peace and security, the United Nations fell short of fulfilling this mandate when it virtually ignored the Yugoslav crisis until it had spiraled out of control. Once involved, the Security Council relied on the parties to abide by its demands to cease fighting, withdraw, and adhere to the on-again, off-again cease-fires, thereby ignoring the underlying realities of the crisis. Ethnic factions living side by side in Yugoslavia could not answer to the rule of law when their sacred homeland was threatened, their brothers shot, and their sisters and mothers raped. The Council's demands and pleas, coming amid the virtual dissolution of Yugoslavia, fell on deaf ears. If the UN had entered much earlier, with a peacekeeping force in place before the war was in full force, negotiations might have been more successful. Instead, the burden falling on Vance and Owen to negotiate a settlement over Bosnia-Herzegovina had become "a pathetic catch-up game, in which political and territorial concessions chase the victories achieved on the ground through the ruthless use of force."[150]

By 1993 bureaucratic hurdles, lack of resources, nondisclosure of evidence, and more subtle means were used to avoid and/or impede the likelihood of international prosecutions. Thus, the Commission of Experts on the former Yugoslavia was not adequately funded for investigations. And when it accumulated evidence perceived as dangerous to the political peace process, it was arbitrarily terminated. The more fundamental decision for the international community, however, was whether to make the concessions necessary to create an effective international mechanism against the totality of sovereign prerogatives; if such a view had held sway, no effective international criminal tribunal could have been created.

It is apparent that the international community failed to provide the ICTY enough support to fulfill its mandate, despite a clear legal obligation to do so. Thus, it should be equally clear that the "success" of the tribunal—defined by the number of suspects it actually brings to trial—was seemingly beyond the tribunal's power to achieve. Unlike national courts, the tribunal does not have its own police force. It is, in the words of the tribunal's first president, "like an armless and legless giant which needs artificial limbs to act and move. These limbs are the state authorities . . . the national prosecutors, judges and police officers. If state authorities fail to carry out their responsibilities, the giant is paralyzed, no matter how determined its efforts."[151] This paralysis quickly dissipated once states were galvanized.

We now turn to the genocide in Rwanda, which led to the establishment of the second ad hoc international criminal tribunal of recent times. It is instructive to note that the UN's haphazard response to the Balkan crisis, marked more by "improvisation and ingenuity than by steadfast determination and willingness to make or risk some sacrifices,"[152] played itself out in Rwanda. Once again, the international community's dithering during the run-up to the genocide, and an ambivalence informed more by realpolitik, betrayed the Rwandan people, leaving the minority Tutsi and moderate Hutu at the mercy of bloodthirsty extremist Hutu.

Notes

1. *Report of the Secretary-General on the Work of the Organization*, UN GAOR, 47th sess., para. 3, UN Doc. A/47/277, S/24111 (1992).

2. In January 1991 with the overthrow of Somali president Siad Barre, fighting between various factions and clans resulted in death and destruction, causing a dire need for emergency humanitarian assistance. See generally, *The Situation in Somalia: Report of the Secretary-General*, UN SCOR, 47th sess., UN Doc. S/23829/Add 1 (1992), 7, 9, 11, 13; *The Situation in Somalia: Report of the Secretary-General*, UN SCOR, 47th sess., UN Doc. S/23693 (1992), 4.

3. Chapter VII allows the United Nations to use military force and to act in areas otherwise reserved to the domestic jurisdiction of states. UN operations in Iraq, Somalia, and Haiti were all authorized under Chapter VII. See SC Res. 678, UN SCOR, 45th sess., Res. and Dec., UN Doc. S/INF/46 (1990), 27; SC Res. 794, UN SCOR, 47th sess., Res. and Dec., UN Doc. S/INF/48 (1992), 63; SC Res. 841, UN SCOR, 48th sess., Res. and Dec., UN Doc. S/INF/49 (1993), 119.

4. Jelena Pejic, "Panel II: Adjudicating Violence: Problems Confronting International Law and Policy on War Crimes and Crimes Against Humanity; the Tribunal and the ICC: Do Precedents Matter?" *Albany Law Review* 60 (1997): 841.

5. See "The Pol Pot Riddle," *The Economist*, 28 June 1997, 47.

6. Anne Bodley, "Weakening the Principle of Sovereignty in International Law: The International Criminal Tribunal for the Former Yugoslavia," *New York University Journal of International Law and Politics* 31 (1999): 417, 431.

7. Ibid.

8. The point is made by two writers of the ICTY who were

close observers of the Security Council reactions to published and televised reports of mass rapes, murder, and torture as part of the systematic Serbian program of "ethnic cleansing" reminiscent of the Nazi genocide.

Once the political will of the major powers was mobilized by public shame and public outrage, Security Council resolutions provided the legal basis for speedy action.

Virginia Morris and Michael P. Scharf, eds., *An Insider's Guide to the International Criminal Tribunal for the Former Yugoslavia,* vol. 1 (Irvington-on-Hudson, NY : Transnational, 1995), xxi.

9. Michael P. Scharf, *Balkan Justice: The Story Behind the First International War Crimes Trial Since Nuremberg* (Durham, NC: Carolina Academic Press, 1997), 21.

10. See Vojin Dimitrijevic, "Nationalities and Minorities in the Yugoslav Federation," in *The Protection of Minorities and Human Rights,* edited by Yoram Dinstein and Mala Tabory (Dordrecht: M. Nijhoff, 1992), 419–434.

11. Scharf, *Balkan Justice,* 24.

12. Dusko Doder and Louise Branson, *Milosevic: Potrait of a Dictator* (New York: The Free Press, 1999), 27. See also Roger Thurow, "Tito's Legacy," *Wall Street Journal,* 8 May 1986, available in 1986 WL-WSJ 258991.

13. Doder and Branson, *Milosevic,* 35–62.

14. Ibid., 63–83.

15. Marcus Tanner, "Slovenia Is at War," *The Independent* (London), 28 June 1991, 1.

16. The troika was composed of the foreign minister of the state holding the presidency and his predecessor and successor as president of the EC Council. It operates within the framework of European Political Co-operation (EPC) in accordance with title II of the Single European Act, 17 and 28 February 1986, reprinted in 25 I.L.M. 503 (1986). EPC promotes the adoption of common positions and common actions by the member states on foreign policy issues. See P. J. G. Kapteyn and P. V. Van Themaat, *Introduction to the Law of the European Communities After the Coming into Force of the Single European Act,* 2nd ed. (Boston: Kluwer Law and Taxation Publishers, 1989), 23–24. Following the practice of the press releases of the European Commission, EPC activities are considered part of the general framework of the EC and are therefore subsumed under the acronym "EC." On midnight 30 June 1991, the rotating presidency of the EC passed from Luxembourg to the Netherlands and shortly afterward EC governments sent a third mission, this time composed of senior diplomats from Luxembourg, the Netherlands, and Portugal, to see if they could help monitor a new and durable cease-fire in Slovenia and a withdrawal of FRY forces.

17. Richard Holbrooke, *To End a War* (New York: Random House, 1998), 29.

18. Arguably, the disintegration of Yugoslavia was later accelerated by the premature recognition on the part of certain influential members of the international community of Slovenia as an independent state. On 15 January 1992, the twelve members of the European Community recognized Slovenia.

19. Jelana Pejic, "Yugoslavia: Time Is Running Out," *Inter Press Service,* 25 June 1991. The Serbian Democratic Party stated that it had nothing against Croatia's and Slovenia's independence, "provided that Serbs have the right to live in one country, be it Yugoslavia or Serbia." Ibid. Of the 4.68 million people in Croatia, 85 percent are ethnic Croats and 11.5 percent, or about 600,000, are ethnic Serbs. Marc Weller, "The International Response to the Dissolution of the Socialist Federal Republic of Yugoslavia," *American Journal of International Law* 86 (1992): 569 (providing a thorough delineation of the events comprising Yugoslavia's dissolution through mid-1992).

20. Age Eknes, "The United Nations' Predicament in the Former Yugoslavia," in *The United Nations and Civil Wars,* edited by Thomas G. Weiss (Boulder: Lynne Rienner, 1995), 114.

21. The original, nonbinding CSCE Final Act of 1975 affirmed, in Principle I, the right of every state to juridical equality, territorial integrity, freedom, and political independence with the protection of the territorial integrity of states, defined in greater detail in Principle IV. Further, the reference to territorial integrity confirms an obligation directed at states, but not at peoples, alluding to an obligation of nonintervention further reinforced in Principle VI of the Final Act. It was perceived by the Serbian-dominated central authority as carte blanche for the forcible implementation of its goals to reunify the federation and consolidate its leadership within it.

22. Marc Fisher, "Slovenia Nears Independence as Croatia Faces Civil War," *Washington Post,* 20 July 1991, 6–7. "Leaders Said to See Croats Destined for War," *Washington Post,* 20 July 1991, A1: A senior German official was quoted as saying "without a peacekeeping force, Croatia is destined to suffer civil war."

23. "The obstacle is a clear Soviet message that Moscow will veto any attempt to use UN forces to settle an internal Yugoslav dispute . . . the Soviets will resist any move that could set a precedent for 'internalizing' nationalist conflicts such as those that plague Soviet President Mikhail Gorbachev's government." "Leaders Said to See Croats Destined for War," *Washington Post,* 20 July 1991, A1.

24. United Nations, *United Nations Year Book* (New York: United Nations, 1991), 214 (describing the EC's introduction into the conflict and peacekeeping efforts thereafter). An EC ministerial troika mission, dispatched to Yugoslavia to facilitate a truce and the return of all forces to their previous positions, worked out a cease-fire agreement on 31 July 1991, with the aid of the Conference on Security and Co-operation in Europe. Jonathan Landay, "Presidency Agrees on Proposed Truce Plan," *UPI,* 31 July 1991. See also "Policing Yugoslavia," *Times* (London), 31 July 1991.

25. See *Report of the Secretary-General Pursuant to Paragraph 3 of Security Council Resolution 713,* UN Doc. S/23169 (1991), 6.

26. Andrew Clark, "Yugoslavia: Fragile Cease-fire Holds in Croatia," *Australian Financial Review,* 10 October 1991.

27. *Report of the Secretary-General,* UN Doc. S/22991 (October 1991). Negotiations were attempted at an EC-sponsored peace conference in Brussels on 27 August 1991; ibid. Moving to The Hague, Netherlands, the Conference on Yugoslavia convened on 7 September 1991, with the goal of resolving a peaceful settlement of the conflict. See generally Weller, "The International Response" (outlining the EC's response to the outbreak of fighting among Croats and Serbs).

28. *Report of the Secretary-General,* UN Doc. S/22991 (October 1991).

29. Article 52(2) provides that member states entering into regional arrangements "shall make every effort to achieve pacific settlement of local disputes through such regional arrangements or by such regional agencies before referring them to the Security Council." UN Charter, art. 52(2).

30. In response to letters from the international community requesting that the United Nations reinforce EC efforts due to the rapidly deteriorating situation in Yugoslavia, a meeting of the UN Security Council was convened on 25 September 1991: Letter of 19 September 1991, UN Doc. S/22903 (Austria); Letter of 19 September 1991, UN Doc. S/23053 (Canada); Letter of 19 September 1991, UN Doc. S/23057 (Hungary); Letter of 19 September 1991, UN Doc. S/23069 (Yugoslavia).

31. See generally Eknes, "The United Nations' Predicament in the Former Yugoslavia."

32. Zbigniew Brzezinski, "Bombs and Blather: The Strategy Deficit: Can Clinton Find America's Missing Foreign Policy?" *Washington Post,* 17 January 1993, C1. The United States led the initial call for respecting Yugoslavia's territorial

integrity, qualifying this appeal: "We particularly call upon the central government and the Yugoslav army to end the bloodshed, to exercise restraint and to commence negotiations immediately." U.S. State Department, 28 June 1991 (regular briefing by Margaret Tutwiler). Additionally, support for maintaining the "territorial integrity" of the Yugoslav federation was voiced by the EC and its members and CSCE: Weller, "The International Response," 570. Within days of the initial independence declarations, the Serb-dominated Yugoslav government outlawed Slovenia's and Croatia's independence declarations and ordered the federal army to seize control of the borders with Slovenia: World News Summary, *Agence France Presse,* 27 June 1991, Paris. The federal defense ministry stated the army would "take all necessary steps" to defend Yugoslavia's territorial integrity; ibid.

33. Weller, "The International Response," 570. This policy of proclaiming territorial integrity, precluding internal attempts at secession, "was perceived by the Serbian-dominated central authority as carte blanche for the forcible implementation of its goals to reunify the federation and consolidate its leadership within it." Ibid., 572.

34. Eknes, "The United Nations' Predicament in the Former Yugoslavia," 115.

35. Deep-seeded animosity and distrust, coupled with the absence of a central authority in Yugoslavia, foretold that the parties were not likely to simply talk through their differences. Without a peacekeeping force to bring order and stability to the region, the charged situation did not permit a negotiated settlement of political differences. Although some regional organizations are outfitted to complement negotiation efforts with the dispatch of peacekeeping forces, the EC is not equipped to resort to peacekeeping. Instead, the EC sent "monitors" to the region that proved incapable of little more than observing the escalating violence. See Amy Lou King, "Bosnia-Herzegvina—Vance-Owen Agenda for a Peaceful Settlement: Did the UN Do Too Little, Too Late, to Support This Endeavor?" *Georgia Journal of International and Comparative Law* 23 (1993): 347, 368–369.

36. Security Council Resolutions 713 (25 September 1991), 757 (30 May 1992), 781 (9 October 1992), and 787 (16 November 1992). These resolutions covered economic and military sanctions and their implementation. See *The United Nations and the Situation in the Former Yugoslavia: Resolutions of the Security Council and Statements by Its President,* 25 September 1991–28 April 1995 (New York: United Nations Department of Public Information, 1995).

37. SC Res. 713, UN SCOR, 3009th mtg., UN Doc. S/23067 (1991). The Council unanimously adopted the five-nation draft proposed by Austria, Belgium, France, the Soviet Union, and the United Kingdom. The resolution noted that, "the continuation of this situation constitutes a threat to international peace and security," recalled the principles "enshrined in the Charter," and stated in the CSCE declaration of September 3 that, "no territorial gains or changes within Yugoslavia brought about by violence are acceptable." SC Res. 713.

38. Ibid. The resolution provided that under Chapter VII of the Charter, "for the purposes of establishing peace and stability in Yugoslavia," a general and complete embargo was to be implemented immediately by all states "on all deliveries of weapons and military equipment to Yugoslavia until the Security Council decides otherwise." Ibid., para. 6.

39. Nick Thorpe, "Yugoslavia: Croatia Digs in for Long War," *The Observer* (London), 13 October 1991, 13. The Bosnian ambassador to the UN, Mohammed Sacirbey, stated that the balance of power between the Muslims and the Serbs was tipped such that the Muslims had two tanks, twenty-four artillery pieces, and no planes, whereas the Serbs had more than 300 tanks, 400 artillery pieces, and at least

sixty planes. Remarks of Ambassador Mohammed Sacirbey Before the American Jewish Committee Ambassador's Forum Luncheon (22 October 1992), available in LEXIS/NEXIS Library, Current File.

40. *Report of the Secretary-General,* UN Doc. S/22991 (October 1991), 2. The appointment of Vance was the result of a 25 September 1991 Security Council resolution inviting Secretary-General Javier Perez de Cueller to offer his assistance in peacemaking efforts and to report back as soon as possible. "Cyrus Vance to Visit Yugoslavia as UN Chief's Envoy," *Reuters,* 9 October 1991. Vance served as secretary of state for just over three years under President Jimmy Carter, resigning in 1980 after opposing a decision to launch an armed rescue mission to free Americans being held hostage in Iran. Ibid.

41. *Report of the Secretary-General,* UN Doc. S/22991 (October 1991), 3, 5. In addition, Vance attended sessions of the Conference on Yugoslavia at The Hague at the invitation of its chairman, Lord Carrington of Britain, and pursued contact with leaders of all factions involved in the Yugoslav conflict. Ibid., 3.

42. Action by the Security Council is symbolized by the adoption of a resolution: Robert E. Riggs and Jack C. Plano, *The United Nations: International Organization and World Politics* (Chicago: Dorsey, 1988), 84.

43. The parties signed the Geneva Agreement, thereby agreeing to an unconditional cease-fire, on 23 November 1991: "Letter Dated 24 November 1991 from the Secretary-General Addressed to the President of the Security Council," UN SCOR, UN Doc. S/23239 (1991). This agreement was the fourteenth thus far since the conflict began. "UN Peacekeeping Operation for Yugoslavia in Question, Cease-fire Must First Be Respected," *UN Chronicle* (New York), March 1992, 72.

44. SC Res. 721, UN SCOR, 3018th mtg., UN Doc. S/Res/721 (1991). Specifically, the Council would not consider the deployment of a UN peacekeeping operation until all parties fully complied with the November cease-fire agreement, which called for the removal of Croatian blockades of all JNA barracks and installations, and the immediate withdrawal from Croatia of blockaded military personnel and weapons. Ibid., para. 2.

45. Jonathan Eyal, "United Nations: Blue Flag of Inconvenience—Former Yugoslavia," *Guardian* (London), 29 January 1993.

46. In July 1996, Karadzic was indicted by the International Criminal Tribunal for the Former Yugoslavia.

47. The term "ethnic cleansing" has been used to designate the practice of "rendering an area ethnically homogeneous by using force or intimidation to remove persons or given groups from the area." *Interim Report of the Commission of Experts Established Pursuant to Security Council Resolution 780* (1992), UN SCOR, Annex 55, UN Doc. 5/25274 (10 February 1993).

48. See for example, *Report of the Secretary-General Pursuant to Security Council Resolution 760 UN SCOR,* UN Doc. S/24080, para. 18 (describing the desperate situation emerging in Bosnia-Herzegovina as "one of the worst humanitarian emergencies of our time").

49. Repeatedly, the Security Council deferred settlement of the dispute in Bosnia to the EC, noting the continuing role that the EC played in achieving a peaceful solution in Yugoslavia through the Conference on Yugoslavia, commending its efforts, and demanding that all parties concerned cooperate fully with the efforts of the EC "to bring about urgently a negotiated political solution respecting the principle that any change of border by force is not acceptable." SC Res. 652, UN SCOR, 2918th mtg., 652 (1992); SC Res. 727, UN SCOR, 3028th mtg., UN Doc. S/Res/727 (1992); SC Res. 740, UN SCOR, 3049th mtg., UN Doc. S/Res/

7/740 (1992); SC Res. 743, UN SCOR, 3055th mtg., UN Doc. S/Res/743 (1992); SC Res. 749, UN SCOR, 3066th mtg., UN Doc. S/Res/749 (1992); SC Res. 757 UNSCOR, 3082nd mtg., UN Doc. S/Res/757 (1992); SC Res. 762, UN SCOR, 3088th mtg., UN Doc. S/Res/762 (1992); SC Res. 764, UN SCOR, 3093rd mtg., UN Doc. S/Res/764 (1992).

50. Referring to the Serb-Croat conflict in Resolution 762, the Council urged "all parties and others concerned to honor their commitments to effect a complete cessation of hostilities and to implement the United Nations peace-keeping plan" (citing the Vance Plan of December 1991). SC Res. 762, UN SCOR, 3088th mtg., UN Doc. S/Res/762 (30 June 1992), para. 2. In Resolution 764, the Council stressed "once again the imperative need to find an urgent negotiated political solution for the situation in Bosnia and Herzegovina." SC Res. 764, UN SCOR, 3093rd mtg., UN Doc. S/Res/764 (13 July 1992).

51. Steve Crawshaw and Tony Barber, "Inside Story: Peace? What Peace?" *The Independent* (London), 30 August 1992, 17.

52. "International Conference on the Former Yugoslavia, 27 August 1992, UN Doc. LC/C4 Final," reprinted in *International Conference on the Former Yugoslavia: Documents Adopted at the London Conference,* 31 I.L.M. 1488 (1992), 1534. The International Conference on the Former Yugoslavia envisaged two stages: (1) the London Conference, convening 26–28 August 1992; and (2) the Geneva Process, convening 3 September 1992, to meet in continuous session in Geneva until a settlement was reached; 31 I.L.M. 1488 (1992), 1534. Although the resignation of EC Conference chairman Lord Carrington indicated the failure of a yearlong mission, the London Conference was intended to be a turning point in the peace process to tackle the obstacles to a settlement of the disputes between the Croats, Bosnian Muslims, and Serbs. See, for example, Judy Dempsey, "Carrington Resigns as EC Peace Envoy to Yugoslavia," *Financial Times*, 26 August 1992, 1.

53. *Report of the Secretary-General on the International Conference on the Former Yugoslavia,* UN SCOR, UN Doc. S/24795 (1992), reprinted in 31 I.L.M. 1549 (1992), 1552, 1558. The London Conference combined the efforts of the UN, the EC, the CSCE, the Organization of the Islamic Conference (OIC), and other international organizations; 31 I.L.M. 1488 (1992).

54. Chris Moncrieff, "Lord Owen Sets Off on Peace Trail," *Associated Press*, 30 August 1992. Lord David Owen, a former Labour minister of the United Kingdom, was one of the founders and subsequent leaders of the now-defunct Social Democratic Party.

55. *International Conference on the Former Yugoslavia: Documents Adopted at the London Conference,* 31 I.L.M. 1488 (1992), 1534, 1552. The permanent cochairs of the London Conference were the head of state government of the presidency of the European Community, British prime minister John Major, and UN Secretary-General Boutros Boutros-Ghali. Vance and Owen managed the operational work of the conference as cochairs of the steering committee, overseeing the work of six working groups on: (1) Bosnia-Herzegovina; (2) humanitarian issues; (3) ethnic and national communities and minorities; (4) succession issues; (5) economic issues; and (6) confidence and security-building and verification measures. Ibid.

56. See ibid., 1554. Although the three parties held divergent views on the future structure of Bosnia-Herzegovina, the cochairs believed that, given the intermingled population of Bosnia, there "appear[ed] to be no viable way to create three territorially distinct States based on ethnic or confessional principles," and thus the establishment of a decentralized state was the only "viable and stable solution that does not acquiesce in already accomplished ethnic cleansing." Ibid., 1559. A state-

ment of principles emerged from the London Conference to serve as the basis of a future negotiated settlement, providing for: the cessation of fighting and the use of force by all parties; the nonrecognition of advantages obtained by the use of force; respect for individual rights and fundamental freedoms as embodied in international humanitarian law; the condemnation of forcible expulsions and illegal detentions; respect for independence, sovereignty, and territorial integrity; compliance with Security Council resolutions; the provision of humanitarian assistance; and cooperation in monitoring, peacekeeping, and arms control operations. Additionally, the conference generated a statement on Bosnia, setting forth the provisions necessary for a political settlement in Bosnia-Herzegovina. See *International Conference on the Former Yugoslavia: Documents Adopted at the London Conference,* 1533, 1537.

57. Secretary-General Boutros-Ghali stated:

All international observers agree that what is happening is a concerted effort by the Serbs of Bosnia-Herzegovina, with the acquiescence of, and at least some support from, JNA, to create "ethnically pure" regions in the context of negotiations on the "canonization" of the Republic in the EC Conference on Bosnia-Herzegovina. (Ibid., para. 5. *Report of the Secretary-General Pursuant to Security Council Resolution 757 UN SCOR,* Annex, UN Doc. S/24075 [1992], para. 15.)

In addition to the more than 900,000 persons displaced from Croatia, at the time of Vance's arrival on 14 April 1992 an estimated 184,000 persons had been displaced from Bosnia-Herzegovina. By 20 April of that year this number had grown to 230,000, and by May more than 520,000 persons had been displaced from Bosnia.

58. See, for example, SC Res. 752 (expansion of UNPROFOR mandate); SC Res. 757, UN SCOR, 3082th mtg., UN Doc. S/Res/760 (1992) (general sanctions imposed); SC Res. 758, UN SCOR, 3083th mtg., UN Doc. (1992); SC Res. 760, UN SCOR, 3086th mtg., UN Doc. S/Res/760 (1992); SC Res. 761, UN SCOR, 3087th mtg., UN Doc. S/Res/761 (1992) (demand that all parties and others concerned cooperate fully with UNPROFOR and international humanitarian agencies and organizations and take all necessary steps to ensure the safety of their personnel); SC Res. 762, UN SCOR, 3088th mtg., para. 2, UN Doc. S/Res/762 (1992) (expanding UNPROFOR's mandate); SC Res. 764, UN SCOR, 3093rd mtg., UN Doc. S/Res/764 (1992) (authorizing UNPROFOR to protect humanitarian assistance); SC Res. 771, UN SCOR, 3106th mtg., UN Doc. S/Res/771 (1992).

59. Morris and Scharf, eds., *An Insider's Guide,* 22.

60. See *Report on the Situation of Human Rights in the Territory of the Former Yugoslavia,* submitted by Tadeusz Mazowiecki, Special Rapporteur of the Commission on Human Rights, pursuant to paragraph 14 of Commission Resolution 1992/S-1/1 of 14 August 1992, E/CN 4/1992/S-1/9, 28 August 1992.

61. Ibid., para. 69.

62. Ibid., para. 70.

63. See, for example, E/CN 4/1992/S-1/10 of 27 October 1992, para. 18, as well as annex 11 (statement by Dr. Clyde Snow). See also *Report of the Special Rapporteur* (transmitted by the Secretary-General to the Security Council and General Assembly), A/47/666; S/24809 of 17 November 1992, para. 140, where Mazowiecki states: "There is growing evidence that war crimes have been committed. Further investigation is needed to determine the extent of such acts and the identity of those responsible, with a view to their prosecution by an international tribunal, if appropriate." See also the later reports of the special rapporteur for more details

on the human rights situation in the former Yugoslavia: E/CN 4/1993/50, 10 February 1993; E/CN 4/1994/3, 5 May 1993; E/CN 4/1994/4, 19 May 1993; E/CN 4/1994/6, 26 August 1993; E/CN 4/1994/8, 6 September 1993; E/CN 4/1994/47, 17 November 1993; E/CNA/1994/11, 21 February 1994; E/CN 4/1995/4, 10 June 1994; E/CN 4/1995/10, 4 August 1994; A/49/641-S/1 994/1252, 4 November 1994; E/CN 4/1995/54, 13 December 1995; E/CN 4/1995/57, 9 January 1995; E/CN 4/1996/3, 21 April 1995; and E/CN 4/1996/6, 5 July 1995. On 27 July 1995, Mazowiecki informed the commission of his decision to resign his mandate. The responsibilities of the special rapporteur on the former Yugoslavia were taken up by Elisabeth Rehn of Finland in September 1995.

64. See SC Res. 780 (1992), adopted by the Security Council at its 3119th meeting, 6 October 1992, reprinted in 31 I.L.M. (1992) 1476.

65. See *Report of the Secretary-General on the Establishment of the Commission of Experts Pursuant to Paragraph 2 of Security Council Resolution 780,* UN Doc. S/24657 (1992).

66. See UN Doc. S/25274, 9 February 1993.

67. See SC Res. 808, UNSCOR, 3175th mtg., UN Doc./803 (1993).

68. M. Cherif Bassiouni and Peter Manikas, *The Law of the International Criminal Tribunal for the Former Yugoslavia* (Irvington-on-Hudson, NY: Transnational, 1996), 40.

69. M. Cherif Bassiouni, "The Commission of Experts Established Pursuant to Security Council Resolution 780: Investigating Violations of International Humanitarian Law in the Former Yugoslavia," *Criminal Law Forum* 5 (1994): 279, 339.

70. While press reports charging responsibility for "ethnic cleansing," "systematic rape," and other systematic violations of international humanitarian law could be ignored, evidence substantiating these allegations was a real threat.

71. See Bassiouni and Manikas, *The Law of the International Criminal Tribunal for the Former Yugoslavia,* 210–212. The Secretary-General's position was contained in *Situation on Human Rights in Bosnia and Herzegovina: Report of the Secretary-General,* UN ESCOR, 51st sess., 15, UN Doc E/CN 4/ 1995/62, 9 February 1995. The yearlong delay in the appointment of Richard Goldstone as prosecutor is evidence of the politicization of the tribunal. The Secretary-General presented his first nomination for the prosecutor to the Security Council in August 1993. During the same month, the UK requested the Security Council to appoint the prosecutor by consensus, thereby effectively ensuring that a candidate would not be approved if one of the major powers opposed the nomination. However, the Security Council's final selection of Goldstone, a South African, as prosecutor did not occur until mid-July 1994. Bassiouni and Manikas, *The Law of the International Criminal Tribunal for the Former Yugoslavia.*

72. Bassiouni, "Commission of Experts," 339.

73. See *Report of the Secretary-General Pursuant to Paragraph 2 of Security Council Resolution 808 (1993),* UN Doc S/25704, 3 May 1993. The ICTY Statute and Rules of Procedure and Evidence are reprinted in *International Criminal Tribunal for the Former Yugoslavia, Basic Documents/Documents de Reference* (New York: United Nations, 1995).

74. S/25704, 3 May 1993, and add. 1, 17 May 1993.

75. France, Italy, and Sweden (on behalf of the CSCE) made proposals. Formal suggestions (in contrast with the unpublished informal submissions of other states) were made by Brazil (UN Doc. A/47/922-S/25540 [1993]); Canada (UN Doc. S/25594 [1993]); Egypt, Iran, Malaysia, Pakistan, Saudi Arabia, Senegal, and Turkey, on behalf of the members of the Organization of the Islamic Conference and

as members of the OIC Contact Group on Bosnia and Herzegovina (UN Doc. A/47/920-S25512 [1993]); Mexico (UN Doc. S/25417 [1993]); Netherlands (UN Doc. S/25716 [1993]); Russian Federation (UN Doc. S/25537 [1993]); Slovenia (UN Doc. S/25652 [1993]); and the United States (UN Doc. S/25575 [1993]). See Morris and Scharf, eds., *An Insider's Guide,* 32, n. 120.

76. See "Letter Dated 19 May 1993 from the Charge D'Affaires A.I. of the Permanent Mission of Yugoslavia (Serbia and Montenegro) to the United Nations Addressed to the Secretary-General," UN Doc. A/48/170-S/25801 (1993), paras. 6 and 10.

77. Ibid., para. 3.

78. The CSCE rapporteurs felt that the jurisdiction of an international tribunal should be limited to the two states—Bosnia-Herzegovina and Croatia—that had agreed to the establishment of such a tribunal. See generally *Proposal for an International War Crimes Tribunal for the Former Yugoslavia,* UN Doc. S/25307 (1993) (Rapporteurs Corell, Turk, and Thune under the CSCE Moscow Human Dimension Mechanism to Bosnia and Herzegovina and Croatia).

79. For example, see the submissions of Brazil, France, and Mexico contained in UN Docs. A/47/922-S/25540, S/25266, and S/25417, respectively. The roles envisaged for the General Assembly did not include the actual adoption of the statute or the establishment of the tribunal. As noted in the French proposal, the General Assembly does not have the authority to adopt mandatory resolutions. See Morris and Scharf, eds., *An Insider's Guide,* 40, n. 144.

80. See generally Dick A. Leurdijk, "The Dayton Agreement: A Tremendous Gamble," *International Peacekeeping* 3 (December 1995–January 1996): 2.

81. These included the EC Conference on Peace in Yugoslavia (Carrington); the UN/EC cosponsored International Conference on the Former Yugoslavia, 26–27 August 1992; and the Vance-Owen Plan (the principal stages of the Vance/Owen Plan are set out in UN Docs. S/24795, annex VII, 31 I.L.M. 1584 [1992]). It should be noted that the argument can be made that the inclusion of Russia in the Contact Group, facilitated largely by the United States, was a mechanism to avoid movement on "hard" issues. On one view the inclusion of Russia appears to create a varied international presence and consensus on Bosnia; it also creates the indefinite inclusion of internal competing agendas in the management of the conflict.

82. See UNSC Res. 1021, 22 November 1995, 35 I.L.M. 257 (1996); UNSC Res. 1022, 22 November 1995, 35 I.L.M. 259 (1996); UNSC Res. 1026, 30 November 1995, 35 I.L.M. 251 (1996).

83. The Dayton Accords confirm the existence of the state yet contain the ingredients that divide it into separate political and legal entities. The accords pay homage to the language of self-reliance while ensuring that a long-term international presence remains a necessary element for the survival of the state. Dayton fortifies the tripartite division of nation, community, and individual in the new Bosnia, where ethnic identity is all, and the body politic is a fractured soul.

84. Dayton Accords.

85. Agreement on the Military Aspects of the Peace Settlement (the General Framework Agreement), Article I, annex 1A. IFOR deployed in Bosnia six days after the signing in Paris of the Dayton Accords on 14 December 1995.

86. IFOR had a one-year mandate to oversee implementation of the military aspects of the peace agreement. These goals were achieved by June 1996. It was replaced by a Stabilization Force (SFOR), a 20,000-strong NATO-led peacekeeping mission. At the end of 1996 the mission's aims became more ambitious. In addition to deterring a resumption of hostilities and promoting a climate in which the

peace process could continue to move forward, they included providing an increased level of selective support, within SFOR's means and capabilities, to civilian organizations.

87. *Fifth Annual Report of the International Tribunal for the Prosecution of Persons Responsible for Serious Violations of the International Humanitarian Law Committed in the Territory of the Former Yugoslavia Since 1991,* UN GAOR, 53rd Sess., at para. 276, U.N. Doc. S/1998/737 (1998).

88. *AP,* "Won't Give Up War Crimes Suspects, Bosnian Serb President Tells U.N.," *Toronto Star,* 9 January 1997, A14; M2, Presswire, Press Briefing Transcript for 10 January 1997, 13 January 1997, available in LEXIS, newsfile; see Susan L. Woodward, "Implementing Peace in Bosnia and Herzegovina: A Post-Dayton Primer and Memorandum of Warning," Brookings Disc. Papers 37 (1996).

89. E. Sciolino, "Accord Reached to End the War in Bosnia; Clinton Pledges U.S. Troops to Keep Peace," *New York Times,* 22 November 1995, A1. The Dayton Accords were initialed on 21 November 1995 by the presidents of Bosnia-Herzegovina, Croatia, and Serbia in Dayton, Ohio, ending the four-year war in the former Yugoslavia.

90. "Dissembling in Serbia," *Asian Wall Street Journal,* 10 February 1997, 12.

91. Physicians for Human Rights, *Medicine Under Siege in Yugoslavia, 1991– 1995: War Crimes in the Balkans* (Boston: Physicians for Human Rights, 1996), 32.

92. Inter-Entity Boundary, annex 2 to the General Framework Agreement, 14 December 1995, 35 I.L.M. 111 (1996).

93. See Paul C. Szasz, "The Dayton Accord: The Balkan Peace Agreement," *Cornell International Law Journal* 30 (1997): 759, 765–766.

94. See "Press Briefing by National Security Adviser Berger on Bosnia," *US Newswire,* 10 July 1997. Later, NATO forces were used to apprehend a handful of low- and middle-level indictees, whereas indicted Bosnian Serb leaders Radovan Karadzic and Ratko Mladic, and Serb president Slobodan Milosevic were given de facto immunity.

95. "Dissembling in Serbia."

96. "War-Crimes Hypocrisy," *Washington Post,* 2 February 1997, C6 (attacking U.S. policy of appeasement of war crimes suspects, reconfirmed when Secretary of State Albright met with Louise Arbour, the new ICTY prosecutor). This *Washington Post* editorial concludes that war crime suspects "have not been arrested because U.S. troops have chosen not to arrest them—because ultimately, President Clinton has failed to order their arrests." See also "Discussions, but No Plans Yet on Catching War Criminals: Pentagon," *Agence France Presse,* 11 February 1997.

97. Michael Scharf, "The Tools for Enforcing International Criminal Justice in the New Millennium: Lessons from the Yugoslavia Tribunal," *DePaul Law Review* 49 (2000): 925, 956–964.

98. With the election of Tony Blair as British prime minister, the United Kingdom began to press NATO for a more forceful policy on arresting indicted war criminals. Surprisingly, it was the UN peacekeeping force in Croatia, and not the NATO force, that made the first arrest. In June 1997, an agent of the prosecutor's office lured indicted war criminal Slavko Dokmanovic out of Serbia and into Eastern Slavonia (Croatia), where he was apprehended by UN peacekeeping forces and delivered to the ICTY.

99. Scharf, "Tools," 952.

100. See "Press Briefing by National Security Adviser Berger on Bosnia." That same day, British forces shot and killed indicted war criminal Simo Drjaca, the former police chief in Prijedor, when he fired upon them as they sought his arrest.

101. See for example, Jonathan Steele, "Dutch Seize War Crimes Suspects," *Guardian* (London), 19 December 1997, 11. See, for example, "Bosnia Serb General Captured, Charged with War Crimes" and "Captured Bosnia War Crime Suspects Now Total About 40," CNN online (25 June 2000), http://europe.cnn.com/2000/WORLD/europe/06/25/bosnia.warcrimes.01/index/html.

102. Scharf, "Tools," 941.

103. See *Annual Report of the International Criminal Tribunal for the Former Yugoslavia* (1996), paras. 167–169. Following Rule 61 hearings in the cases of Nikolic, Karadzic and Mladic, and Rajic, the president of the ICTY notified the Security Council of the refusal of the Republika Srpska, the Federal Republic of Yugoslavia, and Croatia, respectively, to surrender the accused. See "Letter from the President of the International Tribunal for the Prosecution of Persons Responsible for Serious Violations of International Humanitarian Law Committed in the Territory of the Former Yugoslavia to the President of the Security Council," 31 October 1995, UN Doc. S/1995/910 (1995) (Nikolic case); "Letter Dated 11 July 1996 from the President of the International Tribunal for the Prosecution of Persons Responsible for Serious Violations of International Humanitarian Law Committed in the Territory of the Former Yugoslavia Since 1991 Addressed to the President of the Security Council," UN Doc. S/1996/556 (1996) (Karadzic and Mladic case); "Letter Dated 16 September 1996 from the President of the International Tribunal for the Prosecution of Persons Responsible for Serious Violations of International Humanitarian Law Committed in the Territory of the Former Yugoslavia Since 1991 Addressed to the President of the Security Council," UN Doc. S/1996/763 (1996) (Rajic case).

104. See SC Res. 1074, UN SCOR, 3700th mtg., UN Doc. S/RES/1074 (1996), paras. 2 and 6.

105. See *Annual Report of the International Criminal Tribunal for the Former Yugoslavia.*

106. See Daphna Shraga and Ralph Zacklin, "The International Criminal Tribunal for Rwanda," *European Journal of International Law* 7 (1996): 501, 517.

107. Colum Lynch, "Departing War Crimes Tribunal Chief Assails UN Inaction," *Washington Post,* 9 November 1999, A26.

108. Scharf, "Tools," 927–928 (describing the use of "soft" [indirect] enforcement measures), 978. Scharf identified and described seven different "indirect" enforcement mechanisms employed by the ICTY:

> (1) condemnation of non-cooperation by the Assembly of State Parties or the UN Security Council; (2) offers of individual cash rewards for assistance in locating and apprehending indicted war criminals; (3) use of luring by deception to obtain custody over indicted war criminals; (4) freezing the assets of indicted war criminals; (5) offers of economic incentives to governments to induce cooperation; (6) imposition of diplomatic and economic sanctions on non-cooperating governments; and (7) use of military force to effectuate apprehension. Ibid., 927–928.

109. *Prosecutor v. Nikolic,* Indictment, no. IT-94–2, available at ICTY website, 12 February 1999, www.un.org/icty/indictment/english/nik-ii941104e.htm.

110. Theodor Meron, "Answering for War Crimes," *Foreign Affairs Journal* (January 1997): 2.

111. This resulted from a combination of factors, including a change of government in the United Kingdom, the appointment of Madeleine Albright as U.S. secretary of state, the lack of progress in the peace process in the former Yugoslavia, and

prosecutor Arbour's use of secret indictments to reduce potential risks to NATO forces involved in detention actions.

112. Undisclosed indictments may also exist. See "ICTFY Key Figures," ICTY website, 10 January 2001, www.un.org/icty/glance/keyfig-e.htm.

113. See "Fact Sheet on ICTFY Proceedings," ICTY website, 10 January 2001, www.un.org/icty/glance/procfact-e.htm.

114. Proceedings have been completed against: Drazen Erdemovic (pled guilty on 14 January 1998 to one count of a violation of the laws or customs of war and sentenced to five years' imprisonment); Dragan Papic (found not guilty of one count of a crime against humanity on 14 January 2000 and released immediately); Dusko Tadic (found guilty of five counts of violations of the laws or customs of war and six counts of crimes against humanity and sentenced ultimately to a maximum of twenty years' imprisonment on 26 January 2000); Zlatko Aleksovski (found guilty on one count of a violation of the laws or customs of war and ultimately sentenced to seven years' imprisonment on 24 March 2000); and Anto Furundzija (found guilty of two counts of violations of the laws or customs of war and sentenced to ten years' imprisonment, which was upheld on appeal on 21 July 2000). See ibid.

115. See Judicial Supplement 11, *Prosecutor v. Kupreskic and Others,* Case no. IT-95-16-T, available at ICTY website, 14 January 2000 (21 January 2001), www.un.org/icty/Supplement/supp11-e/kupreskic.htm.

116. See Judicial Supplement 7 in ibid.

117. See "Fact Sheet on ICTFY Proceedings," 4.

118. See "Law of War: Tribunal Metes Out Harshest Sentence to Croatian General," *International Enforcement Law Reporter* (April 2000): A1.

119. Prior to this, defendants had been released only due to illness or to mourn family members; see "Law of War: Tribunal Will Grant Bail to Two Defendants," *International Enforcement Law Reporter* (June 2000): C5.

120. See Judicial Supplement 14, *Prosecutor v. Simic and Others,* available at ICTY website (21 January 2001), www.un.org/icty/Supplement/supp14-e/simic2.htm, 1.

121. See *Prosecutor v. Simic and Others,* Case no. IT-95–9, Second Amended Indictment, available at ICTY website, 25 March 1999, www.un.org/icty/indictment/english/sim-2ai981211e.

122. Rule 65 of the Rules of Procedure and Evidence governs provisional release.

123. After the arrest of Slobodan Milosevic, Radovan Karadzic is the most sought-after war criminal. His indictment and that of Milosevic occupied the top spot in the ICTY. The rebel Bosnian Serb leader is regarded as one of the prime architects of the Balkan bloodbath. His continued absence from the ICTY has helped to shatter global faith in the international order. But the noose, it is hoped, is tightening, and like Milosevic his arrest will be a major coup for international justice.

124. Details can be accessed at www.un.org/icty.

125. ICTY Status of Cases, *Milosevic Case* ("Kosovo, Croatia, and Bosnia"), available at the ICTY website, 27 February 2002 (3 July 2002), www.un.org/icty/glance/casestatus.htm.

126. Donor countries pegged millions of dollars in aid on Milosevic's arrest and surrender. The initial recalcitrance gave way to the reality that Milosevic was Serbia and Montenegro's most valuable export. With a restive population and desperate to reconstruct a shattered Yugoslav economy badly in need of donor funds, the government reluctantly toned down its anti-ICTY rhetoric and acted. Sure enough, the purse strings opened as soon as Milosevic was on his way to The Hague.

127. *Prosecutor v. Milosevic,* no. IT-99–37-PT, available at ICTY website, 8 November 2001 (3 July 2002), www.un.org/icty/Supplement/supp26-e/milosevic. htm. Milosevic alleged, inter alia, the illegality of the ICTY because it was created not by the UN General Assembly but by the Security Council; lack of impartiality and/or bias against him so as to deprive him of a fair trial under international human rights standards; and lack of jurisdiction due to head-of-state immunity and/or unlawful transfer from the FRY.

128. "Fact Sheet on ICTFY Proceedings."

129. Ibid.

130. Ibid.

131. Ibid.

132. In 2000, the ICTY issued only two trial judgments.

133. *Prosecutor v. Kordic,* no. IT-95–14/2, available at ICTY website, 2 August 2001 (3 July 2002), www.un.org/icty/Supplement/supp14-e/kordic.htm.

134. *Prosecutor v. Todorovic,* no. IT-95–9/1 (accused sentenced to ten years' imprisonment in return for his plea of guilty), available at ICTY website, 31 July 2001 (3 July 2002), www.un.org/icty/Supplement/supp26-e/todorvic.htm.

135. *Prosecutor v. Mucic,* no. IT-96–21, available at ICTY website, 9 October 2001 (3 July 2002), www.un.org/icty/Supplement/supp28-e/celebibi.htm.

136. *Prosecutor v. Kvocka,* no. IT-98–30/1, available at ICTY website, 2 November 2001 (3 July 2002), www.un.org/icty/kvocka/trialc/judgement/kvo-tj0111102e-1.htm; *Prosecutor v. Sikirica,* no. IT-95–8, available at ICTY website, 13 November 2001, (3 July 2002), www.un.org/icty/sikirica/judgement/sik-tsj011113e.htm.

137. The statutes permit appeals from either party on (1) an error of law invalidating the impugned decision; (2) an error of fact that has occasioned a miscarriage of justice; or (3) an application for review of a decision if new facts emerge that could have been a decisive factor in reaching the impugned decision. Rule 72(B) of the Rules of Procedure and Evidence allows an interlocutory appeal as of right from decisions on preliminary motions challenging jurisdiction and upon good cause being shown. *ICTFY Statute,* arts. 25, 26; *Statute of the International Tribunal for Rwanda,* SC Res. 955, UN SCOR, 49th sess., 3453rd mtg., Annex, UN Doc. S/RES/955 (1994), arts. 24–25, available at ICTR website, www.ictr.org/ENGLISH/basicdocs/statute.html.

138. See Chapter 6.

139. See "Summary of Appeals Chamber Decision on Appeals Against the Decision of the Trial Chamber Rejecting the Defence Motions to Direct the Prosecutor to Investigate the Matter of False Testimony by Witnesses 'CC' and 'E'" (*Referencing Prosecutor v. Rutaganda, Notice of Appeal Against the Decision of Trial Chamber I Dismissing the Defence Motion for an Order to the Prosecutor to Investigate a Case of False Testimony* [Witness "CC"], no. ICTR-96–3-A), available at ICTR website, 26 March 1998, www.ictr.org/ENGLISH/cases/Rutaganda/decisions/sum980608.htm.

140. *Prosecutor v. Delalic,* no. IT-96–22, available at ICTY website, 20 February 2001 (3 July 2002), www.un.org/icty/celebici/appeal/judgement/cel-aj010220e-1.htm.

141. Press Release, "Appeal Judgment in the Celebici Case," available at ICTY website, 20 February 2001 (3 July 2002), www.un.org/icty/pressreal/564-e.htm.

142. *Prosecutor v. Kupreskic,* no. IT-95–16, available at UN website, 14 January 2000 (July 2002), www.un.org/kupreskic/trialc2/judgement/kup-tj000114e-1.htm.

143. Press Release, "International Criminal Tribunal for the Former Yugoslavia, Appeals Judgment Rendered in the 'Kupreskic and Others' Case (Oct. 23, 2001)," available at ICTY website (3 July 2002), www.un.org/icty/pressreal/p629-e.htm. The

three Kupreskics won complete reversals and the judgment ordered their immediate release from detention. The sentences of Josipovic and Santic were reduced from fifteen and twenty-five to twelve and eighteen years, respectively.

144. Stephen Castle, "War Crimes Court Reverses Convictions of Bosnians," *The Independent* (London), 24 October 2001, available at Global Policy website (3 July 2002), www.globalpolicy.org/intljustice/tribunals/2001/2410.htm.

145. "9th Annual Report of the International Tribunal for the Prosecution of Persons Responsible for Serious Violations of International Humanitarian Law Committed in the Territory of the Former Yugoslavia Since 1991," UN Doc. A/57/150 (2002), para. 213.

146. Ibid., para. 221–222.

147. Ibid., para. 207.

148. Ibid., para. 207.

149. Ibid., para. 218.

150. Brzezinski, "Bombs and Blather."

151. Statement of Antonio Cassese, President of the International Criminal Tribunal for the Former Yugoslavia, to the Parliamentary Assembly of the Council of Europe, "Dayton Four Months On: The Parties' Co-operation with the International Criminal Tribunal for the Former Yugoslavia (ICTFY) Under the Dayton Peace Agreement," (25 April 1996).

152. Paul Szasz, Introductory Note, "Documents Regarding the Situation in the Former Yugoslavia," 31 I.L.M. 1421 (1992).

6

Rwanda:
Portrait of a Reluctant
International Community

In 1994 the international community became a spectator to an archetypal genocide—the attempted extermination of an entire people in Rwanda. The genocide was anything but a surprise. Rather, it was the culmination of many years of cynical indifference and willful blindness to the plight of the Rwandan people. In the words of the Rwandan representative to the Security Council,

> Since 1959 Rwanda has repeatedly experienced collective massacres, which, as early as 1964, were described by Pope Paul VI and two Nobel Prize winners—Bertrand Russell and Jean-Paul Sartre—as the most atrocious acts of genocide this century after that of the Jews during the Second World War. But whenever such tragedies occurred the world kept silent and acted as though it did not understand that there was a grave problem of the violation of human rights.[1]

The slaughter required extensive administrative and logistical planning, evidenced by the calculated thoroughness with which it was carried out, as well as by the fact that most of the victims—between 500,000 and 1 million mainly Tutsi persons, politically moderate Hutu leaders, and their families[2]—were killed from 6 April 1994 through the first three weeks of that May. This toll amounted to roughly 10 percent of the national population.[3] Notwithstanding the low-tech nature of the massacres (victims were butchered with machetes, or *panga*, and sticks, tools, and large clubs studded with nails, or *masu*)[4], "the dead of Rwanda accumulated at nearly three times the rate of Jewish dead during the Holocaust. It was the most efficient mass killing since the atomic bombings of Hiroshima and Nagasaki."[5] In this sense, the genocide was well organized, coordinated, and administered;

it was anything but spontaneous and random.[6] During the genocide, murder and mayhem were the laws of the land.

The International Criminal Tribunal for Rwanda grew out of the response of the UN system to this tragedy. Parallel to the UN efforts, the government of Rwanda that came to power by toppling the genocidal regime[7] made a request to the UN Security Council for assistance to bring to justice those responsible.[8] Hailed by UN leadership as moral progress,[9] the ICTR was to merge humanitarian instincts with a purported administrative capacity to control deviant behavior. Virtually overnight, the capacity of the international community to punish in a presumptively nondiscriminatory and salubrious manner seemed to grow exponentially.[10]

On 8 November 1994, the day that the tribunal for Yugoslav issued its first indictment, a second international criminal tribunal was established by the UN Security Council. With the Tutsi slaughter over and the world regretting its passive role, the Security Council decided by Resolution 955 to establish the ICTR (officially, the International Criminal Tribunal for the Prosecution of Persons Responsible for Genocide and Other Serious Violations of International Humanitarian Law Committed in the Territory of Rwanda and Rwandan Citizens Responsible for Genocide and Other Such Violations Committed in the Territory of Neighboring States, Between 1 January 1994 and 31 December 1994).[11] It is charged with prosecuting Rwandans for genocide and other serious violations of international humanitarian law. Like the Yugoslav tribunal, it is called upon to address humanitarian concerns.

A People Betrayed:
The International Community's Indifference

Prior to the genocide, the population of Rwanda consisted of an estimated 85 percent Hutu, 14 percent Tutsi, and 1 percent Twa and others.[12] The ethnic compartmentalization and instrumentalization arguably had its roots in colonial Rwanda, with the colonial powers (first Germany, then Belgium) favoring the minority Tutsi people as the ruling class through a system of patron-client control.[13] On 1 July 1962, Rwanda achieved independence under the Hutu leadership of Gregoire Kayibanda. The relatively benign distinctions between Hutu and Tutsi quickly changed after independence redefined political cleavages and fostered enmity. In the early 1960s, violence was endemic, with large-scale massacres perpetrated in 1963 and 1966, mainly against Tutsi. In July 1973, Juvenal Habyarimana, a Hutu from northern Rwanda, seized control of the government and in 1975 formed the National Revolutionary Movement for Development. The Hutu government of Habyarimana, which ruled Rwanda from 1973, exploited and politicized the interethnic tensions that had been simmering, thereby fostering the marginalization and persecution of Tutsi. Motivated to regain their former position of prestige, and wishing to aid their brothers and sisters, Tutsi paramilitary forces coalesced into the Rwandese Patriotic Front (RPF). The RPF launched small-scale incursions from neighboring countries into Rwandan territory in order to force Habyarimana to share power.

By 1993 it must have been clear to the Habyarimana government that the RPF had become an insurgency movement capable of destabilizing Rwanda and that it would be prudent to explore the possibilities of a cease-fire. RPF commanders were obliged to negotiate with the government in order to translate small-scale military victories into larger political successes.[14] With bloodshed increasing in Rwanda, final meetings were convened in August 1993 between the Rwandan government and the RPF after a year of negotiations. These eventually resulted in political settlement between the RPF and the government and the signing of the Arusha Accords on 4 August 1993.[15] The accords, sponsored by the governments of Tanzania, Belgium, and Germany, as well as by the United Nations, were designed to promote respect for basic human rights and the rule of law, broaden power-sharing in Rwanda, and end the RPF insurgency. Then an 11 August 1993 report by the special rapporteur of the UN Commission on Human Rights on extrajudicial, summary, or arbitrary executions[16] shed light on continuing serious human rights violations and raised the question as to whether events might qualify as "genocide."[17] Arguably, the planning of the genocide in Rwanda involved the complicity of the international community.[18] Such planning was becoming evident even before the end of 1993.[19] Reports reaching the UN certainly pointed to this fact.[20] In the months before the mass killings began, Western "Rwanda watchers" ignored warnings that Hutu militias were mobilizing to exterminate the Tutsi minority.

Amid rising ethnic tensions, the UN was more concerned with safeguarding the Arusha Accords than with embarking on a systematic investigation, which in any event depended on cooperation from the government. In line with securing the diplomatic breakthrough that the Arusha Accords symbolized, the UN Secretary-General on 24 September 1993 apprised the Security Council of a plan to empower an international military force to ensure compliance with Arusha. He recommended that the existing peacekeeping force (UNOMUR)[21] be folded into the United Nations Assistance Mission in Rwanda (UNAMIR).[22] On 5 October 1993, the Security Council adopted Resolution 872, which created UNAMIR for an initial period of six months. Its restrictive mandate was later used as an excuse by the UN for the passive role of UN troops when the genocide came seven months later.

Although the Arusha Accords were considered by many as the first sign of effective power-sharing, they also bolstered accusations by extremist Hutu elements that the Habyarimana regime was merely a puppet of foreign

Tutsi interests who threatened to regain direct control over the government. In the final months of 1993, these extremist Hutu elements began to plan the elimination of Tutsi people by training groups of 300 persons (the Interahamwe) in methods of systematic slaughter.

In early April 1994, President Habyarimana flew to Dar-es-Salaam to attend a meeting with President Ali Hassan Mwinyi of Tanzania, Vice President George Saitoti of Kenya, President Cyprien Ntayamira of Burundi, and President Yoweri Museveni of Uganda concerning the maintenance of peace and security in the region. On 6 April, following the meeting, Habyarimana returned by jet to Kigali accompanied by Ntayamira, who intended to continue on to Bujumbura. As the aircraft circled the Kigali airport to land, it was shot down. All those aboard, including the two presidents, several ministers, and their entourages, died in the crash. The downing of the aircraft triggered massacres throughout the country.

Within thirty to forty minutes of the crash, roadblocks were set up in Kigali by Hutu militia, at which identity cards were checked; Tutsi were singled out and murdered on the spot. The slaughter plunged Rwanda into chaos. Other genocides in history took place in secret.[23] Rwanda was different. There was a UN peacekeeping force on the ground in Rwanda. Its members stood by and watched as killings took place. The rest of the world watched on television. The most damning indictment of the UN's recalcitrance? Weeks before the genocide began, the UN peacekeeping office had flatly rejected requests by UNAMIR's commander, General Romeo Dallaire, to seize large arms caches being acquired and hoarded by extremist Hutu elements.

Once the killings had begun, U.S. and European policymakers insisted on withdrawing peacekeepers, refused to jam radio broadcasts inciting murder, and issued tepid, belated condemnations. To defuse pressure to act, they also refrained from labeling the slaughter "genocide." On 7 April Prime Minister Agathe Unwilingiyimana of Rwanda, as well as ten Belgian peacekeeping soldiers assigned to protect her, were murdered by soldiers of the Rwandan government.[24] In the aftermath, the Belgian backbone of the multinational mission was yanked out. On 9 April 1994, three days into the genocide, General Dallaire, the Canadian commander of 2,500 UN peacekeepers, watched as European troops descended upon the Kigali airport to begin evacuating their citizens. "The new arrivals were clean-shaven, well fed and heavily armed, a marked contrast with the ragged, ill-equipped force that General Dallaire had battled his own headquarters to arm, shelter and feed."[25]

General Dallaire spent the next two weeks watching his last, best hope for assistance from the West disappear. The European evacuation forces that swooped in amid the unfolding genocide to evacuate their citizens departed by 13 April, leaving Tutsi and moderate Hutu to their fates.

Finally, on 21 April, two weeks after the bloodbath began, with reports of some 100,000 Rwandans dead, the Security Council, in perhaps its most shameful hour, slashed the flimsy peacekeeping force further, leaving 450 troops to tackle tens of thousands of killers. The Security Council adopted Resolution 912, which reduced the size of UNAMIR despite pleas from some African countries (nine days before) to have the military capability of the peacekeeping force bolstered.[26] In the critical words of Dallaire, "An operation should begin with the objective and then consider how best to achieve it with minimal risk. Instead, our operation began with an evaluation of risk, and if there was risk, the objective was forgotten."[27]

It was already apparent that the events were not linked to any struggle for power but rather were a systematic genocide by Hutu extremists, perpetrated against the Tutsi minority and politically moderate Hutu. On 30 April 1994 the Security Council issued a presidential statement pointing out that the killings of civilians had "especially" taken place in areas under the control of members or supporters of the interim government of Rwanda (whose representative was still participating in the deliberations of the Security Council). However, the Council circumvented the use of the term *genocide* by instead including an almost direct quote from the Genocide Convention in the text.[28]

As a result of the force reduction, peacekeepers often stranded Tutsi who had sought their protection, leaving them at the mercy of Hutu assailants who prowled nearby. General Dallaire's pleas with the Security Council for troop reinforcements, supplies, and the authority to protect civilians fell on deaf ears. Weeks later, when the UN Security Council would finally conclude what was plain from the start—that a genocide had indeed been taking place—it was too late to do anything.[29] To have admitted otherwise would have bound the parties to the 1948 Genocide Convention[30] to intervene and bring the mass murder to a halt. The Rwandan people would become, in the words of Linda Melvern, a British journalist, "a people betrayed."[31]

Initially the international spotlight was not focused on events in Rwanda. Compounding this was the fact that Rwanda, represented by the Habyarimana government, was a member of the Security Council from January 1994. In effect, the entity spearheading the genocide had full access to the discussions of the Council and had the opportunity to influence decisionmaking to its own ends. Further, the presence of Rwanda on the Security Council also affected the information presented to the Council, limiting its scope and depth.

Most countries in the West decided that the civil anarchy under way was an internal matter—a fight for political power and dominance—and thus was not subject to more robust action by the international community. In the meantime, the West focused on Yugoslavia, the most violent conflict in Europe since World War II. Rwanda, situated in Africa, was far removed. The tiny former Belgian colony had none of the same lure, and without initiative from powerful Western countries there was little that Africa would do except watch.[32] In addition, Rwanda paid for the failures of the international community in the Somali debacle and the resultant "fatigue" from that crisis.[33] Partly due to Mogadishu, as well as the U.S. marginalization of Africa, the United States refrained from intervening or pushing to stop the genocide in Rwanda. With congressional pressure to steer clear of UN operations, the administration of President Bill Clinton was the most adamant opponent of sending in troop reinforcements.[34] U.S. isolationist stereotypes of "African conflicts"[35] became the pretext for passivity as top U.S. officials forbade the use of the term *genocide,* as that would increase moral pressure on the president to take action.[36]

It was not until 17 May 1994, six weeks after the genocide had begun, that the Security Council acknowledged, with the adoption of Resolution 918, that a genocide occurred in Rwanda. By that time 800,000 Tutsi and Hutu moderates lay dead. This despite the UN Secretary-General's acknowledgment of the fact more than two weeks earlier.[37] The Secretary-General was still ahead of the U.S. secretary of state, Warren Christopher, whose stance epitomized U.S. indifference and unwillingness to support or encourage any UN initiatives. The U.S. opposition and failure to act sealed the betrayal of the Rwandan people. Five weeks later Secretary of State Christopher relented, quipping that "if there is any magic in calling it genocide . . . I have no hesitancy in saying that."[38] There was magic, all right, in the sense that using the term would have bound the United States and other governments to act. By the time Christopher made his grudging concession to reality, it was too late—which may have been the idea all along.

Shortly after the Hutu extremists launched the genocide, the RPF undertook a major military offensive, moving from Uganda into northern Rwanda. By mid-July 1994, under the leadership of Paul Kagame, the RPF was able to halt the genocide, force the retreat of the former government of Rwanda and associated militia from Kigali, and assert effective control over the remaining Rwandan territory. Kagame was elevated to vice president and minister of defense in the new government. Most of the individuals responsible for carrying out violations of human rights and humanitarian law fled the country among the more than 2 million refugees to neighboring Burundi, Zaire, and Tanzania for fear of possible Tutsi reprisals and revenge attacks. Numerous criminal suspects fled to francophone West African countries, as well as to Kenya, and as far away as Belgium, Canada, France, Switzerland, and the United States.

The UN failure to prevent, and subsequently to stop, the genocide was a failure by the system. The fundamental failure was a lack of resources and political commitment to Rwanda and the UN presence there. There was a persistent lack of will to act among member states.[39] Early UN attempts to respond to the crisis were characterized by bickering and miserliness.[40] The UN adopted a compartmentalized response, with most agencies developing separate strategies. Donor governments were even more divided on what could and should be done.[41] This compartmentalization led to infighting. The early UN strife hurt all efforts to effect a sustainable response. The United States was to enter the region only after the RPF had emerged victorious, and then only with the restricted mandate of airlifting supplies to refugee camps.[42]

Redeeming the World's Conscience: Responding Through the International Penal Process

With the existence of the International Criminal Tribunal for the Former Yugoslavia, it would have been patently discriminatory for the Security Council not to have considered creating a similar institution for Rwanda. Despite the fact that many Security Council members did not consider Rwanda to be as closely tied to their national interests as was the former Yugoslavia, the Council nevertheless had to respond in kind.[43] Parallel to these efforts, the government of Rwanda[44] made a request to the UN Security Council for assistance to bring those responsible to justice.[45]

The UN Commission on Human Rights met in a special session in May 1994.[46] The commission named a special rapporteur to investigate and instructed the Office of High Commissioner for Human Rights to establish a field presence in Rwanda.[47] Days following the special rapporteur's report outlining the human rights problems, and in response to the massive violations in Rwanda, the Security Council adopted Resolution 935 on 1 July 1994. This resolution recalled that "all persons who commit or authorize the commission of serious violations of international humanitarian law are individually responsible for those violations and should be brought to justice" and requested the Secretary-General

> to establish, as a matter of urgency, an impartial Commission of Experts to examine and analyze information submitted pursuant to the present resolution, together with such further information as the Commission of Experts might obtain, through its own investigations or the efforts of other persons or bodies, including the information made available by the Special Rapporteur on Rwanda, with a view to providing the Secretary-General with its conclusions on the evidence of grave violations of international humanitarian law committed in the territory of Rwanda, including the evidence of possible acts of genocide.[48]

Resolution 935 requested the Secretary-General to report to the Security Council within four months of the establishment of the Commission of

Experts. The history of the commission and its work is fraught with politics. The Rwanda commission lasted only four months, not long enough to effectively fulfill an investigatory mandate. Seemingly, the Security Council wished to ensure that the Rwanda commission would not embark on the same path of aggressive investigation and data collection taken by the Commission of Experts for the former Yugoslavia. The Rwanda commission was given a limited mandate and no means to investigate specific allegations. The three-person commission spent a total of one week in the field and conducted no intensive investigations. Its report was patterned on the final report of the Commission of Experts for the former Yugoslavia but lacked thoroughness. The Rwanda commission's report was based on reports made by other bodies, the media, and previously published reports.

The Commission of Experts observed that both sides to the armed conflict in Rwanda during the period 6 April 1994 to 15 July 1994 were responsible "for serious breaches of international humanitarian law, in particular of obligations set forth in article 3 common to the four Geneva Conventions of 12 August 1949 and in Protocol II additional to the Geneva Conventions and relating to the protection of victims of non-international armed conflicts, of 8 June 1977." With the support of the work already done by the special rapporteur and of the high commissioner's field operation in Rwanda, the Commission of Experts took note of violations committed by elements associated with the former government as well as by members of the RPF. It concluded that

> there exists overwhelming evidence to prove that acts of genocide against the Tutsi group were perpetrated by Hutu elements in a concerted, planned, systematic and methodical way. Abundant evidence shows that these mass exterminations perpetrated by Hutu elements against the Tutsi group as such, during the period mentioned above, constitute genocide within the meaning of article 11 of the Convention on the Prevention and Punishment of the Crime of Genocide, adopted on 9 December 1948. To this point, the Commission has not uncovered any evidence to indicate that Tutsi elements perpetrated acts committed with intent to destroy the Hutu ethnic group as such during the said period, within the meaning of the Genocide Convention of 1948.[49]

The commission therefore recommended international prosecution of persons responsible under international law and that "the Security Council amend the Statute of the International Criminal Tribunal for the former Yugoslavia to ensure that its jurisdiction covers crimes under international law committed during the armed conflict in Rwanda that began on 6 April 1994." On 8 November 1994, the Security Council adopted Resolution 955 creating the ICTR, with the ICTR Statute becoming the resolution's annex. Resolution 955 reiterates the Council's "grave concern at the reports indicating that genocide and other systematic, widespread and flagrant violations of international humanitarian law have been committed in Rwanda," determines "that this situation continues to constitute a threat to international peace and security," and resolves "to put an end to such crimes and to take effective measures to bring to justice the persons who are responsible for them." Resolution 955 underlines the conviction that prosecution of individuals responsible for serious violations of international humanitarian law are intended to contribute to the process of national reconciliation and the restoration and maintenance of peace. Rwanda was the only country to vote against establishing the ICTR; it had originally approached the UN to develop a viable response to the genocide and had advocated the creation of the ICTR to the Security Council.[50]

Rwanda's opposition to the ICTR deserves some review. When the Rwandan government first introduced the idea of an international tribunal, it had some kind of hybrid system in mind: international jurists would work side by side with Rwandan colleagues, but the government would maintain some control. The government pushed for an international tribunal to be established by the UN to cooperate with its own justice system. The resulting organization was different, leading to Rwanda's opposition.[51] Although some have attributed this to the Rwandan government's desire to impose capital punishment,[52] other reasons are worth mentioning.[53] By the time the vote occurred, the UN had departed from Rwandan wishes in two ways. First, the ICTR was to deal more with individual criminals and not with the culture of impunity. Second, the majority in the Security Council believed ICTR neutrality and independence were more important than any connection to the social process in Rwanda. For the Rwandans it became evident that independent justice meant a justice that Rwanda could not influence, including the prosecutorial strategy.[54] Further, the structural distance of the ICTR from the Rwandan social process would make it difficult for the ICTR's work to be relevant and unlikely that its work would address the root causes of the genocide.[55] Additionally, the Rwandans also objected to limited temporal jurisdiction, the structure of the ICTR, the few resources provided for operation, and the fact that the new government would be subject to ICTR jurisdiction for any crimes against humanity it had committed.

Although the ICTR was established as a separate institution, its establishment "at a time when the [ICTY] was already in existence dictated a similar legal approach (and) mandated that certain organizational and institutional links be established in order to ensure a unity of legal approach as well as economy and efficiency of resources."[56] Accordingly, article 15 of the ICTR Statute provides that the Yugoslavia and Rwanda tribunals have a common prosecutor, although assisted by an additional deputy prosecution for the ICTR. Likewise, article 12(2) provides that the five members of the chamber of the ICTY "shall also serve as the members of the chamber of the International Tribunal for Rwanda."[57] The tribunals are organized similarly but separately. Each tribunal has its own registry and its own two Trial Chambers (composed of three judges each). Pursuant to article 28 of the ICTR Statute, which mirrors article 29 of the ICTY Statute, states are obliged to cooperate with and to grant assistance to the international tribunals.[58] These provisions entail the core obligation to accept and carry out UN Security Council decisions to establish the ad hoc tribunals.

Curiously, the tribunals share a common prosecutor and a common Appellate Chamber. According to the Secretary-General, the "institutional links . . . ensure a unity of legal approach, as well as economy and efficiency of resources." The decision to link the two bodies was not based on any valid legal argument. The United States, which pushed for this formula, wanted to avoid delays in selecting the prosecutor, as was the case with the ICTY.[59] But as Professor M. C. Bassiouni notes:

> The choice of a single Prosecutor was particularly ill advised because no person, no matter how talented, can oversee two major sets of prosecutions separated by 10,000 miles. The idea that one can shuttle between The Hague, Netherlands and Arusha, Tanzania as part of a normal work schedule is nothing short of absurd.[60]

The ICTR was a sideshow; the prosecutor for both tribunals is resident in The Hague, as are the members of the Appeals Chamber. Initially, the international press and the UN were preoccupied with the ICTY and gave perfunctory coverage to the ICTR. Such cynicism undercut the rule of law. Not surprisingly, the ICTR's first hearing was held against a backdrop of charges of corruption and mismanagement at the tribunal.[61] A subsequent investigative report concluded that the ICTR was dysfunctional in virtually all areas.[62]

We next look at several developments in the ICTR.

Fulfilling a Mandate: Developments in the ICTR

The ICTR or authorities cooperating with it have detained dozens of suspects.[63] The ICTR has ruled on more than 300 motions.[64] Many of the people tried or indicted were former government ministers, mayors, military commanders, and militia leaders.[65] The ICTR's first judgment following a trial was the conviction of Jean-Paul Akayesu, the *bourgemestre* (local mayor) of the Taba Commune, for genocide.[66] In May 1999, Clement Kayishema, prefect of Kibuye, and Obed Ruzindana, a prominent businessman, were tried together and then convicted of genocide; they were sentenced to life imprisonment and twenty-five years' imprisonment, respectively.[67] On 6 December 1999, the ICTR found former Interahamwe militia leader Georges Rutaganda guilty of genocide and crimes against humanity for extermination and murder.[68] In January 2000 Alfred Musema, director of the Gisovu Tea Factory, was convicted of genocide and crimes against humanity for rape and extermination.[69]

In the pantheon of senior figures apprehended and brought to trial by the ICTR, the most senior individual has been Jean Kambanda, who was the prime minister of Rwanda and head of the interim government from 8 April 1994 until he left the country on or about 17 July 1994—the three months during which the genocide occurred. Kambanda was arrested by Kenyan authorities in July 1997 on the basis of a formal request submitted by the ICTR prosecutor on 9 July 1997, in accordance with the provisions of Rule 40 of the ICTR Rules of Procedure and Evidence. The indictment charged Kambanda with genocide, conspiracy to commit genocide, direct and public incitement to commit genocide, complicity in genocide, and crimes against humanity.[70]

In a major development, Kambanda, during his initial appearance before the ICTR on 1 May 1998, pled guilty to the six counts in his indictment. Kambanda had signed a plea agreement with the prosecutor in which he agreed that he was pleading guilty because he was in fact guilty and acknowledged full responsibility for the crimes alleged.[71] Most significant, the Kambanda judgment predated and was cited by human rights groups in the 1998 case in which the United Kingdom's House of Lords ruled that General Augusto Pinochet, former head of state of Chile, was not immune from prosecution for international crimes such as crimes against humanity, torture, and hostage-taking, overruling a lower court.[72] Even more directly, the Kambanda judgment serves as precedent for the 1999 indictment and transfer to The Hague of Slobodan Milosevic, former president of the FRY, to face trial before the ICTY. Considering the legal parallels between Kambanda's case and that of Milosevic,[73] the ICTY Trial Chamber will, in all probability, rely on the Kambanda judgment.

The ICTR also established precedent in situations where the accused declines to be represented by counsel. The most famous example is Milosevic, who declined to formally appoint a lawyer or accept counsel assigned to represent his interests (thus the appointment of amicus curiae). This situation arose at the ICTR but was dealt with decisively and innovatively. Rule 45 provides that a Trial Chamber may, in the interest of justice, instruct the registrar to assign counsel to represent the interests of the accused. This new rule formalized a power that the ICTR previously exercised under its inherent powers. In *Prosecutor v. Jean-Bosco Barayagwiza, Ferdinand Nahimana, and Hassan Ngeze,*[74] Trial Chamber I instructed the registrar to assign counsel to represent the interests of Barayagwiza, who was indigent; he declined to accept counsel, a move viewed by the Trial Chamber as an attempt to obstruct progress in the trial.

The ICTR was criticized for moving too slowly. Although the ICTR has a multimillion-dollar budget, by early 2000, six years after its establishment, it had completed only four trials, and forty-eight other cases were pending. One reason for the delay was its newness. Creating a tribunal from the ground up is difficult, and the ICTR was not capable of processing cases efficiently yet. The ICTR thus suffered from physical, legal, and procedural impediments. As of 2000, however, the ICTR shook off its lethargy and made significant progress on numerous fronts.

In addition to securing new convictions and concluding several appeals, the ICTR improved its relationship with the Rwandan government. The relationship began under a cloud of strained relations in the aftermath of the Appeals Chamber's 1999 decision to dismiss charges against Barayagwiza.[75] However, in March 2000 the Appeals Chamber decided to overrule its earlier decision to dismiss charges and reinstated the charges, something the Rwandan government saluted as a "victory for victims."[76] Subsequently the ICTR took steps to repair and improve its relationship with the Rwandan government and its citizens. The improved relations may facilitate the investigation and, if appropriate, the indictment and prosecution of persons from the largely Tutsi RPF.[77] The RPF remains in power. The failure of the ICTR to indict RPF members exposed the ICTR as being a "victor's tribunal."[78] The chief prosecutor intends to investigate RPF members and has publicly secured the cooperation of the government.[79]

In 2000 ICTR judges for the first time agreed to requests by the Rwandan government to visit crime scenes.[80] More significant, Chief Prosecutor Carla Del Ponte announced that she would request the Trial Chambers to hold future hearings in Rwanda and that in the future "it might even be possible to . . . [move] the entire Tribunal to Kigali."[81] And in September 2000 the ICTR opened an information and outreach center in Kigali to house a public information area, document repository, and legal library and manage a victims' assistance program.[82] As of October 2000, the Trial Chambers had received two guilty pleas and completed five trials, involving six defendants.[83] The early indictment, confession, and conviction of former prime minister Kambanda was a milestone for establishing legitimacy.[84] Additionally, Omar Serushago, a former Interahamwe militia leader, pled guilty to genocide and crimes against humanity.[85] By the end of 2000, the ICTR had forty-four individuals in custody at its detention facility in Arusha, Tanzania.[86] The ICTR continued to receive international cooperation in apprehending and extraditing indicted high-level political and military leaders.[87] The trial of Georges Ruggiu, a former journalist and broadcaster, ended after the accused changed his plea to guilty on 15 May 2000. Ruggiu was sentenced on 1 June 2000 to twelve years in prison after being found guilty on charges of direct and public incitement to commit genocide and of crimes against humanity.[88]

The ICTR also concluded two landmark appeals during 2000. On 14 February 2000, the Appeals Chamber dismissed the appeal of Omar Serushago, confirming the Trial Chamber's sentence of fifteen years' imprisonment on charges of genocide and crimes against humanity.[89] Serushago thus became "the first person to be definitively convicted and sentenced by the ICTR."[90] The Appeals Chamber also unanimously upheld the conviction of Kambanda.[91] Kambanda thus became "the first head of government to be convicted and punished for genocide by an international criminal tribunal."[92]

As of late 2001, the ICTR had indicted more than seventy individuals.[93] Fifty-two were in custody, and four others arrested in 2001 were detained by other states.[94] One individual was acquitted and conditionally released pending appeal by the prosecutor.[95] The ICTR convicted eight, and the Appeals Chamber confirmed six convictions. At the end of 2001, thirty-one of the accused were in pretrial stages, seventeen were at trial in seven proceedings, and two were pursuing an appeal.[96] In December 2001, six convicted persons were transferred to Mali to serve out their sentences.

The Trial Chambers concluded only one case during 2001. On 7 June 2001, Trial Chamber I acquitted Ignace Bagilishema of all charges and ordered his conditional release pending the prosecutor's appeal.[97] The Trial Chambers commenced three trials involving ten defendants in 2001, including the first female accused of genocide in an international court.[98] The ICTR concluded four appeals from trial court verdicts and sentences during 2001. On 2 June 2001, the Appeals Chamber rejected the appeal of Jean-Paul Akayesu, confirming the trial verdict and sentence.[99] On the same date, the Appeals Chamber confirmed the sentences and verdicts in the cases of Clement Kayishema and Obed Ruzindana.[100] The ICTR also found inadmissible an appeal by the prosecutor in the *Ruzindana* case, as it was untimely filed.[101] On 16 November 2001, the Appeals Chamber issued its ruling on the appeal of Alfred Musema, confirming his life sentence and his conviction for genocide and extermination as a crime against humanity. The Appeals Chamber did, however, reverse his conviction for rape as a crime against humanity based upon new evidence.[102] Perhaps the most startling decision came in the *Bagilishema* case—the first acquittal. Bagilishema, a *bourgemestre* for fourteen years, had been accused of genocide and other crimes.[103] This dramatic development was, however, reversed, and the accused was taken back into custody and his trial subsequently commenced.

Between 1 July 2001 and 30 June 2002, eleven more accused persons were arrested, and fourteen new indictments were submitted, all of which were confirmed. Warrants of arrest were then issued, which in most cases led to the rapid arrest and transfer of indictees.[104] In total, the ICTR had "indicted 80 persons; of whom 60 were in custody and 20 at large. Warrants of arrest were issued for these 20 persons and the cooperation of States was sought to secure their arrest. Of the 60 persons already arrested, 8 were sentenced, 1 was acquitted, 22 are involved in ongoing trials and 29 are in custody awaiting the commencement of their trials."[105]

During the same period the ICTR held trials. Nine trials of twenty-two accused persons were in progress before three Trial Chambers, with three judgments with respect of four defendants being rendered in 2002.[106] The prosecutor revised the future investigation program from the original estimate of 136 new suspects to fourteen, together with ten ongoing investigations. The resulting twenty-four new indictments, which the prosecutor intends to submit for confirmation by the end of 2004, will conclude the investigation program.[107] In addition, the prosecutor identified forty suspects whose prosecution was to be deferred to national jurisdictions for trial. Fifteen of these suspects were in countries that have adopted the principle of universal jurisdiction and could be tried in those countries. The cases of twenty-five other suspects who did not occupy high positions of responsibility could be transferred to Rwandan authorities. For this purpose, the prosecutor sought the introduction of a new rule (Rule 11 *bis,* similar to that of the ICTY) to facilitate the deferral of cases to Rwanda, where indictments have already been confirmed, provided that the death penalty is not imposed.[108]

The prosecutor indicated readiness for trial in seven cases involving thirteen of the twenty-nine persons in custody. However, the Trial Chambers were fully engaged with the ongoing trials of twenty-two defendants until the expiration of the judges' mandate on 23 May 2003 and therefore did not undertake any new trials. The prosecutor also devoted attention to the organization of an evidence database, essential for the preparation and presentation of cases. A special project was implemented with the assistance of the ICTY Evidence Unit to perform an audit of the database and of standard operating procedures for processing and retrieving documentary and other evidence.

Conclusion

In the words of Samantha Powers, "A vast array of international decisions, non-decisions and decisions not to decide ensured that the Rwandan people and the peacekeepers would be abandoned to their fates."[109] Two international investigations of the disaster have already been completed. The UN-commissioned independent inquiry in May 1999 was harshly critical. In July 2000, six years after the massacre, the Organization of African Unity issued pointed criticism. In addition to laying the blame at the feet of the UN and the United States, it called upon Security Council members to pay reparations to survivors of what it called the "preventable genocide."

Establishing the "other" tribunal, the ICTR, was possible because the ICTY had set a precedent for the international community. Thus the UN and the powerful states that control it could not reject a tribunal for

Rwanda. The conflicts had taken place in front of TV cameras, making it impossible to prosecute one group of perpetrators but not the other. Arguably, the Rwanda tribunal was an afterthought.[110]

The ICTR stands as a symbol of failure for the international community to understand historical lessons. The ICTR also has shortcomings. First, the ICTR Statute does not cover the entire normative field of international humanitarian law. Second, the tribunal was designed to address the specific factual situation of Rwanda. And third, the tribunal carries out selective prosecutions, and the focus is often on high-profile defendants.

Although the ICTR's accomplishments are significant, there are many obstacles that could prevent it from fulfilling its mandate. Its relationship with the Rwandan government, delays in prosecution, and challenges to legitimacy and integrity could thwart efforts to achieve accountability. In addition, ongoing instability in the region could lead to a perception that the ICTR is ineffectual and unable to contribute to peace. Although one reason the ICTR was created was to compensate for the inability of the Rwandan courts to render justice, it has suffered from some of the same problems as the Rwandan courts, including violations of due process. Additionally, the ICTR and the Rwandan government have not adequately publicized their proceedings.[111]

The two ad hoc international criminal tribunals are important milestones in the international system. The by-products of international realpolitik,[112] they mark a new pattern in the implementation of international criminal law and a return to the model of Nuremberg. On the legal front, the tribunals are living testimony that a permanent penal tribunal can function. Their establishment helped sustain the drive toward a permanent international criminal court in 1998. We now turn to that issue.

Notes

1. UN SCOR, 49th sess., 3453rd mtg., UN Doc. S/PV 3453 (1994), 13–14.
2. See UN ESCOR Commission on Human Rights, *Report of the Situation of Human Rights in Rwanda Submitted by Mr. R. Degni-Sequi, Special Rapporteur of the Commission on Human Rights,* 51st sess., Provisional Agenda Item 12, UN Doc. E/CN 4/1995/7 (1994), para. 24.
3. See Philip Gourevitch, *We Wish to Inform You That Tomorrow We Will Be Killed with Our Families: Stories from Rwanda* (New York: Farrar, Straus, and Giroux, 1998), 4.
4. See Madeline H. Morris, "The Trials of Concurrent Jurisdiction: The Case of Rwanda," *Duke Journal of Comparative and International Law* 7 (1997): 349, 350.
5. Gourevitch, *We Wish to Inform You,* 4. "That's three hundred and thirty-three and a third murders an hour—or five and a half lives terminated every minute." Ibid., 133. Of course, to these numbers have to be added the "uncounted legions who were maimed but did not die of their wounds, and the systematic and serial

rape of Tutsi women, in order to fully grasp the numbers of aggressive participants and victims in the genocide." Ibid.

6. Most of the individuals responsible for carrying out violations of human rights and humanitarian law fled the country, among the more than 2 million that sought refuge in the neighboring countries of Burundi, Zaire, and Tanzania for fear of possible Tutsi reprisals and revenge attacks. Numerous criminal suspects fled to francophone West African countries, as well as to Kenya, and as far away as Belgium, Canada, France, Switzerland, and the United States.

7. The Rwandan Patriotic Front took power in July 1994. For an overview, see Gerard Prunier, "The Great Lakes Crisis," *Current History* 96 (1997): 193.

8. "Letter Dated 28 September 1994 from the Permanent Representative of Rwanda Addressed to the President of the Security Council," UNSCOR, 49th sess., UN Doc. S/1994/1115 (1994), 4.

9. See Kofi Annan, "Advocating for an International Criminal Court," *Fordham International Law Journal* 21 (1997): 363, 365 ("these tribunals have made significant progress and are setting an important precedent").

10. Carrie Gustafson, "International Criminal Courts: Some Dissident Views on the Continuation of War by Penal Means," *Houston Journal of International Law* 21 (1998): 51, 53.

11. SC Res. 955, 8 November 1994.

12. See generally Gérard Prunier, *The Rwanda Crisis: History of a Genocide* (New York: Columbia University Press, 1995).

13. For a history of the ethnic compartmentalization of Rwanda by the colonial powers and the construction of ethnicity, see generally Alain Destexhe, *Rwanda and Genocide in the Twentieth Century,* translated by Alison Marschner (London and East Haven, CT: Pluto, 1995).

14. Negotiations between the government of Rwanda and the RPF commenced at Arusha, Tanzania, on 10 August 1992. The main issues to be addressed at the Arusha peace negotiations were: the need for multiparty elections and power-sharing in Rwanda; the fostering of peace and respect for the rule of law; and an end to the RPF insurgency. These negotiations did not bear fruit immediately.

15. The agreement provided for a broad role for the United Nations, through what the agreement termed the Neutral International Force (NIF), in the supervision of implementation of the accords during a transitional period that was to last twenty-two months. Previously, in a letter to the Secretary-General on 14 June 1993 (S/25951), the government and the RPF had jointly requested the establishment of such a force and asked the Secretary-General to send a reconnaissance team to Rwanda to plan the force. The parties agreed that the existing OAU Neutral Monitoring Group (NMOG II) might be integrated into the NIF.

16. See the report of Bacre Waly Ndiaye on his mission to Rwanda, 8–17 April 1993, E/CN 4/1994/7/Add. 1, 11 August 1993.

17. Ibid., paras. 78–80.

18. In a letter dated 18 March 1999 (S/1994/339), the Secretary-General informed the Security Council of his intention to appoint an independent inquiry into the actions of the United Nations during the 1994 genocide in Rwanda. In their reply (S/1999/340), the members of the Council expressed support for the initiative in this unique circumstance. In May 1999, the Secretary-General appointed Ingvar Carlsson (former prime minister of Sweden), Han Sung-Joo (former foreign minister of South Korea), and Lieutenant-General (ret.) Rufus M. Kupolati (Nigeria) to conduct the inquiry. Subsequently, the *Report of the Independent Inquiry Into the Actions of the United Nations During the 1994 Genocide in Rwanda,* 15 December 1999, concluded that: "The Independent Inquiry finds that the response of the

United Nations before and during the 1994 genocide in Rwanda failed in a number of fundamental respects. The responsibility for the failings of the United Nations to prevent and stop the genocide in Rwanda lies with a number of different actors, in particular the Secretary-General, the Secretariat, the Security Council, UNAMIR and the broader membership of the United Nations. This international responsibility is one which warrants a clear apology by the Organization and by Member States concerned to the Rwandese people." www.un.org/News/ossg/rwanda-report (full report available).

19. The government effort in 1993 to carry out a census in which all Rwandans had to state their tribe was followed by a slaughter of Tutsi in the north. This would prove to be a dress rehearsal for the genocide. In the run-up to the signing of the Arusha Accords, it was clear that Habyarimana was restructuring the Hutu-dominated administration to put extremists in positions of authority—extremists whose main goal was to conspire to launch a final genocidal strike against the hated Tutsi minority, spearheaded by the Interahamwe.

20. In her book *A People Betrayed: The Role of the West in Rwanda's Genocide* (London and New York: Zed Books, 2000), Linda Melvern offers a vivid picture of the role of Western nations in abetting, ignoring, and allowing Rwanda's genocide. She singles out "accomplices" like France, which, with an eye to preserving its dominance in the region, provided the murderous Hutu regime with arms, money, and even protection (allegations France has denied).

21. The United Nations Observer Mission Uganda-Rwanda, established by SC Res. 846, 22 June 1993.

22. UNAMIR was an operation created in the shadow of Somalia. In particular, the deaths of the Pakistani and U.S. peacekeepers in Somalia in 1993 had a deep effect on the attitude toward the conduct of peacekeeping operations. For instance, the UN commission of inquiry set up to study those deaths whose report came out just as preparations were being made to strengthen UNAMIR in the wake of the genocide concluded that "*the UN should refrain from undertaking further peace enforcement actions within the internal conflicts of States*" (emphasis added): S/1994/653. For the U.S. government the events in Mogadishu were a watershed in its policy toward UN peacekeeping. By May 1994, when the genocide began, President Clinton had enacted PDD25, a presidential directive that placed strict conditions on U.S. support for UN peacekeeping.

23. Genocide of the Armenians by Turkey during World War I and the Nazi extermination of Europe's Jews and Gypsies.

24. UNAMIR had been vested only with a UN Charter Chapter VI mandate to monitor and assist in the implementation of the Arusha Accords. It had neither the capability nor the mandate to enforce peace, which could have been made available to it pursuant to Chapter VII of the Charter. On 21 April, the Security Council adopted Resolution 912, which reduced the size of UNAMIR from 2,500 to 270.

25. Samantha Powers, "Accessory to Murder?" *New York Times,* 11 February 2001.

26. On 13 April, Nigeria had presented a draft resolution in the Security Council on behalf of the Non-Aligned Caucus advocating a strengthening of UNAMIR.

27. Ibid.

28. S/PRST/1994/21.

29. On 30 April 1994, the Security Council issued a presidential statement (S/PRST/1994/21). The Council did not at that stage respond to the substance of the Secretary-General's letter and instead promised to do so later. The Council pointed out that the killings of civilians had "especially" taken place in areas under the control of members or supporters of the interim government of Rwanda (whose representative

was still participating in the deliberations of the Council). The Council circumvented the use of the term "genocide" by instead including an almost direct quote from the Genocide Convention in the text. It was not until 17 May 1994, with the adoption of Resolution 918, that the Security Council acknowledged the genocide in Rwanda.

30. Convention on the Prevention and Punishment of the Crime of Genocide 1951, 78 U.N.T.S. No 1021 ("Genocide Convention"), 277.

31. Melvern, *A People Betrayed.*

32. As noted by Prunier, *The Rwanda Crisis: History of a Genocide,* 261: "If we consider that probably around 800,000 people were slaughtered during the short period . . . the daily killing rate was at least five times that of the Nazi death camps."

33. For the failures of U.S. and UN efforts in Somalia, see Hussein H. Adam, "Somalia: A Terrible Beauty Being Born," in *Collapsed States: The Disintegration and Restoration of Legitimate Authority,* edited by William I. Zartmann (Boulder and London: Lynne Reinner, 1995), 69–89; Michael Begg, "UN Withdrawal from Somalia," *Irish Times* (Dublin), 15 March 1995, 15.

34. U.S. policymakers insisted that the United Nations pinpoint its exit strategy precisely before it would vote to allow even other countries to deploy a rescue mission, and also complained about the cost of any expanded peacekeeping presence.

35. Even if one could grant the argument that the tensions between Hutu and Tutsi were in a sense historical, one could still not justify inaction on that basis. If that were a valid premise for viewing conflicts with racial, ethnic, or religious dimensions, it would be senseless to expend resources on peace efforts between Arabs and Jews in the Middle East or Protestants and Catholics in Northern Ireland. Human Rights Watch, *World Watch 1995* (New York: Human Rights Watch, 1996), 56.

36. Ibid., 46; Joyce Price, "Why Rwanda Was Ignored," *Washington Times,* 31 July 1994, A4.

37. Boutros Boutros-Ghali's letter to the Security Council of 29 April (S/1994/518).

38. Jackson Nyamuya Maogoto, "International Justice Under the Shadow of Realpolitik: Revisting the Establishment of the Ad Hoc International Criminal Tribunals," *Flinders Journal of Law Reform* (2001): 161, 184.

39. *Report of the Independent Inquiry into the Actions of the United Nations During the 1994 Genocide in Rwanda,* available at the UN website, www.un.org/News/ossg/rwanda-report.

40. See, for example, Keith B. Richburg and Stephen L. Buckley, "Rwandan Premier Bitter over Delay of UN Crimes Trials' Foreign Aid," *Washington Post,* 21 October 1994, A30.

41. Joint Evaluation of Emergency Assistance to Rwanda, *International Response to Conflict and Genocide: Lessons from the Rwanda Experience* (Copenhagan: Steering Committee of the Joint Evaluation of Emergency Assistance to Rwanda, 1996).

42. Craig Nelson, "Rwanda: U.S. Keen to Prove its Concern over Refugees' Plight," *The Independent* (London), 1 August 1994, 9.

43. See *Preliminary Report,* 4 October 1994, part VIII(A); UN Doc. S/1994/1125.

44. The Rwandan Patriotic Front took power in July 1994. For an overview, see Prunier, "The Great Lakes Crisis."

45. "Letter Dated 28 September 1994 from the Permanent Representative of Rwanda Addressed to the President of the Security Council," UN SCOR, 49th sess., UN Doc. S/1994/1115 (1994), 4.

46. UN ESCOR, Human Rights Commission, 3rd Special sess., UN Doc. E/CN 4/S-3/1–4 (1994).

47. Ibid. See also Rene Degni-Segui, "Report on the Situation of Human Rights in Rwanda," UN ESCOR, 51st sess., UN Doc. E/CN 4/1995/7 (1994).

48. SC Res. 935, UN SCOR, 49th sess., 3400th mtg., UN Doc. S/Res/935 (1994). The complete name of the Commission is Commission of Experts Established Pursuant to Security Council Resolution 935 (1994) to Examine and Analyse the Grave Violations of International Humanitarian Law in Rwanda, Including Possible Acts of Genocide. See ibid.

49. Preliminary Report of the Independent Commission of Experts in Accordance with Security Council Resolution 935 (1994), Part VIII (A), para. 148. This report is contained as an Annex to the Report of the Secretary-General on Rwanda, UN Doc. S/1994/1125, 4 October 1994. Available at www.un.org/Docs/secu94.htm.

50. "Letter Dated 28 September 1994 from the Permanent Representative of Rwanda Addressed to the President of the Security Council," UN SCOR, 49th sess., UN Doc. S/1994/1115 (1994).

51. UN SCOR, 49th sess., 3453rd mtg., UN Doc. S/PV.3453 (1994), 14.

52. "UN Approves War-Crimes Tribunal: Other Developments," available at *Lexis News Library,* Arcnws File, 17 November 1994, www.lexis.com, 868.

53. See Payam Akhavan, "International Criminal Tribunal for Rwanda: The Politics and Pragmatics of Punishment," *American Journal of International Law* 90 (1996): 501, and Morris, "The Trials of Concurrent Jurisdiction" (both discussing Rwandan objections to the ICTR statute). Although Rwandan government officials often say the ICTR was simply created to soothe the conscience of the international community, the ICTR is certainly more than that, but far from the ideal.

54. Some commentators have noted this disconnection from the internal political process. See Mariann Meier Wang, "The International Tribunal for Rwanda: Opportunities for Impact," *Columbia Human Rights Law Review* 27 (1995): 177, 203. See also Makau Mutua, "Never Again: Questioning the Yugoslav and Rwanda Tribunals," *Temple International and Comparative Law Journal* 11 (1997): 167.

55. For a detailed analysis of the philosophical and structural weaknesses of the ICTR in addressing the genocide, see Jackson Nyamuya Maogoto, "International Justice for Rwanda Missing the Point: Questioning the Relevance of Classical Criminal Law Theory," *Bond Law Review* 13 (2001): 40.

56. *Comprehensive Report of the Secretary-General on Practical Arrangements for the Effective Functioning of the ICTR,* UN Doc. 5/1995/134, 13 February 1995, para. 9.

57. It should also be noted that pursuant to article 14 of its statute, the ICTR adopted the ICTY's Rules of Procedure and Evidence (ICTR/TCIR/2/L.2, respectively IT/32/Rev 9, 5 July 1996).

58. Pursuant to the first paragraphs of these articles, states are under obligation to "cooperate with the International Criminal Tribunal in the investigation and prosecution of persons accused of committing serious violations of international humanitarian law." Pursuant to the second paragraphs of these articles, "states shall comply without undue delay with any request for assistance or an order issued by a Tribunal Chamber, including but not limited to: (a) the identification and location of persons; (b) the taking of testimony; (c) the service of documents; (d) the arrest and detention of persons; (e) the surrender or the transfer of the accused to the International Tribunal."

59. The Russian Federation had vetoed five of the previous eight nominees for the post of chief prosecutor in the ICTY, and the implicit questions raised during the lengthy selection process was whether Russia was determined to wreck the tribunal

or was objecting to nominees from countries belonging to NATO. It is not fanciful to suggest that this did have a bearing on the U.S. proposal that the ICTR share the chief prosecutor with the ICTY. After all, the United States was impatient to see the tribunal up and running in order to curry goodwill after proving to be one of the main stumbling blocks in the run-up to and during the Rwandan genocide.

60. M. Cherif Bassiouni, "From Versailles to Rwanda in Seventy-Five Years: The Need to Establish a Permanent International Criminal Court," *Harvard International Human Rights Journal* 10 (1997): 11, 49.

61. Maogoto, "International Justice Under the Shadow of Realpolitik," 190.

62. *Report of the Secretary-General on the Activities of the Office of Internal Oversight Services,* 51st sess., Agenda Items 139, 141, UN Doc. A/51/789 (1997).

63. See "Report of the International Criminal Tribunal for the Prosecution of Persons Responsible for Genocide and Other Serious Violations of International Humanitarian Law Committed in the Territory of Rwanda and Rwandan Citizens Responsible for Genocide and Other Such Violations Committed in the Territory of Neighbouring States Between 1 January and 31 December 1994," UN GAOR, 54th sess., Provisional Agenda Item 51, UN Doc. A/54/315, S/1999/943 (1999) (Fourth Report of the ICTR), 44.

64. See "International Criminal Tribunal for Rwanda, Tribunal at a Glance," Fact Sheet no. 1, November 1999.

65. Ibid.

66. See *Prosecutor v. Akayesu,* no. ICTR-96–4-A (1 June 2001). Rwanda is organized at four administrative levels: cells, sectors, communes, and the highest level, prefectures. As *bourgmestre* of the Taba commune, Akeyesu was responsible for performing executive functions and maintaining law and public order in the commune.

67. See *Prosecutor v. Kayishema and Ruzindana,* Case no. ICTR-95–1-T (21 May 1999), 35.

68. See *Prosecutor v. Rutaganda,* Case no. ICTR-96–3-T (12 June 1999), available at ICTR website, www.ictr.org.

69. See *Prosecutor v. Musema,* Case no. ICTR-96–13-T (27 January 2000), available at ICTR website, www.ictr.org.

70. See *Prosecutor v. Kambanda,* Case no. ICTR 97–23-DP, Indictment (16 October 1997).

71. See *Prosecutor v. Kambanda,* Case no. ICTR 97–23-S, Plea Agreement Between Jean Kambanda and the Office of the Prosecutor, Annexure A to the Joint Motion for Consideration of Plea Agreement Between Jean Kambanda and the Office of the Prosecutor (29 April 1998).

72. See *Regina v. Bartle and the Commissioner of Police (Appellants) Ex Parte Pinochet (Respondent); Evans and Another and the Commissioner of Police and Others (Appellants) Ex Parte Pinochet (Respondent)* (House of Lords on appeal from Divisional Court of the Queen's Bench Division, 25 November 1998), available at UK Parliament website, www.publications.parliament.uk/pa/ld199899/ldjudmnt/jd981125/pino01.htm.

73. See Kingsley Chiedu Moghalu, "Peace Through Justice: Rwanda's Precedent for the Trial of Milosevic," *Washington Post,* 6 July 1999, A15.

74. *Prosecutor v. Barayagwiza,* Case no. ICTR-97–19-AR72, Decision/Request for Withdrawal of Defense Counsel (31 January 2000).

75. For a summary of this 3 November 1999 decision and reactions to it, see Maury Shenk et al., "International Criminal Tribunal for the Former Yugoslavia and for Rwanda," *International Law* 34 (2000): 683.

76. See Coalition for International Justice, "Barayagwiza to Face Trial," 31 March 2000 (24 February 2001), www.cij.org/content.html.

77. See "Missing," *The Economist* (U.S. ed.), 23 December 2000.

78. See Christina M. Carroll, "An Assessment of the Role and Effectiveness of the International Criminal Tribunal for Rwanda and the Rwandan National Justice System in Dealing with the Mass Atrocities of 1994," *Boston University International Law Journal* 18 (2000): 163. Reasons cited in defense of the past policy to limit indictments to Hutu include the desirability of "indicting and prosecuting the most serious violators first," and the desire to "maintain good relations with the current Tutsi government in order to facilitate its investigation of international humanitarian law violations in Rwanda." However, it has also been established that there is "overwhelming evidence to prove that Tutsis [have] committed . . . serious violations of international humanitarian law" during the 1994 massacres. Ibid.

79. See Coalition for International Justice, "Del Ponte Meets with Kagame" and "ICTR Investigation of RPF Addressed," 14 December 2000 (24 February 2001), www.cij.org/content.html.

80. See Coalition for International Justice, "ICTR Judges to Visit Crime Scenes," 16 August 2000 (24 February 2001), www.cij.org/content.html. In response, Martin Ngoga, Rwanda's representative to the ICTR, stated that the decision by the ICTR indicated that "many things have been put right as far as the workings of the Tribunal and its relationship with Rwanda." Ibid.

81. See "Prosecutor Seeks to Move ICTR Hearings on Genocide to Rwanda," *Xinhua,* 21 November 2000. Currently, all trial proceedings are held at the seat of the court in Arusha, Tanzania. Del Ponte further stated that such a move was now possible because "relations with the government . . . reached a stage where proper guarantees can be given and relied upon for the holding of ICTR trials in Rwanda itself," and that such a move was necessary because the ICTR "must make [its] work more relevant to the people of Rwanda." Ibid.

82. See ICTR Press Release, "ICTR Information Centre Opens in Kigali," 25 September 2000, www.ictr.org/ENGLISH/PRESSREL/2000/241.htm. The victims assistance program will provide "counseling for victims who are witnesses or potential witnesses before the tribunal." Ibid.

83. See International Criminal Tribunal for Rwanda, "ICTR Detainees—Status," 5 October 2000 (7 October 2000), www.ictr.org/ENGLISH/factsheets/detainee.htm.

84. See *Prosecutor v. Kambanda,* Case no. ICTR 97–23-S (4 September 1998), available at ICTR website, www.ictr.org.

85. See J. Coll Metcalfe, "Appeals Court Upholds Serushago Sentence, Officially Concluding Tribunal's First Case," *Internews,* 14 February 2000 (6 March 2000), www.internews.org/PROJECTS/ICTRnewsFeb00.html#feb17.

86. See International Criminal Trial for Rwanda, "Detainees—Status," 15 January 2001 (8 February 2001), www.ictr.org/ENGLISH/factsheets/detainee.htm.

87. In 2000, assisting countries were the United Kingdom, Belgium, France, Denmark, and the United States. Also, Swaziland became the third country to agree to imprison persons convicted by the ICTR.

88. See ICTR Press Release, "Former Journalist Ruggiu Sentenced to Twelve Years in Prison," 1 June 2000, www.ictr.org/ENGLISH/PRESSREL/2000/235.htm.

89. See ICTR Press Release, "Appeals Chamber Confirms Serushago Sentence," 14 February 2000, www.ictr.org/ENGLISH/PRESSREL/2000/221.htm. Serushago was convicted by the Trial Chamber on 14 December 1998.

90. Ibid.

91. Ibid.

92. Ibid.

93. See International Criminal Tribunal for Rwanda, "ICTR Detainees—Status," 7 February 2002 (10 February 2002), www.ictr.org/wwwroot/ENGLISH/factsheets/detainee.htm ("ICTR Detainees").

94. Ibid.

95. International Criminal Tribunal for Rwanda, "Achievements of the ICTR" (2 March 2002), www.ictr.org/ENGLISH/geninfo/achieve.htm.

96. "Trials in Progress," *ICTR Bulletin* 2 (December 2001): 9.

97. International Criminal Tribunal for Rwanda, Press Release, "Tribunal Acquits Bagilishema," 7 June 2001 (3 July 2002), www.ictr.org/wwwroot/ENGLISH/PRESSREL/2001/271.htm.

98. *Prosecutor v. Akayesu,* no. ICTR-96–4-A (1 June 2001).

99. *Le Procureur v. Kayishema,* no. ICTR-95–1-A, 1 June 2001, (3 July 2002), www.ictr.org/wwwroot/FRENCH/cases/KayishemaRuzindana/arret.

100. Ibid.

101. *Alfred Musema v Prosecutor,* no. ICTR-96–13-A, 16 November 2001 (3 July 2002), www.ictr.org/wwwroot/FRENCH/casesw/Musema/judgement/arret; see also "Musema's Genocide Conviction Upheld," *ICTR Bulletin* 2 (December 2001): 2.

102. *Prosecutor v. Bagilishema,* no. ICTR-95-I-T, 7 June 2001 (3 July 2002), www.ictr.org/wwwroot/ENGLISH/cases/Bagilishema/judgement.

103. Ibid.

104. "Seventh Annual Report of the International Criminal Tribunal for the Prosecution of Persons Responsible for Genocide and Other Serious Violations of International Humanitarian Law Committed in the Territory of Rwanda and Rwandan Citizens Responsible for Genocide and Other Such Violations Committed in the Territory of Neighbouring States Between 1 January and 31 December 1994 for the Period from 1 July 2001 to 30 June 2002" (2 July 2002), UN Doc. A/57/163; S/2002/733, paras. 77–78.

105. Ibid., para. 1.

106. Ibid., para. 2.

107. Ibid., para. 9.

108. Ibid., para. 10.

109. S. Powers, "Accessory to Murder?" *New York Times,* 11 February 2001.

110. Mutua, "Never Again," 178.

111. See, for example, 1999 Report of the Special Representative of the UNCHR, 24, 91–98; Amnesty International, "International Criminal Tribunal for Rwanda: Trials and Tribulations," AI Report IOR 40/13/98, 1998, www.amnesty.it/ailib/aipub/1998/SUM/I4000398.htm, sec. 1.2.

112. It is arguable that the Yugoslav and Rwanda tribunals were not established because of the United Nations or the powerful states that control it. They were not established because of an intrinsic value on punishing war criminals or upholding the rule of law. Rather, the mobilization of shame by NGOs and especially the grisly pictures beamed to the world by the television camera created a public relations nightmare and made liars of the centers of Western civilization. Once the political will of the major powers was mobilized by public shame and outrage, Security Council resolutions provided the legal basis for speedy action. See, for example, Virginia Morris and Michael P. Scharf, eds., *An Insider's Guide to the International Criminal Tribunal for the Former Yugoslavia,* vol. 1 (Irvington-on-Hudson, NY: Transnational, 1995). See also David P. Forsythe, "Politics and the International Tribunal for the Former Yugoslavia," *Criminal Law Forum* 5 (1994): 401.

PART 3

Into the New Millennium

7

The International Criminal Court: Challenges and Concessions to the State

The problems that plagued international tribunals in the past, along with the worldwide increase in violence, created the impetus toward a multilateral solution. From World War I to Yugoslavia and Rwanda, ad hoc international tribunals have been subjected to national interests and competing types of jurisprudence. Thus there arose the desire to establish a permanent system,[1] which would eliminate the necessity of establishing an ad hoc tribunal each time. The decision to establish tribunals, not to mention drafting the applicable statutes, takes considerable time during which the evidence of the crimes becomes more difficult to obtain and the political will to prosecute dissipates.[2] Moreover, a political debate is invariably reopened over the provisions of the statute, who will conduct the prosecutions, and who will sit in judgment. Such pressures leave ad hoc tribunals vulnerable to political manipulation.[3]

Creation of a permanent court has long been sought to remove the accusation that has dogged ad hoc tribunals. They are seen as "victors' justice," in part due to the lack of universality and specificity in international law. Although some movement has occurred in the UN to standardize and codify international crimes, the structure for an international court did not keep pace until the 1990s. "From a legal standpoint, *ad hoc* tribunals cannot hope to achieve a desired level of consistency in the interpretation and application of international law because their statutes are inevitably tailored to meet the demands of the specific situation that brought them into being."[4] A related concern is whether the political will exists from crisis to crisis to establish yet another tribunal.[5] Many people fear that judicial fatigue will set in, resulting in crimes going unpunished. Questions are raised concerning why one conflict deserves a tribunal and another does not.[6] For example, the UN established tribunals for the former Yugoslavia and Rwanda but not for Iraq, Somalia, or Sudan. If there were a permanent international criminal court, it is arguable that the will required to begin investigations into atrocities would not be solely dependent upon the politics of the UN or national leaders.

The International Criminal Court was the last great international institution created during the twentieth century. It has the potential to reshape thinking about international law.[7] The ICC Statute places state and nonstate actors side by side in the international arena, and the ICC can put real people in real jails.[8] Establishing the ICC raises hopes that the lines between international law and world order are blurring and that the normative structure being created by international law might influence or even restrain the Hobbesian order established by the politics of states. But classic ideas about sovereignty die hard, and if the road to Rome was long and difficult, the task of establishing an effective ICC may be even more arduous.[9]

The next section discusses UN efforts to codify certain crimes and to establish an international criminal court between 1946 and 1996, which finally culminated in the adoption of the Rome Statute for a Permanent International Criminal Court in 1998. At the end of World War II and the Nuremberg and Tokyo trials, efforts to codify international crimes and to establish such a court to enforce them began in earnest within the UN. Between 1946 and 1996, UN efforts to codify crimes and to establish a court were carefully separated, though they were always intertwined. Although the Cold War hindered the codification process, progress began in 1990 and culminated with the adoption of the Rome Statute in the summer of 1998.

The Road to Rome

During the first session of the UN General Assembly in 1946, the United States sponsored Resolution 95(I), which affirmed "the principles of international law recognized by the Charter of the Nuremberg Tribunal and the judgment of the tribunal."[10] In 1947, the General Assembly directed the Committee on the Codification of International Law, the predecessor of the International Law Commission (ILC),[11] to formulate a general codification of offenses against the peace and security of mankind.[12] The resolution mandated the ILC to: (1) formulate the principles of international law recognized in the Nuremberg Charter and in the judgment of the tribunal; and (2) prepare a draft code of offenses against the peace and security of mankind, indicating the place to be accorded to the principles mentioned in (1) above.[13]

Two years later, in compliance with the resolution, the ILC started to formulate the principles recognized in the Nuremberg Charter and to prepare a draft code of the offenses against the peace and security of mankind.[14] A subcommittee was formed, and a special rapporteur was appointed to prepare a Draft Code of offenses.[15] Concurrently, the task of formulating a draft statute for the establishment of an international criminal court was assigned to another special rapporteur, who submitted his first report to the ILC in March 1950.[16] That report argued that a substantive criminal code and a statute for an international criminal court should complement one another.[17] "Contrary to logic and rational drafting policy, these two codification projects remained separated."[18]

A special committee of the General Assembly was established in 1951, comprising representatives of seventeen states, for the purpose of drafting a convention for establishing an international criminal court.[19] The substantive legal aspects of codification were given to one drafting body, the enforcement counterpart to another body. In 1951 the special committee appointed to draft the statute finished its task, using the model of the International Court of Justice.[20] The discussions and written comments, particularly those of major powers, indicated that the project had no chance of acceptance and was politically premature.[21] Because these states did not want to assume political responsibility for the demise of a permanent international criminal court within a few years of Nuremberg and Tokyo,[22] the committee, with some membership changes, revised the 1951 Draft Statute and finalized revisions in 1953.[23] The 1953 revised Draft Statute was submitted to the General Assembly, which found it necessary to first consider the ILC's work on the Draft Code of offenses. The statute for an international criminal court was therefore shelved until the Draft Code was finalized.[24] The ILC's approved text of the Draft Code, consisting of five articles and listing thirteen separate international crimes, was submitted to the General Assembly in 1954.[25]

Article 2 of the 1954 Draft Code, dealing with aggression, did not define "aggression," because another special committee had been established to develop that definition. The General Assembly therefore postponed further consideration of the 1954 Draft Code until the special committee on the question of defining aggression (a contentious and politically volatile issue) submitted its report.[26] Consequently, the expected domino effect occurred: the 1953 Draft Statute could not be considered before the 1954 Draft Code of offenses, which could not be considered until "aggression" was defined. As a result, the 1953 Draft Statute and the 1954 Draft Code were shelved, pending the definition.[27] After almost a quarter-century of fruitless wrangling, a definition was reached by consensus in 1974 when the General Assembly approved Resolution 3314 on 14 December.[28] It is noteworthy that the definition, which took more than twenty years, was not included in a multilateral convention or voted upon in the resolution that adopted it.

The General Assembly, having previously tabled further consideration of the 1954 Draft Code of offenses, and having tabled consideration of the

1953 Draft Statute because the 1954 Draft Code had not yet been adopted, should have reconsidered these items in 1974. With Cold War politics dominating the scene and World War II fading into memory, the General Assembly did not reconsider the 1954 Draft Code or the 1953 Draft Statute.

Progress on the Draft Code and the Draft Statute continued to languish in the 1980s. Though a new rapporteur of the ILC was appointed in 1982,[29] a final report was not produced until 1991.[30] The report ran into a storm of criticism by governments and scholars and was sent back to the ILC for revision. It was finally adopted in 1996.[31] It was expected to be a foundation for discussion of the ICC (notably crimes), then be pursued in earnest, but that did not happen.[32] Meanwhile the question of an international criminal court came back to the ILC via an unexpected route. In 1989 the General Assembly requested the ILC to prepare a report on an international criminal jurisdiction for prosecuting persons engaged in drug trafficking.[33] The ILC transcended the drug-trafficking question, which was the basis of its original mandate, by covering prosecution of other crimes under international law, including violations of international humanitarian law. The ILC's preliminary report in 1992[34] was favorably received by the General Assembly, with no questions raised as to the expanded scope. Thereafter, the ILC produced a comprehensive text in 1993,[35] which it modified in 1994.[36] The changes made in the ILC's 1994 Draft Statute were intended to answer concerns from some major powers.[37]

The 1994 Draft Statute was the basis upon which the General Assembly in 1994 established the Ad Hoc Committee on the Establishment of an International Criminal Court,[38] and then, in 1995, the Preparatory Committee (PrepCom) for the Establishment of an International Criminal Court.[39] The PrepCom report was submitted to the General Assembly session on 28 October 1996, with a recommendation that the Assembly extend the PrepCom's term with a specific mandate to negotiate proposals, with a view toward producing a consolidated text of a convention, statute, and annexed instruments by 1998[40] to be considered by a plenipotentiary conference—as in fact eventually happened, leading to the adoption of the Rome Statute.[41]

The next section examines the organization and operating principles of the ICC. Many aspects of the Rome Statute challenge tenets of international law. We focus on major features and on the influence of realpolitik based on state interests and national agendas.[42]

Structure and Competence of the ICC

Jurisdiction and Admissibility

Jurisdiction ratione personae. The Rome Statute provides for jurisdiction *ratione personae* over *natural persons,* only thereby excluding organizations or states.[43] A crucial test for the ICC will take place over sovereignty. The individual, not the state, will be subject to jurisdiction, thus posing the question whether states will "run the risk of having their nationals sent to be tried by judges possibly from enemy or rogue nations."[44] States that cede to ICC jurisdiction over citizens would also be tempted to do so only when it suited their political goals.[45] Therefore, the ICC would find cooperation only when a state deems it expedient. Even some proponents of the ICC acknowledge the problem that sovereignty presents:

> States are understandably jealous of their right to investigate and try international criminals in their own courts. National pride leads states to have faith in the competency and fairness of their domestic judicial systems. They do not want to surrender control over criminal cases to another tribunal. Certainly, with the exception of the core crimes, states are capable of prosecuting the majority of international crimes fairly and effectively, and the Statute [for the International Criminal Court] should encourage national prosecutions when feasible. Moreover, victimized states have incentives to pursue cases that an international tribunal might lack.[46]

This observation implies that states may not need the ICC because their own legal systems are capable of handling most issues. Therefore, investigations by the ICC might be ignored. The U.S. delegation attempted to resolve this at the Rome Conference by preserving the right of reservation to specific aspects of the statute. This proposal was defeated. Although the statute can be amended, many proponents are adamantly opposed to it. They fear that amendments to the ICC, particularly by powerful nations, would make it a tool of the UN Security Council and likely administer "victors' justice."[47]

The ILC, in early discussions, proposed adding state culpability.[48] The proposal was rejected as "science fiction."[49] The traditional position is that a state, as a sovereign person, can have no legal responsibility whatever. Publicists and penalists argue that states' sovereignty precludes their criminal responsibility in the same way as individuals. The argument that legal entities are abstractions with policies and operations made and carried out by individuals is theoretically correct, but that ignores the need to deter persons who carry out proscribed acts under the color of state authority, as well as those who use the instrumentalities and capabilities of the state to commit international crimes or facilitate crimes that are, by their nature, magnitude, and scheme, the preserve of states.[50]

The ICC did not specifically include state criminal responsibility and other forms of group responsibility. But it stated that "no provision in this Statute relating to individual criminal responsibility shall affect the responsibility of states under international law." History has shown that for some of the international crimes states and their machinery are the worst culprits.[51] Perhaps the failure to incorporate state culpability in more specific terms is a missed opportunity for the Rome Statute to further the development of international humanitarian law as to state responsibility. An express recognition of state culpability would allow a state to be held internationally responsible if, for example, it fails to implement a convention relating to core international crimes or a convention that obligates it to require the compliance of its citizens with international legal norms.

Jurisdiction ratione materiae. Political negotiation of various international instruments has resulted in the codification of the international undesirability of piracy, hijacking, kidnapping of diplomats, taking of civilian hostages, and drug offenses.[52] Thus the will of the international community has been attached to such conduct by invoking international prescriptive jurisdiction.[53] This ought to put the crimes within the jurisdiction of any international penal tribunal. Although transnational crimes present serious problems, some states felt strongly about their inclusion in the Rome Statute. Thus the statute extends subject matter jurisdiction to only four crimes:[54] genocide, crimes against humanity, war crimes,[55] and aggression.[56] This is narrower than article 20 of the original ILC Draft Statute, which envisaged that the ICC would also be able to hear cases involving transnational crimes.[57]

This restricted subject matter jurisdiction leaves many international crimes to national jurisdictions. The reason rests in the prerogative of states to prosecute and punish such acts.[58] Thus political and ideological considerations, coupled with the political nature of many international crimes, militated against inclusion.

One positive aspect[59] is that restricting subject matter jurisdiction permitted the Diplomatic Conference—which had been convened by the General Assembly at its fifty-second session (after completion of a draft text by the Preparatory Committee between 1996 and April 1998) to finalize and adopt a convention on the establishment of an international criminal court—to strengthen the ICC's compulsory jurisdiction, which, as originally conceived by the ILC, was optional.[60] Because the PrepCom also felt strongly that the ICC Statute should define the crimes within its jurisdiction, rather than simply listing them, as the ILC had done, inclusion meant reaching a consensus on definition.[61]

Jurisdiction ratione loci. The geographic scope of jurisdiction, *ratione loci,* varies depending on the mechanism by which the case comes to the ICC. In the event that the Security Council refers the matter, jurisdiction covers the territory of every state in the world, whether or not party to the statute.[62] In such cases, the statute's scope is unbounded by geography. Thus, even though article 10 attempts to separate the statute from customary international law, and each definition of crimes purports to define the law only for purposes of the ICC Statute,[63] the statute applies to non–state party nationals in certain circumstances and can be applied by the Security Council to all human beings.

If the matter is referred by a state party or initiated *proprio motu* by the prosecutor, however, the ICC's jurisdiction is more restricted—but still extensive. In such instances, jurisdiction extends to the territory of a non–state party only if that state consents to jurisdiction, irrespective of whether the acts were committed in the territory of the consenting state or the accused is a national of the consenting state.[64] The fact that this regime gives the ICC jurisdiction over the citizens of non–state parties, allowing the ICC to exercise jurisdiction in certain circumstances within the territory of non–state parties,[65] is considered by some to be in direct contravention of standing international law, which binds states only to those international agreements to which they consent.[66]

Opponents argue that one of the great dangers of the ICC lies in its broad jurisdiction and the possible expansion and abuse of that jurisdiction. They point out that the ICC can exercise jurisdiction over any national of any state party, even when in the territory of a non–state party, as well as over any individuals, regardless of nationality, within the territory of a state party.[67] This was yet another reason put forward by the U.S. delegation for refusing to sign the ICC Statute.[68] Therefore, the statute signed in Rome may violate national sovereignty by indirectly allowing jurisdiction over the nationals of states that choose not to become state parties.

Complementarity

Although the Rome Statute does not use the term *complementarity,* the preamble describes the new ICC as a "complement" to existing national courts and processes[69]—hence the term. The agreed formula in the Rome Statute is that a state with jurisdictional competence has the first right to institute proceedings, unless the ICC decides that the state "is unwilling or unable genuinely to carry out the investigation or prosecution."[70] The assumption in Rome was that such a determination would be straightforward in either of two situations: (1) where the state, for whatever reason, chooses not to exercise its jurisdictional competence—"the unwilling state"; or (2) where the state's legal and administrative structures have completely broken down. Essentially, only dysfunctional or aberrant sovereignties will forfeit their claim to primacy over the ICC. Technically, this means that a state can prevent a case from proceeding before the ICC merely by launching an investigation.

Though the word *genuinely* appears to require some good-faith element on behalf of the state, a state may commence an investigation for the sole purpose of depriving the ICC of jurisdiction, as long as the state does not exhibit "unwillingness" in doing so (or its "inability" is not apparent).[71] Second, the use of the word *genuinely* may create ambiguities. It is a value-laden term, depending on the context. A state may "genuinely" carry out an investigation, with no intention of prosecuting, by simply seeking to ascertain the facts and then grant an amnesty or pardon. It would seem that this state would have discharged its duty under the ICC Statute. Third, even in the event that the ICC seeks to review national judicial action to determine the genuineness of the process, there are problems. The statute provides no standard for judging its own terms. How long a delay in a national court will the ICC consider unjustifiable? Will it look to the national court system or to other UN court actions like the international tribunals in the former Yugoslavia and Rwanda? When will the ICC deem a national court too partial or dependent? The statute is silent on these issues.

Complementarity strives to harmonize, wherever possible, multiple and competing sources of jurisdiction over international crimes. It developed as a principled and pragmatic way to accommodate the conflicting imperatives of state sovereignty and the need for a permanent international institution to end impunity for atrocities at a time of global proliferation of localized armed conflict. It ensures that the ICC complements, rather than replaces, national judicial systems. In recognizing states' concurrent jurisdiction, the ICC is expected to strengthen enforcement of international humanitarian law by domestic courts, not to replace them.

Consent-Based Versus Universal Jurisdiction

There has been a great deal of discussion as to whether jurisdiction in the statute is "universal" or "consent-based."[72] Most of the confusion has been generated by a failure to separate the principles of jurisdiction upon which the statute is premised from the regime governing the exercise of jurisdiction by the ICC in particular cases. Indeed, jurisdiction over particular cases is premised on three principles, which are widely accepted in international law. First, the universality principle operates as a principle of prescriptive jurisdiction and of adjudicative jurisdiction. If the Security Council refers a case to the ICC, the Court may be asked to pass judgment on the commission of crimes anywhere in the world. The consent of no state is required, even as to the nationals of states not party to the ICC Statute. If the prosecutor or a state refers the case, however, although the universality principle does not disappear, layered upon it is a state consent regime based on two additional, disjunctive principles of jurisdiction: the territorial principle,[73] and the nationality principle.[74] The ICC has jurisdiction over cases referred by states parties (or by the prosecutor *proprio motu*) as long as either the territorial state or the state of the accused's nationality is either a party to the statute or has accepted the jurisdiction of the ICC.

The statute does not expressly address universal jurisdiction, leaving such issues to the complementarity principle and state consent regime.[75] The one clue is the statute's command that the ICC is to exercise its jurisdiction only in cases involving "the most serious crimes of concern to the international community as a whole."[76] This phrase combines a substantive limit on jurisdiction with its underlying premise—that in a world of conflicting sovereigns, both territorial (states) and nonterritorial (the international community as a whole), some system must be adopted to sort permissible from impermissible assertions of jurisdiction.[77]

The failure to express universal jurisdiction affirms the determination of states to retain certain prerogatives, even when international customary law recognizes universal jurisdiction,[78] by blending territorial and national jurisdiction, which is state-centered.[79] The lack of express universal jurisdiction means that offenders may successfully seek refuge in other states. Many states have not incorporated international crimes as the law of the land, or have placed qualifications on the instruments. The "extradite or prosecute" concept is based on recognition on the part of the state of the criminality of the alleged offender's acts. Notwithstanding the international recognition of certain crimes, technically it is unconstitutional to bring a case based on international law in states that do not expressly recognize international law as a source of law, unless enabling legislation has been passed to activate the relevant international rule or norm.

The Office of the Prosecutor

Under the ILC Draft Statute, only states and the Security Council could lodge complaints with the ICC.[80] The Rome Statute goes farther, permitting the prosecutor to bring cases before the ICC on his or her own initiative.[81] Defining the powers of the prosecutor was a contentious issue during the PrepCom I meetings, specifically as to whether the prosecutor should be able to act *proprio motu* or *ex officio,* that is, on his or her own motion, in bringing cases. This issue created a deep schism among the PrepCom I delegates, with many smaller nations, some European nations, and NGOs strongly supporting a prosecutor able to act independently,[82] and many larger countries, including most of the permanent five members of the Security Council, opposing an independent prosecutor.[83] Many states were concerned that the independent prosecutor could become "independent counsel for the universe," accountable to no one and liable to file complaints against states on the basis of political prejudices rather than legal concerns.[84] Ambassador David Scheffer, the head of the U.S. delegation to Rome, suggested that there existed a legitimate reason for referrals to come from member states or the Security Council. He made the following statement:

> The value of having a government refer it or the Security Council refer it is they are accountable to somebody. They are accountable either to their people, their populace, for doing so, or the Security Council is accountable to the United Nations system. We believe that that fundamental principle of accountability should be at the core of referrals to this Court.[85]

The Rome Statute grants broad powers to the prosecutor's office.[86] Article 15 provides that the prosecutor "may initiate investigations *proprio motu* on the basis of information on crimes within the jurisdiction of the Court."[87] Thus, the prosecutor may launch investigations and indict individuals for crimes. There is no requirement that the prosecutor act on the request of a sovereign state or at the direction of an international organization such as the UN Security Council. The prosecutor is independent, without any accountability (other than to the ICC).[88] One of the concerns expressed by nonsigning states is the prosecutor's power to initiate an investigation without supervision. Nothing in the statute, it is argued, appears to limit that power. As a response to these concerns, the Rome Statute contains a complex procedure by which the Pre-Trial Chamber is to closely supervise cases in which the prosecutor exercises his or her *proprio motu* investigation powers.

The prosecutor may commence an investigation only if both the prosecutor and the Pre-Trial Chamber have determined that a "reasonable basis" exists. "Reasonable basis" is not defined in the statute, but article 53 suggests that a finding of reasonable basis has three elements: (1) There is a reasonable basis to believe that a crime within the jurisdiction of the Court has been or is being committed; (2) the case is or would be admissible under article 17; and (3) the investigation serves the interests of justice, taking into account the gravity of the crime and the interests of victims. This is a rather circular definition; but the prosecutor should also consider whether there is "a sufficient legal or factual basis to seek a warrant or summons under Article 58."[89]

For a state or the Security Council, however, the matter is referred to the Court under article 13(a) or under Article 13(b), respectively, and the prosecutor will initiate an investigation pursuant to article 53 unless there is no reasonable basis to proceed. The statute permits the Pre-Trial Chamber to order an investigation or prosecution to proceed if the prosecutor's decision is based solely on a determination that the prosecution would not serve the interests of justice.[90] In this way, the framers attempted to strike a balance between the prerogatives of states and the needs of justice. This concession proved difficult for the United States to accept, however, and remains one of the principal objections of the U.S. government. Opponents of the Court argue that these discretionary considerations by the prosecutor amount to limitations addressing only whether a crime has been committed, whether jurisdiction exists, admissibility of evidence, and other potential overriding political concerns. These reservations, it is argued, are minimal, allowing the prosecutor to have great leeway in initiating investigations.

The Cooperation and Judicial Assistance Regime: Kow-Towing to the State

Part 9 ("International Co-operation and Judicial Assistance") is one of the most complex sections of the Rome Statute. The seventeen articles of this part address the interaction between the ICC and states in the arrest and transfer of suspects and in the conduct of investigations or prosecutions on state territory. Not surprisingly, part 9 is the least "supranational" section. Although article 86 requires state parties to "cooperate fully with the court in its investigation and prosecution of crimes,"[91] the articles that follow are riddled with exceptions and qualifications.[92] First, the statute bifurcates the assistance that the ICC may request of states into two categories: requests for the arrest and surrender of persons, and requests for everything else that the ICC might need to conduct investigations and prosecutions.[93] As a matter of principle, state parties must comply with a request for the arrest and surrender of a person;[94] non–state parties are under no such obligation.[95] The same is true with respect to requests for other forms of assistance.

Although state parties will be required to adapt their national law to ensure that they are able to fulfill their cooperation obligations under the statute,[96] a residuary role remains for national law, which will continue to control the form and procedure governing requests for assistance,[97] as well as the execution of such requests, with very limited exceptions.[98] In the case of conduct, the state is to give priority to the ICC unless the competing request represents an existing international obligation to extradite the person to the requesting state, in which case it is to balance the "relevant factors" in determining whether to give priority to the ICC.[99]

With respect to cooperation, state parties remain under a general obligation of assistance.[100] This assistance may take many forms, some listed in article 93(1), and includes taking evidence, serving documents, facilitating the voluntary appearance of persons as witnesses or experts, questioning persons being investigated or prosecuted, freezing or seizing proceeds, property, assets, and instrumentalities of crimes, and other such matters. Conspicuously absent is subpoena power. That is, neither the judges nor the prosecutor (or defense counsel, presumably) have any express power to compel witnesses to appear.[101]

As classically conceived, the jurisdiction to enforce concerns rules governing the enforcement of law by a state through its courts, as well as through executive, administrative, and police action.[102] As Leila Nadya Sadat and S. Richard Carden observe,

If we extrapolate from this to the enforcement power of the ICC, we see the weakest application of the three jurisdictional components of the statute. Indeed, the Court's enforcement jurisdiction is so feeble that it has the potential to completely undermine the efficacy of the Court, which, in other respects (such as institutional structure and definition of crimes), is likely to be quite strong.[103]

The most obvious point is that the ICC has no police force.[104] Indeed, it was unthinkable, although there was some precedent.[105] But the orders of the ICC, whether arrest warrants, judgments, orders to seize assets, or sentences, will need to be enforced. The delegates were not unaware of this problem, and many provisions address it directly.[106] But virtually all are premised on three principles. First, the ICC will not be permitted to sanction states directly for noncompliance with its orders. Rather, the ICC will be required to make findings of noncompliance and direct those to the Assembly of States Parties and the Security Council, in the case of a Security Council referral to the ICC. Second, the ICC may not compel state compliance with its orders.[107] That is, it may not compel the appearance of witnesses; it may not compel execution of arrest warrants; it may not seize bank accounts or government documents of its own accord. There is no subpoena power; there is no mandamus.[108] Third, the personnel of the ICC will have no right, in most cases, to proceed directly to the execution of their duties on the territories of states but must work through the authorities present in the requested state and be subject to national law.[109] There are three important exceptions. First, pursuant to article 56 an ICC judge may be present "to observe and make recommendations or orders regarding the collection and preservation of evidence and the questioning of persons."[110] Second, the prosecutor may be authorized by the Pre-Trial Chamber to take "specific investigative steps" within the territory of a state party without the cooperation of the state, if the state is unable to execute requests for cooperation because its judicial system has collapsed.[111] Finally, pursuant to article 99(4) the prosecutor may under limited circumstances execute specific requests for assistance (other than arrest warrants)[112] directly on the territory of a state party.[113]

Criminal prosecution is inherently tied to notions of national sovereignty and the control over persons and territory fundamental to that notion. Although international cooperation and judicial assistance as set out in the Rome Statute go to the heart of ICC effectiveness by placing an affirmative obligation on states,[114] this may be impeded by national interests in prohibiting and prosecuting certain types of conduct. In fact, some argue that the Nuremberg Tribunal succeeded only because it in some ways substituted itself for the inability of the German government to try war criminals. "Municipal enforcement rather than international law was . . . [the] crucial characteristic [of the Nuremberg trials]." As for state sovereignty, the framers of the Nuremberg Charter were operating in a vacuum—the sovereignty of the German state as the obstacle barring the enforcement of justice had been destroyed in May and June 1945.

Arguably, the successful establishment of the Yugoslavia and Rwanda ad hoc tribunals represents a departure from Nuremberg. The authority under which they were constituted derives not from state status as an occupied territory but from truly international exercises of Security Council power. Nonetheless, both were constituted in the midst of continuing national disarray, where the functioning national legal system had been subverted and compromised and could not be said to reflect basic due process requirements (Yugoslavia) or had collapsed altogether and did not exist (Rwanda). It is questionable whether a criminal justice mechanism that is expected to operate alongside fully operational national legal systems can do so without difficulty.

There is no guarantee that states would be willing to surrender their nationals to the processes of an international criminal justice system.[115] The Rome Statute establishes an obligation on state parties that are also parties to the underlying treaty proscribing the crime to surrender the accused to ICC jurisdiction.[116] Nonetheless, without an effective mechanism for requiring the compliance of states with the dictates of international law, such a regime continues to rest on voluntary compliance by the custodial state. Similarly, the Rome Statute requires that the custodial state give the ICC priority for the transfer of an accused over the extradition request of another state. The statute concurrently requires that the requesting state consent to the operation of the ICC as a precondition to its exercise of jurisdiction.[117] But what incentive is there for the requesting state to agree to trial in an international tribunal as opposed to trial in its own courts?

Control over persons and territory is the practical factor that exists. This is especially so for high-ranking officials who deliberately destroy evidence or attempt to do so. Classic cases are East Timor and Kosovo. In East Timor, a number of high-ranking Indonesian military officers are believed to have been part of the systematic atrocities committed, but as the UN Human Rights Commission of International Inquiry report[118] indicates, there were deliberate and concerted efforts to destroy evidence of atrocities.[119] The situation is much the same in Kosovo, where hundreds are still missing and the hunt for mass graves continues in earnest.[120] The problem of evidence has dogged the two ad hoc international criminal tribunals, with a number of charges being for lack or insufficiency of evidence.

Finally, the reluctance of those in power to bind themselves may well make it difficult to enforce criminal proscriptions against state-sponsored activity.[121] Cases like the former Yugoslavia may be the exception rather than the rule: an example of an instance where a tribunal can be constituted by the sheer will of the international community united in its condemnation, where the sovereign state so condemned is too weak to resist. Even the ICTY was initially hampered by the fact that many indictees were political and military leaders and thus party to international efforts to dispense with justice in those territories. Although many have since left positions of power and are in The Hague awaiting their fate, some are still on the run and hold considerable influence in their respective fiefdoms, rendering arrest difficult. But in most circumstances, where major powers are involved, where fractious political coalitions exist, or where world interest is simply unfocused, international law will go unenforced. The implications for the international rule of law are serious.

The Lonely Superpower: U.S. Opposition to the ICC

Prior to the Rome Conference, there were troubling signs that the U.S. commitment to the ICC was under strong attack by powerful elements in government. Indeed, as the opening of the Diplomatic Conference drew near, attacks on the ICC grew increasingly shrill. Senator Jesse Helms, the chair of the Senate Foreign Relations Committee, which would ultimately take up ratification, suggested that the ICC would be "dead on arrival" if the United States did not have veto power over which cases could be brought before it.[122] The Pentagon, not realizing that the very provisions it desired to protect future U.S. defendants would protect defendants from all countries and render the ICC much less effective from the outset, also weighed in to oppose the investigation of any U.S. soldiers without prior permission. Thus, the U.S. position at Rome was hardly surprising.[123]

The opposition was deepened by the seven-year "opt out" provision.[124] Although the United States favored a transition period of ten years to allow states "to assess the effectiveness and impartiality of the court," during which time states could opt out of the ICC's jurisdiction, it opposed the opt out provision that was finally adopted.[125] This provision allowed a seven-year opt out period with respect to war crimes only.[126] The effect of this in the U.S. view, when coupled with the ICC's apparent jurisdiction over non–state parties, is that "a country willing to commit war crimes could join the statute and 'opt out' of war crimes jurisdiction for seven years while a non-state party could deploy its soldiers abroad and be [immediately] vulnerable to assertions of jurisdiction."[127]

Second, the United States was opposed to prosecutorial initiative to investigate alleged crimes.[128] The United States was concerned "that it will encourage overwhelming the Court with complaints and risk diversion of its resources, as well as embroil the Court in controversy, political decision-making, and confusion."[129] The United States favored a prosecutor that could act only upon the referral of a state party or the UN Security Council.[130] Third, the United States opposed the inclusion of the crime of aggression because "aggression" is not defined under customary international law, and the statute itself did not define it.[131] The United States also insisted that to assign individual criminal responsibility there had to be "a direct linkage between a prior Security Council decision that a state had committed aggression and the conduct of an individual of that state."[132]

Fourth, the United States opposed the possible inclusion of terrorism and drug crimes.[133] It was the U.S. position that including such crimes would not assist in the fight against them and might actually hinder such efforts.[134] The presumption of growing jurisdiction, not only in territory but also in types of crimes, is evident throughout the statute and in the statements of supporters. For example, it is not sufficient for the ICC to address only a narrow class of international crimes. Some see the ICC as ultimately "act[ing] as a standard setting mechanism in the interpretation and application of international law and provid[ing] a model for national authorities in the administration of criminal justice."[135] Placing the ICC as the interpreter of international criminal law dramatically exceeds the scope and intent of the Rome Statute. However, it might be too ambitious to state that the ICC will provide a model for national administration of criminal law. All states would find that offensive because it implies that they are incapable of developing a legitimate legal system.

Finally, the United States could not agree to the provision that the statute be accepted with no reservations.[136] As Ambassador Scheffer explained, "We believed that at a minimum there were certain provisions of the statute, particularly in the field of State cooperation with the Court, where domestic constitutional requirements and national judicial procedure might require a reasonable opportunity for reservations that did not defeat the intent or purpose of the statute."[137] Clearly, the decision to forbid reservations was based in fears that they would ultimately weaken the ICC by undermining its effectiveness and the uniform applicability of the law. Reservations would have frustrated such goals by creating a complex web of interactions between states, wherein specific provisions would apply between some states but not between others. This approach is incompatible with the idea that the crimes in the ICC Statute are universally condemned. Prohibiting reservations also suggests that the framers were well aware of the constitutive nature of the Rome Statute as the fundamental, organic document of an international institution, which establishes permanent organs and provides rules for their operation. Reservations seem inappropriate in such a case.

Although the U.S. concerns about supporting the Rome Statute may be valid and legitimate, they give U.S. citizens some comfort in the knowledge that their government is not willing to blindly stumble into such an "ill-conceived international regime." However, that is not the whole story. The reasoning camouflages the basic aspect of the ICC: the threat it poses to U.S. sovereignty and hegemony.[138]

Some ICC supporters claim that worries over sovereignty are exaggerated,[139] a sentiment shared by this writer. They argue that "concerns of a runaway court are wildly chimerical" and that "the principle of 'complementarity' would protect against any such tendencies."[140] Attempting to assuage such fears in the U.S. Senate, European commissioner Emma Bonino stated that the ICC "will not . . . undermine national sovereignty."[141] The ICC, she said, "is not designed to replace national courts but to complement them."[142] The chief prosecutor of the Yugoslav tribunal, Justice Louise Arbour of Canada, echoed this, cautioning those worried about potential dangers that "an institution should not be constructed on the assumption that it will be run by incompetent people, acting in bad faith from improper purposes."[143]

In spite of the bitter disagreement over U.S. involvement in the ICC, on 31 December 2000, President Bill Clinton signed the statute on the last day it was open for signature, and thus the United States became a signatory to the Rome Statute.[144] Clinton defended this action by stating that the United States became a signatory in order to "reaffirm [its] strong support for international accountability" and to "remain engaged in making the ICC an instrument of impartial and effective justice."[145] Even these cautious words were not sufficient to calm the statute's strongest opponent, Senator Helms. In an address given shortly after the signing, he stated, "If I do nothing else this year, I will make certain that President Clinton's outrageous and unconscionable decision to sign the Rome Treaty establishing the International Criminal Court is reversed and repealed."[146] Helms repeatedly warned that the Rome Statute would never be ratified on his watch.

Helms and other right-wing hawks prevailed as George W. Bush took the White House. The rather thin arguments that the ICC would force the United States to forfeit some sovereignty and due process to a foreign and possibly unrestrained prosecutor, would place U.S. soldiers in jeopardy, and would even target the president, the National Security Council, and civilian and military officials received intense attention from the new Bush administration. The government intended to "unsign" the ICC Statute. A withdrawal of signature would exceed even the actions of Ronald Reagan's administration, which in 1987 decided it would not seek ratification of an amendment to the Geneva Conventions that Jimmy Carter had signed. But the U.S. government appeared unfazed by the national and international storm it would create, despite critics and allies being quick to criticize the Bush administration's stance and dismissing its concerns as largely unfounded.

Despite some U.S. efforts, enough signatures and ratifications were obtained. Once the magic number had been met, the United States began rendering the ICC redundant even before it was constituted. On 6 May 2002, the United States launched its attack on the ICC by unsigning the statute, a procedure unknown in international law. The Bush administration on 6 May 2002 formally renounced its obligations as a signatory to the 1998 Rome Statute. A simple three-sentence letter to UN Secretary-General Kofi Annan formally ended U.S. participation.[147] In the letter, Undersecretary of State for Arms Control and International Security John Bolton asserted that Washington "does not intend to become a party to the [Rome Statute of the ICC]" and that it "has no legal obligations arising from its signature [to the treaty] on December 31, 2000."[148] The decision to unsign the treaty damaged the U.S. reputation and created a rift with some allies. All of Washington's EU allies (except Greece) had by then ratified the Rome Statute, and several key European leaders, including British prime minister Tony Blair, personally lobbied top administration officials, including President Bush, against renouncing the treaty. EU leaders subsequently warned the United States that any deliberate effort to destroy the ICC could do serious damage to transatlantic relations.

Right-wing hawks in the Bush administration were pleased with the unsigning of the Rome Statute. They argued that the action preserved and upheld U.S. constitutional guarantees and sovereignty and curtailed politically motivated prosecutions of U.S. troops stationed overseas. The hawks, with strong support from Republicans in Congress, went much farther, launching a campaign to undermine the treaty and the ICC through the introduction of the American Servicemen's Protection Act. The bill sought not only to bar any U.S. cooperation with the ICC; it also barred U.S. military aid to other countries unless they agreed to shield U.S. troops in their territory from ICC prosecution. It also sought to ban U.S. troops from taking part in UN peacekeeping operations unless the UN Security Council explicitly exempted them from possible prosecution. On 2 August 2002, Bush signed it into law. Acquiring recognition as the Hague Invasion Act, it authorizes the president to retrieve U.S. nationals "using all means necessary" if they are held in The Hague for trial before the ICC. Dutch protests over this have left the U.S. establishment unrepentant.

But the unsigning was not received well by all in the U.S. government. A group of congressmen expressed strong dissatisfaction with the move:

> According to Article 18 of the Vienna Convention on the Law of Treaties, the United States, as a signatory but not a State Party to the Rome Treaty, would merely have been "obliged to refrain from acts which would defeat the object and purpose" of the treaty. As the jurisdiction of the Court is limited to the most serious crimes of concern to the international community—genocide, crimes against humanity, war crimes, and aggression—it is inconceivable that the United States would undertake any action that would so drastically undermine the treaty as to violate its obligations as a

signatory. "Unsigning" the treaty has damaged the moral credibility of the United States and serves as a US repudiation of the notion that war criminals and perpetrators of genocide should be brought to justice.[149]

It was also observed from other quarters that:

This unprecedented action suggests to the world that the signature of a US president lacks enduring meaning. At the very time, the US seeks signatures and ratifications of anti-terrorist treaties, an "unsigning" by the Bush administration will undermine the power of the international treaty system.[150]

Concerns about sovereignty are based on narrow national interests. The ICC and its prosecutors are not under the control of the UN Security Council, which curtails the U.S. ability to influence or manipulate the institution for whatever reason. With the United States wrapped up in its war on terror, the Bush administration has viewed the ICC as undercutting its security interests.

Regrettably, the ICC Statute entered into force a few weeks after the unsigning, without the moral or material support of the world's sole superpower. The ICC will not receive cooperation from Washington in any way, whether in funding, witnesses, or evidence. In addition, Washington will seek assurances from countries where U.S. troops are deployed that they will not be handed over to the ICC. Optimists, though, argue that the decision to unsign may be largely symbolic. Human rights advocates say that renouncing Clinton's signature will have no legal effect, since the treaty gives the ICC universal jurisdiction. Unsigning the treaty is seen as an act that will not stop the ICC, and the move amounts to nothing more than "an empty gesture" and "a triumph of ideology over any rational assessment of how to combat the worst human rights crimes."[151] But that does not mean that Washington's withdrawal will not have consequences. Apart from the damage in relations with European allies and the U.S. image abroad, the decision may set a dangerous precedent in international law.

This determination to kill the ICC paints a worrying picture. As early as June and July 2002, shortly after the unsigning, the United States threatened to withdraw from peacekeeping operations in East Timor and in Bosnia-Herzegovina unless U.S. peacekeepers were granted immunity from prosecution. Through arm-twisting, it succeeded in extracting a resolution from the Security Council on 12 July 2002 that would restrain the ICC from starting or proceeding with investigations or prosecutions of peacekeepers and other officials of non–state parties for a period of twelve months. From that point forward, the Bush administration has been trying to nullify the potential of the ICC. "Impunity agreements" are the most recent tactic it has deployed. These agreements—variously termed "exemption," "Article 98," or "nonsurrender" agreements—are bilateral treaties that provide that neither country will surrender any current or former government official or national of the other country to an international tribunal without the express consent of that country. This is not limited to the nationals of the two states but could extend to anyone in the pay of either state, including, for instance, those involved in espionage or undercover operations. The impunity agreement amounts to an express assertion of noncooperation with the ICC.

Reflections on the ICC

States rarely punish their own war criminals. Frequently, the end of conflict brings a desire to return to normalcy. Additionally, conflicts often end with a negotiated settlement, with amnesty as a condition for the cessation of hostilities, thus shielding criminals from prosecution. New governments may also include individuals who are responsible for war crimes. Such countries are naturally unwilling to prosecute. Supporters of the ICC claim that a permanent international institution would have the objectivity necessary to bring these criminals, regardless of position, to justice. A structural argument for establishing the ICC also exists. The creation of a permanent court would be beneficial to the international community because it would address one of the main failings of the international justice system: the lack of a permanent and effective enforcement mechanism.

The real threat to the ICC is the prospect that it will be little used. If the Court is to command respect, it must have sufficient jurisdiction to play a real role in the struggle against international crime. There is no danger that the ICC will be trivialized as long as it is making a valuable contribution to criminal justice.[152] Hence, the presumption of supporters is that it will be used and expanded as necessary into the future, thus generating respect. There are legitimate questions involving resources. It seems logical and appropriate for states, rather than the ICC, to prosecute cases if they are willing and able to do so. Certainly, states have developed systems of criminal justice and will not have the difficulties that the ICC is certain to face in terms of gathering evidence, conducting investigations, and arresting suspects. Thus, the ICC will more likely focus on clear-cut cases in which it is easier to secure witnesses and gather evidence. In addition, the statute suggests that the ICC should hear only the most serious cases of truly international concern.[153] Thus, there may be a need to distinguish "major" war criminals from "minor" offenders who should be tried locally, as at Nuremberg.[154] It is likely that the ICC will be largely an institution to raise the symbolic profile of the international enforcement of humanitarian law.

Potentially, states and the Security Council have the ability to reduce the ICC to an ad hoc institution by limiting it to situations where there is international and political consensus. This may be a reaction to sustained criticism from within the UN system or global civil society. The experiences in the former Yugoslavia and Rwanda show that realpolitik is the governing force in international law and that the international community reacts only under sustained pressure and criticism from civil society and the media. States and the UN are reluctant to react to internal state matters, irrespective of the nature of violations. As human rights treaty bodies have demonstrated, mechanisms that provide for state-based complaint procedures have been underutilized to date for this very reason. States are more inclined to make decisions based on political rather than judicial interests whenever the issue of international investigation and prosecution arises. States are keen on registering displeasure and condemnation through diplomatic channels and do not wish to offend the sensitivities of a state by triggering concrete international action. Thus, even within the ICC framework it is unlikely that the state complaint mechanism will be popular for invoking the jurisdiction of the ICC.

Beyond the general threat to national sovereignty, the ICC conflicts with many national constitutions. Supranational jurisdiction cannot be reconciled, and the vague and ambiguous crimes that are defined could not pass constitutional scrutiny in a number of countries. And there are no provisions in the Rome Statute for many basic protections, such as trial by a jury of peers. In many states, the constitution is the supreme law of the land, with all other laws (whether national or international) being subordinate. With countless judicial decisions securing the supremacy of constitutions, it will be interesting to see whether the Rome Statute will ever triumph over a constitutional provision. Also, judicial power is vested in courts, which are ordained and established by national legislatures. Thus, arguably, only a court of the state can exercise jurisdiction over a citizen for any offenses committed within that state. Therefore, at the theoretical and technical levels, the Rome Statute would conflict with a constitution if the ICC attempted to assert jurisdiction over a citizen for offenses committed on a state's territory.

Finally, the ICC fails to address the problem that it identifies. Justice is an attempt to set things right, after the crime has been committed. Any genocide, ethnic cleansing, and mass rapes are committed long before the judicial process can begin. By the time evidence has been gathered and the suspects apprehended, the value of the judicial remedy begins to degrade, particularly when dealing with crimes on a massive scale. The international community desires to end crimes against humanity, war crimes, genocide, and aggression. The experience of generations has been that punishment, though important, is at best a poor remedy for victims. Their greatest desire is to avoid victimization in the first place. Therefore, the best solutions to today's humanitarian crises lie not in adjudication that is too late for the traumatized victims but in prevention. Perhaps Carrie Gustafson is right: justice as envisioned in the ICC should be abandoned because it only perpetuates violence.[155] Perhaps adherence to the tenets of the world's greatest moral and ethical philosophers would provide a better solution to international crime and punishment.[156] Prevention of war and criminal activity, whatever the form, may be difficult to achieve through the ICC.

Conclusion

The process leading to the Rome Statute was extraordinary. States voted on the statute and thereby brought into question the continuing relevance of absolute sovereignty, and the law extends to the entire world (through the Security Council) if the case involves Chapter VII of the UN Charter. The one troubling feature is that the ICC will still operate under the shadow of state sovereignty, with states having the ability to frustrate its work. The complementarity principle and state-consent regime will restrain the exercise of prescriptive jurisdiction, such that it does not exceed what reasonable theories of power distribution and law-making authority suggest. The framers' distrust of their new creation is evidenced by the complex and burdensome procedural regime governing challenges to jurisdiction and admissibility, which may prevent the ICC from fulfilling its primary mission to administer justice. The Rome Statute illustrates the tension between the requirements of international justice and the need of states to retain sovereign prerogatives.

Although many aspects of the Rome Statute challenge tenets of international law, deference was paid to state sovereignty, resulting in the inevitable codification of political compromise. Enforcement jurisdiction is paltry at best. In terms of enforcement, classic paradigms of sovereignty mean that each state is master of its own territory.

Though certain sovereign prerogatives gave way, Rome did not present a triumph for the international penal process. The question of sovereignty colored the negotiations throughout. Perhaps the dominant theme at Rome was the need to reconcile sovereignty with the desire for a functioning international institution. As a matter of law, institutional structure, and process, many prerogatives of sovereignty remain. The existing power structure premised on state sovereignty resisted giving too many concessions to the ICC to facilitate its effectiveness. The final product is a fragile compromise that may or may not succeed. The opposition has a powerful champion in the United States.

Notes

1. David A. Nill, "National Sovereignty: Must It Be Sacrificed to the International Criminal Court?" *BYU Journal of Public Law* 14 (1999): 124.

2. Ibid., 125.

3. See M. Cherif Bassiouni, "From Versailles to Rwanda in Seventy-Five Years: The Need to Establish a Permanent International Criminal Court," *Harvard Human Rights Law Journal* 11 (1997): 60–61.

4. See Jelena Pejic, "Creating a Permanent International Criminal Court: The Obstacles to Independence and Effectiveness," *Columbia Human Rights Law Review* 29 (1998): 293.

5. See "Is a UN International Criminal Court in the U.S. National Interest? Hearing Before the Subcommittee on International Operations of the Senate Committee on Foreign Relations," 35 (testimony of Michael P. Scharf in support of the International Criminal Court).

6. See Pejic, "Creating a Permanent International Criminal Court," 293.

7. Leila Nadya Sadat and S. Richard Carden, "The New International Criminal Court: An Uneasy Revolution," *Georgetown Law Journal* 88 (2000): 383.

8. Ibid.

9. Ibid., 387.

10. GA Res. 95, UN GAOR, 1st sess., UN Doc. A/64/Add.1 (1946). See M. Cherif Bassiouni, "The History of the Draft Code of Crimes Against the Peace and Security of Mankind," *Israel Law Review* 27 (1993): 247; Leo Gross, "Some Observations on the Draft Code of Offences Against the Peace and Security of Mankind," *Israel Yearbook of Human Rights* 13 (1983): 10; Sharon Williams, "The Draft Code of Offences Against the Peace and Security of Mankind," in *International Criminal Law,* edited M. Cherif Bassiouni (Ardsley, NY: Transnational, 1998), vol. 1, 109.

11. GA Res. 174, UN GAOR, 2nd sess., UN Doc. A/519 (1947), 105–10.

12. GA Res. 177, UN GAOR, 2nd sess., UN Doc. A/CN4/4 (1947), 9.

13. Ibid.

14. International Law Commission, *Yearbook of the International Law Commission* (1949), vol. 1, vi (referring to Resolution 174 and Resolution 95).

15. The first report was completed in 1950: *Report of the International Law Commission,* UN GAOR, 5th sess., UN Doc. A/CN4/25 (1950). That title was changed in 1988 to Draft Code of Crimes Against the Peace and Security of Mankind. See *Report of the International Law Commission,* UN GAOR, 40th sess., Supp. no. 10, UN Doc. A/43/10 (1988), 145. The Draft Code of Offences, subsequently the Draft Code of Crimes, was never intended to codify all international crimes.

16. *Report of the International Law Commission on Question of International Criminal Jurisdiction,* UN GAOR, 5th sess., UN Doc. A/CN4/15 (1950).

17. Ibid. See also *Report of the International Law Commission,* UN GAOR, 5th sess., Supp. no. 12, UN Doc. A/1316 (1950), and discussions on this report by the Sixth Committee of the General Assembly, reprinted in Benjamin Ferencz, *An International Criminal Court, a Step Toward World Peace: A Documentary History and Analysis,* vol. 2 (Dobbs Ferry, NY: Oceana, 1980), 265–305.

18. That situation continued in part because of political considerations and later in part because the ILC's 1991 Draft Code of Crimes was not well received. See M. Cherif Bassiouni, "Commentaries on the International Law Commission's 1991 Draft Code of Crimes Against the Peace and Security of Mankind," *Nouvelles Etudes Penales* 11 (1993).

19. See "Report of the Sixth Committee," reprinted in Ferencz, *An International Criminal Court,* 298–305; "Report of the Ad Hoc Committee on the Establishment of an International Criminal Court," reprinted in Ferencz, *An International Criminal Court;* M. Cherif Bassiouni, "Recent United Nations Activities in Connection with the Establishment of a Permanent International Criminal Court and the

Role of the Association Internationale de Droit Penal and the Instituto Superiore Internazionale di Scienze Criminali," *Revue Internationale de Droit Penale* 67 (1996): 127.

20. *Report of the Committee on International Criminal Court Jurisdiction,* UN GAOR, 7th sess., Supp. no. 11, UN Doc. A/2136 (1952), 21–25. See also "Comments Received from Governments Regarding the Report of the Committee on International Criminal Jurisdiction," UN GAOR, 7th sess., UN Doc. A/2186 and UN Doc. A/2186/Add.1. See also "Historical Survey of the Question of International Criminal Jurisdiction, Memorandum by the Secretary-General," UN GAOR, 4th sess., UN Doc. A/CN4/7/Rev 1 (1949), reprinted in Ferencz, *An International Criminal Court,* 399.

21. Although many countries, such as the United Kingdom, believed that the establishment of an international criminal court was desirable in theory, its establishment was doomed by the absence of consensus among the major powers. The Soviet Union believed its sovereignty would be affected by the establishment of such a tribunal. The United States was also not prepared to accept the establishment of such a court at the height of the Cold War. See *Report of the Sixth Committee,* UN GAOR, 7th sess., UN Doc. A/2275 (1952), and discussions on this report by the Sixth Committee reprinted in Ferencz, *An International Criminal Court,* 424–428.

22. In 1952 the Allies were still holding trials in Germany under Allied Control Council Law no. 10.

23. *Report of the Committee on International Criminal Jurisdiction,* UN GAOR, 7th sess., Supp. no. 12, UN Doc. A/2645 (1954), 21. The revised statute made a number of changes to the 1951 Draft Statute in order to encourage more states to accept such a proposal, mostly softening the compulsory jurisdiction of the court by allowing more flexibility and voluntary participation on the part of states, including the opportunity for states to withdraw from the court's jurisdiction upon one year's notice. The special committee was eager to develop a project that was politically acceptable to the major powers, but even so the political climate was still not ripe.

24. GA Res. 898 (IX), UN GAOR, 9th sess., Supp. no. 21, UN Doc. A/2890 (1954), 50.

25. See *Third Report Relating to a Draft Code of Offences Against the Peace and Security of Mankind,* UN GAOR, 6th sess., UN Doc. A/CN4/85 (1954); see also D. H. N. Johnson, "The Draft Code of Offences Against the Peace and Security of Mankind," *International Comparative Law Quarterly* 4 (1955): 445.

26. Resolution 898 (IX). See also *Report of the 1953 Committee on International Criminal Jurisdiction,* UN GAOR, 9th sess., Supp. no. 12, UN Doc. A/2645 (1957); GA Res. 1187 (XII), UN GAOR, 12th sess., Supp. no. 18, UN Doc. A/3805 (1957), 52, which tabled the draft once again.

27. For a more detailed historical chronology and evolution, see Bassiouni, "History of the Draft Code."

28. GA Res. 3314 (XXIX), UN GAOR, 29th sess., Supp. no. 31, UN Doc. A/9631 (1974), 142–143. This resolution has been criticized by some scholars for leaving too many loopholes; see, for example, Allegra Carpenter, "The International Criminal Court and the Crime of Aggression," *Nordic Journal of International Law (Acta Scandinavica Juris Gentium)* 64(2) (1995): 223, 242.

29. See *Report of the International Law Commission on the Work of Its Thirty-Fifth Session,* UN GAOR, 38th sess., Supp. no. 10, UN Doc. A/38/10 (1983), 11–28.

30. *Report of the International Law Commission,* UN GAOR, 46th sess., Supp. no. 10, UN Doc. A/46/10 (1991).

31. Bassiouni, "Commentaries on the 1991 Draft Code."

32. Draft Code of Crimes Against Peace and Security of Mankind: Titles and Articles on the Draft Code of Crimes Against Peace and Security of Mankind adopted by the International Law Commission on its Forty-eighth Session, UN GAOR, 51st sess., UN Doc. A/CN4L532 (1996), revised by UN Doc. A/CN4L532/ Corr 1 and UN Doc. A/CN4L532/Corr 3.

33. GA Res. 43/164, UN GAOR, 43rd sess., Supp. no. 49, UN Doc. A/43/49 (1988), 280; GA Res. 44/39, UN GAOR, 44th sess., Supp. no. 49, UN Doc. A/44/49 (1989), 310. This recommendation was the consequence of a resolution adopted by the special session of the General Assembly of that year on the question of illicit traffic in drugs. Its sponsor was Trinidad and Tobago, whose former prime minister, Arthur N. R. Robinson, was the moving force behind it. Robinson deserves much credit for his untiring efforts to promote an ICC.

34. *Report of the International Law Commission,* UN GAOR, 49th sess., Supp. no. 10, UN Doc. A/47/10 (1992).

35. See *Revised Report of the Working Group on the Draft Statute for an International Criminal Court,* UN GAOR, 48th sess., UN Doc. A/CN4/L490 (1993); *Revised Report of the Working Group on the Draft Statute for an International Criminal Court: Addendum,* UN GAOR, 48th sess., UN Doc. A/CN4/L490/Add.1 (1993).

36. *Report of the International Law Commission on the Work of Its Forty-Sixth Session,* UN GAOR, 49th sess., Supp. no. 10, UN Doc. A/49/10 (1994). See also M. Cherif Bassiouni, "Establishing an International Criminal Court: Historical Survey," *Military Law Review* 149 (1995): 49; Timothy C. Evered, "An International Criminal Court: Recent Proposals and American Concerns," *Pace International Law Review* 6 (1994): 121; Michael P. Scharf, "Getting Serious About an International Criminal Court," *Pace International Law Review* 6 (1994): 103. For an insightful contribution to work on the subject by its Deputy Secretary, see Manuel Rama-Montaldo, "Acerca de Algunos Conceptos Basicos Relativos al derecho Penal International y a una Jurisdiction Penal Internacional," in *International Law in an Evolving World,* edited by Manuel Rama-Montaldo (Montevideo: Fundación de Cultura Universitaria, 1994), 865–893.

37. James Crawford, "The ILC Adopts a Statute for an International Criminal Court," *American Journal of International Law* 89 (1995): 404. Crawford, a distinguished member of the ILC, contributed to the 1994 Draft Statute and also to the Draft Code of Crimes that was adopted in 1996.

38. *Report of the Ad Hoc Committee on the Establishment of an International Criminal Court,* UN GAOR, 50th sess., Supp. no. 22, UN Doc. A/50/22.

39. GA Res. 50/46, UN GAOR, 50th sess., UN Doc. A/RES/50/46 (1995). See also "Summary of the Proceedings of the Preparatory Committee on the Establishment of an International Criminal Court," UN GAOR, 50th sess., Supp. no. 22, UN Doc. A/50/22 (1995).

40. Ibid.

41. Rome Statute of the International Criminal Court, UN Doc. A/CONF 183/9 (Rome Statute), reprinted in 37 I.L.M. 999, adopted by the United Nations Diplomatic Conference of Plenipotentiaries on the Establishment of an International Criminal Court on 17 July 1998 and entered into force on 1 July 2002.

42. For excellent analyses of other aspects of the ICC Statute, see Kenneth S. Gallant, "Individual Human Rights in a New International Organization: The Rome Statute of the International Criminal Court," in *International Criminal Law,* edited M. Cherif Bassiouni, 2nd ed., vol. 3 (Ardsley, NY: Transnational, 1998), 693 (discussing how the Rome Statute protects the individual human rights of defendants

from the ICC). For a skeptical critique of the ICC, see Alfred P. Rubin, "Crime and Punishment," in *International Law Across the Spectrum of Conflict: Essays In Honour of Professor L.C. Green on the Occasion of His Eightieth Birthday,* edited by Michael N. Schmitt (Newport, RI: Naval War College 1999).

43. Ibid., arts. 1, 25(1). The statute does not permit trials in absentia. Thus, the ICC must always have the defendant in its custody to obtain personal jurisdiction, in the sense that U.S. lawyers use the term: see Rome Statute, art. 63(1).

44. Christopher L. Blakesley, "Obstacles to the Creation of a Permanent War Crimes Tribunal," *Fletcher Forum* 18 (1999): 90.

45. Human Rights Watch expresses the concern that nations will avoid jurisdiction by invoking a "national security" privilege. See Human Rights Watch, "Section M: The Protection of National Security," (5 May 2000), www.hrw.org/reports98/icc/jitbwb-15.htm. It states that national security "must be balanced against other important and potentially competing interests. These would include the interests of victims, and of the international community as a whole. Deference to a national security must be tempered by the need to ensure the protection of international security, which is seriously compromised by the commission of heinous crimes and the impunity that so often surrounds them." Ibid.

46. See "Is a UN International Criminal Court in the U.S. National Interest? Hearing Before the Subcommittee on International Operations of the Senate Committee on Foreign Relations," 105th Cong. 1, 29 (1998), 6.

47. See Bryan F. MacPherson, "Building an International Criminal Court," *Connecticticut Journal of International Law* 13 (1998): 42, citing Daniel H. Derby, "An International Criminal Court for the Future," *Transnational Law and Contemporary Problems* 5 (1995): 311.

48. Leila Sadat Wexler, "The Proposed Permanent International Criminal Court: An Appraisal," *Cornell International Law Journal* 29 (1996): 678.

49. Ibid., 680.

50. For example, apartheid is criminalized as a result of the entry into force of the 1973 International Convention on the Suppression and Punishment of Apartheid, 30 November 1973, 1015 U.N.T.S. 243. Apartheid by definition is a product of national policies. Further, since the entry into force of the Genocide Convention, all the genocides committed thus far were the products of state policy. This is so in the cases of the genocides in Cambodia, Iraq, the former Yugoslavia, and Rwanda.

51. See, for example, Amnesty International, *"Disappearances" and Political Killings: Human Rights Crisis of the 1990s—A Manual for Action* (Amsterdam: Amnesty International, 1994); Human Rights Watch, *Iraq's Crime of Genocide: The Anfal Campaign Against the Kurds* (New York: Human Rights Watch, 1995); Catherine Knowles, "Life and Dignity, the Birthright of All Human Beings: An Analysis of the Iraqi Genocide of the Kurds and Effective Enforcement of Human Rights," *Naval Law Review* 45 (1998): 152; Louis Rene Beres, "Iraqi Crimes and International Law: The Imperative to Punish," *Denver Journal of International Law and Policy* 21 (1993): 335; Alan C. Leifer, "Never Again? The 'Concentration Camps' in Bosnia-Herzegovina: A Legal Analysis of Human Rights Abuses," *New Europe Journal Law Review* 2 (1994): 159; John Webb, "Genocide Treaty—Ethnic Cleansing—Substantive and Procedural Hurdles in the Application of the Genocide Convention to Alleged Crimes in the Former Yugoslavia," *Georgia Journal of International and Comparative Law* 23 (1993): 377.

52. "As a general matter, those types of criminal activity which are deemed to be of greatest international concern are of two kinds: those crimes that have an international component and those which have a transnational component. An international element exists where the conduct in question [rises] to the level where it

constitutes an offence against the world community. . . . Thus, international crimes are crimes which constitute a direct threat to world peace and security—that is, those which are committed directly against the territory of one State by another State. Also considered international crimes are those acts that are so egregious that they shock the conscience of the world community, or those which constitute an indirect threat by rising to the level of threatening world peace and security due to the magnitude of the offence." Rupa Bhattacharya, "Establishing a Rule-of-Law International Criminal Justice System," *Texas International Law Journal* 31 (1996): 67.

53. Ibid., 66.

54. Rome Statute, art. 5.

55. A state may opt out of the war crimes jurisdiction of the ICC as regarding nationals or crimes committed on its territory for seven years after the ICC Statute enters into force for the state. See ibid., art. 124. The United States desired, but did not obtain, a similar ten-year opt-out provision respecting crimes against humanity. Although the war crimes opt-out has been criticized in many quarters, over the anticipated long life of the Court's existence it is probably of minor importance, particularly as the opt-out will not apply in the event that the Security Council refers a situation to the Court.

56. The statute does not define "aggression." Article 5(2) provides that the Court shall exercise jurisdiction over that crime once it has been defined. It is interesting to note that delegates chose not to reserve an article in the definition of crimes section for aggression. The definition of "aggression" must be adopted in accordance with articles 121 and 123 of the statute, which detail the process of amending the statute. A state party may propose amendments seven years after the statute enters into force: see Rome Statute, art. 121(1). Adoption of the amendment, absent consensus among the states parties, requires a two-thirds majority vote of states parties; see art. 121(3). If seven-eighths of the states parties adopt an amendment, any state party that did not accept the amendment may withdraw from the statute with immediate effect by giving notice no later than one year after the amendment enters into force, subject to the withdrawal provisions in article 127(2); see art. 121(6). All amendments to article 5 enter into force for those states that adopt the amendment one year after the states deposit instruments of ratification; see art. 121(5). The Court may not exercise jurisdiction over a crime covered by such an amendment if that crime is committed by a national of or on the territory of a state that did not accept the amendment; see art. 121(5).

57. Draft Statute for an International Criminal Court 1994 (ILC), art. 20.

58. "Transnational crimes" are those where "the offensive conduct affects the interests of more than one State . . . includes the citizens of more than one State, or involves means or methods which transcend national boundaries." "Doctrinal Basis for the International Criminalization Process," *Temple International and Comparative Law Journal* 8 (1994): 90. International jurisdiction in these cases arises largely due to conflicting assertions of jurisdiction by two or more states.

59. See Draft Statute for an International Criminal Court 1994 (ILC), art. 20.

60. See Leila Sadat Wexler, "First Committee Report on Jurisdiction, Definition of Crimes, and Complementarity," in *The International Criminal Court: Observations and Issues Before the 1997–98 Preparatory Committee; and Administrative and Financial Implications,* edited by M. Cherif Bassiouni (Association Internationale de Droit Penal, Nouvelles Etudes Penales no. 13, 1997); Wexler, "The Proposed Permanent International Criminal Court: An Appraisal," 699.

61. As the International Law Association (American Branch) Committee noted in its initial report on the ILC draft, the inclusion of treaty crimes had the potential

to complicate the Court's jurisdictional regime, involve the creation of special chambers, and require a filtering mechanism to assure that states did not dump insignificant cases on the Court. Nevertheless, the committee supported the inclusion of at least some treaty crimes within the Court's initial jurisdiction; see Wexler, "First Committee Report on Jurisdiction, Definition of Crimes, and Complementarity," 164–165. For a good discussion of the treatment of treaty crimes during the Rome Statute's negotiation, see Herman von Hebel and Darryl Robinson, "Crimes Within the Jurisdiction of the Court," in *The International Criminal Court: The Making of the Statute—Issues, Negotiations, Results,* edited by Roy S. Lee (The Hague: Kluwer Law International, 1999).

62. See Rome Statute, art. 13(b). Because the Security Council will refer cases only under its Chapter VII powers, referral to the Court, like the establishment of the two ad hoc tribunals, is presumably a measure "not involving the use of force" that the Security Council may adopt to maintain international peace and security. See *Prosecutor v. Tadic,* Case no. IT-94–1-AR72, Decision on the Defense Motion for Interlocutory Appeal on Jurisdiction (Appeals Chamber, 2 October 1995), paras. 34–36.

63. Rome Statute, arts. 6 (genocide), 7(1) (crimes against humanity), and 8(2) (war crimes).

64. Rome Statute, arts. 4(2), 12(2).

65. Ibid.

66. See Vienna Convention on the Law of Treaties, 23 May 1969, UN Doc. A/Conf 39/28, UKTS 58 (1980), 8 I.L.M. 679, art. 34.

67. Rome Statute, art. 12.

68. "Is a UN International Criminal Court in the U.S. National Interest? Hearing Before the Subcommittee on International Operations of the Senate Committee on Foreign Relations," 12 (testimony of Ambassador David J. Scheffer).

69. Rome Statute, art. 17, having regard to art. 1 and the statement of the preamble in para. 10.

70. Rome Statute, art. 17.

71. Wexler, "The Proposed Permanent International Criminal Court," 23–24. "Unwillingness" in turn is defined as situations in which the proceedings were undertaken "for the purpose of shielding the person concerned from criminal responsibility," "there has been an unjustified delay in the proceedings [that is] inconsistent with an intent to bring the person concerned to justice," or "the proceedings were not, or are not being, conducted independently or impartially" and in a manner that is consistent "with an intent to bring the person concerned to justice." Rome Statute, art. 17(2). Inability to prosecute does not raise quite the same problem, for the statute is clear that inability concerns the total or substantial collapse of a state's judicial system. See ibid. In making a determination of "unwillingness" the Court is admonished by the statute to "hav[e] regard to the principles of due process recognized by international law."

72. The U.S. position, for example, is that the Court does not exercise "universal jurisdiction" but that the jurisdictional regime is nevertheless improper because the nationals of non–party states may find themselves before the Court even if their state of nationality objects; see "Is a UN International Criminal Court in the U.S. National Interest?" 76 (testimony of David Scheffer). In a recent speech, Scheffer noted the U.S. success in preserving "sovereign decisionmaking" by rejecting proposals requiring states parties to cooperate automatically with the Court. According to Scheffer, unqualified cooperation was "unrealistic" and possibly unconstitutional; see David J. Scheffer, Speech at the Twelfth Annual U.S. Pacific

Command International Military Operations and Law Conference, Hawaii, 23 February 1999, www.state.gov/www/policy_remarks/1999/990223_scheffer_hawaii.html.

73. See American Law Institute, *Restatement (Third) of the Foreign Relations Law of the United States* (St. Paul: American Law Institute Publishers, 1987), sec. 402(1)(a).

74. See ibid., sec. 402(2).

75. Sadat and Carden, "The New International Criminal Court," 408.

76. Rome Statute, art. 5(1); see also art. 1.

77. As Georges Levasseur has noted, the problem is essentially akin to one of conflict of laws: international criminal law as a body of law may apply where an "individual's behavior (whether a national or a foreigner) has troubled the public order of a country other than his own." Levasseur, "Les crimes contre l'humanite et le probleme de leur prescription," *Journal du Droit Internationale* 93 (1966): 267.

78. M. Cherif Bassiouni, *Crimes Against Humanity in International Law* (The Hague: Kluwer Law International, 1999), 235–240.

79. Conventional international law on the subject of universal jurisdiction is not clear and at best is inconsistent. As Bassiouni notes: "Since 1815, there have been sixty-four international criminal conventions that contain reference to one or more of the recognized theories of jurisdiction. Among those only a few contain a provision that could be interpreted as providing universal jurisdiction." For details, see Bassiouni, *Crimes Against Humanity in International Law,* 227–241; Roger S. Clark, "Offences of International Concern: Multilateral State Treaty Practice in the Forty Years Since Nuremberg," *Nordic Journal of International Law* 57 (1988): 51–63.

80. See Draft Statute for an International Criminal Court 1994 (ILC), arts. 23, 25.

81. See Rome Statute, arts. 13(c), 15(1). Private individuals and NGOs may not file complaints directly with the Court (there is thus no right to proceed as a *partie civile,* in the French sense), although the prosecutor may receive information from NGOs or other reliable sources concerning the possible commission of crimes potentially within the Court's jurisdiction; see art. 15(2). The ILC and most state delegations consistently took the position that individuals should not be able to bring cases to the Court; see Wexler, "The Proposed International Criminal Court: An Appraisal," 696, n. 181; 699, n. 197.

82. The issue arose at PrepCom I (IV) in August 1997 during discussions on article 23 of the ILC Draft. Supporters of an independent prosecutor included Germany, Finland, Norway, Costa Rica, Tanzania, South Korea, Italy, Austria, Trinidad and Tobago, Argentina, Greece, Switzerland, Liechtenstein, and New Zealand. Among the NGOs, both the Lawyers Committee for Human Rights and Human Rights Watch issued reports detailing the need for an independent prosecutor; see Lawyers Committee for Human Rights, "The International Criminal Court Trigger Mechanism and the Need for an Independent Prosecutor" (July 1997); Human Rights Watch, "Commentary for the August 1997 Preparatory Committee Meeting on the Establishment of an International Criminal Court: Materials for Working Groups 1 and 2" (1997). The Lawyers Committee for Human Rights also refuted ideas that an independent prosecutor would be uncontrollable; see Lawyers Committee for Human Rights, "The Accountability of an Ex Officio Prosecutor" (February 1998).

83. Opponents of an independent prosecutor at PrepCom I (IV) included the United States, the Russian Federation, China, France, Israel, India, Malaysia, Egypt, and Syria. The United Kingdom appeared to be undecided.

84. The U.S. objection to an independent prosecutor perhaps stems from the Clinton administration's disenchantment with the investigation of independent counsel Kenneth Starr and from the movement in the United States to allow the independent counsel law, 28 U.S.C. 591–599, to lapse. See "U.S. Justice Department Says Independent Counsel Statute Should Go," *Agence France-Presse,* 3 March 1999, available in 1999 WL 2556408.

85. "Is a UN International Criminal Court in the U.S. National Interest?" 23 (testimony of Ambassador David J. Scheffer).

86. Ibid., 26–28 (testimony of Ambassador Scheffer, acknowledging the powers and limitations of the office of prosecutor). Prosecutors with any semblance of independence are currently disfavored in the United States.

87. Rome Statute, art. 15.

88. Article 15 requires that the prosecutor, upon reaching the conclusion that there is a reasonable basis to go forward with an investigation, must submit a request to the Pre-Trial Chamber for authorization to proceed with the investigation. Ibid.

89. Sadat and Carden, "The New International Criminal Court," 401.

90. Ibid.

91. Rome Statute, art. 86.

92. Sadat and Carden, "The New International Criminal Court," 444.

93. Ibid.

94. By "persons," the ICC Statute is presumably tracking earlier drafts under which "persons" included "suspects," "accused," and "convicted persons." *Report of the Intersessional Meeting from 19 to 30 January 1998 in Zutphen, The Netherlands,* UN Doc. A/AC 249/1998/l/13, 226, n. 281.

95. Rome Statute, art. 79.

96. Ibid., art. 88.

97. See, for example, ibid., arts. 91(2)(c), 96(2)(e), 99(1).

98. One such exception is article 99(4)(a), which permits the prosecutor to execute requests that can be performed without any compulsory measures directly on the territory of a state party, if the state is one in the territory in which the crime is alleged to have been committed and there has been a determination of admissibility in the case. The prosecutor must enter into "all possible consultations" with the requested state party, as well. Ibid., art. 99(4)(a).

99. Ibid., art. 90(7)(b).

100. Ibid., art. 93(1).

101. Article 93(7) does permit the temporary transfer of persons in custody for purposes of identification or for obtaining testimony; however, the state is not required to agree to the transfer, which is subject in any event to the consent of the person transferred; see Rome Statute, art. 93(7).

102. See American Law Institute, *Restatement (Third) of the Foreign Relations Law of the United States,* sec. 401(c).

103. Sadat and Carden, "The New International Criminal Court," 415.

104. As one French writer has astutely remarked, the Court represents "justice sans police." Jean-Eric Schoettl, "Decisions du conseil constitutionnel: Cour Penale Internationale," *L'actualite Juridique-Droit Administratif* (20 March 1990): 230.

105. See Wexler, "The Proposed International Criminal Court: An Appraisal," 673, n. 41 (discussing the proposed statute of the London International Assembly, which provided for an international constabulary charged with the "execution of the orders of the Court and of the Procurator General [of the Court]").

106. See, for example, Rome Statute, article 70, which permits the Court to exercise jurisdiction over offenses against its administration of justice, subject to

conditions to be provided in the Rules of Procedure of Evidence. This article requires states parties to extend their laws covering similar offenses against the Court but notes that international cooperation "under this Article shall be governed by the domestic laws of the requested State." Ibid. art. 70(2). Thus, even this jurisdiction in aid of enforcement is strongly dominated by reference to state law insofar as its execution is concerned. See ibid., art. 71, which permits the Court to sanction persons present before it who disrupt its proceedings or deliberately refuse to comply with its directions by "administrative measures other than imprisonment." This section, which appears to permit the Court some direct enforcement power, seems to apply only to those persons actually in front of the Court (and again would presumably require state cooperation if the sanctions were somehow unenforceable directly).

107. Sadat and Carden, "The New International Criminal Court," 415–416.

108. Ibid.

109. Ibid.

110. Rome Statute, art. 56(2)(e).

111. Ibid., art. 57(3)(d).

112. These are requests that can be executed without any compulsory measures. The statute specifically includes "the interview of or taking evidence from a person on a voluntary basis" and "the examination without modification of a public site or other public place." Rome Statute, art. 99(4).

113. Sadat and Carden, "The New International Criminal Court," 415–416.

114. Rome Statute, part 9, contains the provisions on the nature and type of international cooperation and judicial assistance by states.

115. One instance of the priority of state politics over international justice, for example, is the 17 July 1998 position of the Cambodian government, led by Prime Minister Hun Sen, that his government would not cooperate even if the world required handing over the leaders of the genocidal Khmer Rouge (responsible for close to 2 million deaths during the "Killing Fields" era) to stand trial in an international tribunal. This was in response to opinions regarding Khieu Samphan and Nuon Che, two of Pol Pot's lieutenants, whom Hun was trying to entice to join his government. Also refer to the statement of Bosnia-Herzegovina's president, Biljana Plavsic, on 29 October 1996 that her government had no intention of turning in Radovan Karadzic and Ratko Mladic (generals in the Serb army and among the top three most wanted criminals by the ICTY—the other being Slobodan Milosevic) over to the ICTY. These two generals to date are yet to be arrested and handed over to the ICTY.

116. Rome Statute, art. 89.

117. Ibid., art. 12.

118. Appointed by the Secretary-General to investigate the gross and systematic violations of international humanitarian law in East Timor. This was pursuant to Human Rights Resolution 1999/S-4/1 of 27 September 1999 endorsed by the Economic and Social Council in its decision 1999/293 of 15 November 1999. Evidence of destruction of evidence was also corroborated by the *Report of the Joint Members of Special Rapporteurs of the Commission on Human Rights to East Timor* (A/54/660).

119. Ibid., paras. 143–156.

120. M. Heinrich, "OSCE to Create Kosovo War Crimes Court," *Reuters*, 28 April 2000.

121. Five people—Slobodan Milosevic and four others in the Serbian hierarchy—have been publicly indicted by the Hague tribunal over Kosovo's bloody upheaval in 1999. Ibid. The big question is how one gains access to persons who

wield such immense military and political clout in their states. They control the armed forces and police, so who will arrest them? It all boils down to the prevailing political currents and forces, as the arrest and surrender of Milosevic demonstrates.

122. Barbara Crossette, "Helms Vows to Make War on UN Court," *New York Times,* 27 March 1998, A9.

123. Sadat and Carden, "The New International Criminal Court."

124. Rome Statute, art. 123.

125. "Scheffer on Why the U.S. Opposed International Criminal Court," USIS Washington File 23–07–98 (April 2001), www.usembassy.org.uk/forpo12.html, 3–4.

126. Rome Statute, art. 124.

127. "Scheffer on Why the U.S. Opposed International Criminal Court," 4.

128. Ibid.

129. Ibid.

130. Ibid.

131. Ibid.

132. Ibid.

133. Ibid.

134. Ibid., 4–5.

135. See Lawyers Committee for Human Rights, *International Criminal Court Briefing Series,* vol. 2, no. 3 (New York: Lawyers Committee for Human Rights, 1999).

136. "Scheffer on Why the U.S. Opposed International Criminal Court," 5. Article 120 of the Rome Statute states that "no reservations may be made to this Statute."

137. "Scheffer on Why the U.S. Opposed International Criminal Court," 5.

138. As Sadat and Carden ("The New International Criminal Court") state at 459: "There is also an implicit threat to the current 'constitutional' structure based on the UN Charter, because the Statute circumvents the UN system and the privileged position of the United States as a permanent member of the Security Council."

139. William F. Jasper, "Courting Global Tyranny," *The New American* 189 (August 1998): 14, 15.

140. Ibid.

141. Ibid.

142. Ibid.

143. Ibid.

144. William Jefferson Clinton, President of the United States, Statement on Signature of the International Criminal Court Treaty, Washington, D.C., 31 December 2000 (4 February 2001), www.state.gov/www/global/swci/001231_clinton_icc.html, 1 (Clinton Statement on Signature).

145. He acknowledged that the statute has "significant flaws" and recommended to President George W. Bush not to submit it to the Senate for advice and consent on ratification of the treaty; Clinton Statement on Signature.

146. Senator Jesse Helms, "Towards a Compassionate Conservative Foreign Policy," Address by Senator Jesse Helms, Chairman, Senate Foreign Relations Committee, to the American Enterprise Institute, 11 January 2001 (6 February 2001), www.senate.gov/~foreign/2000/pr011201.htm, 10.

147. Editorial, "New Era in War Crimes Justice," *New York Times,* 4 May 2002, A12.

148. Pierre-Richard Prosper, "US Ambassador for War Crimes Issues Foreign Press Center Briefing," U.S. Department of State website, 6 May 2002, http://fpc.state.gov/9965.htm.

149. "Congressional Letter Sent by Congressman Joseph Crowley and 44 of His Congressional Colleagues," 22 May 2002, http://crowley.house.gov/news/record.asp?id=199.

150. Mark Epstein, director of the World Federalist Association, quoted by Jim Lobe in "Bush 'Unsigns' War Crimes Treaty," 6 May 2002 (16 July 2002), www.alternet.org/story.html?StoryID=13055.

151. Human Rights Watch executive director Kenneth Roth, quoted by Jim Lobe in ibid.

152. See MacPherson, "Building an International Criminal Court," 46.

153. See, for example, Rome Statute, Preamble, arts. 1, 5.

154. Sadat and Carden, "The New International Criminal Court," 459.

155. Ibid.

156. Ibid.

8

International Justice:
Retrospect and Prospect

During the twentieth century, following hundreds of years of history and warfare, nations agreed to use the law to help deter interstate wars. The Covenant of the League of Nations, the Kellogg-Briand Pact, the United Nations Charter, and the Nuremberg Charter for the war crimes tribunal together established a new legal regime in which war was outlawed as an instrument of national policy.[1] Not only is this the current legal position; it also seems to correspond to the ways in which most people thought about war during the twentieth century, namely, as something to be avoided if at all possible. Both morally and legally, the Clausewitzian view of war (i.e., war is politics by other means) became unacceptable.

Prior to the twentieth century, the view that war was a legitimate act of state was accepted by international lawyers as part of the doctrine of sovereignty. "So long as the war-making body had the authority to act, and followed the correct legal procedures, a proper declaration of war for example, war could be waged lawfully, and without any legal interest in the reasons for this act of state."[2] War was sometimes a rational choice for states—and a legitimate choice, too, because a majority of international lawyers believed that the right to declare war without any external approval was inherent to sovereignty. War was a *normal* feature of international relations, a normal part of the functioning of the international system—in no sense pathological (although regrettable).[3]

During the twentieth century, the costs of war rose dramatically while the perceived benefits stalled or fell. National wealth was no longer tied to conquering territory and its raw materials. The early twentieth century saw modern industrial society mature and seemed to mark a transformation, with the benefits of conquest seeming trivial compared to the costs: death, destruction by new weapons, the collapse of the world economy, political instability, and social turmoil. It seemed obvious that war was no longer the profitable enterprise it had been. Moreover, economics and imperialistic instability were reinforced by the notion of total war. Then World War I engulfed the European continent, reducing civilian and military objects alike to rubble. It led to an important sequence of events in history.

The first reaction among many was to assign personal responsibility: in Britain and France the German kaiser was widely blamed. Although Germany might bear a greater responsibility than other countries, the system of international relations itself was culpable, and a variety of different thinkers, politicians, and philanthropists sought ways to prevent a recurrence. Britain and the United States led this "liberal internationalism"—adapting liberal political principles to manage the international system.[4] They focused on domestic politics and the need for international mechanisms to address the internal causes of imperialism and militarism, as well as to devise external controls to curb negative forces. Alongside this, continuing bloodshed and suffering caused many to question the nationalistic, statist, and positivist philosophies ascendant in the nineteenth and early twentieth centuries. These conceptions were weakened by World War I, and it took the Nazi horror and the atrocities committed by the Imperial Japanese Army to convince the world community to reform international law and realize the essential importance of fundamental moral values.

The post–World War II trials were pivotal events for the development of international law. In some ways, they marked a return to natural justice that had given way to legal positivism during the eighteenth century. Natural justice doctrines were resurrected, and infused into the new thought and philosophy behind the trials. This belief helped to ensure that the tribunals would apply international law according to fundamental moral values. This reversed the nineteenth century trend toward maximizing state sovereignty and overlooking morality. The high-profile military tribunals became a deterrence.[5] Before, the right to prosecute war crimes rested almost exclusively with the belligerents.[6] Because this was at the discretion of the state, laws of war were applied sporadically. Under this scheme, states were forced to balance the feasibility of prosecution, the political wisdom of prosecution, and the cleanliness of their own hands.[7]

The two world wars generated a groundswell in diplomatic and legal circles that war represents a breakdown—a malfunctioning—of the international system. The postwar trials at Nuremberg and Tokyo represented the institutional expression of the international rule of law; the process they created would become central to improving the world order. Public opinion, coupled with multilateral agreements, spurred a shift in thought. Most important was the firm, clear, credible stand by international society against unilateral aggression, in favor of self-restraint, and the promise of a multinational response.

But these important developments stalled with the onset of the Cold War. It demonstrated that the basic feature of international relations is that *states pursue interests defined in terms of power.* The state is the key actor in international relations—the institution through which all other bodies operate, the institution that regulates other bodies and decides how they can act. As for *interests,*[8] states have interests, and state interests dominate state behavior.[9] States behave accordingly, not in response to abstract legal, moral, ethical, or altruistic principles. These interests clash. And violence may be the only means to meet core interests.

The end of the Cold War led to reexamination. The mechanisms of international enforcement had routinely been ostracism, economic boycott, censure, cultural isolation, and so on. These failed to curb war and violations of international humanitarian law. Too many atrocities by too many ruthless leaders led many to believe that these mechanisms could not effectively address the crimes. Impunity invited death and suffering. Thus there was the need for institutions that stood above the fray to prosecute violence. This new diplomacy was based on law and authority. The ad hoc international tribunals of the 1990s represented this trend—a return to individual responsibility. And though they were symbols of failure of the stale methods of diplomacy, they also undercut them.

The formation of the tribunals for Yugoslavia and Rwanda ended the dormancy.[10] A new era in the prosecution of war crimes meant that contemporary enforcement mechanisms were now inadequate and that the nature of war had reached a critical point.[11] The Security Council's choice to use the court of law to bring peace is a victory for the rule of law, the anchor of civil society. Yet some thought that prosecuting alleged war criminals was inconsistent with efforts to bring peace to the affected regions. Now, the goals of peace and international criminal justice are no longer seen as mutually exclusive. Rather, they are interdependent and complementary.

Certainly, the ICTY and the ICTR are making progress in fulfilling their mandates. The international community, at first cool, gradually softened. Alleged perpetrators are being arrested. The ICTY grew in resources (more than 1,000 staff members from over sixty-eight countries and a budget of close to $100 million in 2000).[12] Although far from perfect, the ICTY and ICTR[13] have redressed the failure to enforce the postwar legal regime designed to protect basic human rights during armed conflict.

States today better understand the need to enforce norms of international law prohibiting violations of human rights. Judicial mechanisms are an established part of conflict resolution, and proposals for international, national, and mixed tribunals are being put forward. Moreover, the culture of impunity is being challenged by states whose national courts are applying international law. The Pinochet principle[14] is demonstrating that justice has no borders. The International Criminal Court is now a reality thanks to the Rome Statute. The judgments of the ad hoc tribunals do more than determine guilt or innocence; they do more than establish a historical record; they do more than interpret international humanitarian law. They *are* the enforcement of international norms. This is the best proof that the numerous conventions, protocols, and resolutions affirming human dignity represent more than empty promises.

Perhaps the most far-reaching contribution is in breaking the cycle of impunity. War criminals are being called to account for their acts. By ensuring accountability, the tribunals demonstrate that basic human rights are real, that the rule of law is integral to peace, that the jurisprudence of international humanitarian law is expanding. They raised the international community's consciousness regarding the need for states to enforce international norms, and they accelerated the creation of the permanent ICC. Moreover, the trials develop a historical record of what happened, thus guarding against revisionism. The judgments, which typically detail factual circumstances, are an incontrovertible record of the brutality. The judgments also make substantive findings on legal issues, most of which are issues of first impression in the courts.

The tribunals underscore the importance of enforcing international humanitarian law. Many human rights instruments have more meaning and power as a result. Ad hoc tribunals cannot possibly handle all the potential prosecutions because of limited resources, yet they can develop jurisprudence that can be used by other courts in other trials. Thus, they set the stage for national judicial systems, which are better equipped to hear complex prosecutions.

International criminal justice is workable, and it is possible to bring high-ranking individuals to justice. These new developments influenced the establishment of the Special Court for Sierra Leone. Prior to the international community's decision to establish the Special Court as a separate entity, some called for expanding the ICTR mandate in Rwanda to Sierra Leone.[15] As it is, the ICTR Rules of Procedure and Evidence will apply *mutatis mutandis* (with the neccessary changes) to the Special Court. This is an important contribution. It is envisaged that the ad hoc tribunals will provide expertise and advice to the Special Court; consultations among judges, training of prosecutors, investigators, and administrative support staff, and sharing of information, documents, judgments, and other relevant material will occur on a continuing basis.[16]

Despite the progress in the humanization of the law of war, there are limitations to reciprocity, the inalienability of rights, personal autonomy, the definition of "protected persons," thresholds of applicability, crimes against humanity, and due process. There continue to be serious concerns over the observance of rules. This highlights the contrast between the normative framework and the harsh reality of the battlefield. The events in

Bosnia, Kosovo, Sierra Leone, Congo, Somalia, Afghanistan, and, not so long ago, Cambodia, Kuwait, and elsewhere represent a series of massacres, rapes, and mutilations. In the intersection among racial, ethnic, religious, and state interests, the normative has been eroding. International and national criminal tribunals have thus far demonstrated little deterrence. Humanization may have triumphed, but mostly in rhetoric. The gap between norms and reality has always been wide. Today, there is cynicism and doubt. In the long run, humanitarian norms must become a part of worldwide consciousness. For that, the creation of a culture of values is indispensable.

The adoption of the Rome Statute for the International Criminal Court, during the same decade as the establishment of the ad hoc international criminal tribunals, was a response to reality. Although nations recognize that the observance of law is in their interest and that every violation may also lead to consequences, policymakers may believe that the advantages of violation are clear; domestic pressures and nationalistic passions, prides, and prejudices may also compel governments to violate human rights. This realization led to the Rome Statute. The ICC aims to be a strong and effective world institution, but it is dependent on state support. Even this institution, hailed as the symbol of humanity's hopes of peace and justice, is already under siege. Threats and arm-twisting, especially by major powers, can be intense.[17]

Humanitarian law has evolved from detailed proscriptions on wartime conduct to dynamic case law. Yet many of the same difficulties back then remain today. To which conflicts should humanitarian law apply? Which is the most effective means of enforcing humanitarian law for purposes of deterrence? At what cost are we willing to advance the principles of humanitarian law? The ICC promises to alter the landscape by raising new questions and amplifying existing issues. The task of humanitarian law is staggering: to minimize human suffering while allowing for the effective conduct of war; any definition of "war crimes" reflects this tension. Article 8 of the Rome Statute, which gives the ICC subject matter jurisdiction over war crimes, is no exception. It is the product of decades of customary war crimes law as well as an attempt to advance principles of humanitarian law. The ICC will be accepted as a deterrent only if it is supported by the principal powers. The development of international war crimes trials as a means to enforce the laws of war is so significant because such trials overcome the obstacles of state sovereignty and impunity.

The popularity of the human rights movement since World War II has focused on individual rights, the universal application of legal norms, and scrutiny of state action. The ICC cannot afford to ignore this trend. Humanitarian law has expanded its reach through the merger with international human rights law[18] and the attendant implications for the global rule of law.[19] The legal changes now occurring at the international, regional, and domestic levels are coalescing to form a body of law that elaborates the rule of law, state responsibilities, and human rights as the international system itself is transforming. The new global rule of law challenges the prevailing bases and values, and levels the threshold conditions that determine whether an international or national legal regime applies to a given situation. The new humanitarian regime implies change, resulting in a new discourse, extended jurisdiction, reconceptualized personality, and new institutionalization.

Historically, talk of "justice" came after the fact. International adjudicatory processes were prompted by states' past violations of international law; they were used to retroactively rationalize the infringement of state sovereignty.[20] Currently, however, the humanitarian regime arises much earlier in policy debates, particularly regarding intervention in crises. The new regime expands territorial jurisdiction, reaching even intrastate conflicts. The Rome Statute supports this notion; it redefines offenses by dropping the previously required nexus to international armed conflict and extending "international jurisdiction" to internal matters.[21] The current shift reflects how the law of war has moved from the periphery to the core. It challenges the basic category of international human rights law by redefining the threshold conditions of war and peace; expanded jurisdiction implies normalization.

Yet bloodshed flows from Iraq to the former Yugoslavia to Somalia, through Rwanda, Afghanistan, Burundi, Liberia, Sierra Leone, Colombia, the Congo, Chechnya, Indonesia, and Sudan. These and other conflicts are grim reminders that international law continues to fail us all.[22] Let's hope that ICTY and the ICTR are harbingers of future processes.

The international penal institutions discussed here establish a hard fact: tribunals are subject to the will and power of states that seek to safeguard or advance their supreme decisionmaking capability. These tribunals have to conduct their business among states, and they cannot exist without them. The international system does not act in a vacuum; nor does it operate outside realpolitik. Its effectiveness all too often depends on the quality of world politics and the degree of community among members.

States will never totally abandon their warmaking ability, despite the abilities of the UN. Crucial questions remain open: Does the Security Council act in a dictatorial and hypocritical manner that promotes injustice? Do influence and power fall under the command of a small minority of states? These and other related questions continue to plague maximalist proposals for world order.[23] However, there is room for optimism. International inducements and restraints form an important component in promoting the observance of law and obligation. "The fate of the more political norms and agreements will be shaped, if not determined, by the extent to which the principal political forces . . . emphasize the advantages of law observance, by the general state of international order and the climate of interstate relations, by the example of influential nations, and by their stand toward the violations of others."[24]

As we move ahead, new agendas face the international community on international humanitarian law, the implications of the emerging human rights regime, and the relationship among the state, the international community, and individuals. Though the international penal process challenges the preeminence of the state under the Westphalian system to protect the values and interests of individuals and to define moral obligations,[25] the behavior of states is still dominated by the maxim that charity begins at home.

Ad hoc tribunals and prosecutorial processes are no panacea[26] for international humanitarian law violations. Other tools must be used. Attention and resources should be refocused to prevent bloodshed in the first place. If existing means of prosecution can adequately incapacitate offenders, why risk military intervention? If existing means of prosecution can adequately spur reconciliation, why sponsor grassroots reconstruction? Inflated expectations provide an excuse for international actors to cling to the familiar responses. Given the difficulty of mobilizing and coordinating political will to achieve international goals beyond narrow national self-interests, even this minor inertial effect may deter support for the development of additional mechanisms of accountability that better meet the objectives of prosecution.[27]

Notes

1. In contemporary times, war is legitimate only in two circumstances: as an act of self-defense, or as an act of law enforcement to assist others in defending themselves. Until 1945 there was no customary prohibition on the unilateral resort to force if circumstances warranted; and for signatories to particular instruments if certain preliminary procedures had been exhausted states reserved the right to resort to force. The UN Charter introduced to international politics a radically new notion: a general prohibition of the unilateral resort to force by states. The prohibition of the use of force embodied in article 2(4) of the UN Charter proscribes not only war but also any use or threat of force in general. Apart from the now obsolete clauses concerning the former enemy states, the UN Charter contains only two exceptions to the prohibition of force, namely, Security Council enforcement actions pursuant to Chapter VII, and the right to individual and collective self-defense laid down in article 51; see, for example, Ian Brownlie, *International Law and the Use of Force by States* (Oxford: Clarendon, 1963); Yoram Dinstein, *War, Aggression, and Self-Defence,* 3rd ed. (Cambridge: Cambridge University Press, 1994).

2. Chris Brown, *Understanding International Relations* (Basingstoke: Macmillan, 2001), 117.

3. "The self-evidence of this interpretation seemed supported by the historical record of nineteenth-century wars—successful diplomatists such as Bismarck, and imperialists such as Rhodes, fought wars of conquest which did, indeed, seem to bring results." Ibid., 10.

4. Liberal internationalism offered a two-part diagnosis of what went wrong in 1914 and a corresponding two-part prescription for avoiding similar disasters in the future. First, it identified *domestic politics*—which encouraged imperialistic and militaristic thought in which governments targeted the raw feelings of the people and harnessed this to political ends, translated into action by the military. A firm liberal belief was that the "people" do not want war; war comes about because the people are led into it by militarists or autocrats, or because their legitimate aspirations to nationhood are blocked by undemocratic, multinational, imperial systems. An obvious answer here is to promote *democratic political systems* and *self-determination.* The second component of liberal internationalism was its critique of pre-1914 *international institutional structures.* The basic thesis here was that the anarchic pre-1914 system of international relations undermined the prospects for peace. Secret diplomacy led to an alliance system that committed nations to courses of action that had not been sanctioned by parliaments or assemblies. There was no mechanism in 1914 to prevent war, except for the "balance of power"—a notion that was associated with unprincipled power politics. What was deemed necessary was the establishment of new principles of international relations, such as "open covenants openly arrived at," but most of all a new institutional structure for international relations—*a League of Nations.* The basic aim of the League of Nations would be to provide the security that nations attempted, unsuccessfully, to find under the old balance-of-power system. See, for example, ibid., 21–26.

5. In fact, the Nuremberg and Tokyo trials were not the first instance of the use of criminal trials to prosecute violators of international criminal law. After World War I, for example, a commission was established to attempt to allocate criminal responsibility for wartime atrocities, but these tribunals failed to attain the broad acceptance of Nuremberg. See Commission on the Responsibility of the Authors of the War and on Enforcement of Penalties, *Report Presented to the Preliminary Peace Conference,* 29 March 1919, reprinted in *American Journal of International Law* 14 (1920): 115.

6. Remigiusz Bierzanek traces the origin of this distinction to the Romans in "The Prosecution of War Crimes," in *A Treatise on International Criminal Law,* edited by M. Cherif Bassiouni and Ved P. Nanda (Springfield, IL: Thomas, 1973), 561.

7. For a general discussion of the shortcomings and prospects for improved use of domestic prosecution, see *National Implementation of Humanitarian Law: Proceedings of an International Colloquium Held at Bad Homburg,* edited by Michael Bothe et al. (Dordrecht: Martinus Nijhoff, 1990), 73–87.

8. National interests may be complex and difficult to identify in concrete terms, but the realist proposition is that a degree of simplicity can be introduced by assuming that whatever else states seek, they seek *power* in order to achieve other goals. The need for power stems from the anarchical nature of the international system. There is no authoritative system of decisionmaking in international relations; states are obliged to look after themselves in what has become known as a "self-help" system. Power is a complex notion; we can think of power as "capability"—the physical force necessary to achieve a particular goal—but capability is always cashed out in a behavioral relationship. The actual possession of assets has political meaning only in relation to the assets possessed by others.

9. Hans Morgenthau, *Politics Among Nations: The Struggle for Power and Peace,* 5th ed. (New York: Knopf, 1978).

10. No concerted effort was made to recognize or to prosecute war crimes arising out of conflicts in, for example, Korea, the India-Pakistan conflict of 1972, or

the Gulf War of 1991. See Yoram Dinstein and Mala Tabory, *War Crimes in International Law* (The Hague: Martinus Nijhoff, 1996), 130.

11. See Aryeh Neier, *War Crimes: Brutality, Genocide, Terror, and the Struggle for Justice* (New York: Times Books, 1998), 24.

12. ICTY Key Figures, ICTY website (23 January 2001), www.un.org/icty/glance/keyfig-e.htm.

13. The ICTR was formed by the Security Council to address violations of international humanitarian law in Rwanda during 1994: SC Res. 955, UN SCOR, 49th sess., 3453rd mtg., UN Doc. S/RES/955 (1994).

14. The arrest of Augusto Pinochet in the United Kingdom in October 1998 and subsequent decisions by the House of Lords established very important practical and juridical precedents. The case vindicated the principle that neither an individual's status nor any putative amnesty can act as a bar to accountability for acts that violate norms of international law. More recently, negotiations between the United Nations and the government of Sierra Leone leading to the establishment of a proposed "Special Court" to try the perpetrators of such acts have reaffirmed the latter. See *Report of the Secretary-General on the Establishment of a Special Court for Sierra Leone*, UN Doc. S/2000/915, 4 October 2000, www.un.org/Docs/sc/reports/2000/915e.pdf, 22–24.

15. See Kingsley Chiedu Moghalu, "Sierra Leone: No Peace Without Justice," *West African Magazine* (12–18 June 2001), 8.

16. See *Report of the Secretary-General on the Establishment of a Special Court for Sierra Leone*, 12.

17. In May 2002 the Bush administration repudiated the U.S. signature on the Rome Statute. This stands in stark contrast to the statements of the ambassador-at-large for war crimes issues, Pierre-Richard Prosper, that the administration was "not going to war" with the Court. In addition, its campaign moved to the Security Council in an attempt to exempt peacekeepers from the Court's jurisdiction. In the words of Richard Dicker, director of Human Rights Watch's International Justice Program: "Rather than focusing on the goals of the court—to prosecute future Pol Pots or Saddam Husseins—the U.S. government has fixated on guaranteeing itself an ironclad exemption from the Court's jurisdiction. The U.S. attempted to achieve that result when the ICC treaty was drafted in 1998, and failed. It must not be permitted to do so now." "U.S. Attack on War Crimes Court Rejected at U.N.," *Human Rights Watch website* (24 June 2003), www.hrw.org/press/2002/07/icc070302.htm.

18. See generally Tim Dunne and Nicholas J. Wheeler, eds., *Human Rights in Global Politics* (Cambridge: Cambridge University Press, 1999); Louis Henkin, *The Age of Rights* (New York: Columbia University Press, 1990).

19. For a comprehensive exposition of the contemporary law of war, see Theodor Meron, *War Crimes Law Comes of Age* (Oxford: Clarendon, 1998); Theodor Meron, "The Humanization of Humanitarian Law," *American Journal of International Law* 94 (2000): 239.

20. See, for example, Telford Taylor, *The Anatomy of the Nuremberg Trials: A Personal Memoir* (New York: Knopf, 1992); Meron, *War Crimes Law Comes of Age* (offering a comprehensive historical account).

21. For illustrations of these developments, see Rome Statute of the International Criminal Court, United Nations Diplomatic Conference of the Plenipotentiaries on the Establishment of an International Criminal Court, 27 July 1998, Annex 11, UN Doc. A/CONF. 183/9, reprinted in 37 I.L.M. 999 (1998), www.un.org/law/icc/statute/romefra.htm.

22. George Aldrich, "Compliance with International Humanitarian Law," *International Review of the Red Cross* 282 (May–June 1991): 302.

23. Walter S. Jones, *The Logic of International Relations,* 5th ed. (Boston: Little, Brown, 1985), 652.

24. Louis Henkin, *How Nations Behave: Law and Foreign Policy* (New York: Praeger, 1968), 245.

25. M. Frost, *Ethics in International Relations: A Constitutive Theory* (Cambridge: Cambridge University Press, 1996).

26. Some tribunal proponents recognize, for example, that prosecutions "cannot be a substitute for [more] robust action by the United Nations." Antonio Cassese, "On the Current Trends Towards Criminal Prosecution and Punishment of Breaches of International Humanitarian Law," *European Journal of International Law* 9 (1998): 17; see also Provisional Verbatim Record of the 3217th mtg., UN Doc. S/PV 3217 (1993), 27 ("an international tribunal must be but one element of a plan").

27. Jose E. Alvarez, "Rush to Closure: Lessons of the Tadic Judgment," *Michigan Law Review* 96 (1998): 2031 (explaining that the tribunals may be best designed to foster "civil dissensus"). "Attempts to make international criminal tribunals carry as much freight as some of their advocates recommend . . . may endanger alternative processes and possibly undermine competing goals for the international community." Ibid., 2104.

Acronyms

CCL no. 10	Allied Control Council Law no. 10
CSCE	Council for Co-operation and Security in Europe (the security arm of the European Community)
EC	European Community
ECMM	European Community Monitor Mission
ECOSOC	UN Economic and Social Council
EPC	European Political Co-operation
FEC	Far Eastern Commission
ICC	International Criminal Court
ICCPR	International Covenant on Civil and Political Rights
ICESCR	International Covenant on Economic, Social, and Cultural Rights
ICRC	International Committee of the Red Cross
ICTR	International Criminal Tribunal for Rwanda
ICTY	International Criminal Tribunal for the Former Yugoslavia
IFOR	Implementation Force
ILC	International Law Commission
NATO	North Atlantic Treaty Organization
NGOs	nongovernmental organizations
NIF	Neutral International Force
OLA	Office of Legal Affairs (UN)
PrepCom	Preparatory Committee
RPF	Rwandese Patriotic Front
SCAP	Supreme Commander for the Allied Powers
SCSL	Special Court for Sierra Leone
SHAEF	Supreme Headquarters, Allied Expeditionary Force

UDHR	Universal Declaration of Human Rights
UN	United Nations
UNPROFOR	United Nations Protection Force
UNWCC	United Nations War Crimes Commission

Glossary

The author wishes to emphasize the caveat that this glossary is not intended to be a general authoritative meaning of the words and terms but rather has been constructed in relation to the use of the words and terms in the book. Often the meanings may appear broader or narrower than their meanings in other contexts.

Ad hoc tribunal: judicial institution formed for a particular purpose.

American Civil War: The Civil War was caused by a myriad of conflicting pressures, principles, and prejudices, fueled by sectional differences and pride. At the root of all of the problems was the institution of slavery. The whole mess went up in smoke in 1860 when the Southern states (which condoned slavery) seceded, leading the federal government with the support of the Northern states to fight to save the Union.

Armistice: A truce marking the end of armed confrontation in war.

Aut dedere aut judicare: Latin: extradite or prosecute. An international rule representing the position that a state may not shield a person suspected of certain categories of crimes. Instead, it is *required* either to exercise jurisdiction over the crimes or to extradite the person to a state able and willing to do so or to surrender the person to an international criminal court with jurisdiction over the suspect and the crime.

Battle of Solferino: This battle fought on 21 June 1859 was a decisive engagement in the Italian Campaign in the Franco-Austrian War. It took place near the village of Solferino, Italy. The horrific suffering of wounded soldiers left on the battlefield was to have a long-term effect on the future conduct of military actions owing to the efforts of Henri Dunant, a Swiss businessman.

Bolshevik Revolution: The October 1917 revolution led to the Communists coming to power in Russia and gave birth to the Soviet Union in 1922 after a bloody civil war.

Bolshevism: A school of thought espousing a combination of revolutionary and political realism. It aims to prove that the alliance between the proletariat and the oppressed masses of the rural and urban petit bourgeoisie is possible only through the political overthrow of the traditional petit-bourgeois parties.

Bourgmestre: French: mayor.

Central Powers: The military alliance during World War I between Germany, the Austro-Hungarian Empire, the Ottoman Empire (Turkey), and the Kingdom of Bulgaria.

Clausewitzian War: Labeled after the Prussian general Carl von Clausewitz (1780–1831) who advocated "absolute war"—in war the party seeking to win should inflict upon the enemy as much harm as is necessary to ensure a decisive victory.

Cold War: The essential duopoly of power resting with the two superpowers (the United States and the USSR) left by World War II. This led to the East-West competition for hegemonic leadership that crippled international cooperation on many fronts and fostered numerous wars of proxy.

Collective security: One type of coalition-building strategy in which a group of nations agree not to attack each other and to defend each other against an attack from one of the others, if such an attack is made. The principle is that "an attack against one is an attack against all."

Complementarity: The preamble of the Rome Statute describes the International Criminal Court as a "complement" to existing national courts and processes—hence the coining of the term *complementarity*. A state with jurisdictional competence has the first right to institute proceedings.

Crimes against humanity: The term has come to mean anything atrocious committed on a systematic or large scale. To some extent, crimes against humanity overlap with genocide and war crimes. Crimes against humanity apply in the context of war and peace.

De facto: Latin: In fact.

De jure: Latin: By right, or legally.

De lege ferenda: Latin: What the law ought to be.

Entente powers: The military alliance during World War I between France, Britain, and Russia, which comprised the core of the Western Allied powers.

Ethnic cleansing: The term has been used to designate the practice of rendering an area ethnically homogeneous by using force or intimidation to remove persons or given groups from the area.

Ex post facto: Latin: By reason of a subsequent act.

Fascism: Form of authoritarian government that repudiates the doctrine of pacifism.

Franco-Prussian War: The war between France and Prussia in 1870–1871 provoked by Otto von Bismarck (the Prussian chancellor) as part of his plan to create a unified German Empire.

Geneva Conventions: The four 1949 Geneva Conventions that constitute the core of international humanitarian law in regard to rules, duties, and obligations in the waging of warfare.

Genocide: An international crime characterized by promotion and execution of policies by a state or its agents that result in the deaths of a substantial portion of a group. The characteristics by which members of the group are identified by the state are defined primarily in terms of their communal characteristics, i.e., ethnicity, religion, or nationality.

Hague Conferences: The two international peace conferences of 1899 and 1907 held at The Hague leading to the codification of the laws of war and a recognition of the need for arms limitation and avenues for pacific settlement of interstate feuds.

"Hard" enforcement: In the context of international justice refers to direct use of force whether by domestic law enforcement agents or multinational forces to track down and apprehend war criminals.

Hegemony: the leadership and/or dominance by one state over others.

Holocaust: The World War II genocide of 6 million Jews by Nazi Germany. This term is seemingly reserved for this specific time and set of events through usage.

Humanist: Person who believes in meaningful, fulfilling lives based on reason and compassion, and acts accordingly.

Humanitarian intervention: It may be defined as the use of force in order to stop or oppose massive violations of the most fundamental human rights in a third state, provided that the victims are not nationals of the intervening state(s).

Intelligentsia: Intellectuals or highly educated people. Usually taken to comprise a social group characterized by status privileges, rank, and influence.

Interahamwe: Kinyarandwa: Those who fight together. A band of militia composed of extremist Hutu elements trained to massacre Tutsi and moderate Hutu in Rwanda.

International criminal law: As used in this book refers to those violations of international humanitarian and human rights law generally recognized as international crimes.

International humanitarian law: The body of rules that, in situations of armed conflict, protects people who are not or are no longer participating in the hostilities. Its central purpose is to limit and prevent human suffering.

International jurisdiction: Concerns the power of the state or international penal institution to affect people, property, and circumstances both within and without the domestic sphere.

International penal process: As used in this book refers to the enforcement of international criminal law through institutionalization of its substantive provisions in courts that have a markedly international dimension. That is, courts constituted either by multiple states for the benefit of the international community or by the international community to vindicate its interests.

Juridical entity: A legal entity created by national or international law.

Juridical person: A legal person created by national or international law.

Jurisdiction: From Latin *jurisdictio:* administration of the law. The authority or power of a court or tribunal to hear a particular case or dispute.

Jurisdiction ratione loci: Latin: Geographic jurisdiction over particular places.

Jurisdiction ratione materiae: Latin: Subject matter jurisdiction.

Jus ad bellum: Latin: The right to initiate war. The rights of states to start wars.

Jus cogens: Latin: Compulsory law. A peremptory norm of international law; one that all states must observe.

Jus contra bellum: Latin: Law on the prevention of war.

Jus gentium: Latin: The law of nations.

Jus in bello: Latin: The law during war. The law regulating combat or the waging of war.

Jus militaire: Latin: Law of arms governing professional soldiers.

Jus naturale: Latin: Natural law. Law inherent in nature that may be ascertained by reason.

Kellogg-Briand Pact: This pact providing for the renunciation of war as an instrument of national policy marked the first formal step toward outlawing war as an accepted right of states subject to their sovereign prerogative.

Kreigraison: German: The argument that under conditions of extreme military necessity, the rules of war should be ignored. In other words, why follow the rules of war, especially if the other side is not?

Laws and customs of war: Broadly, these are recognized and accepted norms with regard to the general affair of waging warfare, which regulates a broad array of activities including the means and methods as well as treatment of prisoners of war. In many ways these are mirrored by international humanitarian law.

Le Contrat Social: French: The Social Contract. It is the title of Jean-Jacque Rousseau's seminal treatise on politics that propounded the doctrine that government gets its authority over the citizenry by a willing consent on the part of the citizenry, not through divine right.

Lex lata: Latin: What the law is.

Liberal internationalism: The adaptation of broadly liberal political principles to the management of the international system post–World War I. This thought focused on addressing the internal causes of imperialism and militarism and establishment of international controls to curb these internally generated negative forces.

Lieber Code: *General Orders No. 100, Instructions for the Government of Armies of the United States in the Field*, issued by U.S. president Abraham Lincoln during the American Civil War.

Military necessity: Those measures that are indispensable for securing the ends of war, and that are lawful according to the modern laws and customs of war.

Municipal jurisdiction: Concerns the power of the state to affect people, property, and circumstances within its domestic sphere.

Mutatis mutandis: Latin: Things being changed that are to be changed, or with the necessary changes.

Neutrality: Status of a nation that refrains from participation in a war between other states and maintains an impartial attitude toward the belligerents.

Nulla poena sine lege: Latin: No penalty without a law. In law, the principle that one cannot be penalized for doing something that isn't prohibited by law.

Nullum crimen sine lege: Latin: Penal law cannot be enacted retroactively.

Ottoman Empire: The largest and most influential of the Muslim empires that revolved around modern-day Turkey. The end to the empire came with the secularization of Turkey after World War I along European models of government.

Paris Peace Conference: The centerpoint of post–World War I efforts by the victorious Western Allies to not only redefine international relations, but also to resolve Europe's prevalent militarism and imperialism through a series of negotiated treaties.

Passive personality principle: This permits the exercise of jurisdiction over a crime committed outside the territory of the state based solely upon the nationality of the victim.

Peace of Westphalia: Peace treaty signed in October 1648 that ended the Thirty Years' War, which revolved around conflict between Catholic and Protestant forces.

Peace Treaty of Lausanne: Treaty through which Turkey recovered full sovereign rights over all its territory, its foreign zones of influence and capitulations were abolished, and the end of the Ottoman Empire resulted.

Peace Treaty of Sevres: Imposed by the Western Allies on the Ottoman Empire after World War I virtually destroyed Turkey as a national state.

Pinochet principle: Chilean dictator Augusto Pinochet's arrest and trial in the U.K. set a precedent that reigning tyrants who have traditionally been beyond the reach of the law when at home and enjoy diplomatic immunity when traveling are now open to prosecution should they have committed or been complicit in international crimes nothwithstanding the principle of diplomatic immunity.

Principle of proportionality: The amount of destruction permitted in war must be proportionate to the importance of the objective.

Proprio motu: Latin: By one's own motion; of one's own initiative.

Realpolitik: German: Practical politics. It is broadly used in this book to denote power politics by states designed to produce or achieve certain desired outcomes whether domestically or internationally based on legal, moral, or ideological agendas.

Reichsgericht: German Supreme Court sitting at Leipzig where German war criminals were tried in the aftermath of World War I.

Rome Statute: Rome Statute of the International Criminal Court adopted in 1998. It entered into force on 1 July 2002. It will investigate and prosecute people accused of genocide, crimes against humanity, war crimes, and aggression (when this is eventually defined) committed from this date onwards.

Schlieffen Plan: Military masterplan drawn by Alfred von Schlieffen, German chief of staff (1862–1906), targeting France and Russia in order to consolidate Germany's position on the continent and to confirm its status as a world power.

"Soft" enforcement: In the context of international justice refers to indirect means of meeting the goal of apprehending war criminals including condemnation of noncooperation by the UN Security Council, offers of economic incentives to governments to induce cooperation, and imposition of diplomatic and economic sanctions on noncooperating governments.

State egoism: In a broad sense, the term means self-centered acts by states that make the advancement of a state's agenda for whatever reason the end and motive of action.

Territorial jurisdiction: The principle that a country has the power to prosecute all offenses committed or alleged to have been committed within its territorial limits.

Universal jurisdiction: The principle that the courts of any country may prosecute any person whatever his/her nationality and wherever he/she may have committed certain international crimes.

War criminal: Broadly refers to persons who violate the laws and customs of war.

Westphalian sovereignty: The concept asserts the supremacy of the state in its territorial sphere and its political independence in external relations, i.e., exclusion of external actors from authority structures within a given territory.

Selected Bibliography

Akhavan, P. "International Criminal Tribunal for Rwanda: The Politics and Pragmatics of Punishment." *American Journal of International Law* 90 (1996).

Ambrosius, L. E., ed. *A Crisis of Republicanism*. Lincoln: University of Nebraska Press, 1990.

American Law Institute. *Restatement (Third) of the Foreign Relations Law of the United States*. St. Paul: American Law Institute, 1987.

Amnesty International. *"Disappearances" and Political Killings: Human Rights Crisis of the 1990s—A Manual for Action*. Amsterdam: Amnesty International, 1994.

Baker, G. S., and M. N. Drucquer, eds. *Halleck's International Law or Rules Regulating the Intercourse of States in Peace and War,* 4th ed. London: K. Paul, Trench, Trubner, 1908.

Ballis, W. B. *The Legal Position of War: Changes in Its Practice and Theory from Plato to Vattel*. New York: Garland Publishers, 1973.

Bardakjian, K. *Hitler and the Armenian Genocide*. Cambridge, MA: Zoryan Institute, 1985.

Bassiouni, M. C. "Commentaries on the International Law Commission's 1991 Draft Code of Crimes Against the Peace and Security of Mankind." *Nouvelles Etudes Penales* 11 (1993).

———. "Establishing an International Criminal Court: Historical Survey." *Military Law Review* 149 (1995): 49–63.

———. "Former Yugoslavia: Investigating Violations of International Humanitarian Law and Establishing an International Criminal Tribunal." *Fordham International Law Journal* 18 (1995): 1191–1211.

———. "From Versailles to Rwanda in Seventy-Five Years: The Need to Establish a Permanent International Criminal Court." *Harvard Human Rights Law Journal* 11 (1997): 11–62.

———. "The History of the Draft Code of Crimes Against the Peace and Security of Mankind." *Israel Law Review* 27 (1993).

———. "The Time Has Come for an International Criminal Court." *Indiana International and Comparative Law Review* 1 (1991): 1–35.

———. *Crimes Against Humanity in International Criminal Law*. Boston: Martinus Nijhoff, 1992.

————. *Crimes Against Humanity in International Criminal Law,* 2nd rev. ed. The Hague and Boston: Kluwer Law International, 1999.

————. *International Criminal Law.* Dobbs Ferry, NY: Transnational, 1986–1987.

Bassiouni, M. C., ed. *International Criminal Law,* 2nd ed. Ardsley, NY: Transnational Publishers, 1998.

Bassiouni, M. C., and V. P. Nanda, eds. *A Treatise on International Criminal Law: Crimes and Punishment.* Springfield, IL: Thomas, 1973.

Bedjaoui, M. *International Law: Achievements and Prospects.* Paris: UNESCO, 1991.

Beres, L. R. "Iraqi Crimes and International Law: The Imperative to Punish." *Denver Journal of International Law and Policy* 21 (1993): 335–360.

Berriedale, A. K. *The Causes of War.* London: Nelson, 1940.

————. *War Government of the British Dominions.* Oxford: Clarendon, 1921.

Bhattacharya, R. "Establishing a Rule-of-Law International Criminal Justice System." *Texas International Law Journal* 31 (1996): 57–99.

Blakesley, C. L. "Obstacles to the Creation of a Permanent War Crimes Tribunal." *Fletcher Forum* 18 (1994): 77–102.

Bodley, A. "Weakening the Principle of Sovereignty in International Law: The International Criminal Tribunal for the Former Yugoslavia." *New York University Journal of International Law and Politics* 31 (1999).

Boissier, P. *From Solferino to Tsushima: History of the International Committee of the Red Cross.* Geneva: Henry Dunant Institute, 1963.

Bothe, M., et al. *New Rules for Victims of Armed Conflicts.* The Hague and Boston: Martinus Nijhoff, 1982.

Bothe, M., et al., eds. *National Implementation of Humanitarian Law: Proceedings of an International Colloquium Held at Bad Homburg.* Dordrecht: Martinus Nijhoff, 1990.

Boyajian, D. H. *Armenia: The Case for a Forgotten Genocide.* Westwood, NJ: Educational Book Crafters, 1972.

Brown, C. *Understanding International Relations.* Basingstoke, UK: Macmillan, 2001.

Brownlie, I. *International Law and the Use of Force by States.* Oxford: Clarendon, 1963.

Bullock, A. *Hitler: A Study in Tyranny.* London: Odhams, 1952.

Carpenter, A. "The International Criminal Court and the Crime of Aggression." *Nordic Journal of International Law* 64 (1995).

Cassese, A. *International Law in a Divided World.* Oxford: Clarendon, 1994.

Churchill, W. *The World Crisis: The Aftermath.* London: Thorton Butterworth, 1929.

Clark, R. S. "Offences of International Concern: Multilateral State Treaty Practice in the Forty Years Since Nuremberg." *Nordic Journal of International Law* 57 (1988).

Comment. "Security Council Resolution 808: A Step Toward a Permanent International Criminal Court for the Prosecution of International Crimes and Human Rights Violations." *Golden Gate University Law Review* 25 (1995): 435–461.

Comprehensive Report of the Secretary-General on Practical Arrangements for the Effective Functioning of the ICTR; UN Doc. 5/1995/134 (1995).

Crawford, J. "The ILC Adopts a Statute for an International Criminal Court." *American Journal of International Law* 89 (1995): 404–416.

Dadrian, V. N. *The History of the Armenian Genocide: Ethnic Conflict from the Balkans to Anatolia to the Caucasus.* Providence, RI: Berghahn Books, 1995.

Deak, I. "Post–World War II Political Justice in a Historical Perspective." *Military Law Review* 149 (1995): 137–144.

Derby, D. H. "An International Criminal Court for the Future." *Transnational Law and Contemporary Problems* 5 (1995): 307–318.

Destexhe, A. *Rwanda and Genocide in the Twentieth Century.* Trans. Alison Marschner. East Haven, CT: Pluto, 1995.

De Vitoria, F. *Francisci de Victoria de Indis et de Jure Belli Reflectiones.* Ed. James Scott Ernest and trans. Ernest Nys. Washington, DC: Carnegie Institute of Washington, 1917.

Dinstein, Y. *The Defence of "Obedience to Superior Orders" in International Law.* Leyden: A. W. Sijthoff, 1965.

———. *War, Aggression, and Self-Defence,* 3rd ed. Cambridge: Cambridge University Press, 1994.

Dinstein, Y., and M. Tabory. *War Crimes in International Law.* The Hague: Martinus Nijhoff, 1996.

Dinstein, Y., and M. Tabory, eds. *The Protection of Minorities and Human Rights.* Dordrecht: M. Nijhoff, 1992.

Doder, D., and L. Branson. *Milosevic: Potrait of a Dictator.* New York: The Free Press, 1999.

Dunant, H. *A Memory of Solferino,* English ed. Washington, DC: American Red Cross, 1959.

Dunne, T., and N. J. Wheeler, eds. *Human Rights in Global Politics.* Cambridge: Cambridge University Press, 1999.

Evered, T. C. "An International Criminal Court: Recent Proposals and American Concerns." *Pace International Law Review* 6 (1994): 121–157.

Fay, S. B. *The Origins of the World War.* New York: Macmillan, 1930.

Ferencz, B. *An International Criminal Court, a Step Toward World Peace: A Documentary History and Analysis.* Dobbs Ferry, NY: Oceana, 1980.

First Annual Report of the International Tribunal for the Prosecution of Persons Responsible for Serious Violations of International Humanitarian Law Committed in the Territory of the Former Yugoslavia Since 1991. UN GAOR, 49th sess., UN Doc. A/49/342, S/1994/1007 (1994).

Fischer, F. *Germany's Aims in the First World War.* New York: W. W. Norton, 1967.

Freidel, F. *Francis Lieber, Nineteenth-Century Liberal.* Baton Rouge: Louisiana State University Press, 1947.

Frost, M. *Ethics in International Relations: A Constitutive Theory.* Cambridge: Cambridge University Press, 1996.

Gaddis, J. H. *The United States and the Origins of the Cold War.* New York: Columbia University Press, 1972.

Garner, J. W. "Punishment of Offenders Against the Laws and Customs of War." *American Journal of International Law* 14 (1920).

Gilpin, R. *War and Change in World Politics.* Cambridge: Cambridge University Press, 1981.

Gourevitch, P. *We Wish to Inform You That Tomorrow We Will Be Killed with Our Families: Stories from Rwanda.* New York: Farrar, Straus, and Giroux, 1998.

Green, L. C. *Superior Orders in National and International Law.* Leyden: A. W. Sijthoff, 1976.

Gross, L. "Some Observations on the Draft Code of Offences Against the Peace and Security of Mankind." *Israel Yearbook of Human Rights* 13 (1983).

Grotius, H. *The Rights of War and Peace: Including the Law of Nature and of Nations.* Trans. A. C. Campbell. Washington, DC: M. W. Dunne, 1901.

Hall, C. K. "The First Proposal for a Permanent International Criminal Court." *International Review of the Red Cross* 322 (March 1998).

Hankey, Lord. *The Supreme Control at the Paris Peace Conference 1919: A Commentary.* London: Allen and Unwin, 1963.

Harries, M., and S. Harries. *Soldiers of the Sun: The Rise and Fall of the Imperial Japanese Army.* New York: Random House, 1991.

Hart, B. H. L. *A History of the World War, 1914–1918.* London: Faber and Faber, 1934.

Hartigan, R. S. *Lieber's Code and the Law of War.* Chicago: Precedent, 1983.

Henkin, L. *How Nations Behave: Law and Foreign Policy.* New York: Praeger, 1968.

———. *The Age of Rights.* New York: Columbia University Press, 1990.

Hilberg, R. *The Destruction of the European Jews,* rev. ed. New York: Holmes and Meier, 1985.

Historical Survey of the Question of International Criminal Jurisdiction, Memorandum by the Secretary-General. UN GAOR, 4th sess., UN Doc. A/CN4/7/ Rev 1 (1949).

Holbrooke, R. *To End a War.* New York: Random House, 1998.

Holsti, K. J. *Peace and War: Armed Conflicts and International Order, 1648– 1989.* Cambridge: Cambridge University Press, 1991.

Honor, H. *Romanticism.* London: Allen Lane, 1979.

Howard, M. *Franco-Prussian War: The German Invasion of France, 1870–71.* London and New York: Methuen, 1981.

Human Rights Watch. *Iraq's Crime of Genocide: The Anfal Campaign Against the Kurds.* New York: Human Rights Watch, 1995.

———. *World Watch 1995.* New York: Human Rights Watch, 1996.

Interim Report of the Commission of Experts Established Pursuant to Security Council Resolution 780. UN SCOR, Annex 55, UN Doc. 5/25274 (1993).

International Law Commission. *Yearbook of the International Law Commission* 1 (1949).

Johnson, D. H. N. "The Draft Code of Offences Against the Peace and Security of Mankind." *International Comparative Law Quarterly* 4 (1955).

Jones, J. R. W. D. *The Practice of the International Criminal Tribunals for the Former Yugoslavia and Rwanda.* Irvington-on-Hudson, NY: Transnational, 1998.

Jones, W. S. *The Logic of International Relations,* 5th ed. Boston: Little, Brown, 1985.

Kapteyn, P. J. G., and P. V. Van Themaat. *Introduction to the Law of the European Communities After the Coming into Force of the Single European Act,* 2nd ed. Boston: Kluwer Law and Taxation Publishers, 1989.

Kegley, C. W. Jr., and E. R. Wittkopf. *World Politics: Trend and Transformations.* New York: St. Martin's, 1995.

Kennedy, D. "Primitive Legal Scholarship." *Harvard International Law Journal* 27 (1986).

Knowles, C. "Life and Dignity, the Birthright of All Human Beings: An Analysis of the Iraqi Genocide of the Kurds and Effective Enforcement of Human Rights." *Naval Law Review* 45 (1998).

Kochavi, A. J. *Prelude to Nuremberg: Allied War Crimes Policy and the Question of Punishment.* Chapel Hill: University of North Carolina Press, 1998.

Kuper, L. *Genocide: Its Political Use in the Twentieth Century.* New Haven, CT: Yale University Press, 1981.

Lauterpacht, H. *The Function of Law in the International Community.* Hamden, CT: Archon Books, 1966.

Lauterpacht, H., ed. *Oppenheim's International Law.* London: Longmans, 1952.

Lawrence, T. J. *The Principles of International Law,* 7th ed. Boston: D. C. Heath, 1923.

Lawyers Committee for Human Rights. *International Criminal Court Briefing Series.* New York: Lawyers Committee for Human Rights, 1999.

Lee, R. S., ed. *The International Criminal Court: The Making of the Statute—Issues, Negotiations, Results.* The Hague: Kluwer Law International, 1999.

Leifer, A. C. "Never Again? The 'Concentration Camps' in Bosnia-Herzegovina: A Legal Analysis of Human Rights Abuses." *New Europe Journal Law Review* 2 (1994).

Leurdijk, D. A. "The Dayton Agreement: A Tremendous Gamble." *International Peacekeeping* 3 (December 1995–January 1996).

Levie, H. *Terrorism in War: The Law of War Crimes.* Dobbs Ferry, NY: Oceana, 1993.

Levy, J. S. "Preferences, Constraints, and Choices in July 1914." *International Security* 15 (1990–1991).

MacPherson, B. F. "Building an International Criminal Court." *Connecticut Journal of International Law* 13 (1998): 1–59.

Mallison, W. Jr. *Studies in the Law of Warfare: Submarines in General and Limited Warfare.* Washington, DC: U.S. Government Printing Office, 1966.

Maogoto, J. N. "International Justice for Rwanda Missing the Point: Questioning the Relevance of Classical Criminal Law Theory." *Bond Law Review* 13 (2001): 190–223.

———. "International Justice Under the Shadow of Realpolitik: Revisting the Establishment of the Ad Hoc International Criminal Tribunals." *Flinders Journal of Law Reform* 5 (2001): 161–198.

McCoubrey, H. *International Humanitarian Law: The Regulation of Armed Conflicts.* Aldershot, UK: Dartmouth, 1990.

McDougal, M. S., and F. P. Feliciano. *Law and Minimum World Public Order.* New Haven, CT: Yale University Press, 1961.

Melanson, R. A. *Writing History and Making Policy: The Cold War, Vietnam, and Revisionism.* Lanham, MD: University Press of America, 1983.

Melvern, L. *A People Betrayed: The Role of the West in Rwanda's Genocide.* London and New York: Zed Books, 2000.

Meron, T. *Human Rights and Humanitarian Norms as Customary Law* (Oxford: Clarendon Press, 1989).

———. "The Humanization of Humanitarian Law." *American Journal of International Law* 94 (2000): 239–278.

———. *War Crimes Law Comes of Age: Essays.* Oxford: Clarendon, 1998.

Morgenthau, H. *Politics Among Nations: The Struggle for Power and Peace,* 5th ed. New York: Knopf, 1978.

Morris, J. *The German Air Raids on Great Britain, 1914–1918.* London: S. Low, Marston, 1920.

Morris, M. H. "The Trials of Concurrent Jurisdiction: The Case of Rwanda." *Duke Journal of Comparative and International Law* 7 (1997): 349–374.

Morris, V., and M. P. Scharf, eds. *An Insider's Guide to the International Criminal Tribunal for the Former Yugoslavia.* Irvington-on-Hudson, NY: Transnational, 1995.

Muller-Rappard, E. *L'ordre superieur militaire et la responsibilite penale du subordonne*. Paris: A. Pedone, 1965.

Mullins, C. *The Leipzig Trials: An Account of the War Criminals' Trials and a Study of German Mentality*. London: H.F. & G. Witherby, 1921.

Mutua, M. "Never Again: Questioning the Yugoslav and Rwanda Tribunals." *Temple International and Comparative Law Journal* 11 (1997): 167–187.

Neier, A. *War Crimes: Brutality, Genocide, Terror, and the Struggle for Justice*. New York: Times Books, 1998.

Nill, D. A. "National Sovereignty: Must It Be Sacrificed to the International Criminal Court?" *BYU Journal of Public Law* 14 (1999): 119–150.

Noone, G. P. "The History and Evolution of the Law of War Prior to World War II." *Naval Law Review* 47 (2000).

O'Connell, D. P. *The Influence of Law on Sea Power*. Manchester, UK: Manchester University Press, 1975.

———. "International Law and Contemporary Naval Operations." *British Year Book of International Law* 44 (1970).

O'Donnell, D. "Trends in the Application of International Humanitarian Law by United Nations Human Rights Mechanisms." *International Review of the Red Cross* 324 (September 1998).

Oppenheim, L. *International Law: A Treatise*, 1st ed. London: Longmans, Green, 1905–1906.

Orel, S., and S. Yuca. *Ermenilerce Talat Pasa'ya Atfedilen Telegraflar In Gercek Yuzu* [The Talât Pasha "Telegrams": Historical Fact or Armenian Fiction?]. Nicosia: K. Rustem and Brother, 1983.

Orentlicher, D. "Bearing Witness: The Art and Science of Human Rights Fact-Finding." *Harvard Human Rights Journal* 3 (1990).

Ozkaya, N. *Le peuple Armenien et les tentatives de rendre en servitude le peuple Turc* [The Armenian People and the Attempts to Subjugate the Turkish People]. Istanbul: 1971.

Pal, R. B. *Dissentient Judgment of Justice R. B. Pal*. Calcutta: Sanval, 1953.

Pearson, G. *Towards One World: An Outline of World History from 1600 to 1960*. Cambridge: Cambridge University Press, 1962.

Pejic, J. "Creating a Permanent International Criminal Court: The Obstacles to Independence and Effectiveness." *Columbia Human Rights Law Review* 29 (1998): 291–353.

———. "Panel II, Adjudicating Violence: Problems Confronting International Law and Policy on War Crimes and Crimes Against Humanity." *Albany Law Review* 60 (1997): 841–860.

Pflanze, O. *Bismarck and the Development of Germany: The Period of Unification, 1815–1871*. Princeton, NJ: Princeton University Press, 1963.

Pictet, J. *ICRC Commentary on the Geneva Convention (I) for the Amelioration of the Condition of the Wounded and Sick in Armed Forces in the Field*. Geneva: International Committee of the Red Cross, 1952.

Ponting, C. *Progress and Barbarism: The World in the Twentieth Century*. London: Chatto and Windus, 1998.

Poolman, K. *Zeppelins Against London*. New York: John Day, 1961.

Prunier, G. "The Great Lakes Crisis." *Current History* 96 (1997): 841–860.

———. *The Rwanda Crisis: History of a Genocide*. New York: Columbia University Press, 1995.

Raleigh, W. A., and H. A. Jones. *The War in the Air: Being the Story of the Part Played in the Great War by the Royal Air Force*. Oxford: Clarendon, 1922–1927.

Report of the 1953 Committee on International Criminal Jurisdiction. UN GAOR, 9th sess., Supp. no. 12, UN Doc. A/2645 (1957).

Report of the Commission on Responsibilities of the Conference of Paris on the Violation of the Laws and Customs of War. Carnegie Endowment for International Peace, 1919.

Report of the Committee on International Criminal Court Jurisdiction. UN GAOR, 7th sess., Supp. no. 11, UN Doc. A/2136 (1952).

Report of the Committee on International Criminal Jurisdiction. UN GAOR, 7th sess., Supp. no. 12, UN Doc. A/2645 (1954).

Report of the Group of Experts for Cambodia Pursuant to General Assembly Resolution 52/135. UN GAOR, 53rd sess., Agenda Item 110(b), UN Doc. A/53/850 and S/1999/231 (1999).

Report of the International Law Commission on Question of International Criminal Jurisdiction. UN GAOR, 5th sess., UN Doc. A/CN4/15 (1950).

Report of the International Law Commission on the Work of Its Forty-Sixth Session. UN GAOR, 49th sess., Supp. no. 10, UN Doc. A/49/10 (1994).

Report of the International Law Commission. UN GAOR, 40th sess., Supp. no. 10, UN Doc. A/43/10 (1988).

Report of the International Law Commission. UN GAOR, 46th sess., Supp. no. 10, UN Doc. A/46/10 (1991).

Report of the International Law Commission. UN GAOR, 5th sess., UN Doc. A/CN4/25 (1950).

Report of the International Law Commission. UN GAOR, 5th sess., UN Doc. A/CN4/25 (1950).

Report of the Secretary-General on the Work of the Organization. UN GAOR, 47th sess., UN Doc. A/47/277, S/24111 (1992).

Report of the Secretary-General on the Activities of the Office of Internal Oversight Services. 51st sess., Agenda Item 139, 141 UN Doc. A/51/789 (1997).

Report of the Secretary-General on the Establishment of a Special Court for Sierra Leone. UN Doc. S/2000/915 (2000).

Report of the Secretary-General on the Establishment of the Commission of Experts Pursuant to Paragraph 2 of Security Council Resolution 780. UN Doc. S/24657 (1992).

Report of the Secretary-General on the International Conference on the Former Yugoslavia. UN SCOR, UN Doc. S/24795 (1992).

Report of the Secretary-General Pursuant to Paragraph 2 of Security Council Resolution 808 (1993). UN Doc. S/25704 (1993).

Report of the Secretary-General Pursuant to Paragraph 3 of Security Council Resolution 713. UN Doc. S/23169 (1991).

Revised Report of the Working Group on the Draft Statute for an International Criminal Court. UN GAOR, 48th Sess, UN Doc. A/CN4/L490 (1993).

Rich, N. *Great Power Diplomacy, 1814–1914.* Hanover, NH: University Press of New England, 1992.

Riddell, G. A. R. *Lord Riddell's Intimate Diary of the Peace Conference and After, 1918–1923.* London: Gollancz, 1933.

Riggs, R. E., and J. C. Plano. *The United Nations: International Organization and World Politics.* Chicago: Dorsey, 1988.

Ritter, G. *The Schlieffen Plan: Critique of a Myth.* Trans. Andrew and Eva Wilson. London: O. Wolff, 1958.

Rudin, H. R. *Armistice 1918.* New Haven, CT: Yale University Press, 1944.

Sadat, L. N., and S. R. Carden. "The New International Criminal Court: An Uneasy Revolution." *Georgetown Law Journal* 88 (2000): 381–459.

Scharf, M. P. *Balkan Justice: The Story Behind the First International War Crimes Trial Since Nuremberg.* Durham, NC: Carolina Academic Press, 1997.

———. "Getting Serious About an International Criminal Court." *Pace International Law Review* 6 (1994): 103–119.

Schindler, D., and J. Toman, eds. *The Laws of Armed Conflicts: A Collection of Conventions, Resolutions, and Other Documents*, 3rd rev. ed. Dordrecht: Nijhoff, 1988.

Schlesinger, A. Jr. *The Cycles of American History.* London: Penguin Books, 1986.

Schmitt, M. N., ed. *International Law Across the Spectrum of Conflict: Essays in Honor of Professor L. C. Green on the Occasion of His Eightieth Birthday.* Newport, RI: Naval War College 1999.

Schwarzenberger, G. *International Law.* London: Stevens & Sons, 1957–1986.

———. *International Law as Applied by Courts and Tribunals.* London: Stevens & Sons, 1968.

———. *Power Politics: A Study of International Society.* London: Stevens & Sons, 1951.

Schwelb, E. "Crimes Against Humanity." *British Yearbook of International Law* 23 (1946).

Scoble, H. M., and L. S. Wiseberg. "Human Rights and Amnesty International." *Annals of the American Academy of Political and Social Science* (1974).

Shestack, J. J. "Sisyphus Endures: The International Human Rights NGO." *New York Law School Law Review* 24 (1978).

Shirer, W. L. *The Rise and Fall of the Third Reich: A History of Nazi Germany.* London: Pan Books, 1979.

Shraga, D., and R. Zacklin. "The International Criminal Tribunal for Rwanda." *European Journal of International Law* 7 (1996).

Simma, B. *The Charter of the United Nations: A Commentary.* Oxford: Oxford University Press, 1995.

Simpson, G. "'Throwing a Little Remembering on the Past': The International Criminal Court and the Politics of Sovereignty." *University of California Davis Journal of International Law and Policy* 5 (1999): 133–146.

———. "Didactic and Dissident Stories in War Crimes Trials." *Alberta Law Review* 60 (1997).

The Situation in Somalia: Report of the Secretary-General. UN SCOR, 47th sess., UN Doc. S/23693 (1992); UN SCOR, 47th sess., UN Doc. S/23829/Add 1 (1992).

Smith, B. F. *The American Road to Nuremberg: The Documentary Record, 1944–1945.* Stanford: Hoover Institution Press, 1982.

Sprout, H., and M. Sprout. *The Rise of American Naval Power, 1776–1918,* 2nd ed. Princeton, NJ: Princeton University Press, 1967.

Stone, J. *Legal Control of International Conflict.* Sydney: Maitland, 1954.

Stowell, E. C., and H. C. Munro, eds. *International Cases: Arbitrations and Incidents Illustrative of International Law as Practiced by Independent States.* Boston and New York: Houghton Mifflin, 1916.

Straubing, H. E., ed. *The Last Magnificent War and Eyewitness Accounts of World War I.* New York: Paragon House, 1989.

Strisower, L. *Der Kriegund die Volkenechtsordmung* [War and the Law on Regulation of Nations]. Wein: Manz, 1919.

Sunga, L. S. *The Emerging System of International Criminal Law: Developments in Codification and Implementation.* The Hague: Kluwer Law International, 1997.

Taylor, A. J. P. *The Struggle for Mastery in Europe, 1848–1918.* Oxford: Clarendon, 1954.

Taylor, L. *A Trial of Generals: Homma, Yamashita, MacArthur.* South Bend, IN: Icarus, 1981.

Taylor, T. *The Anatomy of the Nuremberg Trials: A Personal Memoir.* New York: Knopf, 1992.

Third Report Relating to a Draft Code of Offences Against the Peace and Security of Mankind. UN GAOR, 6th sess., U.N. Doc. A/CN4/85 (1954).

Trainin, A. N. "Le tribunal militaire international et le proces de Nuremberg." *Revue Internationale de Droit Penal* 17 (1946).

Trimble, P. R. "International Law, World Order, and Critical Legal Studies." *Stanford Law Review* 42 (1990).

Tuchman, B. *The Guns of August.* New York: Macmillan, 1962.

Turner, L. C. F. *The First World War.* Melbourne and Canberra: Cheshire, 1967.

Tusa, A., and J. Tusa. *The Nuremberg Trial.* New York: Atheneum, 1984.

U.S. Department of State. *Report of Robert H. Jackson, United States Representative to the International Conference on Military Trials.* Pub. no. 3080. Washington, DC: U.S. Government Printing Office, 1949.

Vagts, D. F. "The Hague Conventions and Arms Control." *American Journal of International Law* 94 (2000): 31–41.

Van Evera, S. "Primed for Peace: Europe After the Cold War." *International Security* 15 (1990–1991).

Verlag, G. S. *Bilanz Des Zweitan Weltkreiges Erkenntinisse und Verpflichtungen Fur Die Zunkundt* [Balance of World War II: Insights and Duties for the Future]. Oldenburg: Stalling, 1953.

von Clausewitz, C. *On War.* Ed. and trans. Michael Howard and Peter Paret. Princeton, NJ: Princeton University Press, 1976.

Von Wegerer, A. *Der Ausbruch des von Weltkrieges, 1914* [The Outbreak of the World War, 1914]. Hamburg: Hanseatische Verlagsanstalt, 1943.

Wang, M. M. "The International Tribunal for Rwanda: Opportunities for Impact." *Columbia Human Rights Law Review* 27 (1995).

Webb, J. "Genocide Treaty—Ethnic Cleansing—Substantive and Procedural Hurdles in the Application of the Genocide Convention to Alleged Crimes in the Former Yugoslavia." *Georgia Journal of International and Comparative Law* 23 (1993).

Webster, C. K. *The Congress of Vienna.* London: H.M. Stationery Office, 1920.

Weiss, Thomas G., ed. *The United Nations and Civil Wars.* Boulder: Lynne Rienner, 1995.

Weissbrodt, D. "The Role of International Nongovernmental Organizations in the Implementation of Human Rights." *Texas International Law Journal* 12 (1977).

Wexler, L. S. "The Proposed Permanent International Criminal Court: An Appraisal." *Cornell International Law Journal* 29 (1996).

White, Colin M. *The Gotha Summer: The German Daytime Air Raids on England, May to August 1917.* London: R. Hale, 1986.

Whitney, H. R. *Tyranny on Trial: The Trial of the Major German War Criminals at the End of World War II at Nuremberg, Germany, 1945–1946,* rev. ed. Dallas, TX: Southern Methodist University Press, 1999.

Willis, J. F. *Prologue to Nuremberg: The Politics and Diplomacy of Punishing War Criminals of the First World War.* Westport, CT: Greenwood, 1982.

Wilson, H. *The Congress of Vienna: A Study in Allied Unity, 1812–1822.* London: Constable, 1946.

Wright, Q. "The Legality of the Kaiser." *American Political Science Review* 13 (1919).

———. *A Study in War.* Chicago: University of Chicago Press, 1965.

Zartmann, W. I., ed. *Collapsed States: The Disintegration and Restoration of Legitimate Authority.* Boulder: Lynne Reinner, 1995.

Index

Accountability, 6–7, 9, 11, 18, 27, 64, 95, 106, 130, 193, 212, 218, 231, 238, 241
Ad hoc international criminal tribunals. *See* Ad hoc tribunal
Ad hoc tribunal, 9–10, 102, 109, 137, 145, 188, 203, 215, 229, 241, 247
Additional Protocols, 129–130, 131, 135
Aggression, 10, 39, 54 107–110, 115, 141, 146, 205, 208, 217
Akayesu, Jean-Paul, 188, 191, 198, 200
Allied Powers, 41, 79, 87, 90, 92, 97, 99, 102, 105, 119
American Civil War, 19
Amnesty, 27, 62, 200, 222, 228, 243
Arbour, Louise, 174–175
Armenia, 38, 40, 42–44, 47–48, 58, 195
Armenian genocide. *See* Armenia
Armistice, 23, 29, 59
Army, Imperial Japanese. *See* Japan
Arusha Accords, 181, 195–196
Authority, 4, 8, 10–11, 27, 37, 48–49, 79, 86, 91–92, 156, 159, 183, 195, 207, 215, 223, 235, 237
Axis Powers, 79, 83, 94, 97–98, 106

Bagilishema, Ignace, 191, 200
Balkan Conflict. *See* Balkans
Balkans, 143, 145–146

Bassiouni, M. Cherif, 9, 12, 21, 28, 53–54, 57, 63, 70, 108, 154, 188, 224
Battle of Solferino, 19, 30
Belligerents, 33, 47, 130
Bildt, Carl, 158
Blaskic, Tihomir, 160
Bodley, Anne, 144, 165
Bolshevik, 45, 55, 64, 69
Bolshevik Revolution. *See* Bolshevik
Bolshevism. *See* Bolshevik
Bonino, Emma, 218
Bosnia, 6, 143, 146, 149, 150–151, 153. *See also* Balkans
Bourgemestre, 198

Central Powers, 40, 48
Charles, Duke of Burgundy, 21
Christopher, Warren, 184
Citizens, 8, 29, 48, 56–57, 83, 98, 207–209, 217, 228
Citizenship. *See* Citizens
Clausewitz, Carl von, 3, 30
Clausewitzian war, 4
Codification, 1, 6, 8, 16, 19, 24, 27
Cold War, 108–109, 125–127, 136, 144–145, 204, 206
Collective security, 19, 64, 79, 81, 109
Communist, 118, 145–146
Communist partisan forces. *See* Communist
Communist Party members. *See* Communist

Complementarity, 209–211, 218, 223, 228–229
Compulsory jurisdiction, 26, 208, 225
Concurrent jurisdiction. *See* Jurisdiction
Crimes against humanity, 5, 13, 21, 25, 33, 37, 49, 55, 62, 94–96, 99, 102, 127, 132, 156, 160–161, 163, 187–189, 208, 222
Crimes against peace. *See* Aggression
Criminal jurisdiction. *See* Compulsory jurisdiction; Jurisdiction
Criminal sanctions. *See* Sanctions

Decisionmakers, 135

Economic sanctions. *See* Sanctions
Emperor, 46, 49, 54
Emperor Hirohito, 104–105
Emperor Napoleon III, 23
Enforcement, 3–6, 15, 20–21, 23–24, 46–47, 51, 58, 64, 70, 79, 99, 108, 143, 154, 158, 205, 210, 213–214, 237, 241
Entente powers, 40, 248
Ethnic cleansing, 150–152, 165

Fascism, 77
Former Yugoslavia. *See* Yugoslavia
Franco-Prussian War, 20, 22, 32, 248

Galic, Stanislav, 161
Geneva Conventions, 129–133, 135, 152, 160–161, 186
Genocide, 38, 42, 44, 58, 61–62, 84, 86, 143, 157, 161, 165, 179–182, 184, 208, 219
Germany, 5, 37–40, 77–78, 80, 82–84
Greater Serbia. *See* Balkans; Serbia
Grotius, Hugo, 17–18, 28–29

Hagenbach, Peter Von, 21, 28
Hague Conferences, 24, 26, 33
"Hard" enforcement. *See* Enforcement
Hegemony, 38, 78, 82
Himmler, Heinrich, 93, 111
Hiroshima, 83
Holocaust, 84, 98, 102
Humanitarian intervention. *See* Intervention
Human rights, 5–6, 9, 11, 68, 81, 83, 107, 143–144, 150–151, 154, 179,

181, 184, 215, 220, 237–238. *See also* International humanitarian law
Human rights violations. *See* Human rights; Massacres
Hungarian Revolt, 45
Hurst, Cecil, 90, 112

ICTR Statute, 186–188, 193, 197
Immunity, 55, 73, 103, 174, 177, 221
Imperial rescript, 42–43, 106
Impunity, 20, 62, 64, 126, 187, 210, 220–221, 227, 237–239
Indictees, 160, 162, 174, 191
Inherent jurisdiction. *See* Jurisdiction
Interahamwe, 182, 188, 190, 195
Inter alia, 95, 122, 151, 163, 177
International community, 3, 8, 17, 23, 29, 64, 79, 126, 131–132, 134, 137, 144–145, 148, 155, 180–181, 184, 208, 211
International crimes, 37, 64, 189
International Criminal Court, 6, 12, 20, 22, 127, 153, 193, 203–204, 208, 218, 237, 239
International criminal law, 9, 63, 107, 127, 132, 217, 242
International humanitarian law, 1, 3–6, 16, 18, 21, 23, 56, 79, 107, 143–144, 151, 180, 186–187, 193, 206, 208, 237–238. *See also* Laws and customs of war
International jurisdiction, 8, 22, 64, 228, 240
International law, 2, 3, 5–6, 8, 16, 18, 24, 27, 37, 44, 51–52, 85, 93–94, 96, 99, 143, 154, 164, 186, 203–204, 206, 209, 214, 236–238, 240
International law violations. *See* International law
International norms, 1, 5–7, 128, 238. *See also* Human rights; International humanitarian law
International obligations, 6, 21, 24, 64, 79
International penal process, 9, 11, 20, 24, 37, 44, 62, 79, 100, 151–152, 164, 223, 241
International politics. *See* Realpolitik
International system, 3–4, 17, 21, 57, 77, 126, 136, 193, 235–236
Intervention, 42–43, 45

Ittihadist leaders. *See* Ittihadists
Ittihadists, 60
Izetbegovic, Alija, 149

Jaequemeyns, Rolin, 48
Japan, 48–51, 55, 63, 77–78, 81–83, 86
Judicial proceedings, 63, 84
Juridicization, 8
Jurisdiction, 5, 17, 21–22, 26, 37, 44, 49–50, 91, 95, 107, 155, 186–187, 192, 206–213
Jus ad bellum, 1, 12, 16
Jus in bello, 1, 12

Kagame, Paul, 184, 199
Kaiser, 62, 71–72
Kambanda, Jean, 189–191, 198
Karadzic, Radovan, 150, 157, 161, 163, 169, 175
Kayibanda, Gregoire, 180
Kayishema, Clement, 188, 191, 198, 200
Kellogg-Briand Pact, 80–81, 104, 115
Kemal, Mustafa, 58, 60, 62, 74
Kemal, Yusuf 60
Kemalism, 59, 74
Kemalists. *See* Kemalism
Kordic, Dario, 161, 177
Krajisnik, Momcilo, 161
Krstic, Radislav, 161, 162
Kugel Erlass (the Bullet Decree), 85

Laws and customs of war, 17, 25, 46–50, 66, 132. *See also* International humanitarian law
Lieber Code, 19–20

Major war criminals. *See* War criminals
Maogoto, Jackson Nyamuya, 196–198
Martens, Fedor Fedorovitch, 25, 33
Massacres, 40, 42, 44, 47, 58, 60, 150–151, 179–180, 182, 239. *See also* International humanitarian law
McDonald, Gabrielle Kirk, 159
Melvern, Linda, 183, 195–196
Meron, Ted, 138–141, 160, 175
Military law, 20, 73, 95
Military necessity, 15, 19–20, 41
Military regulations. *See* Military law
Military retaliation. *See* Reprisals

Military tribunal. *See* Nuremberg Tribunal; Tokyo Tribunal
Moynier, Gustave, 20–24, 32
Municipal jurisdiction, 107, 250. *See also* Jurisdiction
Musema, Alfred, 188, 192, 198, 200
Museveni, Yoweri, 182
Mussolini, Benito, 81–82, 110
Mwinyi, Ali Hassan, 182

Nacht und Nebel Erlass (the Night and Fog Decree), 85
Nazi, 42, 57, 83–84, 89, 93, 96–98, 100, 106
Nazi atrocities. *See* Nazi
Nazi regime. *See* Nazi
Nikolic, Dragan, 159, 175
Noncooperation, 159, 221
Noninternational, 128–129, 131, 133
Nonsurrender, 220
Ntayamira, Cyprien, 182
Nuremberg Charter, 92–96, 100, 204
Nuremberg Tribunal, 92, 95, 97, 99, 100–102, 107

Ottoman, 38, 42–43, 58–59, 64
Ottoman Empire. *See* Ottoman; Turkey

Papic, Dragan, 160, 176
Paris Peace Conference, 44–45, 66
Pasa, Talat, 43, 59, 68
Peace of Westphalia, 2, 16–18, 250
Pell, Herbert, 91, 112
Penal process. *See* International penal process
Political power, 183
Politis, Nicolas, 47
Prijedor, 162, 174
Prijedor region. *See* Prijedor
Prosecute, 17, 19, 25, 40, 44, 48, 53, 55, 79, 91–92, 94, 132–133, 144, 151, 155, 193, 203, 211, 221, 236–237

Rape of Nanking, 87
Realpolitik, 4, 7, 8, 10–11, 125
Reprisals, 84, 90, 93, 128
Respublica Christiana, 16–17
Rome Conference, 207, 216. *See also* Hague Conferences; Paris Peace Conference

Rome Statute, 6, 9, 12, 133, 136, 217–219, 223, 238–239. *See also* International Criminal Court
Rousseau, Jean-Jacques, 18, 29
Ruggiu, Georges, 190, 199
Rutaganda, Georges, 188, 198
Ruzidana, Obed, 188, 192, 198, 200
Rwanda, 6, 12, 137, 143, 165, 179–189, 192–195, 203–204, 210, 215

Saitoti, George, 182
Sanctions, 8, 21, 26, 49, 81, 158–159
Schlieffen Plan, 39, 65–66
Security Council, 143–144, 148–155, 158–159, 179–181, 183–186, 207–208, 237, 240. *See also* UN Charter
Serbia, 37–39, 46, 145–150, 153, 159
Serushago, Omar, 190–191
Shawcross, Hartley, 99
"Soft" enforcement. *See* Enforcement
Staal, Baron de, 25
State authority. *See* Authority
State cooperation, 160, 162, 217, 232
State jurisdiction. *See* Jurisdiction
Statist, 6, 236

Tadic, Dusko, 159, 161, 176
Tadic, Miroslav, 161
Takayanagi Kenzo, 103, 120
Territorial jurisdiction. *See* Jurisdiction

Tito, Josip Broz, 145–146, 166
Tokyo Charter, 96, 102, 107, 120
Tokyo Tribunal, 92, 101–103, 105–107
Tomoyuki Yamashita, 103, 120
Treaty of Lausanne, 38, 98, 102
Treaty of Sevres, 37–38, 51, 58, 60, 62
Turkey, 37, 40, 42–44, 57–58, 60
Tutsi. *See* Rwanda

Ultranationalism, 129
UN Charter, 126, 128, 143, 147–148, 223
United Nations. *See* UN Charter
Universal jurisdiction, 132, 210–211. *See also* Jurisdiction
Unsign, 218–220, 234
Unwilingiyimana, Agathe, 183

War criminals, 20, 26, 48, 50, 56, 59, 88–90, 92, 106, 145, 156, 237
War guilt. *See* International crimes; War criminals
Westphalia. *See* Westphalian sovereignty; Peace of Westphalia
Westphalian sovereignty, 6

Yugoslavia, 7, 12, 137, 143–146, 148–150, 154–155, 164, 184–186, 237

Zaric, Simo, 161

About the Book

From the very early stages in the development of international law, the nature of the state-centric international system has dictated that law play second fiddle to the hard realities of power politics. *War Crimes and Realpolitik* explores the evolution and operation of the international criminal justice system, highlighting the influences of politics.

Maogoto takes the reader behind the scenes of the conflict between justice and realpolitik. Showing how states, in furthering their political agendas, sometimes hinder the enforceability of international criminal law, he delineates the state interests that often control international legal norms and institutions and even manipulate public perceptions. Ranging from the period just after World War I to the recent establishment of the International Criminal Court, he provides a thorough exposition of the politics and processes of international penal institutions in the state- driven international system.

Jackson Nyamuya Maogoto is lecturer in law at the University of Newcastle in Australia.